TRADE AND TRADERS
IN MID-VICTORIAN LIVERPOOL

for Mum and Dad

Trade and traders in mid-Victorian Liverpool

Mercantile business and the making of a world port

GRAEME J. MILNE

LIVERPOOL UNIVERSITY PRESS

First published 2000 by
Liverpool University Press
4 Cambridge Street
Liverpool L69 7ZU

British Library Cataloguing-in-Publication Data
A British Library CIP record is available

ISBN 0 85323 606 2 *cased*
ISBN 0 85323 616 X *paperback*

Typeset by Carnegie Publishing Ltd, Chatsworth Road, Lancaster
Printed and bound in the European Union by
Bell and Bain Ltd, Glasgow

CONTENTS

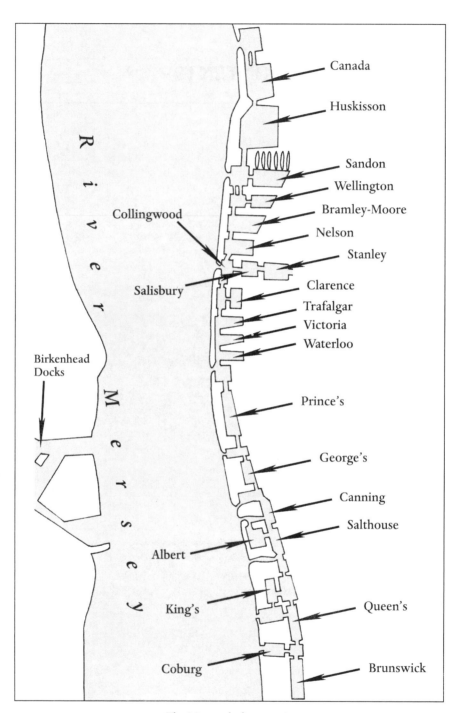

Canada

Huskisson

Sandon
Wellington
Bramley-Moore

Collingwood

Nelson

Stanley

Salisbury

Clarence

Trafalgar
Victoria
Waterloo

Birkenhead
Docks

Prince's

George's

Canning

Salthouse

Albert

King's

Queen's

Coburg

Brunswick

The Mersey docks, *c.* 1860.

PREFACE

Liverpool presents a challenge to historians. Most people assume that a lot has already been written about it – I received much well-meant advice in the early part of this project that nineteenth-century Liverpool had been 'done', and that I ought to find something more original to study. It is certainly true that there is no shortage of original evidence ('primary sources' in historian-speak), but whatever people think, very little of it has been subjected to serious historical analysis. The last large-scale economic history of Liverpool – F. E. Hyde's *Liverpool and the Mersey* – was published in 1971, so we now have a generation's worth of studies of other ports, and analysis of more general issues in trade, shipping and mercantile business, to compare with the primary evidence, to say nothing of major aspects of the port's operation that have never been analysed at all.

Many of the sources used in this book have been undervalued by historians, and one useful by-product of this research is to demonstrate some of the different angles from which the port can be studied. Even then, I am very aware of roads not taken – of subjects, briefly mentioned in the chapters that follow, that should have entire books written about them. Plans to commemorate Liverpool's 800th 'birthday' in 2007 with a new generation of serious historical study are already taking shape, however, so there is reason to be optimistic that justice will be done to the still-hidden Liverpool before too long.

The historians who write those books will, as I do now, owe a great debt to the archivists and librarians who serve as custodians of Liverpool's past. I am grateful for the help and interest of staff at NMGM's Merseyside Maritime Museum Archives and Library; the University of Liverpool Library, Archives and Special Collections; Liverpool Record Office; Lancashire Record Office, Preston; the Guildhall Library, London; the Bank of England Archives, London; the Public Record Office, Kew; Perkins Library, Duke University, North Carolina; the British Library, St Pancras; University College Library, London; and ING Barings Limited, London.

Economic historians spend most of their lives worrying about money – how it worked in the past, and how to get enough in the present to find out how it worked in the past. Parts of this project could not be attempted single-handed, and financial support from a number of sources made it possible to employ research assistants for short periods. The University of Liverpool Research Development Fund paid Graham Tonks to transform a mass of manuscript figures into a new core set of statistics for Liverpool's port revenue, and the foundations of many parts of this book would be much weaker without his labours. NMGM provided a month's salary for Sheryllynne Haggerty to work with the Liverpool Dock Registers: her efforts set some new standards for the treatment of this heinously complex but vital source. Some transcription work from the Customs Bills of Entry (B series) was undertaken by Jackie McMannion and Debbie Coffey, both of NMGM's Central Services Division, and the files they generated were a considerable help in the analysis of cotton traders.

I am also grateful to the organisers of, and audiences at, seminar programmes and conferences for listening to earlier versions of some of the material presented here: the Port Projects group meetings at Hull and Leeds; the British Commission for Maritime History at King's College, London; and the Economic History Association Annual Meeting at Durham, North Carolina. Many other people helped get this book written, directly or otherwise. Thank you – Bruce Anderson, Neil Ashcroft, Will Ashworth, John Belchem, Robin Bloxsidge, Nancy Cox, Peter Davies, Skip Fischer, Sheryllynne Haggerty, Gordon Jackson, Adrian Jarvis, Drew Keeling, Robert Lee, Sari Mäenpää, Helen Power, Michael Power, Mike Stammers, Mike Tadman, Arthur West, David Williams, and Gill Wilson. I have to single out Di Ascott, whose enthusiasm for obscure Liverpool sources pointed the work in new directions more than once.

NOTE ON CONVENTIONS

Relatively little needs to be said about nomenclature, spelling and transcription. One slight oddity which readers may notice is in the naming of the Liverpool docks. There is a surprising lack of consistency in the historical record with regard to apostrophes: clearly, King's Dock (named after George III) should, according to modern rules, have an apostrophe, but it very often appears in Dock Board and other material as Kings Dock. The same applies to Prince's/Princes, Queen's/Queens, and so on. I have used apostrophes, usually dropped the word 'Dock' in sections where there are a lot of them, and put the date of opening of the dock in brackets where this information seems helpful. Thus, for example, Albert (1846) and Prince's (1821) appear in chapter 4 as important docks specialising in high-value commodities.

Many of the primary sources used in the book – Parliamentary Papers especially – have notoriously clumsy titles. They are therefore cited in the footnotes in abbreviated form. The full titles, and any necessary explanation for the way each source has been used, appear in the Notes on Sources section at the end of the book.

Prices have been left in the original sterling pounds (£), shillings (s) and pence (d).

List of tables

List of figures

Chapter 1

INTRODUCTION:
BOOM, BUST, CRISIS AND OPPORTUNITY

This book is about change and choice. We should stress both – historians sometimes see change as an impersonal force, sweeping individuals powerless before it, but people make choices in response to change, and those choices in turn drive further change. Economic historians in particular tend to play down the role of the individual in order to explain broader trends and avoid being bogged down in irrelevant detail, but this process can be – and all too often is – taken too far. This book tries to maintain a sense of human agency, of the ability of people to control their situations, even in times of radical and apparently inexorable change.

Mid-Victorian Liverpool is an excellent laboratory in which to explore these issues. England's leading Atlantic port city was a cauldron of growth and diversity, providing its traders with a complex and challenging environment in which to make and lose money. Contemporary commentators stress the pace and scale of change in the port: bigger ships, many made of iron and powered by steam, were using the port every year; they carried a diversifying range of goods in ever-greater quantities; and the dock system itself had to be expanded to cope, stretching further each year along the Mersey waterfront. Indeed, the very bricks and mortar of the dock estate competed with the greatest achievements of ancient civilisations: the Albert Dock warehouses – their 'vastness surpasses the pyramid of Cheops' – stood as a potent visual symbol of the times.[1] Observers were also struck by the global range of the port as manifested in Liverpool's connections with 'every port of any importance in every quarter of the globe'.[2] Running through all this was that other great Victorian fascination – the galloping pace of technological progress. The new forms of transport and telecommunications harnessed by Liverpool traders were indeed central to the port's development, and contemporaries and historians alike have ascribed hefty symbolic weight to the interplay between trade and technology.[3] In the first twelve months of the reign of Queen Victoria, noted Liverpool's most enthusiastic promoter, the railway stretched from Lancashire to London, the first steamship travelled from Britain to America and the electric telegraph heralded an age of instant communication: these three great undertakings had 'given a wonderful impulse, not merely to

---

1 Local historian James Picton nonetheless despised their utilitarian appearance. See J. A. Picton, *Memorials of Liverpool*, 2 vols, London, 1873, vol. 1, p. 520.
2 T. Baines, *History of the commerce and town of Liverpool*, London, 1852, p. 840.
3 See, most notably, D. R. Headrick, *The tentacles of progress: Technology transfer in the age of imperialism, 1850–1940*, Oxford, 1988.

the prosperity of Liverpool, but to that of the British Empire, of Europe and America, and of the whole human race'.[4]

And yet ... historians need to be careful about letting any one group of contemporaries set the agenda. Even those who saw steam shipping as the harbinger of a new age often recognised the complexities inherent in the economics of change: Cunard's John Burns still doubted as late as 1860 whether sail would ever be superseded in bulk trades like coal-carrying.[5] Some saw the rapid expansion of Liverpool's dock system in the 1840s not as a step forward in the provision of national infrastructure, but as a dangerous consolidation of old monopoly power in the hands of the Liverpool Corporation. Where Victorian enthusiasts saw change as progress, many Liverpool traders were conscious of the hard choices facing them, and of the fact that there would be losers as well as winners. Being cautious enough to avoid the more dangerous snakes, yet adventurous enough to climb the more promising ladders was never an easy balance to strike, and neither the zealotry of some contemporaries nor the hindsight of historians should be allowed to trivialise the decisions faced by traders.

This introductory chapter has two tasks. The first part considers previous efforts to analyse the Liverpool trading community. Historians have drawn a range of conclusions from the study of nineteenth-century Liverpool, but just as important are the sources they used and the methods they adopted: it is important to highlight the successes and limitations of earlier studies, and identify avenues for further exploration. The second section of the chapter explains the structure of the book and the way in which the analysis is organised. While the main themes of change and choice run throughout, it is necessary to consider them from a number of perspectives, and a brief survey of the book, chapter by chapter, is a useful guide to the overall argument.

HISTORIANS AND NINETEENTH-CENTURY LIVERPOOL

Historians have long recognised that there are important lessons to be learned from the study of nineteenth-century Liverpool, although they have often struggled to make sense of the patterns they unearth. Much of the problem stems, explicitly or implicitly, from the perception that the town was different, that it was a place of greater extremes than most, and not quite in the mainstream of British history: Liverpool has resisted the tendency of urban historians to rigidly pigeon-hole towns into categories. Perhaps, as some scholars have realised, this owes more to the narrow boundaries historians sometimes put on their work than to any real abnormality about Liverpool.[6] In recent years, those undertaking wider comparative work on port cities have begun to identify a range of economic, social and cultural issues that tend

4   Baines, History, p. 642.
5   BPP, Merchant shipping (1860), evidence of John Burns, q. 2,020.
6   J. Belchem, 'The peculiarities of Liverpool', in Popular politics, riot and labour: Essays in Liverpool history, 1790–1940, ed. J. Belchem, Liverpool, 1992, pp. 1–20; p. 1.

to make such places different.[7] Liverpool is easier to understand as a European port city than as an English provincial town – which of course would have been no surprise to members of its trading community, who generally had a broader view of the world than historians do.

Liverpool's value to the historian of the nineteenth century stems from its trading dynamism and its great mix of social, economic and political forces. Commerce, directly and indirectly, gave Liverpool a particular character, whether in comparison with its industrial northern neighbours or with its agrarian hinterland around the rim of the Irish Sea. By mid-century, Liverpool's mercantile classes already had a long heritage of close involvement in the government of their old chartered town, while the industrial élites of the new manufacturing towns elsewhere in the north of England struggled to gain control of corrupt and obsolete political structures. The Liverpool town council managed the development of the port until the late 1850s, so that questions of politics and commerce were closely linked and leadership in both spheres often resided in the same individuals.[8]

The magnet of commerce and prosperity attracted generations of migrants from all parts of Britain and Ireland and sometimes from further afield. Their legacy was multi-faceted. Most obviously, they brought religious and cultural affiliations to bear on the development of the town, both in the first half of the century when the division between Anglicans and Dissenters permeated the town's cultural politics, and in later years when the influx of Irish Roman Catholics added a new dimension.[9] Commerce also required a 'part-time' population of merchant seamen, which added to the heterogeneous character of the town, as did the large transient populations of European settlers who formed the core of Liverpool's passenger trades to the Americas after mid-century.[10] Such heterogeneity created tensions. The semi-detached status of the town's seafarers, absent from their families for extensive periods, fed into an uncertain social structure, not helped by the obvious contrast with the great wealth of some shipowners and merchants. Confident, commercial Liverpool may have been symbolised by the building of St George's Hall, but prominent critics of the time commented that the money might have been better spent on the other Liverpool, a town with England's worst slums and poorest public health.[11]

This ambivalence of confidence in mid-century is rarely to be found in the town's promoters, but is briefly apparent in the writings of Thomas Baines, among the most

---

7   For a survey of key themes, see W. R. Lee, 'The socio-economic and demographic characteristics of port cities', *Urban History*, Vol. 25, 1998, pp. 147–72.

8   M. J. Power, 'Councillors and commerce in Liverpool, 1650–1750', *Urban History*, Vol. 24, 1997, pp. 301–23; N. Ritchie-Noakes, *Liverpool's historic waterfront*, London, 1984, p. 6.

9   The standard works on Liverpool politics and religion include F. Neal, *Sectarian violence: The Liverpool experience, 1819–1914, an aspect of Anglo-Irish history*, Manchester, 1988; P. J. Waller, *Democracy and sectarianism: A political and social history of Liverpool, 1868–1939*, Liverpool, 1981; N. Collins, *Politics and elections in nineteenth century Liverpool*, Aldershot, 1994.

10 For the social history of maritime Liverpool, see T. Lane, *Liverpool: Gateway of empire*, London, 1987.

11 Neal, *Sectarian violence*, pp. 93–94.

vocal champions of Liverpool's economic boom. Baines' *History of the commerce and town of Liverpool*, published in 1852, is a great compendium of precise figures, reflecting both Baines' own determination to prove Liverpool's status as the most dynamic town in the nation, and also the more general Victorian obsession with collecting statistics – Baines offers page after page of them, from the 1,751 public houses in Liverpool in July 1839 to the 42 million cubic feet of gas required to light the town's streets a decade later.[12] It is all the more striking, therefore, that one of the few points in his narrative where Baines becomes defensive is in his account of the crisis years of the later 1840s, against a backdrop of political agitation and unprecedented in-migration from Ireland.[13] Baines departs from his usual volley of figures to launch a suspiciously vague defence of the town. 'Immense sums' were being spent on improvements; 'two, if not three, times' the cost of public buildings was being devoted to sanitary engineering, for which 'many admirable plans of improvement have been devised'.[14] For a man who used so few words and so many precisely calculated numbers, such fudging stands out, and is indicative of the conflicting demands of commerce and community in a major port.

Where better than Liverpool, then, to study the activities and attitudes of a trading community? That community had a notable reputation in the nineteenth century as a dynamic – perhaps too dynamic – group willing to exploit opportunities and seize trade wherever it was available. Various well-known comments about Liverpool traders' willingness to act pragmatically appear in surveys of the period, starting from the later eighteenth century, when the port's economy was becoming much more diverse. The slave trade and the activities of Liverpool privateers have caused periodic reassessments of the ethics and practices of the port's leading figures. Liverpool traders favoured government regulation when it worked in their favour and opposed it when it interfered with their operations: needless to say, opinions were divided as to whether that attitude stemmed from pragmatism and flexibility, or from a general lack of principle.[15]

This sometimes shady reputation continued to colour outside views of Liverpool in the mid-nineteenth century. Writers for the London *Times*, fond of playing the moral arbiter of the nation's commercial classes and confident in their metropolitan superiority, often sniped at Liverpool traders. The paper was especially keen to expose unsound businesses, and complained that the financial health of firms was surrounded by too much secrecy in Liverpool: the port's traders repelled questions about financial affairs 'with a zeal which shows a greater sensitiveness for the reckless speculator than for the legitimate trader'.[16] It was with great satisfaction that *The Times* quoted

---

12   Baines, *History*, pp. 655, 678.
13   For a recent analysis of the crisis, see J. Belchem, 'Liverpool in 1848: Image, identity and issues', *Transactions of the Historic Society of Lancashire & Cheshire*, Vol. 147, 1998, pp. 1–26.
14   Baines, *History*, p. 677. Baines went on to make a career of promoting Liverpool, taking charge of the town's Parliamentary Office in London.
15   M. J. Power, 'The growth of Liverpool', in *Popular politics, riot and labour: Essays in Liverpool history, 1790–1940*, ed. J. Belchem, Liverpool, 1992, pp. 21–37; pp. 25–28.
16   *The Times*, 24 Aug. 1857, p. 4.

an anonymous Liverpool merchant in 1857 as arguing that 'if you could sweep the Liverpool Stock Exchange from the face of the earth you would indeed be a public benefactor'.[17] Visitors to Liverpool were struck by the way commercial attitudes seemed to colour the thinking of all sections of the community – even the clergymen drove hard bargains over funeral costs.[18]

Such views were not, of course, left unchallenged: Liverpool's community was just as aggressive in its opinions about competitors. Liverpool shipowners complained that Londoners had a monopoly on lucrative government contracts and trading privileges: London owners and government departments worked a cosy arrangement in which carrying troops had become 'a City annuity that had lapsed into two or three firms'.[19] Long-standing tensions between the Liverpool Shipowners' Association and the London-based General Shipowners Society made it difficult for the industry to muster a united front against repeal of the Navigation Acts in the late 1840s.[20] In the 1850s, Liverpool shipowners experimenting with iron vessels argued that the Lloyd's Register Committee was a reactionary London clique whose attachment to old technology was holding back entrepreneurial progress, and the Liverpool Underwriters went on to create their own rival register.[21] Liverpool traders took pride in their achievements, and regularly wrote to correct press stories that put their competitors in an undeservedly good light – especially if the article in question had been written by one of the 'fossils' of *The Times*.[22] When that paper credited Hull with the largest manufactured cargo sent through the Suez Canal in its first months of operation, Harrisons of Liverpool was quick to put the record straight and note that the firm's own *Cordova* had carried a much larger load.[23] Liverpudlians could also give as good as they got in the slanderous epithet stakes: 'Hull merchant' was a local term of abuse for the bookmaking and gambling fraternity.[24]

Unfortunately, efforts to study the activities and attitudes of this trading community in the round have been few and far between. Most work on Liverpool traders has focused on the activities of small sections of the community, and often on individuals and firms that were unusually prominent. The best known body of work has come to be referred to as the 'Liverpool School' of maritime economic and business history. Mainly represented by the work of Hyde, Davies and Marriner, the impressive output of Liverpool University's economic historians from the late 1950s included a number of monographs on Liverpool's major shipping operators of the later nineteenth century. The work of the Liverpool School was classic, corporate business history as

---

17 *The Times*, 28 Aug. 1857, p. 5.
18 Nathaniel Hawthorne, *The English notebooks*, New York, 1941, p. 16.
19 James Baines to the Editor, *The Times*, 2 Apr. 1855, p. 4.
20 S. Palmer, *Politics, shipping and the repeal of the Navigation Acts*, Manchester, 1990, p. 33.
21 Underwriters' Minutes, vol. 6, p. 10; see also letter of Edward Bates, Liverpool shipowner, c. Feb.–April 1858, quoted in M. K. Stammers, 'An extraordinary letter', *Bulletin of the Liverpool Nautical Research Society*, Vol. 41, 1997, pp. 34–35.
22 BPP, Merchant shipping (1860), evidence of John Burns, q. 2,324.
23 *The Times*, 17 Feb. 1870, p. 5.
24 *Liverpool Mercury*, 1 Jan. 1863, p. 5.

developed in the United States prior to the Second World War. Its core approach was the exploitation of large company archives, such as those belonging to Cunard, Blue Funnel and Elder Dempster, tracing the developments of fleets and corporate structures through surviving business sources, and revealing a great deal about the operations of the port's major players.[25] These books remain at the heart of the extensive genre of shipping company history, and continue to inspire periodic re-evaluations of the histories of particular companies.[26]

For a number of obvious reasons, though, the Liverpool School could not reveal a very comprehensive picture of the trading community. Seeing the trade of a port like Liverpool through the eyes of the big companies is not just a problem of scale, but also of kind. Davis noted in the late 1970s that 'most of the companies with published histories are on the liner side – both cargo and passenger – of the shipping industry', and that such companies were unusual until the late nineteenth century.[27] The historiographical situation has changed little since, and the problem remains that smaller operators were not necessarily smaller versions of the big companies, but dealt in rather different kinds of trade.

Broadly speaking, the focus of the Liverpool School was on large liner companies at the expense of smaller shipping operators, and on shipping companies in general at the expense of other members of the trading community: merchants, brokers and agents play little part in most of the house histories of the steamship firms. Such patterns are common enough in business history. Access to the archives of the major players is rarely easy, and historians, for all their claims to impartiality, are always bound to some extent by the expectations of the firm in question. In particular, firms rarely appreciate having their records used as part of a larger project, and understandably wish to be the focus – usually the sole focus – of attention in the finished book.[28] In addition, like most classic business history in any industry, the chronological coverage of most of this work was heavily biased to the late nineteenth and early twentieth centuries: while many of these volumes make reference to earlier periods, it is usually only as a prelude, or a biographical sketch of the early life of the company's founder.

Historians are naturally drawn to firms with complete, well-preserved archives, but this can lead to a loss of perspective. Significant evidence is not evidence of significance. Just because a firm left a complete archive of its activities does not necessarily mean that the firm was very important in the trading community of its

---

25 See, for example, P. N. Davies, *The trade makers: Elder Dempster in West Africa, 1852–1972*, London, 1973; F. E. Hyde, *Blue Funnel: A history of Alfred Holt & Co. of Liverpool, 1865–1914*, Liverpool, 1957; also his *Cunard and the North Atlantic, 1840–1973: A history of shipping and financial management*, London, 1975.

26 For example, M. Falkus, *The Blue Funnel legend: A history of the Ocean Steam Ship Company, 1865–1973*, Basingstoke, 1990.

27 R. Davis, 'Maritime history: Progress and problems', in *Business and businessmen: Studies in business economic and accounting history*, ed. S. Marriner, Liverpool, 1978, pp. 169–97; p. 170.

28 Such problems are well covered in D. Coleman, 'The uses and abuses of business history', *Business History*, Vol. 29, 1987, pp. 141–56; p. 142.

time. Some small and relatively inconsequential firms have left large and interesting archives, or have had histories written by insiders with access to material that no longer exists; some huge firms have left little behind to directly describe their business.[29] The business records of individual firms are also notoriously transient documents, which in many cases seem not to have been valued by those who produced them: the routine and casual destruction of records shortly after they had been generated was commonplace. Court cases involving trading firms were sometimes hampered by a lack of surviving documentation only months after the events in question: one example from the 1860s found that a firm's order books were being used as waste-paper by an employee who was also involved in running a fishmonger's shop.[30]

In addition, and perhaps more importantly, reliance on the surviving records of individual firms can produce excellent works of internal, structural business history that nonetheless seem oddly adrift from the world in which the firm operated. Only in a few cases, when the nature of the business in question encouraged historians to explore connections between companies, were broader questions asked about the world beyond the firm. Marriner's work on Rathbones offers valuable insights, examining the collaborative strategies employed by this commodity trading firm, while Anderson's work on credit and insurance dealt, almost by definition, with the networks of co-operation and investment that linked businesses.[31]

It was partly in an effort to move away from the focus on individual firms that another group of historians, working in the 1960s, turned to an alternative range of sources and began to investigate the first half of the nineteenth century. They recognised the significance of the great upheavals in Liverpool's trade during the first two decades of the century – the Napoleonic Wars, the ending of the slave trade, and the war with the United States in 1812 – and sought to trace the development of the port in the generation thereafter. Faced with very few surviving records from trading firms in the first half of the century, Williams and Neal pioneered lateral approaches to the study of trading communities. In general, such methods rely on the records of official institutions that had some overseeing function – various branches of central and local government keep records of trade, the ownership of vessels and the ownership of companies. Here historians benefit from the fact that economic and commercial activity is something governments and other official bodies are usually keen to keep an eye on, and that such scrutiny generates records.

The two major sources used by Williams and Neal were the Customs Bills of Entry and the Liverpool Register of Shipping. It is useful here to outline briefly the strengths of these sources. The first point to make is that the Bills and the Register

29   Examples from this study would be the extensive letters of Daniel Williams, a minor Latin America merchant, and the rather sparse records of the Inman steamship line.
30   R. Stevens, *On the stowage of ships and their cargoes*, 5th edn, London, 1869, p. 70.
31   S. Marriner, *Rathbones of Liverpool, 1845–73*, Liverpool, 1961; B. L. Anderson, 'Institutional investment before the First World War: The Union Marine Insurance Company', in *Business and businessmen: Studies in business economic and accounting history*, ed. S. Marriner, Liverpool, 1978, pp. 169–97.

are particularly able to cast light on *traders*, as well as on *trade*. These sources are a great leveller: they record details of the activities of traders regardless of the scale of their operations or the nature of their business. Williams based his work on incoming voyages recorded in the Bills of Entry, which include vessels belonging to everyone from the largest operators to the smallest, and itemise cargo consigned to major merchants and occasional dabblers in trade alike.[32] Only a tiny proportion of these traders left business records behind, and those that did are much more likely to come from the top rather than the bottom of the scale. The Register has an analogous set of data allowing us to identify shipowners. Each vessel registered has its owners recorded, along with their places of residence, their occupations and the number of shares they held: changes in ownership over time are also recorded. Neal revealed patterns in the number, occupations and regional distribution of shipowners. Like the Bills, the Register is impartial: the ownership of everything from Atlantic passenger liners to coasters has to be recorded and is consequently visible to the historian.[33]

Anyone spending a few minutes with the Bills or the Register will therefore read the names of more members of the trading community than are contained in the entire collected works of the Liverpool School. Unfortunately, the very strength of these sources can also lead to problems, because the sheer volume of officially-collected material on trading activity can threaten to swamp the historian. Williams and Neal rapidly reached the limit of what was feasible given the manual sorting and processing methods used by historians before the development of computerised databases. Williams was forced to limit his investigations to the three major import trades, and extension of these methods into other trades, or further into the century, was not possible until recently. For this very good practical reason, therefore, such methods have not been systematically applied to the second half of the nineteenth century, during which time the volume of trade, and therefore of surviving records, became very much greater.

It is indeed rapidly evident to the historian approaching nineteenth-century Liverpool for the first time that the largest chronological gap in our knowledge is in mid-century: too early to interest historians of the large steam companies, and too late to be easily tackled by the manual methods of the pioneering users of the major systematic sources. Yet it is equally obvious that the mid-century period has enormous potential for a study of Liverpool. It was an era of considerable and rapid change, and of dramatic and well documented crises, in which Liverpool traders played an important part – how better to assess the abilities of a business community than

32 D. M. Williams, 'The function of the merchant in specific Liverpool import trades, 1820–50', unpub. MA dissertation, University of Liverpool, 1963; also his 'Merchanting in the first half of the nineteenth century: The Liverpool timber trade', *Business History*, Vol. 8, 1966, pp. 103–21; and his 'Liverpool merchants and the cotton trade, 1820–1850', in *Liverpool and Merseyside: Essays in the economic and social history of the port and its hinterland*, ed. J. R. Harris, Liverpool, 1969, pp. 182–211.

33 F. Neal, 'Liverpool shipping in the early nineteenth century', in *Liverpool and Merseyside: Essays in the economic and social history of the port and its hinterland*, ed. J. R. Harris, Liverpool, 1969, pp. 147–81.

through its response to, and initiation of, such major changes in the trading environment? Economic historians have long recognised it as an era of major change in the global economy, in Britain's development as a great power, and particularly in the conduct of international trade. Despite much debate and reassessment over the years, there is still good evidence to support earlier commentators who saw the era from about 1850 to the early 1870s as the 'Great Victorian Boom', or the age of 'Mid- Victorian Prosperity'.[34] From the perspective of trading ports, the period between 1840 and 1870 saw a rapid expansion in trade, at rates well above the growth rate of industrial production.[35] This phenomenon had important consequences, raising the profile of merchants, shipowners and ports relative to that of manufacturers and industrial cities. As will be discussed throughout part one of this book, there were also important shifts in the nature of the world's trades, with reductions in shipping costs making bulk transport of relatively low-value goods more profitable, or, in some cases, affordable for the first time.

A major factor in the changing face of maritime trade in this period was of course the shift from sailing ships to steam. The mid-century decades are by far the most fluid in Liverpool's experience of this question, yet there has been no systematic examination of the role played by the port's shipowners in this crucial change, nor of the full range of consequences for the port and its traders. This gap exists despite some excellent work on the sail/steam transition in particular regional trades.[36] Mid-century shipowners had to take major decisions about their use of shipping at a time when steamships were a risky, unproven but potentially very lucrative investment: this is a particularly valuable period in which to study the business choices of shipowners.

The role of the trading community in other aspects of the maritime economy can readily be explored in the rapidly shifting circumstances of mid-century. A dramatic expansion of the Liverpool docks was needed to cope with new traffic – not just an unprecedented increase in the volume of trade, but also changes in the type and size of vessels carrying it. The trading community was closely involved in this expansion, both in lobbying for it and in implementing it. The mid-century decades saw important shifts in the way the Mersey dock estate was administered, giving historians valuable evidence for the relationship between traders and the institutional structures which helped – or hindered – their activities.[37]

---

34 For the issues, see R. A. Church, *The Great Victorian Boom, 1850–1873*, London, 1975.

35 S. Kuznets, 'Quantitative aspects of the economic growth of nations, X, level and structure of foreign trade: Long term trends', *Economic Development and Cultural Change*, Vol. 15, no. 2 part ii, 1967, pp. 1–140; pp. 69–73.

36 For the Mediterranean, see P. Cottrell, 'Liverpool shipowners, the Mediterranean and the transition from sail to steam during the mid-nineteenth century', in *From wheelhouse to counting house: Essays in maritime economic history in honour of Professor Peter Neville Davies*, ed. L. R. Fischer, St John's, Newfoundland, 1992, pp. 153–202; for West Africa, see M. Lynn, 'From sail to steam: The impact of the steamship services on the British palm oil trade with West Africa, 1850–1890', *Journal of African History*, Vol. 30, 1989, pp. 227–45.

37 The 'company history' of the Mersey port authority is S. Mountfield, *Western gateway: A history of the Mersey Docks and Harbour Board*, Liverpool, 1965.

It is worth making one final point in support of the mid-nineteenth century as important historical territory. It was an era of considerable disruption and crisis in international trade and commerce, caused by wars, and historians (like dramatists) get some of their best material from conflict and upheaval. The American Civil War (1861–65), for example, is widely regarded as having been a defining phase in the relationship between Britain and the United States, and caused considerable economic dislocation in the cotton processing districts around Manchester. Yet there has been little attempt to analyse the effect of the conflict on Liverpool, which was at the time Britain's busiest cotton port and the terminal for the North American liner services. Liverpool traders are assumed to have been pro-Confederate because of their investments in the cotton trade, and the port as a whole is assumed to have suffered when that trade was curtailed, but little systematic work has been done to determine the reality of the situation.[38] Other wars have attracted still less attention from a Liverpool perspective. Perhaps because it was not a major naval port, historians have seen little need to include Liverpool's role in foreign and colonial wars, despite the heavy involvement of the port's merchant shipping in transporting troops and supplies during the Crimean War (1853–54) and the Abyssinian campaign (1867–68).

Such conflicts emphasise the point that Liverpool operated as part of a wider world of trade, globalisation and empire, and this period is characterised by the re-thinking of a number of issues relating to imperial and non-imperial trade. British planners rapidly reached the conclusion that it was not necessary to actually occupy some countries in order to dominate them. Naval power, diplomacy and commercial treaties could keep many parts of the world safe for British manufactured goods without the expense of formal empire. Even where force was considered necessary, it should only be temporary, and careful enlistment of local support would point the region in the right economic and political direction. Not everyone was always convinced, of course. In the aftermath of the Abyssinian campaign in 1868, the *Economist* noted with measured sarcasm that 'the three or four millions of treasure expended among the tribes of the Red Sea may possibly assist them to become, by slow degrees, consumers of English calicoes and hardware'.[39]

If all this has persuaded us *why* we should focus on mid-century, we still need to be confident of *how* to do it. Thanks to the development of computers, and particularly of database software, we can now take forward the approaches of historians like Williams and Neal. The defining methodology of this book is therefore a lateral approach to the trading community – rather than relying on papers generated directly by traders, it uses sources recorded by official bodies which give us an indirect picture of the activities of traders. The Bills of Entry and Ship Register, in the form of

---

38 J. D. Pelzer, 'Liverpool and the American Civil War', *History Today*, March 1990, pp. 46–52, is a rare study of the topic. Neil Ashcroft is undertaking a major reassessment of the Civil War and the Atlantic economy: see his 'British trade with the Confederacy and the effectiveness of Union maritime strategy during the Civil War', *International Journal of Maritime History*, Vol. 10, 1998, pp. 155–76.

39 *Economist*, 'Commercial history and review of 1868' (1869), p. 2.

computerised samples from the mid-century decades, can now provide the core quantitative framework for much of the book, showing the activities of traders and their relative importance.

There are also lateral ways to approach the more qualitative aspects of life in a trading community – what traders thought, and what their attitudes were to the changes and choices around them. One vital and often overlooked source is the rapidly expanding volume of material contained in the British Parliamentary Papers during this period. Britain's global interests ensured that not much happened any-where without having some implication for British imperial and commercial policy. Various branches of government sought to investigate and oversee almost every aspect of domestic and foreign affairs. Such information-gathering, in the form of both routine reports and special enquiries, reflects the range of British interests from the mid-nineteenth century, and the development of a more effective official machine. The Earl of Clarendon, when inaugurating a new system of reporting in 1857, noted that it would be a character-building process for junior diplomats, as well as providing London with more useful economic intelligence.[40]

As can be seen from the Notes on Sources at the end of this book, Parliament held a large number of enquiries into trading questions in mid-century, and many of them either directly involved Liverpool, or heard evidence from Liverpool traders alongside other members of the nation's commercial classes. Most dock-building projects had to be authorised by Parliament through the tortuous Private Bill process, and Committees therefore heard extensive evidence from a wide range of interested parties. The vital point for the historian is that evidence was collected and printed in full, with verbatim records of questions asked and answered. Of course, contem-poraries often recorded their views in contexts that encouraged them to either exaggerate or diminish the changes before them. Those who invested in steam, for example, had to promote it, both to reinforce their own business decisions, and to persuade port authorities to spend considerable sums accommodating large and demanding vessels: sailing ship owners naturally had the converse interest, arguing that steamers were being given preferential treatment, far out of proportion to their actual contribution to the nation's trade. In addition, most traders' views that have survived come from the major, nationally recognised figures who have been studied by historians, or who gave evidence to Parliamentary Committees, and not from the ranks of the small businesses that made up most of the industry. Such biases are readily recognisable, however, and if used carefully, Parliamentary Papers cast valuable light on the activities of individual traders – many individuals who have left no business papers or correspondence behind may nevertheless be found in the proceedings of the Parliamentary Committees, registering their opinions on the major commercial questions of the day.

The other great lateral source exploited in this book is the records of financial institutions. The Bank of England's local agent in particular maintained an extensive correspondence with London, recording opinions on the reliability and credit-

40 BPP, Embassy reports (1857), p. ii.

worthiness of Liverpool trading firms. Major financial upheavals and bankruptcies were discussed in detail alongside the success stories of the port's trading community. Again, the broader activities of otherwise obscure firms can be reconstructed from their appearance in the records of a third party.[41]

It is clear, therefore, that not only is the mid-nineteenth century a vital and revealing period, but it is by no means lacking in material for the historian. This book adopts a combined quantitative and qualitative approach, through analysis of major, yet previously neglected, sources. It seeks lateral approaches to the attitudes and activities of traders, relying less on the scarce records that they personally left behind, and more on the records generated when they came into contact with government and regulators. By these means, it asks new questions about the trading community as an interactive whole rather than trying to extrapolate general conclusions from the activities of a particular firm.

STRUCTURE AND ARGUMENT

This book is divided into three parts. Broadly, part one sets the scene with a discussion of trends and patterns in shipping, trade and port development. Part two takes interaction as its major theme, assessing the choices made by different kinds of traders in the context of the broader profile of the mercantile community. Almost every issue facing traders, whether it was specialisation, growth, credit or reputation, required some form of collaborative or competitive interaction with other firms – no merchant is an island.[42] Part three then considers other indicators of the attitudes and activities of Liverpool traders through their dealings with official institutions, both on a national and imperial scale and at the level of their own port authority. Readers who are primarily interested in business cultures and attitudes can probably start with part two, and use part one for reference, while those seeking a broad view of Liverpool ought to start at the beginning.

The aim of part one, then, is to establish a framework for the major changes that occurred in mid-century Liverpool's trading environment. This is not as easy as it sounds. The central problem stems from a broad failure in much economic history to relate statistical data to the lives and concerns of contemporaries. In big-picture macro-economics, imports, exports, gross national product and a range of other measures of economic development are relatively easy to measure on a national level but much harder to analyse in terms of individual localities, cities or regions. Economic history textbooks are well stocked with statistical series constructed from governmental and other sources, but the evidence becomes much more fragmented when we move below the level of the nation-state into a local context that was, arguably, more relevant to the decision-making needs of contemporary business.

In addition, when local evidence is available, we need to ask what it meant to

---

41 For the most impressive recent use of such material, see S. Chapman, *Merchant enterprise in Britain: From the Industrial Revolution to World War I*, Cambridge, Cambridge UP, 1992.

42 Thanks to Gordon Jackson for this apt comment.

contemporaries. Historians cannot simply select a set of figures as the definitive picture of a given activity, because contemporaries were not unanimous on how best to measure things. An example might help. The total tonnage of shipping handled by each of Liverpool's docks in relation to the length of its quays may seem to be just another measure of activity in the port, among several available and used later in this book. Historians – including this one – would argue that it is not really a very good measure of a port's traffic: it ignores the different working arrangements of sail and steam and becomes even more confusing when used to assess the activity of different commodity trades. But the Mersey Docks & Harbour Board (MDHB) considered this to be one of its most useful indicators, citing such figures in its own decision-making processes and when presenting evidence to government. Therein lies the balancing act: we have to be conscious that a particular indicator is giving us a distorted picture of the past, but also sensitive to the fact that important decisions might have been taken on the basis of those flawed measures. We have to weigh our sense of statistical superiority against the knowledge that contemporaries were the people who actually had to do the job on the ground.

When it comes to analysing the trading activity of a particular port, therefore, various complex and subtle measures are needed. The strengths and weaknesses of all the available indicators need to be explored, and in aggregate they then offer the most comprehensive available picture of the port's operation. Part one adopts this approach, using three complementary perspectives on the work of the port. The first, in chapter two, outlines the changing patterns of shipping using the port. It might be assumed that this chapter would be about the rapid development and growth of steam shipping, and that is indeed the single most obvious trend clear to contemporaries and historians alike. When considered in more detail, though, Liverpool's experience with this transition involved many variables. Historians often overlook the continued growth of sail on many routes throughout the middle decades of the century, and Liverpool provides the ideal case-study for the changing patterns of shipping in a port that traded with most parts of the world. The 'transition from sail to steam' in the port of Liverpool was in fact a series of shifts and adjustments, evolutionary and revolutionary, that touched each regional trade at different times, and in aggregate resulted in a long-term relative decline of sail.

In addition, we need to be careful about using phrases like 'Liverpool shipping'. Many historians would assume that meant shipping *registered* in the port, but we also need to examine in some detail the bigger picture of shipping *using* the port. Vessels of many different nations used Liverpool: their distribution across the various regional trades differed considerably, as did their response to the advent of steam. Naturally, Liverpool's own registered vessels are crucial to understanding the port's shipowners, but visiting ships put just as much strain on the port's resources ton for ton, and the competition they offered was perceived as a significant threat. Chapter two therefore places Liverpool shipping in broader context, offering a variety of indicators which point to the capabilities of the port's merchant fleet in relation to other major operators.

Chapter three takes another approach, exploring issues relating to Liverpool's regional and commodity trades. Trade has been neglected by economic historians in the modern era, and largely eclipsed by work on industry. This is unfortunate, because a better understanding of the processes of trade and the work of traders illuminates important aspects of economic development, and is particularly useful in analysing questions of control and influence over change. Liverpool's traders were under considerable pressure from manufacturers to diversify in the international markets of the era, but they took care to set their own agenda, and only explore new trades when it was in their own commercial interest. The range and sophistication of Liverpool's commodity trading did develop markedly in this period with the opening up of new trades and radical changes in older ones, although large sections of the community remained oriented to the port's traditional bulk trades. The crucial issues here are persuasion and control: any port risked being marginalised over time by shifting patterns of trade and the changing influence of particular commodity markets, and trading communities had to ensure that suppliers and customers continued to use their services.

A third angle is explored in chapter four, which brings in evidence usually neglected in studies of trade and shipping, but which is nonetheless central to the activity of a major port. The provision and development of strategic infrastructure is such an obvious element in the history of a port that it has all too often been seen simply as background and subjected to little scrutiny. In addition, work that does pay attention to docks and harbours is often technical engineering history that focuses on how such facilities were built: rarely have historians asked whether dock facilities actually met the needs of a port's users or how efficiently they were operated. Liverpool's uniquely voluminous MDHB archive facilitates a much more detailed analysis of the dock system than is possible for most other ports. The distribution of different commodity trades across the dock system; the ability of the system to accommodate steam shipping alongside sail; and a range of alternative measures of the working efficiency of the docks are all examined in this chapter.

The three chapters in part one therefore establish key patterns and demonstrate the potential of examining the overall profile of the port's activities from as many angles as possible. Hopefully, some of this analysis is informative in itself, but its main purpose is to provide the foundation for the rest of the book. Part two moves beyond the trades themselves and considers the processes by which Liverpool's trading community made them happen.

Perhaps the most obvious way to organise an analysis of a trading community in easily digestible chapters would be to follow an occupational division, and have a chapter on shipowners, another on merchants, a third on brokers, and so on. That would, however, defeat part of the object of the book: any attempt to take a broader view of the port's activities that starts by imposing the same old boundaries is not likely to be very successful. Occupational divisions in the trading community remained vague in this period and beyond. Although it will be argued that merchanting, shipowning and the other trading functions became more specialised and profession-alised in this period, they still inhabited a rather nebulous space, each closely connected with every other part of the trading systems of the port – many individuals moved in different directions around this space in the course of their careers, usually being more one thing than another, but not necessarily taking major leaps in any clear direction. Devoting a lot of space at the outset to defining people as 'shipowners', 'merchants', or whatever, tends to obscure more than it reveals. It is better to focus on some of the issues that were central to the working of the port and its traders, drawing evidence from as broad a range of activity as possible. The term 'trader' is itself used as a generic expression throughout this book, not to suggest that all who worked in Liverpool's mercantile businesses were the same, but as a reminder that they faced many common issues: more particular labels like 'shipowner' are used when there is a good reason to highlight a genuinely different perspective.

Indeed, specialisation is a question that needs to be addressed and debated, rather than just assumed. Chapter five considers the range of specialisation evident among Liverpool's traders, and prevailing attitudes toward differing degrees of focus. In a time of expansion, as markets diversified and commodities became more sophisticated, ever-more minute specialisms became attractive as a means of reducing risk and ensuring that traders knew exactly what they were doing. The process was not irreversible, however, as economic crises led to a reluctance on the part of some operators to work with a lengthy chain of specialist firms, and some attempts were made to bring elements in the trading process into the direct control of the firm. There were also considerable differences in attitude and tradition from one sector of the port's trade to another, with some maintaining high levels of traditional integrated business while others fragmented.

Chapter six shifts perspective to strategies for raising finance and expanding business activity. While some firms grew dramatically in mid-century – in terms of capital, turnover and employees – many perfectly viable businesses remained small, with few staff and relatively low levels of activity. Small firms, long the staple element in British business, were both sustainable in their own right and, in some cases, capable of being the foundation of much larger enterprises. Change was often most dramatic in shipowning, where capital requirements pushed a greater level of corporate change, but traders of all kinds had a variety of approaches available to them in consolidating their activities and achieving what seems to have been a mercantile mantra of the period – to make a little capital go a long way.

Chapter seven considers questions of risk, reputation and information, which were the often intangible lubricants of the system discussed in chapters five and six. The shadowy means by which banks and other traders decided the credit-worthiness of a firm were often central to the progress of the trading community but are difficult for historians to assess. Firms operated in a web of information and obligation, relying on friends and family for support in difficult times and working to maintain a good name in the broader community. They had to avoid the more dangerous pitfalls of operating long-distance trade with extended – sometimes over-stretched – lines of credit in an era of global upheaval and uncertainty, and had to walk a thin line between entrepreneurship and recklessness. In addition, firms operating in new markets, or adopting new and untested business structures – such as the joint-stock shipping companies – had to persuade a sceptical public that they were safe and reliable.

What does part two contribute to the historiography? Its main feature is the development of a more holistic approach to trading activity. In particular, it contributes to an increasing trend in business history, which, as it matures as a discipline, is less concerned with individual firms, and more determined to explore business culture and environment. In the context of trade, that implies that we need to pay attention to different degrees of collaboration and competition, and to the connections between firms in the trading matrix rather than to the boundaries between them. Such thinking has been the foundation of more recent attempts to write the business history of major *industries*, as opposed to that of major *companies*, and the mercantile sector needs to take its place alongside the better-known manufacturing branch of the economy.

Part three pursues another important but neglected path, placing Liverpool's traders in a broader institutional framework, and linking economics and politics to assess the interface between the trading community and the official bodies that regulated its activity. Traders were vulnerable to decisions taken at local, national and international level, but they also profited from government protection and contracts. In the local context, in Liverpool, matters were made more complex by the creation of an elected port authority: leading traders had to accept responsibility for the management of the port while criticising its operation.

Chapter eight considers the tensions inherent in the relationship between national government and traders. Complex and ever-more-demanding rules and regulations ran alongside lucrative opportunities for traders to win official contracts in an era of imperial expansion. The value of mail contracts to the major steamship lines is well established, but little has been done on the efforts of smaller shipowners to secure such subsidies. Carrying passengers on government contracts – whether troops or emigrants – is more neglected still, despite the fact that troop-carrying in particular was a valuable business for a large number of shipowners. Liverpool shipowners actively sought contracts to service every major conflict from the Crimean War onwards and carried tens of thousands of state-sponsored emigrants to the fledgling colony of Australia. This chapter assesses the drive behind this effort to establish Liverpool as a serious alternative to London as a provider of government contract services.

If chapter eight explores the role of Liverpool's traders on the imperial stage, chapter nine addresses more local issues, in the shape of the relationship between the trading community and the port authority. The nineteenth century saw a steady rise in the influence of leading traders in the management of the port, but also a fragmentation of the trading interest. In addition, the port authority was increasingly scrutinised by Parliamentary Committees, as factions in the port sought to wield influence beyond their local support. Leading members of the trading community played significant roles in decision-making in the port, developed a complex pattern of 'hat wearing', and struggled to balance the influence that particular trades had in driving the development of the dock system. The shift in administration of the port from town council to public trust coincided with a great increase in trade, but also with vocal disputes between branches of the trading interest. It took place against the backdrop of a continuing and acrimonious conflict between Liverpool and Birkenhead, which was in no way resolved by the amalgamation of the two dock estates under one management. There is a case to be made that management of the dock estate became *less* effective after traders were given the right to elect the members of the Board, because they fell into factional disputes rather than operating as a dedicated trading interest: this chapter will offer the first detailed analysis of the pressures on the management of the port in this crucial period.

Chapter ten offers a brief overview of the book's findings and in particular considers the extent to which different trades were able both to respond to changing circumstances, and to drive that change in their own interests. It highlights the role of Liverpool's traders in the mercantile globalisation of the mid-nineteenth century, and offers an assessment of their successes and failures.

Finally, having outlined what is in the book, it is worth making a brief comment on what is not. All books have relatively arbitrary boundaries, or else they would never be finished. Like most previous efforts, this book gets its evidence from Liverpool's overseas trade: the coastal and Irish Sea economy that had Liverpool as its regional focus remains a major gap in our knowledge, and a key priority for future research. We also need much more on the rich social and labour history tied up in the complex connections involving shipowners, mariners and port workers, and the broader social, political and associational activities of the trading classes themselves. The contribution of sectors of Liverpool's economy that were not directly mercantile in nature remains neglected here, as do broader questions of Liverpool as a cultural melting pot, a home for traders, seamen and migrants from all parts of an ever-widening world. These topics, and many others, could be studied in much more detail using some of the sources cited here as a starting point, and it is to be hoped that this book will serve as just that.

Change and choice, then, run as central themes throughout the book. The other fundamental question that permeates structure and argument alike is that of multiple perspectives – the study of a major trading community cannot be effectively conducted from any one viewpoint. The priorities and motives of those who owned ships, of those who traded goods, of those who designed and managed docks, and of a range of other mercantile and commercial interests, must be considered in turn and a broader picture built up than has been the case in previous studies. That is the key strategy and aim of the chapters that follow.

Part I

Patterns and contexts

These chapters consider Liverpool's development in the mid-nineteenth century from three key perspectives: changes in the composition and operation of the shipping that used the port; shifting priorities in the consolidation and growth of the port's trade routes and markets; and the building and working of Liverpool's path-breaking dock system in an era of increasing pressure on resources and facilities. There are many common threads, of course. The rising use of steam shipping, for example, had profound implications for those who wanted to own ships, for those who wanted reliable carriage for their commodities, and for those who had to efficiently manage a dock system becoming congested with ever-larger vessels. Adopting different angles of approach to such problems offers valuable insights, and the aim of these chapters is to build a more integrated profile of Liverpool's development and operation in this era.

Chapter 2

SHIPPING IN AN ERA OF TRANSITION AND OPPORTUNITY

Contemporaries often identified innovation in shipping as the single most obvious indication that mid-century Liverpool was a place of great change and progress – steamships, like their close relatives the railway locomotives, were literally transporting Victorian Britain to new heights of economic and imperial dominance. Nonetheless, it is also clear that sail proved remarkably persistent, and that new, larger and more technically sophisticated sailing ships continued to be used on some major trading routes several decades after steam became the norm on others.

This chapter assesses the nature of these complex patterns of shipping development. The first section offers a critique of previous analysis of the issue, and highlights potentially fruitful new avenues. The second places Liverpool's shipping in the context of British ports, and demonstrates that historians need to be sensitive to the perceptions and priorities of contemporaries if we are to come to a balanced assessment of the port's history. The third section looks in more detail at the powerful role of the US merchant fleet in 1850s Liverpool, because it was an issue of great concern to contemporaries, and represents the background against which change in the port needs to be assessed. The remaining sections focus on contrasting patterns in sail and steam, with particular reference to Liverpool's own registered shipping.

SAIL, STEAM AND HISTORIANS

A great deal of historical research has been devoted to the development of shipping in the nineteenth century. Shipping was an industry – perhaps *the* industry – of global importance in the period, and central to the economic processes that defined an increasingly integrated world market by the beginning of the twentieth century. As such, it offers a range of valuable evidence for historians investigating a number of key issues, quite apart from any intrinsic interest it may have itself. Shipping can be a useful case study of the adoption of new technology, of the changing nature of government and international regulation, of the growth of large-scale companies, and of the relationship between the transport sector and other elements in the economy. This section highlights some of the approaches and findings of such previous work on shipping.

Studies of the industry as a whole have taken a long view of the transition from sail to steam as the key trend in nineteenth-century shipping, from steam's experimental beginnings on short coastal voyages early in the century to its dominance of global trade networks by the end. The striking element in much of this work is the gradual nature of the changes described, and the continued importance of sailing ships until much later in the century than would popularly be supposed. Writing in the 1950s, Graham provocatively referred to the 'ascendancy' of the sailing ship in the *second* half of the nineteenth century, refuting the tendency of historians to assume the dominance of steam from an early date. In fact, sail's persistence had been evident to commentators nearer the time: Kirkaldy's assessment on the eve of the First World War was that 'the really interesting period of the British sailing ship lies between the years 1850 and 1890'.[1]

This continued focus on sail is sound historical practice, not romantic nostalgia. It forces consideration of a complex range of factors in the sail/steam transition, rather than falling into the trap of assuming the inevitable and inexorable superiority of steam over the noble but doomed sailing ship. By taking long-running series of statistics from national merchant fleets, economic historians have been able to consider the relative impact of technological, regulatory and economic factors. Long-term trends in freight rates, the growth of world trade, technological improvements and the changing relative costs of sail and steam have all been brought to the equation. Early steam ships had a high fuel consumption, and naturally had to carry their fuel with them, leaving little room for cargo. Broadly speaking, they could only compete with sail if steam technology was rapidly improved, if the market prices of key commodities shifted to allow higher transport costs to be absorbed, or if government regulation or subsidy favoured steamship operators at the expense of sail.

All of these did in fact happen, and a series of debates in the 1950s and 1960s analysed the relative influence of the various possible factors. Economic historians usually argue that the most important single factor was technological change, and in particular, the greatly improved fuel economy of steam engines.[2] The total costs and capabilities of steamships changed more rapidly in the mid-nineteenth century than the equivalent measures for sail. All else being equal, the newest, most efficient steamships of the early 1870s could compete economically with sailing ships on routes of around 5,000 miles – even a decade before, such voyages had been hopelessly expensive for steamers unless they had large government subsidies for carrying international mail. Further development followed from the 1870s onward, with steam operating on ever-longer voyages as engine and fabrication technology improved.[3]

---

1   G. S. Graham, 'The ascendancy of the sailing ship, 1855–1885', *Economic History Review*, Vol. 9, 1956, pp. 74–88; A. W. Kirkaldy, *British shipping: Its history, organisation and importance*, London, 1914, p. 25.

2   For debate over the relative importance of various factors, see C. K. Harley, 'The shift from sailing ships to steamships, 1850–1890: A study in technological change and its diffusion', in *Essays on a mature economy: Britain after 1840*, ed. D. N. McCloskey, Princeton, 1971, pp. 215–37; also his 'Ocean freight rates and productivity, 1740–1913: The primacy of mechanical invention reaffirmed', *Journal of Economic History*, Vol. 48, 1988, pp. 851–76; D. C. North, 'Ocean freight rates and economic development, 1750–1913', *Journal of Economic History*, Vol. 18, 1958, pp. 537–55.

3   Harley, 'The shift from sailing ships', pp. 219–20.

It should be stressed that while steam may have changed more quickly, sail was not a static or stagnant sector in this period. Some shipowners believed that the continuing evolutionary development of sail offered a more promising future than the more radical leap to steam. There was considerable technological development in sail during mid-century, especially with the refinement of the iron sailing vessel. Iron ships could be made much bigger than wooden ones, giving a boost to sail's economics of scale. Large sailing ships in mid-century often had a small steam engine fitted for manoeuvring in port and on calm seas, creating the 'outstanding form of mixed technology'.[4] Many of the choices between sail and steam therefore stayed marginal for a long time. Even in trades where steam rapidly became the norm, short-term fluctuations in freight rates could shift the balance, with periodic revivals in the use of sailing ships during cyclical depressions.[5] Technological refinement of sail on most routes peaked in the 1850s and 1860s, as demonstrated by the setting of commercial sailing records from Europe to the East and Australia that have never been beaten, but the South American nitrate traders were still improving the capabilities of their huge steel sailing ships in the first decade of the twentieth century.[6]

Identifying the technological innovations at the heart of the process establishes frameworks for further analysis, but should not obscure the complex web of issues surrounding change in shipping. There is an increasing awareness among historians that technological change should not be studied in isolation, or in a narrow engineering or manufacturing context. This approach works on two levels. First, inventions need to be viewed in connection with other associated technologies: this is often referred to as the 'path-specific' question.[7] Steamships needed technological advances in engines to run in tandem with iron fabrication in hull-building, and in the design and manufacture of propellers.[8] Early steamers were notorious for problems with engines that were too powerful for the propeller shafts and housings, and with wasted capacity in engines because boilers were not efficient enough – steam shipping as a whole could only progress as fast as the slowest element in the array of new technologies that had to work in concert.

Secondly, and most important for this current work, we need to understand steamships in the 'real' economic and regulatory world, rather than in the protected and artificial environment of government shipping subsidies. Just as a particular invention has to take its place in a technological and economic context, so individuals and firms are part of a broader commercial web. Technology, economics and local circumstances are all central to the explanation. The mere existence of a technology is not enough to guarantee its universal adoption: it has to be seen as useful,

---

4   D. M. Williams and J. M. Hutchings, 'Shipowners and iron sailing ships: The first twenty years, 1838–1857', in *Peoples of the northern seas*, ed. L. R. Fischer and W. Minchinton, St John's, Newfoundland, 1992, pp. 115–33; p. 115.

5   Graham, 'The ascendancy of the sailing ship', pp. 84–85.

6   Kirkaldy, *British shipping*, p. 575.

7   N. Rosenberg, *Exploring the black box: Technology, economics and history*, Cambridge, 1994, pp. 19–22.

8   Graham, 'The ascendancy of the sailing ship', p. 75.

economically viable and appropriate *in the context of the time*, and not just with the benefit of the historian's hindsight. For many sailing-ship owners in mid-century, a sudden shift to steam made no rational sense, and far from writing these people off as conservative and backward-looking, we should give them credit for a sound awareness of their business. There is ample evidence that technologies and practices can persist over considerable periods of time because keeping them remains, overall, less expensive than replacing them: this is all the more likely in industries in which the initial capital investment is high compared with ongoing running costs. The windmill-owners of Kent in the 1860s continued to use wind-power until their mills fell to bits, and only then adopted steam.[9] The wooden sailing ship industry, in both its building and operating sectors, faced similar issues of being locked into established investments. North American shipbuilders were not ignorant of the new iron technology, nor necessarily prejudiced against it, but they nonetheless had to operate in an environment of raw material supply, capital assets and wages that made continued production of wooden vessels their only realistic option.[10] While in the long run such industries were clearly in decline, they provided a short-run living for those working in them – and when change is so slow that the short run might extend over a working life, it is hard to be critical of those who took the decisions to persist with existing practices rather than make a leap to new technologies.

We need a more balanced perspective. The clarity of the big picture is a valuable thing to have in mind when analysing the much messier circumstances of individual trades and ports, and the continuous improvement in steam performance across the period forms the key thread around which the other factors clustered. Nonetheless, those messier circumstances have to be confronted if we are to assess the human dimension. To grasp the issues here, it might help to consider an analogous case – the recent debates amongst historians over the Industrial Revolution. Taken at its broadest, industrialisation can be seen as a gradual process, with an extended, decades-long period of 'proto-industrialisation' slowly developing into a reformed economy, with more significant change in some industries than in others. From the viewpoint of the individual mill-owner or textile-worker, though, events could appear much more radical, and a whole raft of issues which were of vital concern to contemporaries tend to be lost in the general picture. Explaining change by means of statistical series that span decades and centuries is a vital historical tool, therefore, but we also need methods that retain a sense of human scale. In the case of the sail/steam transition, we need to be aware of the gradualist conclusions derived from the big picture while also recognising that the transition was clearly revolutionary from the viewpoint of those who had to live and work through it in particular ports and trading communities.

Addressing the motives and priorities of individual firms is a reminder that much existing writing on shipping companies focuses on a particular branch of the industry,

  9 N. Rosenberg, 'Factors affecting the diffusion of technology', *Explorations in Economic History*, Vol. 10, 1972, pp. 3–34; p. 25.
 10 C. K. Harley, 'On the persistence of old techniques: The case of North American wooden shipbuilding', *Journal of Economic History*, Vol. 33, 1973, pp. 372–98; p. 388.

and one which is likely to produce a narrow perspective. Most studies of individual firms have attempted to assess the methods by which pioneering companies drove the adoption of steam, often against the background of Liverpool's contribution to the technical advances of the era.[11] Unfortunately, there is a self-fulfilling logic at work here, and this approach has often made the adoption of steam appear inevitable. The individual corporate histories of the major steamship firms were written, obviously, because Cunard and the like were just that – major steamship firms. Their exceptional nature makes them targets for study, but also leaves them with little to reveal about the sail/steam transition. These 'national flagship' companies, with their huge government subsidies, were natural 'early-adopters' of the new technology.[12] Their protected revenues ensured a relatively short delay between the first practical manifestation of the technology and its adoption on particular routes. In addition, the most significant transition made by Samuel Cunard (and by his US contemporary Edward Collins) was not from sail to steam, but from one form of packet service to another: neither had come through the ranks of ordinary cargo shipping.[13]

'The real competition between sail and steam was fought by humble tramps carrying bulk cargoes,' but only occasionally does the existing literature focus on the firms that operated such shipping.[14] Some of the most insightful studies have come from historians of the Scandinavian fleets. Lacking major corporate archives and flagship companies to study for the nineteenth century, Scandinavian scholars have been forced to consider the sail/steam transition from the perspective of less glamorous but much more representative operators.[15] Other historians taking a close look at particular trades and ports have stressed the interconnection of factors involved in the adoption of new technology and the adaptation of older forms and practices in response. The rise of steam in Britain's African trade is a good example: it led to the reorientation of mercantile and shipping activity in a number of leading ports,

11 F. E. Hyde, *Liverpool and the Mersey: An economic history of a port, 1700–1970*, Newton Abbot, 1971, pp. 52–54.

12 There is a useful literature on subsidies and contracts: K. S. MacKenzie, ' "They lost the smell": The Canadian steam merchant marine, 1853–1903', *Northern Mariner*, Vol. 6, 1996, pp. 1–29; F. Harcourt, 'The P&O company: Flagships of imperialism', in *Charted and uncharted waters: Proceedings of a conference on the study of British maritime history*, ed. S. Palmer and G. Williams, London, 1981, pp. 6–28, and 'British oceanic mail contracts in the age of steam, 1838–1914', *Journal of Transport History*, 3rd series, Vol. 9, 1988, pp. 1–18; A. J. Arnold and R. G. Greenhill, 'Contractors' bounties or due consideration?: Evidence on the commercial nature of the Royal Mail Steam Packet Company's mail contracts, 1842–1905', in *Management, finance and industrial relations in maritime industries*, ed. S. Ville and D. M. Williams, St John's, Newfoundland, 1994, pp. 111–37. See also chapter eight.

13 F. E. Hyde, *Cunard and the North Atlantic, 1840–1973: A history of shipping and financial management*, London, 1975, pp. 2, 37.

14 Y. Kaukiainen, 'Coal and canvas: Aspects of the competition between steam and sail, c. 1870–1914', *International Journal of Maritime History*, Vol. 4, 1992, pp. 175–91; p. 187.

15 See articles by O. Gjølberg, O. Hornby and C. Nilsson, M. Fritz, and Y. Kaukiainen, in a special issue of *Scandinavian Economic History Review*, Vol. 28, 1980. (Full citations in the Bibliography.)

and was inextricably linked to trading structures and business relationships that had developed over half a century.[16]

A focus on particular ports and trades also confirms that, for all its gradualism, the sail/steam transition could seem much more sudden at a local level. The idea of a 'crucial decade' in the structure of a particular trade comes across in the literature: the Atlantic cotton exports of New Orleans, for example, switched from 10% to 70% carriage by steam during the 1870s.[17] Technological and economic circumstances could change gradually until they reached a crucial imbalance in the particular market, trade or port in question, giving rise to a rapid shift to steam. Such locally dramatic changes have rarely been investigated in their own right, yet they were the forum for crucial decision-making by shipowners and trading communities. In addition, in the context of the global market, a shift to steam in one trade might encourage sail in others. The Suez Canal may have encouraged the building of steamers, but that in turn created a buoyant market in used sailing ships, which were put to good use in the South America guano trade.[18] There is also the well-observed sense in which the rise of steam generated a need for sail during a crucial period – Britain's exported coal, much of which went to fill coal bunkers in strategic ports world-wide, was carried, of course, in sailing ships. Faced with such patterns, contemporaries could reasonably conclude in 1860 that 'not a single ton of the sailing shipping of the Kingdom has been displaced by the introduction of steam navigation'.[19] Such connections are central to a better understanding of the reasons for adopting steam: the assumption that the rise of the steamship was an inexorable process, and that anyone with any sense would have recognised it as a good thing, does lesser owners no favours – they faced difficult choices in adopting steam that have been oversimplified.

We therefore need an alternative framework for the study of sail and steam, one that is more sensitive to local variation than the macro-economic approach, while telling us more about the real world of shipping than the business histories of flagship companies. Fortunately, a number of avenues for further study have already been suggested in the existing literature. Only by looking at Liverpool's shipping as a whole, rather than studying the activities of the specialised fleets of the major operators, can we reach a more rounded perspective on the shift from sail to steam. This chapter introduces a number of indicators which will collectively provide a new framework for the transition as it was played out in the Liverpool trading community.

LIVERPOOL SHIPPING, BRITISH SHIPPING AND THE QUESTION OF PERSPECTIVE

The first step is to place Liverpool's sail/steam transition in a national context, comparing it with its leading rival – London – and with the British merchant marine in general. Previous research into the rise of steam in Liverpool has revealed a

---

16   M. Lynn, 'From sail to steam: The impact of the steamship services on the British palm oil trade with West Africa, 1850–1890', *Journal of African History*, Vol. 30, 1989, pp. 227–45.

17   Harley, 'The shift from sailing ships', p. 223.

18   *Liverpool Telegraph & Shipping Gazette*, 3 Jan. 1871, p. 4.

19   BPP, Merchant shipping (1860), p. vii.

continued attachment to sail in Liverpool in mid-century. The port's shipowning community 'appears to have clung stubbornly to wind propulsion until the 1870s', but then made a more rapid switch to steam, catching up with the much earlier transition made by London and the east coast ports. Steam accounted for 10% of Liverpool's registered tonnage in 1864, a figure that had already been reached in London back in 1850.[20]

It is important, however, to ask how that conclusion was reached, not because there is any doubt about its accuracy, but because there are several ways to measure shipping, and all offer potentially different views and conclusions. It is also vital that this should not become a dry technical debate between historians – different ways of measuring and analysing shipping reflect different perspectives held by contemporaries. Historians may argue amongst themselves over the validity of particular sources and methods, but we need to remember that we are also in a sense arguing with contemporaries, and trying to ascertain what they intended when they compiled the original figures in the first place.

The compilation of different sets of shipping statistics in the mid-nineteenth century – and therefore the available perspectives on the question of sail and steam – was driven by a range of motives and priorities. The British government placed great weight on the registration of shipping, and sought to compare the total tonnage of the British (and often imperial) merchant marine with that of competing countries: accordingly, these figures will tell us a lot about the nationality of shipping, but sometimes rather less about what it carried or where it went. The above-mentioned conclusion that Liverpool remained committed to sail is derived from this officially collected data on the port's *registered* shipping. Such statistics are widely used by historians, who agree with the original compilers that these figures place the activities of shipowners in the context of their competitors elsewhere.[21] Comparing tonnage registered in London and Liverpool, or in the UK and US, offers an indicator of the relative dynamism of shipowning in a port or country, and their relative attachment to sail and steam. As well as the insights offered by registration data, into competition between ports and countries, there are also practical reasons for focusing on these statistics. Registration data survive for many ports and countries over long periods, thus allowing extensive studies to be made assessing change in patterns over time.

There are, of course, some well-known problems. The first is that registration figures are hard to relate to the actual use of vessels. It is impossible to tell from the registration figures, for example, in which trade any given ship was being used. Given that ports have very different trading profiles, this makes matters difficult. Obviously, in the mid-nineteenth century when steam coasters were more common than

20 P. L. Cottrell, 'The steamship on the Mersey, 1815–80: Investment and ownership', in *Shipping trade and commerce: Essays in memory of Ralph Davies*, ed. P. L. Cottrell and D. H. Aldcroft, Leicester, 1981, pp. 137–63; pp. 138–42.

21 F. Neal, 'Liverpool shipping in the early nineteenth century', in *Liverpool and Merseyside: Essays in the economic and social history of the port and its hinterland*, ed. J. R. Harris, Liverpool, 1969, pp. 147–81; p. 149.

long-distance overseas steamers, a port with a lot of coastal or short sea trade could appear to be more 'advanced' in steam than a port with a lot of long-distance overseas trade, which was still being conducted with good reason in sailing ships. Differences in focus like this are at the root of some disagreements between historians over the relative role of sail and steam. Short voyages were, in general, more typical of the activity of the British merchant fleet in mid-century – continental Europe was Britain's biggest market, and steamers were already dominating the short sea trades in the 1850s. From this perspective, contemporary commentators were right to focus on steam's achievements.[22] On the other hand, historians who have stressed the continuing role of sail are also making valid points, but they are more pertinent to Britain's long-distance trades.[23] For a port like Liverpool, which was expanding its activities in trade with the Far East and Latin America, a continued commitment to sail in mid-century is a sign of sensible business practice, not backwardness. The historian needs to measure the dynamism of a trading community by its use of the most appropriate technology, not the most 'advanced'.

The second problem with registration data stems from the registration of vessels in one port and their operation from another. A significant proportion of Liverpool's early steam liners appear in the port's traffic statistics but not in its shipping register, because vessels operated by the Cunard organisation were registered on the Clyde rather than the Mersey.[24] These included both the transatlantic liners which operated mail and passenger services between Liverpool and New York, and the Mediterranean cargo vessels operated by the company. To all intents and purposes, these vessels were based in Liverpool: they were operated by managing agents D&C MacIver and Burns & MacIver respectively, both firms being as established a part of the Liverpool owning and operating community by mid-century as any of the 'native' Liverpool shipping families. The problem of vessel *registration* bearing no relation to vessel *use* is therefore beginning to be a problem for historians in the mid-nineteenth century, long before more recent concerns about flags of convenience.

What are the alternatives to registration data? The most obvious is to find a measure of the traffic *using* a port. Naturally, this will be different from the registered tonnage, because not all of the traffic using a port was registered there, and registered shipping does not always operate from its home port: while the two sets of figures will have some overlap, they are measures of rather different things. Practically, there is a problem with traffic statistics in that they were less often collected, and it is therefore harder to undertake international comparative studies. For historians of nineteenth-century Britain, however, there is no excuse for neglecting the alternative perspective provided by traffic statistics, which were collected by central government and by local port officials alike.

---

22 J. R. T. Hughes and S. Reiter, 'The first 1,945 British steamships', *Journal of the American Statistical Association*, Vol. 53, 1958, pp. 360–81; p. 361.

23 Graham, 'The ascendancy of the sailing ship', p. 81.

24 G. Jackson and C. Munn, 'Trade, commerce and finance', in *Glasgow: Volume II, 1830–1912*, ed. W. H. Fraser and I. Maver, Manchester, 1996, pp. 52–95; p. 65.

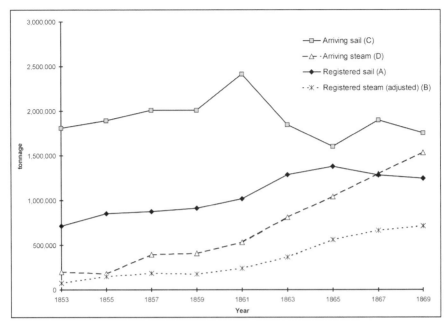

Figure 2.1 Contrasting patterns in arriving and registered shipping, Liverpool, 1853–69
Source: BPP Annual Statements of Trade and Navigation.

Figure 2.1 tests the two sources, and shows the rather different patterns of change in mid-century Liverpool that emerge. In terms of shipping registered in Liverpool, sail and steam tonnage both rose across the period, although sail (series A) levelled off in the later 1860s while steam (series B) continued to rise.[25] When we consider the total shipping arriving in Liverpool, we see a much sharper rise in steam (series D), while sail tonnage rose and fell across the period, returning to roughly its mid-1850s point by the end of the 1860s (series C).

Even from these very general figures, we get a rather different picture of some aspects of Liverpool's shipping depending on the method of measurement chosen. Considering alternative perspectives on the port's shipping is therefore a useful way of identifying anomalies and patterns that need further investigation. Liverpool's own registered sailing fleet, for example, grew in the early 1860s at a time when the port saw a drop in its overall sail traffic. This points to Liverpool owners pursuing shipping strategies that were out of step with the broader shipping community using the port, and will be investigated in the next section of the chapter. It is also clear that steam

25 The registered steam tonnage of the port has been multiplied by three. There is some dispute over the appropriate figure to use, but historians generally argue that steamships did three times the work of sail and that this should be allowed for in this sort of presentation. In fact, for this graph and the others in this section, the shape of the line is more important than the actual numbers. Graham, 'The ascendancy of the sailing ship', p. 86.

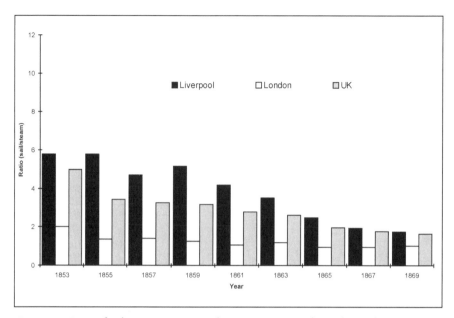

Figure 2.2 Ratio of sail to steam (registered tonnage), Liverpool, London and UK, 1853–69
Source: BPP Annual Statements of Trade and Navigation.

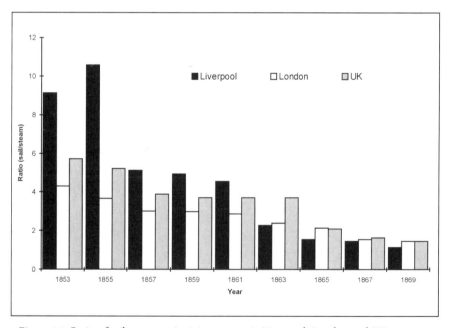

Figure 2.3 Ratio of sail to steam (arriving tonnage), Liverpool, London and UK, 1853–69
Source: BPP Annual Statements of Trade and Navigation.

traffic grew faster than steam registration throughout the 1860s, suggesting that Liverpool's users were more committed to steam than its own resident shipowners were: again, this point will be explored in a later section.

For the moment, it is revealing to place Liverpool's sail/steam figures in the context of the overall UK shipping profile. Figures 2.2 and 2.3 should be looked at in tandem, because they show the results of comparing Liverpool through the different indicators. The crucial point to look for in both graphs is the difference in height between the Liverpool columns on the one hand, and those of London and the overall UK figure on the other. Consider Figure 2.2 (registered shipping). Here the gap between Liverpool and London remained marked throughout the period, although Liverpool did draw level with the overall UK figure by the later-1860s. Now consider Figure 2.3 (arriving shipping) – here the gap between Liverpool and the others is also large in the mid-1850s, but narrows quickly, so that by the early 1860s Liverpool's figures are level with and subsequently below the others.

What do these patterns mean in real life? We can think of the registration data in Figure 2.2 as representing the view from Whitehall of the civil servants compiling the reports for the nation's ship registration statistics. The traffic statistics in Figure 2.3, on the other hand, offer the view from the quayside in Liverpool. Clearly, our observer on the Liverpool docks would have been much more impressed by the port's adoption of steam than someone reading the registration statistics in the Parliamentary Papers. On paper, from the registration data, Liverpool looked to be trailing behind, with far more sailing ships than steamers well into the nineteenth century. Thus the port's registration figures show more sailing ships in relation to steamers than London, and hence the conclusions of earlier historians that Liverpool lagged in the adoption of steam. The view from the quayside, though, was one of a much more rapid rise of steam, alongside continuing use of sail.

Both perspectives are technically accurate, but is it possible to conclude that one or the other is a more relevant measure of the priorities and attitudes of Liverpool's trading community? Various aspects of this question will be considered in the sections that follow, but at the level of particular ports, it is debatable whether registration statistics meant as much to contemporaries as they do to historians. When Liverpool owners in the later 1850s expressed fear for their market share, it was in relation not to the shipping registration figures of other British ports, but rather to the impressive fleets of large US sailing vessels that docked daily on the Mersey. The steam fleets of London or Hull rarely appear in the testimony of Liverpool traders – American strength was the key reason why 'half of our shipowners have been all but ruined'.[26]

While not ignoring registration statistics, then, this chapter gives more weight to trends visible in the port traffic records than has usually been the case in port history. Taking the different perspectives together, we gain a far more rounded picture of dramatic change in the port during the mid-nineteenth century.

---

26   Letter from 'A shipowner, Liverpool', *The Times*, 21 May 1859, p. 11.

THE AMERICAN QUESTION

Liverpool's experience with the United States fleet, and especially with the formidable scale and efficiency of the largest American sailing ships in the mid-nineteenth century, makes a particularly valuable case-study. As we saw in the last section, the overall pattern of sailing tonnage using the port rose and fell in mid-century, but not to any dramatic extent. This apparently unexciting pattern is actually quite remarkable, because the composition of Liverpool sailing traffic changed radically in these years, without having much effect on the overall figures for the port. The size, nationality and construction of sailing ships using Liverpool all underwent significant shifts in a short period. This section explores these changes, and their implications.

The national composition of Liverpool's traffic was an important issue in mid-century. The spectre of foreign competition haunted the shipping industry in this period, and was brought to a head in the debates surrounding the repeal of the Navigation Acts in 1849.[27] Under the Acts, British shipowners had enjoyed a comfortable monopoly over colonial trade, but had also witnessed the rise of other nations' fleets as world trade expanded more generally in the first half of the century. In particular, the increasing dominance of United States shipping on the North Atlantic from the 1830s onward was most obvious in Britain's leading Atlantic port – nothing could have driven home the reality of foreign marine supremacy more strongly than the number of American merchant ships arriving daily at the Liverpool docks by mid-century.[28] The importance of the US merchant fleet to Liverpool in the 1850s is shown in Table 2.1, which breaks down arriving sail tonnage in 1855 by the region from which it came, and by the registry of the vessels concerned. The port's trading community had, for a generation, faced the situation in which much of its key trade was carried in US vessels: in 1855 no less than four in every five tons of shipping arriving in Liverpool from the northern United States carried a US flag, and the figure for the cotton ports of the south was only slightly behind.

More alarming still for British shipowners were the inroads being made into other trades by the US fleet during the 1850s. Liverpool's timber trade with Canada was one of the port's oldest overseas trades, and one which had gained in significance from the late eighteenth century: Canada was British colonial territory which British shipowners were accustomed to seeing as their own market. In addition, Liverpool shipowners and merchants had become complacent in the apparent economic logic of combining ship delivery with timber transport. Ships were built in Canada, loaded with timber and any other available cargo, and then sent to Britain to be sold to British owners, re-registered, and operated on other routes.[29] Extensive networks of closely-related firms, such as that centred on the Rankin and Gilmour families, operated the timber trade in a closely integrated web of shipping, forestry and

---

27 The best study of this complex question is S. Palmer, *Politics, shipping and the repeal of the Navigation Acts*, Manchester, 1990.

28 Kirkaldy, *British shipping*, p. 26.

29 Hyde, *Liverpool and the Mersey*, p. 39.

Table 2.1 Arriving tonnage, 1855, showing regional origin, registry and sail/steam division

Registry		Baltic tons	%	Mediterranean tons	%	Africa tons	%	Far East tons	%	US South tons	%	US North tons	%	Canada tons	%	W. Indies tons	%	S. America tons	%
Sail	Canada									6,789	6			29,714	49	689	5	618	2
	US	444	5	1,195	2			1,655	6	87,217	72	84,569	82	24,420	40	282	2	3,963	12
	Liverpool	157	2	7,770	13	6,024	98	14,055	51	20,367	17	1,800	2	4,958	8	6,585	51	19,363	58
	Other UK			17,901	31	135	2	10,688	39	6,622	5	698	1	1,258	2	4,084	32	5,828	17
	Other	8,847	94	14,557	25			1,105	4							1,154	9	3,566	11
Steam	Liverpool			10,412	18							1,310	1						
	US											10,036	10						
	Other UK			5,755	10							4,398	4						
	Other			348	1														
Total		9,448	100	57,938	100	6,159	100	27,503	100	120,995	100	102,811	100	60,350	100	12,794	100	33,338	100

Source: BE (1855 sample). Vessels arriving in February, June and October 1855.

saw-milling.[30] Nevertheless, the Canadian market was a key target for US shipping in the mid-1850s. By 1855 US-flagged vessels made up 40% of the port's incoming sailing tonnage from Canada, and were rapidly drawing level with Canadian-registered shipping (Table 2.1).

The high profile of US shipping in the decade after the repeal of the Navigation Acts reinforced long-standing fears about the superiority of the American merchant fleet: the abilities of the Americans were part of the popular maritime culture of mid-century Britain.[31] US vessels were well built from excellent yet cheap timber in long-established yards, and their captains had a reputation for sobriety and diligence. As early as the 1830s, the abilities of American master mariners were being singled out as a key factor in their sailing packets taking the North Atlantic trades from British competitors.[32] The government emigration officer in Liverpool reported in 1851 that American captains were 'a superior order of men', often having the additional motivation of being part-owners of their vessels.[33] Such comments are much harder to find in relation to British mariners, although historians have long recognised that various groups in mid-century Britain had an interest in denigrating British seafarers. In the 1840s in particular, amid debates over the Navigation Acts, the competence of mariners became a major political issue. Those arguing that the British maritime economy would benefit from competition had an interest in characterising Britain's shipping as backward and its personnel as incompetent, feeding into popular fear and dislike of the maritime professions.[34]

Liverpool traders themselves had various explanations for the strength of the American fleet, some more convincing than others. A common theme at the Parliamentary investigation into the state of merchant shipping in 1860 was the brutality of the regimes operated on US vessels, with men being worked much harder than was reasonable, under threat of brass knuckles: this, it was alleged, enabled the Americans to work with far fewer crew members than the more humane British.[35] James Beazely, a vocal proponent of this view, had little regard for seamen of any nationality – challenged to explain why mariners would put up with such brutality he alleged widespread drunkenness and stupidity. His only explanation for the

30 J. Rankin, *A history of our firm: Some account of the firm of Pollock, Gilmour & Co., and its offshoots and connections*, Liverpool, 1908, is a survey of the dozen or so firms in Scotland, England and the various Canadian territories that worked as a kind of federal multinational.

31 D. M. Williams, 'The rise of United States merchant shipping on the North Atlantic, 1800–1850: The British perception and response', in *Global crossroads and the American seas*, ed. C. Reynolds, Missoula, Montana, 1988, pp. 67–83; J. J. Safford, 'The United States merchant marine in foreign trade, 1800–1939', in *Business history of shipping: Strategy and structure*, ed. T. Yui and K. Nakagawa, Tokyo, 1985, pp. 91–118, pp. 92–93; R. A. Killmarx, *America's maritime legacy: A history of the US merchant marine and shipbuilding industry since colonial times*, Boulder, 1979, chap. 2.

32 BPP, Shipwrecks (1836), evidence of Charles Lorimer, qq. 1486–95.

33 BPP, Passengers' Act (1851), evidence of Lt T. E. Hodder, q. 1343.

34 The most recent major study is C. Singleton, 'The competence, training and education of the British nineteenth-century master mariner', unpublished PhD dissertation, University of London, 1996.

35 *The Times*, 17 July 1860, p. 12.

willingness of British seamen to sign on American ships was the poor character of the men concerned: 'We all know the character of Jack, that he does not think, and often does not know where he is going till he gets on board the ship.'[36]

A few of Beazely's fellow shipowners took a more rational position. William Lamport was willing to concede that wages might be a factor, noting that American owners paid their seamen at least 10% more than the normal wage on a British ship. In Lamport's view, this actually negated any financial savings available to US owners from having smaller crews, because their extra wages bills cancelled out their smaller crew sizes.[37] Historians have long been aware that US vessels were run with fewer crew than their British counterparts. Part of the American advantage was simply economy of scale. They tended to use larger vessels on average than other flags, and large sailing ships needed proportionately fewer men than small ones – a 1,000 ton ship did not need twice the crew of a 500 ton vessel. Even when this is taken into account, however, British shipowners were failing to get close to their American counterparts in mid-century, and the US fleet was improving its operational efficiency year by year.[38]

Furthermore, Lamport was seriously underestimating the level of crew savings on American vessels. Rather than 8–10%, as he claimed, US vessels were operating with around 30% fewer men than their Liverpool counterparts by the mid-1850s. In 1855, Liverpool-registered vessels over 1,000 tons needed one sailor for every 35 tons: the equivalent American figure was one crew member for no less than 47 tons.[39] If higher wages were also a factor in raising crew motivation and productivity, then the overall effect of US practices made a significant difference to fleet efficiency.

Some aspects of Liverpool's profile of sailing traffic in the mid-1850s therefore seemed to vindicate the worst fears of the protectionists – British shipping was unable to compete with foreigners, and with the Americans in particular, who stood to take over even its formerly secure trades. It is important not to get carried away, however. Another look at Table 2.1 demonstrates that British shipowners had reason for reassurance. US shipping was not making great inroads into Liverpool's traffic, apart from in its own trade, and that of Canada. South America, widely regarded as an expanding speciality of Liverpool traders, was dominated by British vessels: 75% of arriving tonnage in 1855. Only 2% of the port's long-standing West Indian traffic was American by registry, and 83% British.

It is of course possible that the US fleet would have continued to expand its role in British imperial markets, but it was overtaken by events. The subsequent direction of US shipping in Liverpool was determined by one of the most dramatic shifts in the port's trading history: the US merchant fleet largely vanished from the seas during

36 BPP, Merchant shipping (1860), evidence of James Beazely, qq. 2242–44.

37 BPP, Merchant shipping (1860), evidence of W. J. Lamport, qq. 2778, 2810.

38 D. M. Williams, 'Crew size in trans-Atlantic trades in the mid-nineteenth century', in *Working men who got wet*, ed. R. Ommer and G. Panting, St John's, Newfoundland, 1980, pp. 107–53; pp. 121–22.

39 Calculated from BE (1855).

the American Civil War and did not recover afterwards. The collapse of the American fleet is well known to historians, who disagree to some extent over whether the war was a crucial factor, or the final straw for an industry that was already past its peak. Improvements in British wooden ship design inspired by the new tonnage measurement law of 1854 may have been rapidly reducing the gap between UK and US shipping standards in the later 1850s anyway.[40] It is more certain that the US government, with its protectionist, agrarian priorities, was responsible for the failure to rebuild the fleet after the war.[41] Some American vessels were registered as British in an effort to keep trading under a neutral flag, especially in the early stages of the conflict.[42] Many American shipowners went further as the war continued, selling their largest vessels abroad during the conflict rather than risk losing them to raiders, or having them requisitioned by their own side: afterwards, the US government sought to punish such activity and boost domestic investment by prohibiting the return of these vessels to the US flag.[43] By that time, in any case, British steamship operators were making serious inroads into transatlantic emigrant trades, attacking the lucrative westward traffic that had long been of vital importance to US shipping.

In the Liverpool context, the particularly high volume of US shipping in the 1850s made the fall still more dramatic during the following decade. While US-registered sailing ships continued to arrive in Liverpool, their share of arriving tonnage had almost halved by 1863, and again by 1870: in that year, only 14% of sailing tonnage arriving in the port was US registered, down from 48% in 1855. Only in cotton – their longest-standing, most specialised trade – did US ships continue to play a serious role, but even there they had almost been overtaken by Liverpool-registered ships by the late 1860s. On the once-threatened Canadian routes, the level of arriving sail tonnage carrying a US flag fell to less than a quarter of its 1855 level.[44]

In one sense, historians should not exaggerate the overall impact of this collapse on the US maritime economy, because coastal shipping and inland waterways continued to carry an important proportion of the nation's trade, and this made a great deal of sense in the era of westward expansion and Manifest Destiny.[45] US sail tonnage registered for overseas trade may have fallen almost in half in the decade after 1860, but the nation's inland waterways fleet continued to expand. On the Atlantic routes, though – and particularly in the context of our current focus on Liverpool – the effect was a radical realignment of the national profiles of merchant shipping. The Civil War created an unprecedented shift in Liverpool's traffic, and the port's own shipowners moved quickly to take advantage.

---

40 Graham, 'The ascendancy of the sailing ship', p. 79.
41 Safford, 'The United States merchant marine', pp. 96–97.
42 *The Times*, 23 Jan. 1861, p. 12.
43 Killmarx, *America's maritime legacy*, p. 67.
44 BE (1855, 1863, 1870).
45 P. N. Davies, 'British shipping and world trade: Rise and decline, 1820–1939', in *Business history of shipping: Strategy and structure*, ed. T. Yui and K. Nakagawa, Tokyo, 1985, pp. 39–85; table 2.

PERSISTENCE IN SAIL

The most important point to be stressed in this section is that the collapse of the US sail fleet did not mark the end of sail in the port of Liverpool. Nor did the sharp rise in steam traffic in the port (see next section) create an immediate decline in sail. Shipowners and operators clearly felt that there was enough business left for sailing ships to make it worth their while taking up where the Americans had been forced to leave off, in the sail trades.

Table 2.2 Characteristics of arriving sail tonnage, by registration

	1855			1863			1870		
Registry	Total tonnage	Mean tonnage	As % of total arriving sail tonnage	Total tonnage	Mean tonnage	As % of total arriving sail tonnage	Total tonnage	Mean tonnage	As % of total arriving sail tonnage
US	203,908	1,046	48	110,631	1,302	25	59,584	993	15
Liverpool	89,217	485	21	135,463	574	31	137,971	738	35
Other UK	52,895	231	12	92,077	287	21	90,690	353	23
Canada	38,104	595	9	41,932	626	10	37,720	674	9
Germany	10,783	245	3	15,203	323	3	15,309	356	4
Spain	5,476	203	1	7,688	285	2	7,630	332	2
Holland	3,467	193	1	3,094	221	1	4,270	225	1
Norway	3,020	232	1	2,628	263	1	15,568	318	4
France	2,508	96	1	2,787	147	1	4,297	215	1
Italy	1,527	218	0	3,929	246	1	8,770	418	2
Other	13,590		3	22,782		5	15,089		4
Total	**424,495**		**100**	**438,214**		**100**	**396,898**		**100**

Source: BE (Samples). Vessels arriving in February, June and October.

A number of points can be made about Liverpool's evolving experience of sail in the 1860s. Table 2.2 shows the changing proportions of national flags using the port in the third quarter of the century. The most dramatic shift, obviously, is found in the first row, which shows the collapse of the US fleet. Liverpool's own fleet (row 2) moved to become the largest single registration by the early 1860s, and will be discussed in more detail shortly. Of the other 'flags', UK tonnage outside Liverpool almost doubled its share. This increase was remarkably fragmented, however, with a large number of ports contributing only one or two vessels to the total: of all UK port registries, only London and Glasgow routinely accounted for more than 1% of Liverpool's sail traffic. Canadian-registered traffic remained broadly constant, while other nationalities made minor gains in their share of the port's activities.

The only pronounced increase in market share, albeit from a very low base, is that of the Norwegian fleet. Importantly, though, the Norwegians had broken out of the old pattern of working between their home country and the UK, and were making an impact in cross trades with third parties. Only 30% of Norwegian sailing tonnage arriving in Liverpool in 1870 came from Norway or its surrounding countries, while 14% carried timber from Canada, 11% worked in the South American animal hides trade, and 24% sailed from the southern United States.[46]

Liverpool's own registered sail fleet therefore clearly emerges as the single force that took most advantage of the collapse of the US fleet. Liverpool's increase in average tonnage was also more marked than that of its rivals. This is a useful starting point for a closer discussion of Liverpool's own sailing fleet. Not only did the overall figures increase, but the fleet became heavily weighted toward the larger end of the scale. Only 7% of Liverpool-registered sailing ships active in overseas trade were over the 1,000 ton mark in 1855, but by 1870, this had increased to 31%.[47] Given that the US fleet was, in effect, the benchmark against which all sailing fleets measured themselves in the 1850s, it is worth comparing the Liverpool and US fleets as they appeared in the port in this period.

Table 2.3 Characteristics of Liverpool-registered sailing ships in overseas trade

	1855			1863			1870		
	% of total	mean age	mean tonnage	% of total	mean age	mean tonnage	% of total	mean age	mean tonnage
Wood sail									
Country where built									
Britain	36	11	339	31	13	381	15	12	435
Canada	56	7	658	37	7	566	42	10	915
US	4	7	518	22	11	943	7	17	1083
Other	0			2			2		
Iron sail									
Country where built									
Britain	3	8	575	9	4	492	33	7	677

Note: Vessels built in 'other' countries are too few in number to make further analysis worthwhile.

Source: BE (Samples). Liverpool-registered vessels only; further details then traced in the Liverpool Register of Shipping.

Liverpool's improved sail fleet was created on two fronts: by using bigger wooden vessels and by investing in the new iron sailing ships. The upper section of Table 2.3 shows the ongoing use of larger wooden ships. Clearly, Liverpool owners were heavily reliant on Canadian-built ships, especially at the largest end of their operations: Canadian-built ships were almost twice as large on average as their British-built counterparts in the Liverpool fleet. This is a reflection, though, of the ambivalence with which British shipowners looked upon Canadian shipping in this period. Sailing ships from the maritime provinces were cheaply built and considered eminently

46   BE (1870).
47   BE (1855, 1870).

suitable for the bulk cotton and timber trades, but owners working on long-distance routes in more hazardous seas maintained a preference for British-built vessels.[48] Canadian shipbuilders tried to counter such attitudes by improving their product – from the early 1850s, brokers were praising the new lines and better build of colonial ships, and the willingness of builders to have ships coppered before sale rather than leaving this for the new owners to deal with.[49] Nonetheless, perceptions of the superiority of British-built shipping permeated the industry: Lloyds would only certify Canadian vessels at the top rate (A1) for six or seven years, as against the best British vessels which might retain that classification for twice as long. The comparative roles of British and Canadian-built ships therefore show that, overall, Liverpool owners were getting the most from their vessels: both groups have average ages throughout the period that are broadly in line with the oldest Lloyds classification, suggesting that wooden vessels were being used to their maximum effect.

Should we go further, and argue that continued attachment to wooden sailing ships suggests decline and conservatism? There is, after all, a thin line between making the most of an investment, on the one hand, and risking lives and cargo in obsolete ships on the other. The average ages of both Canadian and British-built wooden vessels increased slightly over the period (Table 2.3), suggesting a tendency to hold on to vessels longer than before, but the changes are not dramatic: there is no sense on the basis of these figures that Liverpool owners were clinging desperately to ageing obsolete vessels.

This conclusion is further supported by two related strands of evidence. First, if the owners of Liverpool's wooden ships were extreme conservatives in the 1860s, one would expect to see them buying up large numbers of second-hand US sailing ships during the American Civil War, and eking every last ounce of service from them. Many of the US-built vessels that appear in significant numbers in the Liverpool fleet in the early 1860s (Table 2.3, 1863 columns) were indeed acquired in exactly that fashion. Liverpool's owners took good advantage of the American crisis, selectively buying the largest vessels available. In 1863, Liverpool firms bought 137 US ships, totalling 122,924 tons: this was 22% of the number of such ships sold to British subjects, but no less than 37% of the tonnage.[50] Some of these American vessels were still in use in Liverpool in 1870, but their proportion of the overall sailing traffic of the port had declined markedly since the boom period during the war. In addition, the expansion of US-built tonnage in Liverpool's own sail fleet in the early 1860s was only accompanied by a *relative* fall in British- and Canadian-built tonnage: in absolute terms this tonnage stayed broadly constant over the period. It is clear therefore that the acquisition of significant US-built tonnage on the second-hand market in the early 1860s was not the last throw of Liverpool's wood-sail operators as the rest of the port rushed to iron or steam: instead, it should be seen as an opportunistic reinforcement of continuing patterns.

48   BPP, Shipwrecks (1843), evidence of George Kendall, q. 2560.
49   Tonge, Curry & Co. circular, quoted in *The Times*, 6 Jan. 1852, p. 3.
50   Calculated from BPP, American vessels (1863).

In addition, Liverpool emerged relatively unscathed from enquiries in the early 1870s aimed at identifying failings in Britain's shipping safety practices. Of 168 vessels ordered to be repaired by government surveyors in 1874, only 14 came from Liverpool.[51] While criticism of the standard of vessels used in the timber trade especially remained common in the later nineteenth century, Liverpool's own ship-owners could claim that they placed considerable emphasis on safety, and indeed that they saw it as a crucial element in the maintenance of their commercial reputations.

This determination to drive whatever improvements were possible within the context of wooden sailing ships is also evident in the relative crewing levels of Liverpool's fleet over time. The Americans, as has been mentioned, were far better at running ships with small crews than were British shipowners, but the mid-century decades nonetheless saw a marked improvement in Liverpool's crew/ton figures. Liverpool never reached the efficient crew levels of the Americans or the Canadians, but its crewing levels were being actively reduced in mid-century, especially in the largest sailing ships. Liverpool vessels over 1,000 tons needed one crew member for every 35 tons in 1855, but one to 45 tons by 1870.[52] Historians working in more detail with crew/ton ratios have analysed patterns in relation to the rig of the ship and the trade in which it was used, as well as placing these issues in a broader context of the working conditions of maritime labour. Work on the merchant fleets of Atlantic Canada, for example, has stressed changing technology, but also a deliberate reduction in crew levels and increase in the demands made of the remaining sailors.[53] None-theless, even the material discussed in this section is sufficient to demonstrate an ongoing commitment to wooden sailing ships on the part of a significant sector of Liverpool's trading community, and also – more importantly – to establish that this was a dynamic sector, able to expand and develop its fleet and use it more efficiently in mid-century.

The other side of Liverpool's continued employment of sailing ships – iron construction – is shown in the bottom part of Table 2.3. Iron made its most rapid impact in the Liverpool sail fleet in the later 1860s, rising to one-third of the active sail tonnage by 1870. This interest in iron vessels needs to be considered against contemporary opinion, which was very divided. Iron ships in tropical latitudes suffered badly from hull fouling, and as a result were often very slow in the later stages of long voyages: vessels trading in the Far East made 'a good passage out, and a bad passage home'.[54] There was also a significant problem with compass deviation in iron vessels. While manageable on short sea and coastal voyages, this was potentially disastrous in long-distance trades where vessels were out of sight of land for weeks – precisely the trades in which Liverpool owners wanted to use large sailing ships and

---

51 Calculated from BPP, Ships detained (1876).

52 Calculated from BE (1855, 1870).

53 Williams, 'Crew size in trans-Atlantic trades', pp. 112–20; E. W. Sagar, *Seafaring labour: The merchant marine of Atlantic Canada, 1820–1914*, Kingston, 1989, chap. 7.

54 BPP, East India communication (1862), evidence of David Wilson, q. 319; Graham, 'The ascendancy of the sailing ship', p. 76.

were keen to experiment with iron. The port's traders took the problem seriously enough to form a Committee to investigate the question and lobby the Board of Trade.[55] Nonetheless, others could refer to 'the acknowledged superiority of iron vessels, in point of durability, carrying capacity and economy of working'.[56]

Iron sailing ships are often seen as a half-way house between wooden sailing and steamships, particularly because the sail auxiliary vessels of the 1850s seemed such a logical mixture of technology. Such vessels combined the economy of a sailing ship with the ability of a steamer to make progress in calm weather. The problem, of course, was that such vessels had much higher operating costs than either pure sail or pure steam. Engines large enough to do more than just manoeuvre the ship in port were costly, and needed a specialised crew to run them; carrying enough sails to drive the ship also required a sailing crew and another tranche of capital. Shipowners found by the late 1850s that adding slightly to the steam element allowed them to do away entirely with the sail, or vice versa: economically, it was more efficient to be one or the other.[57] The iron sailing ships that became so prominent in the Liverpool fleet by the 1860s were therefore large, modern vessels designed for the long-distance bulk trades. Liverpool dominated the British market in such ships, in sharp contrast with London's commitment to auxiliary vessels.[58]

Before moving on to consider Liverpool's adoption of the new steam technology, a few points should be made about sail in conclusion. The rising proportion of Liverpool's sail traffic that was British- or colonial-registered in this period was a striking turn around for an industry that reached mid-century in fear of foreign competition. Liverpool shipowners took the lead in filling the shipping vacuum left by the Civil War, and in adopting new practices and larger ships to take their existing businesses forward by evolution rather than revolution.

STEAM: THE LIMITED REVOLUTION

Liverpool's adoption of steam is a more familiar process than its persistence in sail, and many of the patterns have been described elsewhere.[59] It is important to stress that while dramatic, Liverpool's early increase in ocean steam traffic was narrowly focused. The Mediterranean and northern US trades made up 79% of Liverpool's arriving steam tonnage in the mid-1850s, and still accounted for just over 70% in 1870.[60] Most of the overall increase in Liverpool's steam traffic was in these regions,

---

55 Underwriters, Minutes, vol. 6, p. 15.
56 British Shipowners' Company, prospectus printed in *Gore's Advertiser*, 7 Apr. 1864, p. 3.
57 A. Holt, 'Review of the progress of steam shipping during the last quarter of a century,' *Minutes of proceedings of the Institution of Civil Engineers*, Vol. 51, 1877–8, pp. 2–135; p. 9.
58 Williams and Hutchings, 'Shipowners and iron sailing ships', pp. 127–29.
59 Cottrell, 'The steamship on the Mersey'; also his 'Liverpool shipowners, the Mediterranean and the transition from sail to steam during the mid-nineteenth century', in *From wheelhouse to counting house: Essays in maritime economic history in honour of Professor Peter Neville Davies*, ed. L. R. Fischer, St John's, Newfoundland, 1992, pp. 153–202.
60 BE (1855, 1870).

as an increasing number of operators ran ever-larger vessels on proven routes. These trades also saw the only real replacement of sail with steam in Liverpool during the period, with steam tonnage increasing rapidly and sail tonnage falling in absolute as well as relative terms. Finally, they fit the model mentioned earlier in this chapter of a transition that happened within a 'crucial decade' or so. By 1870, arriving steamship tonnage outnumbered sail by more than four to one in Liverpool's Mediterranean trades, and by five to one with the northern US ports.

If these two routes dominated Liverpool's early ocean steam trades, there is an equally striking pattern in the registry of the vessels themselves. No less than 86% of arriving steam tonnage in 1870 was registered in either Liverpool or Glasgow.[61] These vessels therefore provide much useful evidence, and their profile is shown in Figure 2.4. The first point to make is the contrast in the number and size of steamships between 1855 and 1870. Series A and B show the tonnage profile of Liverpool and Glasgow vessels using Liverpool in 1855: they are broadly similar in pattern, with most vessels in the 400–800 ton range, and only a few of Cunard's Glasgow-registered ships in the 1,200 ton range on the right-hand end of the curve. As is obvious from the 1870 patterns (series C and D), though, steam shipping in Liverpool expanded dramatically both in number and size during the 1860s – not only were there many more vessels in the smaller tonnage range, but significant numbers of larger ships in the 1,500 to 2,000 ton range were in use by this point.

The 1870 patterns (series C and D) also point to increasing specialisation in the size of steamers used by the major operators on particular routes. Consider Glasgow-registered vessels first. Series D has two clear peaks. That on the right-hand end of the graph is mainly the Cunard/Burns & MacIver fleet, working in the US and Mediterranean trades, while the left-hand area, around the 600 ton mark, represents smaller steamers, mainly handled by Henderson Brs, working the Italian fruit trades.[62]

Liverpool's own registered steam fleet in 1870 (series C) was more diverse, with frequent use of vessels in much of the range from 300 to 2,500 tons. Nonetheless, there are at least four discernible peaks worthy of particular focus. The very largest vessels, in the 2,500 ton range at the far right of series C, were the new cargo liners operated on the US routes by firms like the National Steam Navigation Co. Much of the area round the 2,000 ton point is made up of Atlantic liners belonging to William Inman, and the largest, newest ships of the Bibby Mediterranean fleet.

Ships in the 1,000–2,000 ton range were by this point the workhorses of a number of trades, most particularly in the Mediterranean: this is reflected in the large area in the middle of series C. Such vessels were also a useful compromise for some of Liverpool's newest steam operators, because they were large enough to carry considerable cargoes yet not so large as to be barred from the undeveloped harbours of Africa and South America: these trades will be considered in more detail in the next section. Finally, the smallest category, at the left of series C, reflects the continued

---

61 BE (1870).
62 For example, BE 28/2/1870/15, 8/6/1870/6.

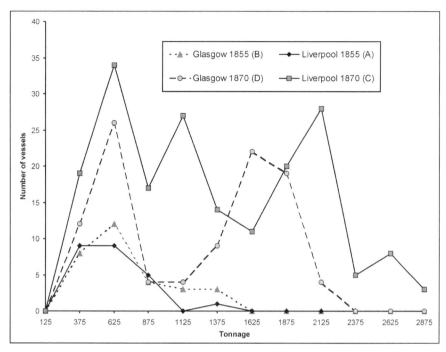

Figure 2.4 Contrasting profiles of Liverpool- and Glasgow-registered ocean steamers using
Liverpool, 1855 and 1870
Source: BE (Samples).

use by Liverpool owners of large numbers of 600-ton steamers on the shorter sea
routes to Europe.

The key point to emerge from this section is that much of the dramatic rise of
steam shipping using the port of Liverpool was closely focused on two major trades.
It was also concentrated in the hands of a relatively small number of Liverpool and
Glasgow firms that managed the expansion within little more than a decade. Like
the port's experience with sail, the early adoption of steam on the two main routes
involved a consolidation of control in Liverpool. Just as Atlantic sail had been the
preserve of the Americans, so Mediterranean sail had relied on vessels and operators
from outside Liverpool. In this case, though, there was no single dominant player –
Mediterranean sail was a scattered business conducted by small shipping firms from
a wide range of British and continental ports.[63] In 1855, as steam was beginning to
establish itself, no fewer than 72 ports of registry contributed vessels to Liverpool's
sail trade with the Mediterranean.[64] The following decade saw that activity decline
dramatically, and with it the diversity of smaller operators.

Liverpool's steam operators also established footholds in a range of other trades

63 Cottrell, 'Liverpool shipowners'.
64 BE (1855).

in mid-century, although none reached the take-off point for a large-scale shift to steam. Indeed, some showed no signs of interest in steam beyond a few highly specialised and unusual activities – carrying the mail, mostly – and contemporaries would have been hard pressed to visualise a Mediterranean-style transition in many of the port's trades. Nevertheless, where steam firms did establish themselves in niche trades, the shift to Liverpool ownership patterns is a feature across the board. As steam routes superimposed themselves on top of existing, and ongoing, sail patterns, so Liverpool owners became prominent in areas otherwise dominated by foreign shipping. The Baltic is a good example. There is a clear division between traffic from Hamburg and that from elsewhere in the region. Liverpool's Hamburg trade in 1870 was conducted by the regularly scheduled, Liverpool-registered steamers of Donald Currie & Co.[65] The rest of the region's trade with the Mersey continued to be carried in sailing ships, a trade that changed little in the middle decades of the century – vessels increased in average size, but just over half of the sailing tonnage from the region was registered in Prussia or elsewhere in the north of Germany throughout the period, and the rest was shared among the Scandinavian fleets. Ample traffic in bulk goods like timber and grain remained for the sailing ships, which had long-established connections with Liverpool agenting firms.[66]

Liverpool's South American traders adopted a similar pattern of selective intro-duction of steam services, although there is also a complicating factor in this period of the adoption of iron sailing ships. Liverpool's own shipowners continued to use wooden sailing ships, added another level of iron sail, and then selectively deployed steamers in addition to that. Arriving sail tonnage from South America doubled in Liverpool in the decade after 1855, and the new iron clippers increased the average tonnage of sailing ships from the region. As well as expanding existing long-distance trades in South America, Liverpool's owners took the process a logical step further, using large sailing ships to open a grain trade with the west coast of the United States during the 1860s.

Most regional trades therefore show the beginnings of the sail/steam transition in mid-century, but had not reached the point of critical momentum by 1870. These trades are therefore very revealing, highlighting as they do the complexity of sail/steam and the variety of factors involved in gradual transitions. They also demonstrate the range of factors involved in the transition, only one of which was the technological change itself. These trades will therefore be considered again in the next chapter, and placed in the broader context of commodity markets and diversification strategies.

---

65 *Sutherland* (SR 1867/021, BE 26/10/1870/5) and *Navarre* (SR 1866/155, BE 14/10/1870/15); for Currie's Baltic enterprise, see A. Porter, *Victorian shipping, business and imperial policy: Donald Currie, the Castle Line and southern Africa*, Woodbridge, 1986, pp. 34–36.

66 For example, *Express* (BE 4/6/1870/1) and *Peter Rolt* (BE 11/6/1870/13), both N. German-registered sailing ships carrying timber to Liverpool, where their affairs were handled by Bahr, Behrend & Co.

This chapter has sketched the profile of Liverpool's shipping in the mid-nineteenth century, and has reinforced the centrality of the transition from sail to steam. It has also, however, highlighted some of the subtleties of that process – such changes meant different things in different regional trades, and have to be considered in a broad economic and business framework in addition to the more common attention paid to technology and innovation. Questions of sail and steam were not matters of abstract intellectual debate among shipowners. As will be discussed in the rest of part one, the shipping operations of the port were fundamentally linked to the commodity trades pursued by Liverpool merchants, and to the development and operation of the port's docks and other key infrastructure.

The most striking pattern in both sail and steam, however, is the shift in control toward Liverpool's own shipping operators. On the Mediterranean and northern United States routes, Liverpool-based steamers rapidly dominated trades that had previously been the preserve of others, whether the much-feared Americans on the North Atlantic, or the broadly-scattered community of small schooner operators trading with southern Europe. The various sail/steam transitions of mid-century Liverpool were therefore accompanied by transitions in ownership also, toward British, and particularly Liverpool, shipping operators. The increased role of Liverpool-registered and Liverpool-based shipping points to a consolidation of economic power by the port's own trading community, a key thread that will be considered from a number of perspectives throughout the book.

Chapter 3

TRADE, DIVERSIFICATION, REGIONS AND COMMODITIES

This chapter considers the range of trades that made Liverpool a crucial contributor to Britain's overseas commercial economy in the mid-nineteenth century. This has been a neglected element in historical writing. Maritime history has usually focused on ships rather than cargoes or regional trading systems, and the economic history of the modern era as a whole pays more attention to industry than to trade. In addition, the history of particular commodities tends to be written in terms of their production and/or manufacture rather than their trade – there are, for example, many more books on the agricultural production of cotton in the American South and on the manufacture of textiles in the Lancashire mills, than on the mercantile processes that carried the raw cotton from one to the other. What work there is on Liverpool's trade has also suffered from a similar problem to that of its shipping, in that historians have concentrated on the big players. Any book on Liverpool will make the same general observations about the port's trade, with its familiar pattern of cotton, grain and timber being imported and coal, salt and manufactured goods being exported.[1] While correct, this broad picture conceals a multiplicity of smaller trades which collectively provided a living for a significant proportion of the Liverpool trading community. The great diversity of trade lurking underneath the well-known staples made the port more attractive to merchants and shippers, confident that they could sell almost anything, and find a return cargo without much difficulty. Although very hard to quantify, the collective contribution of the lesser trades to the port's overall prosperity needs to be considered along with the major staple commodities.

In addition, these commodity trades should not themselves be seen in isolation. The first section of this chapter sketches the broader context of Liverpool's mercantile activity, considers the relative importance historians have given to trade, and argues that greater awareness of the realities of the provincial trading environment would add an important dimension to our understanding of the process of industrialisation and the development of the British economy. The remaining sections consider approaches to the history of Liverpool's regional and commodity trades, using the issue of diversification as an interpretative theme. Diversification is sometimes seen as an unequivocally positive trend, but contemporaries were less certain, and had to balance the potential benefit against the risk of moving away from well-known and established markets and practices.

1   For an overview, see F. E. Hyde, *Liverpool and the Mersey: An economic history of a port, 1700–1970*, Newton Abbot, 1971, chapter 3.

Rather than recount statistical series for these various trades, a number of which are available elsewhere, it is important to analyse the often conflicting influences that drove change in the port's trading patterns. Trading opportunities were promoted by traders themselves seeking new markets and profits, but also by a number of external forces. British imperial expansion in the nineteenth century was a commercial as well as a military business. Traders expected to benefit, at least indirectly, from the growing influence of the British in various parts of the world. Changes in trading practice were also driven by customers, whether producers of raw materials, manufacturers of finished goods, or – increasingly – the unpredictable consumers of fashion and luxury status symbols. Finally, trade was, of course, closely tied to transport and communications, and the complicated pattern of steamship adoption in regional trades shifted the economic arguments for and against the carriage of certain commodities on those routes. Through all this, Liverpool traders worked to maintain, and where possible expand, the influence of their port and its markets on an increasingly global stage.

PERSPECTIVES ON TRADE, DEVELOPMENT AND CONTROL

Trade has sometimes seemed to be the Cinderella subject of modern economic history, especially in Britain. The key reason appears to be that a generation of historians in the third quarter of the twentieth century developed a rather narrow obsession with the study of industry, and devoted all their efforts to ever-more-minute aspects of the 'industrial revolution'. Many historians have assumed that because Britain was the first European nation to embark on large-scale industrialisation, manufacturing industry itself was the crucial element in the country's prosperity in the nineteenth century. The relative decline in British industry, as other countries in turn developed their manufacturing and raw material sectors, is then seen as a central explanation for British economic decline from about 1870 onward. When trade appears at all in such work, it is usually in a negative sense: a large amount of academic time and effort was spent in the 1970s demonstrating that overseas trade was only a relatively small contributory factor to Britain's industrial 'take-off' in the later eighteenth century.[2]

More recently, doubts have been expressed about this argument. Part of the problem that economic historians have in dealing with trade stems from the assumptions they make in order to simplify analysis. Debates on trade and economic growth in the late eighteenth and early nineteenth centuries have been conducted in terms of values, wages and prices, which are readily convertible into convenient sets of competing statistics. But endless refinement of these figures (to several decimal places, even) has still left us remarkably ignorant of the real processes by which such trading activity was integrated with the broader economy. Much of the reason stems from the failure of economic modelling to take into account precisely the factors that make trade so complex in the first place. Information, for example, is fundamental to any

---

2   See, for example, R. Davis, *The industrial revolution and British overseas trade*, Leicester, 1979, p. 63; D. N. McCloskey, '1780–1860: A survey', in *The economic history of Britain since 1700*, ed. D. N. McCloskey and R. Floud, 2nd edn, 3 vols, Cambridge, 1994, vol. 1, pp. 242–70; pp. 255–58.

trading system, but many economic models assume that information is perfect, and equally available to all participants. The dead-ends created by such approaches have led some historians to take a step back and consider the indirect consequences of trade. Trade did not just involve moving goods from A to B, but required increasingly sophisticated mechanisms of credit and finance, which in turn became available to other sectors of the economy in ways far removed from any that can be explained by gross national product statistics.[3]

Some scholars have gone still further in their focus on the service and commercial sides of the British economy, arguing that it was in these sectors – not in manufacturing industry – that the core strength of the nation's development took place from the seventeenth century onward. In the century after 1750, this commercial wealth was of course greatly supplemented by rapid industrial growth, but industry did not replace commerce. Under this model, Britain's modern economic history has not been a series of phases in which agriculture and commerce gave way to industry, which was ultimately replaced in turn by the service economy of the later twentieth century. Rather, commerce and services were central to the economy throughout. Industry, financed by the established wealth of land and commerce, prospered in its innovative period, but was inevitably overtaken by the efforts of countries with better natural resources, and did not represent a fundamental shift in the key strengths of the British economy.[4]

Some moderation is required. An approach that belittles industry makes no more sense than one that belittles trade in the explanation of British economic change. In particular, debates about industrialisation need to be broader. Historians should stop assuming that 'industrialisation' and 'the role of manufacturing industry' are the same thing. Industrialisation is a process involving a wide range of elements, from transport to training, power supply to marketing. The factory is a vital piece in the jigsaw, but only as vital as any of the others, and a more holistic approach is increasingly being sought.[5]

Knowing more about trade will help to achieve this broader goal. Even those historians who have done most to balance the high profile of manufacturing industry have based their work heavily on evidence drawn from commerce and finance, rather than commodity trades. Inevitably, such work tends also to be centred on London and the institutions of the City, with relatively little attention paid to the provinces. The foremost practitioners of this avenue of enquiry argue that the provinces operated on a very different system of finance from that of the City, and that this was one of the key factors underpinning the apparent lack of contact between the service and industrial sectors in the Victorian era.[6]

---

3 P. Hudson, *The industrial revolution*, London, 1992, p. 188.

4 W. D. Rubinstein, *Capitalism, culture and decline in modern Britain, 1750–1990*, London, 1993, chap. 1.

5 See, for example, S. D. Chapman, review of G. Timmins, *Made in Lancashire*, in *Economic History Review*, Vol. 52, 1999, pp. 578–79.

6 P. J. Cain and A. G. Hopkins, *British imperialism: Innovation and expansion, 1688–1914*, London, 1993, p. 187.

The activities of traders in the provincial ports may therefore cast useful light on the relationship between trade and industry during the Victorian expansion of the British economy. Economic change drove shifts in regional definition, changing perspectives on the relationships between towns and counties and the shape of local financial and social networks. But while industrialisation changed Britain's regions, it did not abolish them or make them a redundant framework for the analysis of the period.[7] On the contrary, regional issues permeated decision-making and fund-raising with regard to major eighteenth-century infrastructural developments like canals, which in turn defined routes and markets for later generations. In the north-west of England, local culture and tradition makes much of the divide between Liverpool and Manchester, stemming in part from the economic and occupational division between trade and manufacturing. Yet a division of labour can be an effective means of organising a regional economy, rather than a source of tension and conflict. Historians studying networks of credit in late eighteenth-century Lancashire found an integrated and largely self-sufficient system capable of balancing the commodity and financial flows between traders and industrialists without much reference to the London institutions.[8]

Of course, a working relationship is not necessarily an equal one. Traders and manufacturers recognised the importance of each other, but there is ample evidence to suggest that control over commodity and financial channels was generally located in the ports and the trading communities rather than in the factories. Those who control the buying and selling of goods are in an enormously powerful position in any economy. In addition, ports that could dominate *sales* of a particular commodity could make themselves important far beyond their actual *handling* of commodities – traders would be drawn to the market to conduct business. Commodity markets, capital sources and financial institutions could focus money and influence in particular places, often overriding national boundaries. Hamburg, for example, was the venue for most of northern Europe's corn sales, although by no means all the corn actually passed through the town; London's role in global finance ensured that more Californian gold was shipped there than to New York in the 1850s.[9]

In Liverpool, the development of the cotton market in the first half of the nineteenth century saw a marked concentration of power in the hands of the port's merchants. This was not necessarily to the disadvantage of manufacturers – indeed, manufacturers initiated some elements in the process through their wish to save costs by dealing more directly with the importers. Having previously bought from dealers in Manchester, they shifted their orientation toward brokers based in Liverpool as the century went on.[10] Liverpool's extensive warehousing facilities also focused power

7 P. Hudson, 'The regional perspective', in *Regions and industries: A perspective on the industrial revolution in Britain*, ed. P. Hudson, Cambridge, 1989, pp. 5–38.

8 B. L. Anderson, 'The Lancashire bill system and its Liverpool practitioners: The case of a slave merchant', in *Trade and transport: Essays in economic history in honour of T. S. Willan*, ed. W. H. Chaloner and B. M. Ratcliffe, Manchester, 1977, pp. 59–96.

9 BPP, Commercial reports (1855), pp. 106, 189.

10 T. Ellison, *The cotton trade of Great Britain*, London, 1886, reprint 1968, p. 176.

and control in the hands of traders rather than manufacturers, through the mainte-nance of large stocks of cotton which could be bought and sold at the convenience of traders. In the late 1860s, the location of real power in the cotton business is clear from the stock figures. Warehouses in Britain's major ports held 498,000 bales of cotton, while the spinners themselves had widely scattered stocks that totalled only 80,000 bales. In addition, 71% of the total British port stock was in Liverpool.[11] In normal years, Liverpool's traders were encumbered with having to bear the storage costs of the cotton, while manufacturers benefited from only having to store enough to supply their mills in the short term, but the American Civil War brought home the reality of this arrangement: Liverpool's traders could make more money specu-lating in their cotton stock than they could selling it to manufacturers, and supplies stopped reaching the mills. The Liverpool commercial press hailed the 'vigour' of the port's cotton market in the early 1860s, arguing that everyone involved in cotton was doing well, except – and they were usually mentioned as an afterthought – the unfortunate mill-workers.[12]

The power and priorities of traders in times of unusual strain in the international economy led, therefore, to some peculiar commodity flows. Liverpool imported *and* exported cotton from and to New York during the American Civil War: depending on the prices on the Liverpool market, it was sometimes better for New York traders to send whatever cotton they could find to Liverpool rather than sell it to the New England textile manufacturers, while at other times it made sense to buy some of Liverpool's stockpile and ship it back across the Atlantic. One such boom early in 1863 saw the Cunard and Inman shipping firms put extra steamers on the New York run to cope with the demand for cargo space.[13] Opportunities became greater still with increased cotton shipments from the Far East – traders on the Liverpool–New York axis had considerable stocks of cotton from an ever-diversifying supply network to buy and sell amongst themselves, while cotton mills across Europe and America sat idle and labour forces faced destitution.[14] Although cotton was always an extreme case, other commodities were sometimes subject to similar manipulation. Corn traders kept a close watch on fluctuating prices and exchange rates during the 1860s, and while conditions generally favoured large imports of cereals, there were occasions when it was profitable to ship American cereals back to New York after a spell in the Liverpool warehouses.[15]

At some times, and in some trades, the dominance of commodity traders could therefore reach the point where the broader world seemed an abstract irrelevance. Most of the time, though, Liverpool's traders were all too aware of the diversity and complexity of affairs beyond the inward-looking, largely artificial speculative market

11 *Economist*, 'Commercial history and review of 1868', 1869, p. 29.
12 For example, *Gore's Advertiser*, 1 Jan. 1863, p. 3.
13 *Liverpool Chronicle*, 2 Jan. 1864, p. 2; *Gore's Advertiser*, 19 Feb. 1863, p. 1.
14 Ellison, *Cotton trade*, pp. 93–96.
15 G. J. S. Broomhall and J. H. Hubback, *Corn trade memories, recent and remote*, Liverpool, 1930, pp. 46–47.

in cotton. Making money from trade could require complex arrangements for overseeing multi-lateral commodity flows, which might or might not actually involve the goods themselves appearing in the trader's home port. This was the vital point. The continued prosperity of a port like Liverpool required the maintenance of control over the trading process on a number of levels. Traders had to define their markets, allowing their customers – industrialists, primary producers and consumers, at home and abroad – to influence but never control the trading chain. They had to take rapid advantage of new trading opportunities to ensure that commodities either flowed via Liverpool or were subject to the prices and standards established by the Liverpool market. In an age of rapid change, whether economic, political, imperial or regulatory, these were considerable tasks.

FLEXIBILITY AND DIVERSIFICATION

Probably the most serious question facing Liverpool's traders was how to manage change, seek new trades and markets, and cope with external pressures without taking unacceptable risks, either in the trading process itself or in the broader question of maintaining control relative to those elsewhere in the commodity chain. Anecdotally, Liverpool traders appear to have had some success, in that they had acquired by the eighteenth century a reputation for seizing opportunities and developing new markets. They were not alone in this – diversification was one of the most successful tactics of traders in the provincial ports seeking a way to bypass the entrenched monopolies and privileges of the old mercantile firms and imperial trading companies based in London. England's medieval traders looked east, to the great continental markets with their chain of connections across Europe to Asia. By the sixteenth century the English had found that some money could be made in the Atlantic (by robbing the Spanish, if nothing else), and the gradual development of English colonies in the Americas eventually created a range of more legitimate trades. Traders from Liverpool, Bristol and Glasgow, as well as a new generation of London merchants, competed for this new business in the eighteenth century.[16]

Diversification was sometimes a proactive policy developed on a trader's own initiative, and sometimes a reaction to crisis. Various events in the early nineteenth century either required or encouraged Liverpool traders to shift direction. The most obvious was the abolition of the British slave trade in 1807. Although Liverpool's historians have been keen to marginalise the 'comparatively few' traders active in the business, the central role of the trade in the later decades of the eighteenth century cannot be explained away.[17] By its very nature, the slave trade was closely integrated with other lucrative lines of activity. It had developed from Liverpool's previous trade with the West Indies, and by the time of abolition a range of broader

16 Recent work on early modern merchant communities includes D. Hancock, *Citizens of the world: London merchants and the integration of the British Atlantic community, 1735–1785*, Cambridge, 1995; K. Morgan, *Bristol and the Atlantic trade in the eighteenth century*, Cambridge, 1993.

17 Hyde, *Liverpool and the Mersey*, pp. 31–34.

activities in plantation owning, sugar trading and processing had become established elements, both in the Liverpool economy and specifically in the affairs of major slave traders. These, of course, survived abolition: slave traders did not have to radically reorient their businesses in order to remain active. In addition, any blow to the port's activities was cushioned by simultaneous imperial expansion in the same period which opened new markets in the Caribbean and Central America – the most notable of these territories were Demerara and Berbice, the future British Guiana. Liverpool traders like John Gladstone, seeking trade not yet controlled by the established operators, moved quickly to supply the trading needs of the new plantations, and in time became owners of prosperous sugar operations.

External factors could therefore offer opportunities as well as threats, but in either case, the trading community's response required some flexibility. That was greatly helped by Liverpool's hinterland, which proved capable of both producing and absorbing an unusual range of goods in the century after 1750. Geography is often cited as a key factor in Liverpool's prominence, although generally in terms of its westward-facing ease of access to Atlantic routes. Arguably, the more significant locational aspect of Liverpool's development was its surrounding territories. As well as the growing textile industry in Lancashire and Yorkshire, which is usually mentioned as the market for the port's cotton and wool trades, there is the less well remembered market around the Irish Sea. Liverpool's Irish trade in the seventeenth and eighteenth centuries established important trading foundations upon which could subsequently be constructed a more diversified and expansionist approach.[18] The need for a political and economic gateway to Ireland in the late medieval and early modern periods initially favoured Chester, and if the River Dee had not silted up, Liverpool might have been slower to develop. As it was, being on the next river up the coast from the Dee allowed Liverpool to fill a vacuum. Being on the west coast, but further from continental Europe than Bristol, say, made Liverpool a safer base for Atlantic commerce in times of war with France. The Irish context remained vital, however. Irish linen was shipped to Liverpool in the first instance, before joining outward cargoes of other manufactures gathered from the port's eastern hinterland.[19] Periodically, older trading patterns would take on new importance depending on external circumstances. Irish corn traders who had settled in Liverpool during the 1830s and 1840s found themselves central players in the famine crisis, as old patterns of emigration and food supply across the Irish Sea had to be urgently merged with a much wider overseas trading environment.[20]

Building new activities on long-established foundations is a theme that emerges across the community. The evolution of attitudes toward particular commodities demonstrates that while Liverpool had a long-term attachment to a few staple

18 J. Langton, 'Liverpool and its hinterland in the late eighteenth century', in *Commerce, industry and transport: Studies in economic change on Merseyside*, ed. B. L. Anderson and P. J. M. Stoney, Liverpool, 1983, pp. 1–25; p. 2.

19 T. Baines, *History of the commerce and town of Liverpool*, London, 1852, p. 758.

20 Broomhall and Hubback, *Corn trade memories*, p. 242.

commodities, the circumstances of these key trades changed dramatically over time. Trade and manufacture of textiles, with a range of raw materials and finished products, had long been an important element in the British economy, evolving through a series of phases prior to the sector's most famous period of growth during the late eighteenth and nineteenth centuries. Textiles always involved a significant trading element, usually with an international dimension. The medieval textile industry was pan-European, with steady exchange of wool, finished products, and specialised labour forces.[21] By the later eighteenth century, cotton was the rising textile, despite the difficulties of growing the crop in European climates – securing sources for it further afield became a key priority of merchants and imperial planners alike. Early in the nineteenth century, Britain had hopes of an imperial cotton industry: British West Indian colonies, and particularly the territories on mainland South America captured during the Napoleonic Wars, were promising sources for cotton production. Demerara and Berbice produced more cotton than sugar in the early years of the century, and Liverpool's connections with the region ensured a significant role in the trade.

Keeping cotton at the heart of the port's operations over the next half-century required a considerable shift of focus on the part of Liverpool's traders. Serious competition from the southern United States rapidly swamped the British colonial industry, which switched to sugar and other tropical products: by mid-century, the slave plantations of the US South were, overwhelmingly, Liverpool's prime source of cotton.

Such a concentration of resources and investment was not to everyone's taste, and the textile manufacturers in particular feared monopolies and restrictive practices at various points on the supply chain. During the second quarter of the century, there had been increasing demands for a reduction in Britain's reliance on United States cotton. Most of the pressure for diversification came from Liverpool's customers. Lancashire mill-owners argued that cotton came from a dangerously limited range of sources, and that Liverpool merchants had a complacent and cosy relationship with their American producers, all of which conspired to raise prices and deprive the users of the product of the benefits of competition. The Manchester Chamber of Commerce and Cotton Supply Association lobbied government to take a more active stance in promoting the Indian cotton supply. The Chamber of Commerce sent an agent to India in the early 1850s to investigate the state of cotton cultivation in the sub-continent, and increasingly demanded formal government intervention to build the transport infrastructure regarded as a necessary prerequisite of any serious expansion in the Indian crop. Despite widespread criticism of the East India Company in the wake of the 1857 uprising, however, the Manchester lobby was unable to capitalise on this and make the cotton supply question a central part of the government's plans to reform the Indian economy.[22]

21   The key texts are J. de L. Mann, *The cloth industry in the west of England from 1640 to 1880*, Oxford, 1971; T. H. Lloyd, *The English wool trade in the middle ages*, Cambridge, 1977.
22   P. Harnetty, *Imperialism and free trade: Lancashire and India in the mid-nineteenth century*, Manchester, 1972, pp. 36–41; Ellison, *Cotton trade*, p. 90.

As Liverpool's traders knew only too well, diversification could have costs as well as benefits, and was not something to be undertaken for the sake of it, or as a favour to another economic interest group. As long as Indian cotton was considered inferior by the manufacturers, and attracted a lower price, it was also unattractive to traders, who were not going to invest in large stocks of it simply on the off-chance that there might be a failure in the main supply from the American South. If there was such a failure, alternative supplies would be developed as necessary, but not before. Leading traders were therefore sanguine about the Civil War, believing that either it would be a temporary interruption of American supplies, or, if longer-lasting, that Indian cotton would be developed to compensate.[23] Broadly speaking, a shortage of supply meant an increase in prices, so the net value of a merchant's business was unaffected by such events. Those calling for diversification of the cotton supply before the American Civil War were asking traders, or government, to fund that diversification for no clear gain. The Manchester interest was widely criticised by traders and government officials in Liverpool, Whitehall and India for demanding that others take risks for their benefit.[24] With the onset of the American Civil War in 1861, the worst fears of the manufacturers were realised, as the largest single source of cotton was cut almost instantly and the spectre of war-profiteering among those merchants and brokers who had stockpiles was all too apparent.

The changing patterns of Liverpool's cotton imports in the mid-nineteenth century show that the port's cotton market was powerful enough to set the diversification agenda throughout the American conflict. Mercantile incomes were not dependent on the quantity of cotton being imported, but on its price and on the available stocks within the port. The rising price of cotton encouraged traders to revisit the possibilities of the Indian source. Although Indian cotton was perceived to be of poorer quality than the American crop, and liable to higher carriage costs because of distance, rising prices across the board could, for the first time, cancel out that handicap. Indian cotton accordingly became a significant element in Liverpool's cotton stocks. The quantity of Indian cotton imported in the Civil War years never exceeded half the amount of US cotton brought in during a typical pre-war year, but its value told a different story: even with concerns about the quality of the product, that smaller quantity was worth more in 1864 than the total import of US cotton had been in 1860.[25]

Elsewhere, however, possible sources of cotton were less likely to be viable, even in an era of rising prices. There was an attempt to revive the old colonial West Indian cotton industry, especially in the Bahamas, where the climate and territory were well suited to cotton. The Cotton Supply Association tried to encourage the business by sending six cotton gins in 1862, but these were found to be far inferior to those manufactured in the United States, or even the locally-made hand-operated

---

23   See comments by J. Tobin quoted in *Liverpool Daily Post*, 30 Oct. 1861, p. 5.

24   Harnetty, *Imperialism and free trade*, pp. 42–43.

25   W. Sandford, table of cotton quantities and values prepared for John Cheetham, MP (1867), British Library, 74/1882.d2.

machines. The real problem, though, was that no-one anticipated a lasting future for cotton in the islands, and major investment seemed pointless. The Civil War would not last forever, it was reasoned, and as soon as it ended the cotton traders and manufacturers would go back to dealing in US cotton, abandoning the Bahamas once again.[26]

Flexibility and diversification were not always appropriate responses from the viewpoint of the trading community, therefore, and the issue should be seen as a battleground between competing visions of who should control the direction of key trades in difficult times. Manufacturers obviously would have preferred a multiplicity of sources of goods from which to choose on the basis of quality and price. Traders had a different agenda, favouring sufficient supply of items they had a good chance of selling. Traders explored diversified markets when there seemed to be some prospect of mercantile gain, and not out of some abstract sense of the greater economic good. Diversification offered new trading firms lucrative but risky opportunities to break into the ranks of the mercantile community; presented hard choices to established traders faced with a decline in their fortunes; fuelled at least part of the agenda behind imperial expansion; and served as an ongoing source of tension between traders and their customers. The next section considers the implications of this issue for Liverpool's trading profile in the mid-Victorian era.

THE DYNAMICS OF REGIONAL AND COMMODITY TRADES

There are a number of ways to assess the changing direction and composition of the port's regional and commodity trades, although measuring the relative importance of a number of trades is obviously a difficult task. As with the shipping patterns considered in chapter two, there are a number of possible indicators, all of which offer a slightly different angle on the problem. In addition, historians need to achieve working compromises in their use of sources in such large and complicated issues: some sources are quick and easy to use but relatively uninformative, while others have huge potential but would take years to process, even with computerisation.

This section begins with a general picture and then focuses more closely on particular issues in key trades. The broad patterns are derived from the port authority's own income from fees and rates, which is in general terms a reflection of the volume of each trade and the value of the major commodities characteristic of the region. It is also a useful indicator in terms of strategic decision-making: as will be discussed in chapter four, the MDHB had to balance the needs of different regional trading interests, and its assessment of the merits of each case involved an awareness of how important the trade in question was to the prosperity of the port.

Figure 3.1 therefore offers a broad profile of the relative roles of Liverpool's major regional trades, by charting the MDHB's revenue as recorded in the port authority annual statistical reports. Obviously, the United States provided Liverpool's single most valuable regional trade in the third quarter of the century. Only in 1865, with

26 BPP, Colonial reports (1863), p. 16.

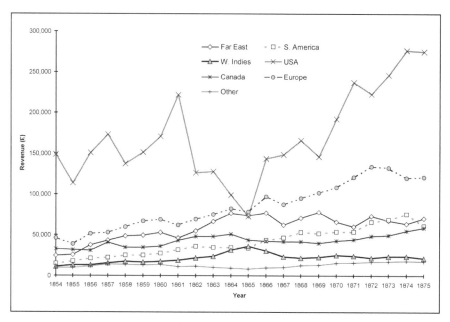

Figure 3.1 Regional revenue collected by MDHB, 1854–75
Source: Dock Revenue statements.

the culmination of damage caused by the American Civil War, did other trades reach the level of US commerce. Perhaps surprisingly, Liverpool's second most valuable trade was that with continental Europe, which shows a rising trend throughout the period. As has been noted, one of the most commonly-quoted arguments for Liverpool's rise as a major port is that it did not focus on Europe, and that its ships were able to sail to the Americas without going near to the European continent in time of war. In the comparatively peaceful times of the mid-nineteenth century, however, the continent became increasingly important to Liverpool, as a market for exported manufactures and as a source of foodstuffs and raw materials. In addition, Liverpool sought to be Europe's gateway to the west, by channelling goods to and from the Americas. While numerous continental ports would have been more logical geographical choices in such a role, Liverpool's strength in shipping and markets gave it considerable pulling power.

Liverpool's third trade in this period was consistently that from the Far East, although it was closely followed by one of the port's oldest trades (Canada), and one of its newest (South America). The West Indian trade – another long-standing element in Liverpool's commerce – was broadly steady throughout the mid-century years, with a peak during the American Civil War as smuggled cotton from the southern states was brought back via ports in the Caribbean.

Although a useful scene-setter, the MDHB classification hides important variations within regions, and it is necessary to have a closer look at patterns in North American trade in the era of the Civil War in particular. In addition, Liverpool had a number of new trades, rising sharply in mid-century and catching headlines, but not yet significant enough to make a noticeable impact on the broad statistics. Finally, as was noted in chapter two, these rather gentle patterns of regional trade disguise considerable upheavals in the sail/steam composition of the port's traffic, and the implications of changing modes of transport for the viability of individual commodity trades needs to be assessed.

The first step is to move beyond the general regional categories favoured by the port authority and look more closely at patterns within key trades. Table 3.1 shows a more detailed regional breakdown of arriving traffic in the port in mid-century, based simply on the number of vessels arriving from each overseas port. This points to important patterns. The changing volume and direction of trade in the Americas brings home the impact of the Civil War on Liverpool's regional connections. Most obviously, direct contact with the southern states collapsed in the early 1860s, although it had broadly returned to its pre-war level by the end of the decade. The collateral impact of the conflict on Liverpool's regional outlook is more complex. Contact with the northern US was considerably boosted during the war. Liverpool's West Indian trade also expanded, as traders sought ways of bypassing the blockaded ports of the South.[27] The conflict had an impact further afield also. Far Eastern traffic grew in Liverpool as Bombay cotton became a serious substitute for the American crop. In all of these cases, though, the peak of the early 1860s was not a sustainable pattern, and trade dropped again somewhat.

The most spectacular new trade in the period is that with the western United States. There were two dynamics at work here. First, California's development was rapid in mid-century, even before the large-scale westward expansion of United States interests in the aftermath of the Civil War. Gold was significant of course, but the 'miner forty-niners' were not the only California entrepreneurs in mid-century. Farmers and millers have attracted less attention, but they nonetheless made the territory self-sufficient in grain and flour by the 1850s, and had begun exploring export markets in Australia. The high quality of the grain was immediately noted by the distilling industry, and Liverpool's initially-limited involvement in the region grew rapidly from the 1850s.[28] Liverpool's existing activity in the Pacific was also a factor in channelling California's trade in the port's direction. Liverpool traders were already working in the western ports of South America, and some saw a northward extension of their operations as a logical step. Most famously, Balfour, Williamson & Co., having acquired considerable experience trading from Chile with large, efficient sailing ships, established a firm in San Francisco in the late 1860s.[29] There is evidence that

27 For the latest research in this area, see N. Ashcroft, 'British trade with the Confederacy and the effectiveness of Union maritime strategy during the Civil War', *International Journal of Maritime History*, Vol. 10, 1998, pp. 155–76.

28 BPP, Commercial reports (1855), p. 189.

29 Forres, *Balfour Williamson & Company and associated firms: Memoirs of a merchant house*, London, 1929, pp. 33–37.

Table 3.1 Number of arriving voyages from each global region, 1855, 1863 and 1870

	1855	1863	1870
Africa	75	88	113
Central America	80	91	101
S. America	403	572	636
Baltic	153	182	183
Biscay	164	192	167
Canada	442	520	425
Channel	360	281	499
Far East	259	448	310
Mediterranean	1077	1162	1063
North Atlantic	11	26	17
US (North)	319	619	489
US (South)	552	8	518
US (West)	3	27	123
W. Indies	178	385	305
Other/unknown	126	84	85
Total	**4202**	**4685**	**5034**

Source: BE. All arriving voyages in each year.

Liverpool firms put a great deal of effort into developing the California trade, especially relative to their counterparts in London. At least one San Francisco firm preferred to have goods carried from London to Liverpool and then have Liverpool ships take them to California: 'the shipowners of London must be very ignorant of the inducements that California trade can offer, to continue in their old course of sending such worthless vessels to its shores'.[30] To be fair, it may have been less ignorance than the long-standing problem of having a limited number of large, fast sailing ships – Liverpool's specialisation in precisely the sort of ships likely to appeal to the Californians was well-established.

Some trades had more complex patterns that make them hard to spot in the general statistics of the port. Liverpool's Australian trade is the most obvious example. Liverpool had a considerable volume of direct outward traffic to Australia in mid-century, but this was much more concerned with emigrants than with goods. More to the point, its direct inward traffic was very rare: most ships coming back to Liverpool from Australia came via ports in India or went on to the Pacific coast of South America where return cargoes were easier to come by. Such patterns were actually a mixed blessing for Australia's own economic development. Although the country's place in the broader Far East economy encouraged shipping to carry goods and passengers from Britain in the first place, it could be hard for Australian producers to persuade shipping firms to take wool or other animal products back again when

---

30 R. Stevens, *On the stowage of ships and their cargoes*, 5th edn, London, 1869, p. 494.

earnings were likely to be higher from cargoes collected elsewhere.[31] James Baines'
Astarte returned to Liverpool from Australia in June 1870 via the west coast of South
America, carrying a cargo of guano.[32] Others left from Liverpool but returned to
London in the first instance – the fleet operated in the 1850s and 1860s by Baines
and Thomas MacKay had flexible patterns of operation and firms resident in both
ports to handle the vessels.[33] They therefore appeared in Liverpool's statistics as
coastal arrivals when they came back to the port for another group of emigrants.
Stopping in London was more likely if gold was the main return cargo, although
some vessels did go directly to Liverpool with gold. Pilkington & Wilson's *Shalimar*
brought 50 boxes of gold dust to Liverpool in 1855, consigned to 18 different firms,
individuals and banks.[34] Indeed, Liverpool operators claimed to be so efficient that
they could overcome problems of distance, both at home and abroad. In a high-profile
'race' in 1855, gold carried on Baines' *Marco Polo* to Liverpool, and then carried south
by train, still reached the Bank of England faster than London's fastest vessel could
make the direct journey – Baines, of course, made the most of the publicity.[35]

Developing new markets was never without its hazards. Liverpool's South America
traders had worked hard to expand the region's trade since the 1820s, but by
mid-century were still suffering from some of the classic problems associated with
the region. The major issue was one of scale. Even the more developed areas of
South America could easily be swamped by the volume and variety of manufactured
goods available to traders. Initial attempts to move into the region after the fall of
Iberian imperial control had been wildly over-optimistic, with traders finding that
they shortly acquired warehouses full of goods that were beyond the purchasing
power of the local population. In mid-century, firms starting in the business could
still fall into the trap of over-trading. Stephen Williamson, writing from Valparaiso,
Chile, complained that his Liverpool partners were sending far too many goods:
Arthur Balfour, it seemed, 'imagines that goods can be sold here like cotton or flour
on the Liverpool market'.[36]

These new trades were largely conducted in sailing ships, and often in the new
iron ships that became a Liverpool speciality in the 1860s. Elsewhere, established
regional and commodity traders had to develop strategies for the incorporation of
steam into their operations. Sometimes they did this directly by making full use of
the changing technology, but in other cases the process was more subtle, as traders
adjusted their existing activities to take advantage of faster mail, for example, without
actually having their goods carried by steamer.

Two aspects of steam's development need to be considered. First is the question
of routes. As chapter two demonstrated, steam was only economic on certain routes

31   F. Broeze, 'The cost of distance: Shipping and the early Australian economy, 1788–1850', *Eco-
      nomic History Review*, Vol. 28, 1975, pp. 582–97; p. 592.
32   BE 18/6/1870/4.
33   Bank, 21 Jan. 1858.
34   BE 9/6/1855/1.
35   *The Times*, 6 Mar. 1855, p. 8.
36   Stephen Williamson letter book, 15 Feb. 1858, Balfour Williamson papers, box 4.

for a large part of the nineteenth century, and tended to connect a relatively small number of key locations on fixed timetables, in comparison with the old sailing ship patterns which were much more universal in their coverage. Second is the question of commodities. Not all commodities were valuable or perishable enough to justify the extra costs of steam transport. Traders had more choice as steam became common, but each new option brought its own risks.

The limited deployment of steam on certain routes was a crucial issue facing traders. It was a question not just of distance, but of identifying routes that would generate sufficient levels of trade to make the heavy investments of the steamship firms worthwhile. Steam-driven globalisation was not without complications and casualties, and global connections did not mean that everywhere was connected to everywhere else directly – there were often fast and slow tracks. The rise of steam could isolate some of the world's trading regions that had previously been much more important, and leave others dependent on feeder services to the nearest major steam port. Mauritius, for example, had long been a key stopover and refuge for sailing ships rounding the Cape of Good Hope on their way to the East. It had been claimed by a succession of European powers – Portugal, the Netherlands, France and finally Britain – since the early sixteenth century, and favoured as a naval base precisely because of its strategic location.[37] By the 1860s, regular steam lines using the Red Sea route (even with the inconveniences of a land crossing of Egypt) began to shift the focus of trade to the east, and the Suez Canal, of course, bypassed the island completely. A depressed colonial official predicted that Mauritius would soon cease to be 'on the high road of the Eastern world'.[38]

This was the sort of fate awaiting any port that could not establish a major role in the new steam networks, and one of Liverpool's central aims in this period was to ensure that it was not relegated to the slow lane. The increasing development of multi-lateral trading patterns, centred on Liverpool but not necessarily channelling all their shipping through the port, points to Liverpool's success in establishing itself as a key hub for large sectors of the world's trade. Such issues became still more important with the development of large-scale steam fleets and the need for firms to operate a 'hub and feeder' system.

The commodity question was closely connected. The broad evolutionary pattern of sail, steam and commodity trades is clear and well-known to historians – steamships started carrying a small range of high-value or perishable commodities, and gradually expanded their role into a wider range of goods, while sailing ships were left carrying a few, mainly bulk, classes of cargo. By 1870, steam cargoes tended to be much more fragmented and diverse than sail cargoes. For example, a sailing ship from the Mediterranean in 1870 was likely to have only a single class of item on board – cereals, usually, or cotton – while a steamer from the same region would generally have several different kinds of goods, often ranging from fruit through spices to

37 M. Havinden and D. Meredith, *Colonialism and development: Britain and its tropical colonies, 1850–1960*, London, 1993.
38 BPP, Colonial reports (1870), p. 74.

marble artworks.[39] Clearly, this diversification of steamship cargoes was closely tied to the activities of commodity traders, and in particular to the relationship between those traders and the operators of the new steam services. Those are issues best dealt with in chapter five. Here, it is worth considering such patterns in more detail for selected trades in order to demonstrate the multi-faceted impact of steam services on commodity patterns.

By far the most common pattern was for steam to cherry-pick goods of low bulk but high value, and operate a packet service on specific routes. Donald Currie's service from Hamburg to Liverpool specialised in miscellaneous consignments, most of which are described vaguely in customs records under the generic labels 'glasswares', 'manufactures' and 'merchandise': *Sutherland* arrived in Liverpool in February 1870 carrying more than 1,200 'packets' of 'merchandise' as part of a cargo largely composed of small items.[40] The long-established Baltic timber and grain trades continued to reach Liverpool by sail, however, broadly undisturbed by the new steam traffic. Liverpool's Canadian trades worked in much the same way. Steam shipping grew from a mere 4% of arriving tonnage from Canada in 1855 to 27% in 1870, but did so without much impact on the traditional practices of the timber trade.[41] The steamers carried perishables such as meat, while the timber trade stuck firmly to sailing ships. Sail tonnage remained steady across the period, and steam was super-imposed, rather than replacing sail.

Elsewhere in the Americas, many contemporary accounts divide the South American trades into east and west coast trade in this period, and that reflects, among other things, the introduction of steam services to key ports in Brazil and the River Plate, while sail persisted much longer in Chile and Peru. The activities of Balfour, Williamson & Co. are nicely symbolic: their commodity trade with Chile was carried in sailing ships throughout this period, but their communications between branches went by steam, taking advantage of the mail route from Liverpool via Panama. Liverpool's Latin America traders developed their business in mid-century in an area frequently used by historians as a classic case-study of 'indirect empire', of commercially secure yet administratively cheap influence over less-developed nations.[42]

Liverpool's African trades are also important indicators of the attitudes of some traders to Britain's developing role in the world, although trading patterns were very different because of the peculiar geography of the region. Steamers were able to navigate much more freely along the West African coast than sailing ships – the winds and currents made it notoriously difficult for sailing vessels to call at the numerous trading stations at river mouths.[43] Steamships therefore opened up many more stops on the coast, rather than operating from a favoured terminus as in other

---

39   BE (1870).

40   BE 4/2/1870/11.

41   BE (1855, 1870).

42   Cain and Hopkins, *British imperialism*, chap. 9.

43   M. Lynn, 'From sail to steam: The impact of the steamship services on the British palm oil trade with West Africa, 1850–1890', *Journal of African History*, Vol. 30, 1989, pp. 227–45; p. 230.

regional trades. African traders in mid-century were happy to have British influence stop short of colonisation, however. If treaties with local rulers could be enforced stopping the slave trade and guaranteeing free trade, this was preferable to having British authorities on the ground – customs duties, noted one Liverpool trader, were always heavier in formal colonies than in nominally independent states.[44]

Sometimes external events gave a sudden impetus to the decision-making processes surrounding steam. One trade requiring special attention is with the Far East, because the Suez Canal added a major new factor to the ongoing relationship between sail and steam.[45] Steam was, at least in theory, given a great advantage by the shortening of the voyage from Europe to India. Historians have tended to hail the opening of the Canal as a great watershed in maritime history: 'the greatest discontinuity in the shipping history of the late nineteenth century'.[46] It must be stressed, though, that European steamship operators ran steam services to India via the Middle East long before the Canal was opened: P&O operated steamers on either side of the divide, and passengers and goods were transshipped by land between the two. One voyage late in 1856 required the transit – by camel – of 4,150 packages, 2,054 cases and £557,000 in specie between Cairo and Suez.[47] Although extremely inconvenient, such practices had already cut voyage times compared with the route round the Cape of Good Hope.

Operating the Far East route as two shorter voyages required considerable organisation, however: only firms like P&O and their French counterparts Messageries Impériales had the logistical resources to operate on such a scale. P&O had its own dock facilities in Singapore, while the French used established British merchant houses in India as agents for the purchase and supply of coal.[48] The only way for Liverpool operators to work in a similar fashion was to reach collaborative agreements with shipping firms active in the Indian Ocean. James Moss & Co., Mediterranean steamship operators, advertised a service from Liverpool to Bombay in the late 1860s, in which they carried passengers to Egypt at times designed to link with a complementary service at the other side run by the Bombay & Bengal Steamship Co.[49]

The Canal, however, made the Suez route available to any steamship owner with a suitable vessel, eliminating the need for negotiations with other firms or railway companies. This is perhaps its key significance from a business viewpoint: the canal did not so much bring steam to the East, as enable smaller shipping firms to operate

44   BPP, West Africa (1865), evidence of James Tobin, q. 5234.
45   The classic study is D. A. Farnie, East and west of Suez: The Suez Canal in history, 1854–1956, Oxford, 1969.
46   M. Fletcher, 'The Suez Canal and world shipping, 1869–1914', Journal of Economic History, Vol. 18, 1958, pp. 556–73; p. 556; D. R. Headrick, The tentacles of progress: Technology transfer in the age of imperialism, 1850–1940, Oxford, 1988, pp. 25–27; C. K. Harley, 'Aspects of the economics of shipping, 1850–1913', in Change and adaptation in the North Atlantic fleets in the 19th century, ed. L. R. Fischer and G. Panting, St John's, Newfoundland, 1984, pp. 169–86; p. 176.
47   The Times, 17 Nov. 1856, p. 10.
48   BPP, East India communication (1862), evidence of David Wilson, qq. 322–33.
49   Clayton Brs, Liverpool ABC timetables and shipping directory, Liverpool, 1868; p. 115.

in this lucrative market. The canal also sharply differentiated sail from steam, because only steam could use the Canal effectively because of high towing charges and contrary winds in the Red Sea. Liverpool's traders had invested heavily in sailing traffic with the East during the 1860s, expanding their use of sail at this time by a factor of three in tonnage terms. These trades were also a potentially lucrative testing ground for improved steam technology in the form of compound engines. Working in both technologies, Liverpool operators recognised that the Canal had shifted the sail/steam demarcation line decisively in steam's favour, but continued to see prospects for sail in the bulk trades. Railway iron and coal outward, and cotton back, would still be a 'fair business' for sailing ship operators round the Cape of Good Hope.[50] Liverpool's steam traders grasped the Suez advantage, however, and rapidly expanded services in the early 1870s. Indeed, they were probably, like everyone else, taken aback by the speed with which steam came to dominate the India and China trades: Suez revitalised Liverpool's ambitions in the Far East trades.[51] Compound engines and cheaper coal by the later 1870s led Alfred Holt to observe that his fuel costs in the China trades were becoming a minor part of his operating expenses – dues paid for passage through the Suez Canal were of more concern to him.[52]

It should be remembered that even the pioneering steamship routes did not see the total elimination of sail in mid-century. As has been noted, Liverpool's trade with the northern United States was one of the port's first areas of steamship expansion. The pattern of commodity groups divided by sail and steam is, broadly, a mirror image from 1855 to 1870. In 1855, 24 broad categories appear on sailing ships, and 15 on steam. In 1870, the picture is reversed, with only 17 groups appearing on sailing ships and 25 on steam – as steam proved economical for a wider range of goods, sail retreated into niche markets.[53] Foodstuffs were always common on the Atlantic routes, but fruit was carried by steamer well before grain was. Furs rarely appear on sailing ships, but were an important steam cargo in the early 1860s. Cotton grew in importance on the route in mid-century, with New York established as America's third most important cotton port by 1850, after New Orleans and Mobile.[54] A regular sailing ship cargo in the 1850s, cotton had become a steam commodity by the later 1860s. This is not to argue that sail's remaining commodities on the US routes were insignificant. The most common groups in 1870 were dyestuffs and petrochemicals, mainly shipped from Baltimore and Wilmington rather than Boston and New York. Sail therefore continued to play a significant role in the carriage of industrial materials on the Atlantic after a broad range of consumer durables and perishables had switched to large-scale transport by steam.

50 Charles Turner, MP, addressing a British Shipowners' Association meeting in Liverpool, *The Times*, 25 Jan. 1870, p. 7.
51 Hyde, *Liverpool and the Mersey*, pp. 95–96.
52 A. Holt, 'Review of the progress of steam shipping during the last quarter of a century,' *Minutes of proceedings of the Institution of Civil Engineers*, Vol. 51, 1877–8, pp. 2–135; p. 73.
53 Calculated from BE (1855, 1870). For commodity classification, see the Notes on Sources.
54 R. A. Killmarx, *America's maritime legacy: A history of the US merchant marine and shipbuilding industry since colonial times*, Boulder, 1979, p. 47.

Control over the management and direction of extensive, and rapidly diversifying, regional trading networks was therefore at the heart of Liverpool's 'mission' in the mid-nineteenth century. That control came to be manifested in a number of ways, both in relation to other ports and with regard to other parties in the commodity chain running from raw material to finished product. Liverpool traders took the initiative in developing new markets when such diversification was in their interest, but fiercely resisted such undertakings for the benefit of others. This is not to say that they were immune to the needs of their customers, and a number of changes in the operation of particular trades in this period suggest a determination to meet demands in such a way as to retain the initiative within the trading community. The trick was to be a major entrepôt through which the new steam trades and their feeder services would continue to flow even in an era of significant change and readjustment in global trading patterns. Liverpool, broadly speaking, managed to achieve that, and some of the reasons for that success are considered in more detail in the rest of the book.

Chapter 4

ACCOMMODATING DIVERSITY: PORT INFRASTRUCTURE

Change and diversity have been recurring themes in this book so far: the aim of this chapter is to consider how successful the port of Liverpool was in accommodating them. This is not a question frequently asked by historians, who tend to take the physical infrastructure of a port for granted. It is often assumed that there was an inevitability about dock building, and that no particularly complex decisions were required: the more trade there was, the more docks were needed. Such assumptions disguise the complexity of providing appropriate accommodation for different trades and different kinds of shipping, to say nothing of the financial and logistical challenges of managing a major port. Such questions were always politically controversial – disputes over the running and management of ports were frequent, and relations between traders and port authorities became particularly fraught when new dock building was under discussion.

The provision of strategic infrastructure was central to achieving the aims of the trading community. The pragmatic and innovative adoption of the various available shipping technologies discussed in chapter two depended on having suitable facilities in which to load, unload and maintain those vessels. Liverpool's ability to control commodity flows and markets, as considered in chapter three, relied on structures and systems capable of moving and storing extraordinary quantities of bulk goods and luxuries alike. The construction and operation of the Liverpool dock estate was a vital element in the success or failure of the trading community, and in the broadest terms, the commitment of that community to the provision of dock infrastructure was clear in this period. Capital directed at dock works on Merseyside far outstripped that devoted to public utilities, was usually greater than that tied to railways, and in some years even came close to the levels of capital on which the region's dramatic housing expansion was based.[1] Nonetheless, the scale of an investment does not guarantee its effectiveness, and the long-term viability of the port could be severely constrained if the capabilities of dock facilities did not closely match the technical and quantitative demands placed upon them.

It is necessary, therefore, to raise a number of issues in the provision of port infrastructure which will illuminate some of the problems faced by the trading community and the port authority in dealing with the growth of trade in Liverpool. The first section sets the context with a brief survey of the development of the dock

1 A. G. Kenwood, 'Fixed capital formation on Merseyside, 1800–1913', *Economic History Review*, Vol. 31, 1978, pp. 214–37; p. 225.

estate up to the middle decades of the nineteenth century, considering the reasons why the port grew in the ways that it did, and the physical and political 'baggage' inherited by the port authority when it was reformed in the 1850s. The second section considers major issues of tension in the direction of the port in mid-century, as the port authority struggled to balance the needs of specialised trades against more general traffic, of sailing ships against steamers, and of bulk staple goods against lucrative luxury trades. The third section examines measures of efficiency in the system, both operational and financial, and considers the success of the port authority in managing an effective dock system. Discussion of these issues here establishes the foundation for a broader analysis, in chapter nine, of the politics of port management in mid-century. It should be stressed that this chapter is not a comprehensive survey of the construction and trading activity of each dock: a number of useful descriptions of that sort already exist, and the priority here is to highlight major themes.[2]

THE DYNAMICS OF PORT DEVELOPMENT

Previous historians of the port of Liverpool are broadly agreed that, looked at solely from the viewpoint of civil engineering, it is an unlikely place to build a major port. The Mersey is an extremely inhospitable river. Its tidal range is considerable, it is exposed to north-westerly gales, and it plays host to a number of dangerous sandbanks. Other coastal towns – Glasgow, Southampton, Hull – are much more obvious places for maritime trade, with vessels being able to tie up on the riverbank itself, or in sheltered inlets requiring a bare minimum of civil engineering.[3] In the broader locational terms considered in the previous chapter, though, Liverpool's development made considerable sense. Local geography may have made the port difficult, but a more strategic view of the Mersey's location offered various reasons to try to overcome such problems.

What made Liverpool exceptional in the early eighteenth century was its determination to overcome its disadvantages physically by means of systematic dock building. Although docks were not a completely new concept at that time, Liverpool's willingness and ability to invest heavily in such strategic infrastructure rapidly established the port as a rising power in British trade.[4] The construction, and subsequent expansion, of a commercial dock system on the Mersey met a number of political and economic agendas, all of which in the end boiled down to the wish

---

2 See, for example, T. Baines, *Liverpool in 1859*, London, 1859, pp. 78–112; K. McCarron and A. Jarvis, *Give a dock a good name?*, Birkenhead, 1992; N. Ritchie-Noakes, *Liverpool's historic waterfront*, London, 1984.

3 G. Jackson and C. Munn, 'Trade, commerce and finance', in *Glasgow, volume II: 1830–1912*, ed. W. H. Fraser and I. Maver, Manchester, 1996, pp. 52–95; pp. 53–55.

4 G. Jackson, *The history and archaeology of ports*, Tadworth, 1983, chap. 3; D. Swann, 'The pace and progress of port investment in England, 1660–1830', *Yorkshire Bulletin of Economic and Social Research*, Vol. 12, 1960, pp. 32–44; F. E. Hyde, *Liverpool and the Mersey: An economic history of a port, 1700–1970*, Newton Abbot, 1971, pp. 11–15; S. Mountfield, *Western gateway: A history of the Mersey Docks and Harbour Board*, Liverpool, 1965, chap. 1.

to control the direction of the port. Historians have recently begun to pay more attention to the politics of Liverpool's economic development. The port's traders, growing in wealth and influence in the later seventeenth century, gained control of the town council under the new charter of 1695 and celebrated by commissioning the world's first commercial dock.[5] This did not simply make their own trading operations safer and easier, however. The development of a formal dock system ensured that some elements of commercial wealth – dock dues and rents – became a key source of income for the town, and that Liverpool did not simply act as a staging post for the transient goods and wealth of other towns. In modern jargon, Liverpool, as a break-bulk point, was creating a value-added service that would channel at least some of the profit of trade into the town, whatever traders and shipowners chose to do with their own incomes.

Steady expansion of trade in the eighteenth century was therefore matched by steady expansion of dock facilities, but Liverpool's commitment to the development of its dock system moved up a gear in the second quarter of the nineteenth century, when the expansion of the estate acquired a considerable momentum. This is the backdrop against which the attitudes of Liverpool's leading traders of the 1850s and 1860s have to be considered. They had witnessed a dramatic expansion of the dock estate during their working lives. Back in 1821, when Prince's Dock was opened, Liverpool had nine docks with a total of just over 46 acres of enclosed water. This was almost four times the accommodation available half a century earlier, but was itself dwarfed by development in the next three decades. Through a combination of major new building and a number of reconstruction and modernising projects on the existing estate, Liverpool opened about 44 acres of dock space in the 1830s, 50 acres in the 1840s and 72 acres in the 1850s.[6]

By the mid-1850s, though, doubts were creeping in on a number of levels. A political storm had been rumbling for some time over the failure of the Birkenhead docks, on the other bank of the Mersey, to establish themselves as a serious rival to Liverpool, and matters came to a head with the forced amalgamation of the two systems under the new Mersey Docks & Harbour Board (MDHB) in 1858. Commercial and technical questions had always had to coexist with political issues, of course, but the tension now became overwhelming – central government required the bulk of port investment on the Mersey to be targeted at Birkenhead during the 1860s, at a time when the trading community remained firmly rooted in Liverpool. Dock expansion in Liverpool, so dramatic in earlier decades, was severely curtailed for more than a decade after 1858.

The politics of the Birkenhead question will be discussed more fully in chapter nine. For the moment, it is important to stress that the shifts in shipping and commodity trades so evident in mid-century had a disruptive effect on the port's

5   M. J. Power, 'Councillors and commerce in Liverpool, 1650–1750', *Urban History*, Vol. 24, 1997, pp. 301–23.

6   A convenient tabulation of Liverpool's dock development is the MDHB pocket yearbook, 1920, reproduced in A. Jarvis, *Liverpool central docks, 1799–1905*, Stroud, 1991, pp. 230–34.

expansion at much the same time as the Birkenhead fiasco. We need to establish the relationship between these different elements of growth and change, because pressure on dock facilities does not necessarily vary in proportion to the simple volume of traffic. Different kinds of ships, and different commodities, make demands that may be more or less proportionate to their tonnage or volume. Historians need to take a more sophisticated view of the relationship between expanding trade and expanding port facilities, rather than rely on long-established figures for overall shipping tonnage.

The first point to make is that by the mid-1850s, not all contemporaries were convinced of the need for constant expansion. Those who had to live through the mid-century period found many patterns in the port's trade confusing in the short term. Few had doubted the need for more dock space in the 1840s, reminded daily by the number of ships left waiting in the river unable to gain access to the docks, either because tides were not high enough to get them over old, shallow dock entrances, or because the docks themselves were full. One witness reckoned in 1845 that only one in eight vessels arriving in the Mersey had been able to gain access to the docks within a day of their arrival.[7] Within fifteen years, though, that dock space had been doubled, and the rate of growth in tonnage using the port was no longer so clear. The broad trend was, of course, upward, but this was an era of pronounced short-term fluctuations in shipping. Figure 4.1 demonstrates the volatility of Liverpool's shipping during the 1850s and 1860s. Traffic was as likely to contract as expand in these years, and the port authority's ability to plan was hampered by the unpredictable development of shipping patterns. There were always voices in the port opposed to new dock building, and they gained credibility in an era which saw such marked gains and slumps in traffic: it was tempting to wait for a more recognisable pattern to develop.[8]

Such uncertainty was fuelled by alternative ways of looking at changes in the port's traffic. It was clear that while a few exceptionally large vessels were placing unprecedented strain on the port's resources, the great bulk of Liverpool's traders were expanding their operations in a steady, much more manageable form. The key question was the depth of water required by the largest ships – building deep dock gates was a much more difficult and expensive engineering question than building wide gates, or long quays. Even in the mid-1850s, however, dock engineers could still argue that vessels were not increasing greatly in maximum draft, and that the overall scale of the problem was not so great as to justify huge expenditure and expansion.[9] In part, such comments were politically driven – the Birkenhead lobby at the time was trying to portray Liverpool as complacent and short-sighted, and Liverpool's officials therefore had an interest in publicly playing down the problem while working hard to address it behind the scenes. There were in fact good reasons to suppose that the maximum draft of ships would not be increased radically by

---

7   The figure was 213 vessels of a total of 1,625 arriving during a six-month period: BPP, Birkenhead Company's Docks Bill (1845), evidence of Lt Hookey, p. 145.

8   Mountfield, *Western gateway*, p. 25.

9   BPP, Birkenhead Docks (1856), evidence of John Bernard Hartley, p. 114.

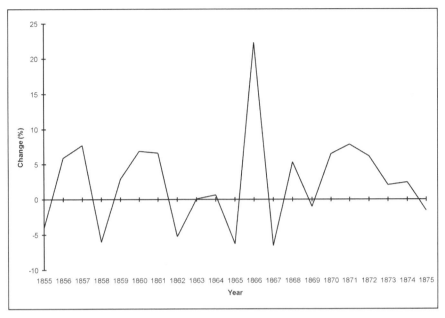

Figure 4.1 Rate of change in tonnage handled by Liverpool docks
Source: Dock Revenue statements.

shipbuilders: Lloyds required ships to have extra structural support if holds were
more than 23 ft deep, so there was an incentive to keep within such limits.[10] The
available evidence does point to relatively little change in maximum draft in this
period: the deepest vessel entering the Liverpool docks in 1855 had a draft of 22.5
ft, while the equivalent in 1870 was 24 ft.[11]

The problem was in fact very real, but did not stem from the 'headline' growth
of the port's biggest ships. Rather, it stemmed from the great expansion in the number
of ships with drafts in the upper reaches of the scale. Figure 4.2 shows the changing
pattern of vessel drafts across the period, demonstrating in particular a marked
increase in the number of vessels with drafts greater than 18 ft. Many of these ships
could not use the port's older docks because of their shallow entrances, and had to
compete for space in the newest docks. This is the crucial issue. Liverpool's expanding
shipping may not have looked too daunting when averaged across the whole dock
system, but that was precisely the point – it could not be spread across the whole
system. Much of this growth in traffic, involving an ever-increasing number of vessels
with drafts in the 18–22 ft range, could only be accommodated in a few, newer docks.

In addition, many of these vessels belonged to the port's rapidly expanding steam

10 BPP, Birkenhead Docks (1856), evidence of John Jones, p. 316.
11 Respectively *Emerald Isle*, a US-registered sailing clipper agented by W. Tapscott & Co. (DR,
    Bramley Moore, 17 Feb. 1855), and *Persia*, handled by Hargrove & Jackson in the Far East trades
    (DR, Waterloo, 10 Oct. 1870).

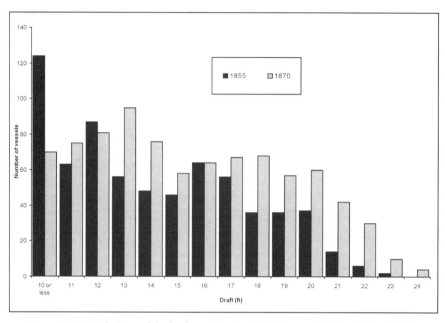

Figure 4.2 Distribution of draft of vessels using the Liverpool docks, 1855 and 1870
Source: Dock Registers (Samples, 1855, 1870).

fleets, which had a high public profile. Once again, there was a political thread alongside the technical one. Ever since Atlantic steamers began to operate from the port, Liverpool had recognised that providing suitable dock space for them was vital to maintaining the port's reputation as a modern, efficient venue for trade. Asked to provide facilities for a new generation of ocean paddle steamers in the 1840s, the Dock Committee sought assurances that such vessels were actually on the ship-builders' books, then publicly undertook to build appropriate accommodation.[12]

By the 1860s, keeping such promises was a much more difficult matter. The port authority could only keep pace by pursuing two key strategic avenues. First, at least some new, deep dock facilities had to be built on a regular basis, so that the newest, largest vessels could always be accommodated. The second necessity was a regular review of the older docks. In the mid-nineteenth century in particular, when many of Liverpool's most lucrative trades were still using sailing ships, it was possible for older docks to earn significant revenue handling a wide range of overseas traffic before eventually being turned over to coasters. For this to work smoothly, though, remodelling and adapting to specialised activities had to be a regular process.

This raises another additional pressure on the dock system in mid-century – finding time to undertake these renovations became increasingly difficult. Overseas traffic in Liverpool became less seasonal in this period. Figure 4.3 shows the fluctuating patterns

12   BPP, Liverpool Docks (1848), evidence of John Bramley Moore, pp. 13–14.

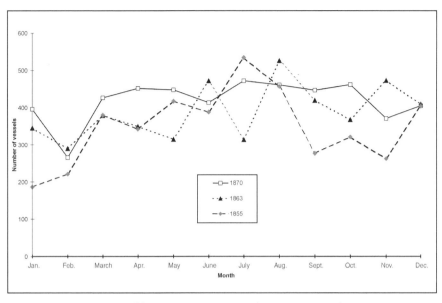

Figure 4.3 Monthly variations in arriving shipping, Liverpool, 1855–70
Source: BE. All arriving voyages, 1855, 1863, 1870.

of monthly arrivals in Liverpool. By 1870, the dock system had fewer 'quiet' months than in earlier decades – the 1870 series is clearly smoother than those of the earlier years, with a much less pronounced winter trough and summer peak. The total number of overseas vessels arriving in the port increased by almost 1,000 between 1855 and 1870, but the difference between the busiest and quietest month dropped dramatically from 347 in 1855 to only 206 in 1870.[13] This pattern points to increased pressure on facilities and reduced opportunities for dock maintenance and alterations during quieter periods, to say nothing of the considerable implications for the handling and marketing of particular trades, which will be discussed in more detail in later sections of this chapter.

Despite all these difficulties, previous studies have shown that Liverpool's dramatic dock expansion in the later 1840s and 1850s was broadly successful in matching the increasingly complex needs of the trading community.[14] Various measures of that success will be considered in the next section. It is all the more important to stress, therefore, the sudden breakdown of the pattern of growth in the 1860s. Even with the heavy investment insisted upon by Parliament, the Birkenhead docks attracted relatively little trade, while traders working from the Liverpool docks saw little new development despite the changes in traffic just outlined. This sudden shift in the direction of port development is at the heart of conflict between traders and the port

13 Incoming voyages in BE (All voyages, 1855, 1863, 1870).
14 Jackson, *History and archaeology of ports*, p. 80.

authority in mid-century, and is the background against which we need to analyse the operational realities of the dock system.

Operating the dock system in mid-century was therefore often a question of taking difficult decisions and making compromises. It had been much easier just to build new facilities, as in the 1840s – although the port's engineers deserve considerable credit for their work in expanding Liverpool's docks, they were nonetheless working in an era of relatively generous funding, and could build their way out of trouble. When external politics eliminated this option, other ways had to be found to manage the port and accommodate ever-more-diverse and complex trade. Although many of the measures taken by the port authority in mid-century have the air of pressured, coerced expedience, some were in fact based on longer experience in running the port – the quest for efficiency was not new in this period, although it became more urgent. The next section considers Liverpool's evolving attitudes to the different demands placed on port facilities over time, and considers some of the 'baggage' carried by the port at mid-century.

SPECIALISATION, FLEXIBILITY AND CHANGE

Even by the end of the eighteenth century, not all docks were alike: port planners had already begun to explore the idea of targeting specialised facilities at particular trades. The concept was seductive, promising a close match of infrastructure to the technical requirements of particular trades, and therefore a more efficient use of the port's resources. The construction of docks for particular trades also demonstrated an important commitment on the part of the port authority to its major customers, and encouraged further expansion of key trades. Traders themselves often favoured the development of specialised facilities, partly because their businesses could be conducted more efficiently, but also because bringing together all those active in a given trade meant that they could keep an eye on their competitors. Traders feared being placed at a disadvantage by their location within the dock system – those operating from a central dock might do better business than their competitors who worked from a more distant dock. A specialist facility in the north or south docks might not be very convenient for the offices and businesses in the town centre, but at least all members of a particular trade would suffer the same. In addition, there was a sense that traders grouped together with a common interest could negotiate with the port authority from a greater position of strength. Traders handling sailing ship cargoes from the United States sought exclusive use of Bramley-Moore Dock in 1864, and petitioned to move as a group to Victoria in 1868. This trade, while still important, was no longer the force it had been in the 1850s, but its ability to speak with one voice by sending a deputation of its leading members to negotiate with the Board enabled it to maintain some control over its dock accommodation.[15]

Against these general benefits, though, the port authority had to weigh a number of important problems, some of which were immediately apparent while others only

15   MDHB, WUP (Unbound), B141 vol. 1, 2 Mar. 1864, 9 Dec. 1868.

emerged over time. Some specialised facilities were more specialised – and usually more expensive – than others. Few objected to allocating sheds or berths to a given trade, but when specialisation required additional engineering, it became a political risk. Considerable sums, it might be argued, were being spent on a favoured few, while most users of the port struggled to find quay space in overcrowded general-purpose docks.

The other major difficulty was obsolescence. In the longer term, specialised facilities suffered even more acutely than 'ordinary' infrastructure from shifts in shipping technology and trading practices. The flexibility needed to accommodate such change was largely incompatible with the provision of highly specialised docks. If a number of the system's docks were built for particular trades that then outgrew them, any change of use tended to require substantial investment in modification and rebuilding. Specialisation could, therefore, offer important benefits to trade and port alike, but only if the port authority had mechanisms in place to deal with change over time.

The changing distribution of trades across the docks is therefore central to any assessment of the effectiveness of the port authority in matching the needs of its customers. The issue that looms largest in the historiography, and in much contemporary comment, is that of the accommodation of steamships. This is indeed a vital question, but it needs to be addressed from more than one viewpoint. In particular, we need to remember that the impressive growth of steam in the 1850s and 1860s was not accompanied by a significant fall in sail tonnage – the port authority could not assume that there would be a natural process whereby sail would, literally, make way for steam.

It is well established that ocean steamships brought about a major overhaul in the way ports were managed. The received wisdom was that steamships could only be efficiently accommodated in specialised docks, and that these had to be arranged rather differently from the established practices. Partly, there was a perceived risk of fire caused by sparks or, more seriously, by boiler explosions. Such fears were probably always exaggerated: the greatest threat to ships in dock was probably from cooking fires and smoking, which the authorities tried to ban on sailing ships and steamers alike. Nonetheless, Liverpool's first steam dock, Clarence (1830), was built well away from the rest of the system and its timber, cotton and other inflammable cargoes. By the early 1840s, however, it was clear that quarantine was not a long-term solution. Steam was being used on oceanic routes, vessels were getting much bigger, and land was expensive: the idea of building a very large steam dock with a firebreak of open ground around it in the heart of Liverpool was never a serious option. The expansion of the docks in the 1840s had to consider steam as an integrated part of the system.

The more important element in making steam different in terms of dock use was the pressure of steam liner timetables. Steamship owners objected to vessels being boxed in or made to wait for berths.[16] Each steamer therefore required a greater area of the dock than its dimensions would necessarily suggest, because other ships could not be parked in the space between it and the dock exit. Sail docks had traditionally

16   Jackson, *History and archaeology of ports*, pp. 74–75.

been organised differently: sailing ships were often berthed alongside one another, because it was accepted in most trades that vessels were in no particular rush to load or unload. Looked at from the sailing viewpoint, steamers in a dock restricted the available space by far more than an equivalent tonnage of sailing ships did, simply because of the way they were worked.

It would be wrong, however, to draw too sharp a distinction between sail and steam. Some historians – like some steamship owners – have been too ready to accept the idea that sail was a relatively relaxed business, free from the stresses of the strict steam liner timetables. Sail operators, especially those working long-distance routes in dangerous seas, begged to differ. For a Far East trader even a week's delay in Liverpool, at particular times of the year, was 'of great importance; at a critical season, it involves the necessity of the vessel taking a longer route ... [and] would very often throw her into a contrary monsoon in returning'.[17] Canadian timber ships sometimes tried to fit two round-trip voyages into the year, but a few days' delay on the Mersey in late July could lead to the underwriters raising insurance premiums, fearing a return voyage in icy seas.[18] Delays were not the only problem faced by ships berthed closely together: one unfortunate trader reported a case in which two of his ships were berthed next to one another and cargo intended for Venezuela left Liverpool on the Valparaiso ship, 'at great cost'.[19] The question is not so much one of steam operations distancing themselves from sail, as one of some operators – sail and steam alike – seeking more efficient ways to get the most from their extensive investments in ships. While the port authority saw rapid turn-round for the growing steam fleets as one of its highest priorities, we should remember that other port users also had an interest in increased efficiency.

How, then, did the Liverpool dock estate accommodate sail and steam in mid-century? Figure 4.4 demonstrates the changing pattern of sail and steam accommodation in some key docks. It is worth examining these figures in a little more depth. By the mid-1850s, Liverpool's steam traffic was concentrated in Nelson (1848) and Huskisson (1852) – between them, these docks handled 82% of arriving steam tonnage in 1855. Indeed, steam's progress in the 1850s seemed easily managed, with two main regional trades in two main docks: the Mediterranean traffic was focused on Nelson, while Huskisson handled the US trade.

During the 1860s, matters became more complex, with, as has been discussed, a considerable rise in steam shipping and little expansion of the dock estate. The extension of dock facilities that did take place was rapidly taken over by steam. Huskisson remained central to the steam trade, dealing with an even greater tonnage of both Mediterranean and North American steamers after it was extended in the early 1860s. Wellington (1850), Nelson and Coburg (1840) were also playing a role, the last as a result of significant modernisation in 1858. By 1870, steam became much more scattered across the system. Only seven of Liverpool's docks handled steamers

17 BPP, Birkenhead Commissioners' Docks (1844), evidence of William Potter, p. 35.
18 BPP, Birkenhead Docks (1848), evidence of Duncan Gibb, p. 81.
19 BPP, Liverpool Docks (1855), evidence of Joseph Mondell, p. 92.

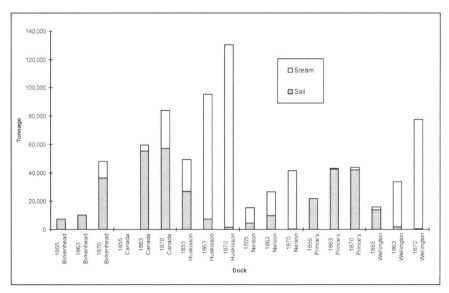

Figure 4.4 Proportion of sail/steam tonnage using key docks
Source: BE (Samples 1855, 1863, 1870).
Note: Canada was not opened until after the 1855 sample.

in 1855, but by 1870, no fewer than twenty docks saw some steam traffic. Smaller steamers had to find berths in older docks like Prince's: the smallest steamers working the European trades could fit physically into older docks, and the port authority forced them to use such facilities rather than mix with the large steamers in the new, deeper docks. This was not popular: Mediterranean steam traders working from Queen's were clearly offended by being assigned to 'what was always a sailing dock'.[20]

That said, most steam traffic managed to congregate in particular docks, following the time-honoured habit of clustering particular trades. Most steamers from West Africa used Coburg, for example, most services running to European ports on the English Channel used Huskisson, and the great majority of steamers from North Sea and Baltic ports used Nelson. While steam shipping was permeating the working of the system in a much more thorough manner than before, the Board did manage to maintain sail/steam segregation across a large part of the system even during the sharp rise in steam traffic after 1860.

Canada (1858) is clearly the dock with the greatest mix of sail and steam, and therefore an impressive symbol of the conflicting pressures on the new Dock Board in the late 1850s. Its construction and operation combined a number of issues of specialisation and adaptation, and offer useful evidence in explaining the Board's tactics in making conflicting interests fit into inadequate facilities. As originally planned, Canada was to be the solution to a long-running problem of how to

20 BPP, MDHB Bill (1873), evidence of Walter Glyn, q. 778.

accommodate the Liverpool timber trade. Under constraints imposed by central government at the instigation of the Birkenhead lobby, however, it also proved to be the only major dock to be built in the later 1850s. With steam's rapid expansion in the 1860s, Canada became the point at which the two pressures converged.

We need to take a step back and explain the process by which the timber trade came to be one of the port authority's key preoccupations. Liverpool handled timber rather differently from many contemporary ports, investing in specialised docks. Many ports handled timber by unloading it over the side of the vessel into the water, floating it into storage ponds, and then eventually moving it to large yards and sheds for seasoning.[21] Liverpool's timber trade was based on land-storage, however. The port's timber docks were built with sloping quays, enabling long beams to be unloaded through hatches in the front of the specialised vessels working the trade. Timber quays led directly to large storage yards, minimising the handling of what was one of the port's heaviest and most awkward cargoes. Nor was it just difficult to handle: as this was a relatively low-value commodity, handling had to be kept to a minimum to keep the trade economic.[22] Open storage often did not come cheap, and it should not be assumed that the lack of sheds and warehouses made timber docks an easier financial prospect for the port authority: considerable areas of land had to be purchased from local landowners, who were generally able to make large sums from the transaction.[23]

The distribution of timber across the dock system, and the changing use of the docks built to accommodate it, cast some light on the adaptation of specialised facilities. Brunswick Dock (1832) was custom-built for timber, and for a quarter of a century the trade duly dominated the work of the dock. Even in the early 1840s, however, the trade had expanded considerably and was becoming a victim of its own success. Although pressure on facilities for all trades was acute in the 1840s, the timber trade was politically one of the best organised and most vocal in its demands for new facilities. As usual, however, the trade wanted to move *en masse* or not at all. It was generally accepted that any traders shifting their operations away from the south docks would be isolated and disadvantaged. Timber traders first sought expansion in the crammed south docks, which was not realistic, and then agreed to move to new facilities at the north end of the estate. While they complained about this dislocation from their traditional base, they did not object too loudly in case the port authority took the opportunity to move timber's operations to Birkenhead.[24]

Dock building plans in the late 1840s therefore included much that was targeted at resolving timber's problems. A large dock at the north end of the Liverpool system was envisaged, which would allow timber to be stored afloat or dragged onto large

21   Jackson, *History and archaeology of ports*, pp. 59–61.

22   BPP, Liverpool Docks (1855), evidence of Robert Rankin, p. 103.

23   N. Ritchie-Noakes and M. Clarke, 'The dock engineer and the development of the port of Liverpool', in *Liverpool shipping, trade and industry*, ed. V. Burton, Liverpool, 1989, pp. 91–108; p. 97.

24   BPP, Birkenhead Docks (1856), evidence of Charles Turner, p. 364.

adjacent storage yards. Overall, there would be 100 acres of land storage, around 50 acres of float space, and 61 acres of working dock, dwarfing Brunswick's 12 acres of water.[25] This plan was never implemented, because by this point all dock building in Liverpool was subject to objections from the Birkenhead lobby. Huge schemes like this, or the earlier (and successful) plan that led to the opening of six new central docks on the same day in 1848, gave way to much more compromised programmes. Canada, the still-impressive element salvaged from the original plans, was all too rapidly overtaken by the expansion of traffic in the port.

The pattern of timber's move from its traditional southern docks to the new facility at Canada is clear from the figures. Of the pine boards landed in Liverpool in 1855, 41% went to Brunswick, and 12% each to Garston and Huskisson. Another 25% was recorded as arriving on the river, although most of this would have gone to Brunswick when space became available. By 1870, the long-awaited consolidation had been achieved – Canada handled 93% of Liverpool's board trade. Traffic in deals remained more scattered, although Canada had still claimed 70% of the port's total by 1870.[26]

The apparent ability of the timber trade to make full use of whatever space it was given in the new dock symbolised trouble for the future. Leading timber traders feared that a mix of timber ships and steam liners would be the start of a process which would erode the facilities available to the port's older trades. Although they had been willing to allow other operators access to timber docks during the traditional quiet season when traffic from the ice-bound Canadian ports was slack, there was always a concern that such access would be the thin end of a wedge.[27] These fears were expressed still more forcibly when the Board began giving other steam operators access to Canada in the early 1860s.[28] Indeed, alarm bells had been ringing in the ranks of the timber trade before Canada even opened. In 1858, the Board refused to define Canada as being intended 'exclusively' for timber – major steamship owner William Inman insisted that 'especially' was a more appropriate word, leaving room for flexibility later.[29]

The Board took increasing advantage of that flexibility as the 1860s progressed. Throughout its first decade of operation Canada was dominated by North American timber ships, with an important Baltic timber element as well. Its sheer size relative to other Liverpool docks made it possible to accommodate other large vessels, however, and ships from the United States used Canada for grain and meat cargoes in the early 1860s, and an increasing quantity of cotton after 1865. After a prolonged argument at the Dock Board, steamship operators began to be allocated space on those quays in Canada that were not designed specially for timber, and more general cargoes, sail and steam, began to be handled by Canada.

Although this diversification angered the timber trade, it was clear from the port

25 BPP, Liverpool Docks (1848), evidence of John Bernard Hartley, p. 20.
26 Figures calculated from BE (1855, 1870).
27 *Liverpool Courier*, 2 Oct. 1863.
28 See complaints by timber trader John Farnworth at the Dock Board, reported in *Gore's Advertiser*, 8 Oct. 1863, p. 1.
29 MDHB, Minutes, 25 Mar. 1858.

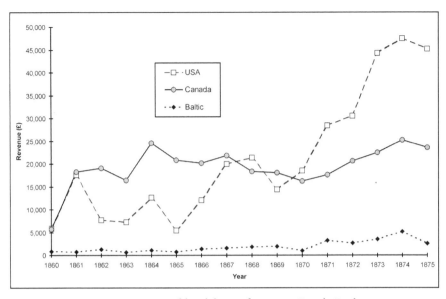

Figure 4.5 Regional breakdown of revenue, Canada Dock
Source: Dock Revenue statements.

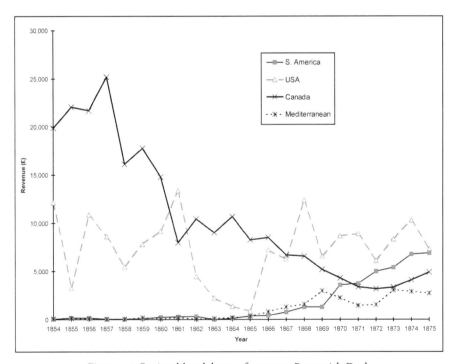

Figure 4.6 Regional breakdown of revenue, Brunswick Dock
Source: Dock Revenue statements.

authority's figures that cramming more steamers into Canada considerably increased the dock's value to the Board in terms of revenue. As Figure 4.5 shows, revenue from British North America – mainly timber – was broadly steady in Canada's first fifteen years of operation, while revenue from the United States was the dock's significant growth sector. Such figures reinforced the Board's view that timber's importance should not be allowed to overshadow the potential of other, still more lucrative, activities. As will be discussed in chapter nine, however, maintaining a working balance between the competing interests using Canada remained a considerable problem for the port authority.

If the Board hoped that Canada's original design would be flexible enough to accommodate diverse trades, it also faced the harder task of adapting older timber docks to deal with new demands. Timber's old home in the Brunswick Dock has useful lessons for the adaptability of specialised port facilities. Figure 4.6 shows the regional breakdown of Brunswick's revenue in mid-century. Timber's move to the north docks is clear from the drop in Canadian revenue, although cotton from the United States propped up the dock's returns in the late 1850s. Brunswick's revenue troughed in 1864–5 during the American Civil War and then picked up again in the rest of the decade. There is a further rise in the 1870s, although the dock then went into a decline that was only reversed by extensive modernisation early in the 20th century.[30] The dock could not recapture the sort of revenue brought in during its timber heyday. Nonetheless, Brunswick expanded its traffic in cotton from the southern United States, and also played host to a few small steamships from South America and the Mediterranean. Such adaptation was hampered by the inflexibility of Brunswick's original infrastructure, and in particular the highly specialised sloping quay. This was recognised by the port authority, and the quay was finally removed early in the 1870s, with an attendant growth in traffic. The fact that it took until the 1870s to carry this out, though, is in itself a measure of the relative paralysis of the system in mid-century. The Dock Committee had originally planned to redevelop Brunswick – the 'second best site in the town' – back in the mid-1840s, as one of the beneficial spin-offs of the original plan to move timber to a huge north dock.[31]

The timber trade raises one more point about Liverpool's approach to the channelling and control of trade, and that leads to the broader question that is explored in the remainder of this section. Much of the difficulty in handling timber was not in unloading but in storage. Traders argued that the port was losing business because charges were high in the crowded south docks. Timber traders often had to store their goods for some time – clearly, timber arrivals were at their busiest in the autumn, but building timber would often not be bought by the construction industry until the following year. Storage costs amounted to a third of the traders' expenses in handling a typical cargo.[32] While the port authority believed that its major

30 Figures from Dock revenue statements.
31 BPP, Liverpool Docks (1848), evidence of John Bramley Moore, p. 9.
32 Storage space in the packed south docks was charged at 1s 3d per square yard: BPP, Liverpool Docks (1848), evidence of John Bramley Moore, pp. 7–8.

competitors charged even more, there was evidence that smaller ports could undercut Liverpool. The Welsh building industry, it was argued, imported timber directly into a number of small ports – it cost more in freight charges, but avoided a range of other costs associated with the Liverpool market.[33]

The port authority and the trading community therefore had to strike a difficult balance in the question of storage. Traders needed to be able to control stocks of a broad range of commodities, without incurring such expense that their profits from the eventual sale would be wiped out or customers would go elsewhere. At the same time, the port authority needed sufficient income from specialised facilities to service the debts incurred in building and maintaining them. This was true of the large storage yards used by the timber trade, but it was most obvious in the question of warehousing.

Liverpool's approach to warehousing in mid-century is probably most famously symbolised in the opening of the Albert complex in 1846. Jesse Hartley's great brick structures are for many the classic dock warehouses – secure, fireproof, and capable of handling and storing huge quantities of the port's key commodities. Albert came at the end of a half-century in which warehousing had transformed the mercantile practices of British business. Before the 1803 Warehousing Act, traders had to pay duties on most goods when they were imported, and could only claim their funds back after the goods had subsequently been re-exported. Naturally, this required traders to tie up significant sums of money in Customs duties, and discriminated against smaller traders who could not afford such duties. The Act, however, put the bonded warehouse concept at the disposal of traders, allowing them to store goods duty free until they were exported again, or pay duties when the goods were sold domestically, rather than when they were imported. The overall result, of course, was a significant increase in the ability of traders to control their costs, and therefore to expand their activities.[34]

Warehousing, in short, was all about power and control. This operated on a number of levels. Some commodities, like tobacco, were subject to close control by the government's revenue authorities: handling such goods in special bonded and secure warehouses allowed this scrutiny to be undertaken. Tobacco was therefore the earliest cargo to have dedicated warehousing in Liverpool. King's Dock had a tobacco warehouse from the late eighteenth century, to which was added a second, larger building designed for the same purpose in 1811. That early nineteenth-century development was overdue, in the opinion of the port's traders, especially given the complex control systems exercised by the Customs. When the warehouse was full, traders had to cart tobacco from the ship to a private warehouse, then to King's for official weighing at the first available opportunity, then back to a private warehouse for storage, and then to King's again for final weighing at the time of sale. Needless

---

33 BPP, Liverpool Docks (1848), evidence of James Smith, p. 17.

34 E. H. Rideout, 'The development of the Liverpool warehousing system', *Transactions of the Historic Society of Lancashire & Cheshire*, Vol. 82, 1930, pp. 1–41; pp. 1–3.

to say, the tobacco merchants incurred considerable excess costs and no-one benefited except the carters.[35]

Such problems were serious, but usually short-lived: when they worked well, warehouses close to the dock estate offered traders considerable advantages and reduced costs. As was noted in the last chapter, Liverpool traders and brokers maintained extensive stocks of key commodities – cotton, most obviously – in their efforts to control key markets. Warehouses were an essential component in that structure, warehouse owners were wealthy and powerful, and private warehousing in Liverpool was big business by mid-century. One representative of the trade believed that the town had around 1,400 warehouses in the mid-1840s, 1,000 of which were used for cargoes arriving at the docks, and the remainder for storing manufactured goods prior to export.[36] Inevitably, therefore, moves in mid-century to build dock warehouses which would be controlled by the port authority represented a threat to the considerable vested interests of private warehouse owners. The politics of this issue will be better addressed in chapter nine – this section will offer an overview of the working of the warehouse and storage system.

To assess the working of such docks in mid-century, it is worth considering Albert in some detail. The dock was modelled on the large London warehouse docks, and specifically designed to perform similar functions and attract the same lucrative trades. Liverpool had long lagged far behind London in this regard. The St Katherine's complex in east London was widely admired for the security and efficiency of its operations.[37] Particular trades demanded such facilities if they were to operate in the port. Far East trade was a prize well worth having, and Liverpool had been gradually working in that direction since the withdrawal of the East India Company's monopoly earlier in the century. With the Company no longer able to marshal all the region's trade into London, the provincial ports sought ways to attract eastern traffic. Liverpool realised that long-standing tradition would be hard to overcome – London could always claim to be the 'natural' home of the Far East trades, and significant incentives were needed to persuade traders that other ports had the necessary facilities. Liverpool cut its dock dues in 1844 specifically, it was claimed, to attract long-haul shipping from the Far East.[38] Albert's opening shortly thereafter represented a further thread in the port authority's effort to attract lucrative new trades.

Albert was, for a time, highly successful in catering for Far East trades. In 1855, at the end of its first decade of operation, Albert was earning 52% of Liverpool's total revenue from the region. Albert's revenue from the Far East continued to grow in absolute terms during the 1860s, and despite losing some of its share to other docks, it remained the eastern trades' single most important dock on the Mersey until the mid-1870s. As late as 1870, Albert was earning 29% of Liverpool's total Far East revenue, just over twice that of its nearest rival, Prince's. Other docks had begun

---

35 Nicholas Henry & Co. (Liverpool) to Ephriam MacQuillen (Richmond, Virginia), 22 April 1803, in Perkins Library, Duke University, Samuel Smith Downey papers, box 2.

36 BPP, Liverpool Docks (1848), evidence of Richard Harbord, p. 29.

37 Warehouse report (1839), pp. 10–11.

38 BPP, Birkenhead Docks (1848), evidence of John Bramley Moore, p. 139.

to account for an increasing share of the region's trade by the mid-1860s, though, and Prince's, Wapping, Queen's and Stanley all managed more than 10% of total revenue in 1863.[39]

Albert's principal Far Eastern cargoes included silk, cotton and tea from China and animal horns, cotton, jute, sugar, rice, wool and various seeds and spices and dye-stuffs from India. There is good evidence that the silk, cotton and wool traders found Albert particularly convenient for their work. The bonded warehouse regime allowed goods to be inspected and sorted before weighing and sale, and Albert's warehouses had good natural lighting on the upper floor.[40] The entire silk trade, according to the Chief Clerk of the dock estate warehouses, moved from scattered private warehouses to Albert when these facilities first became available. There is some evidence that this may not have been too great an exaggeration: Albert handled 87% of Liverpool's Chinese silk imports by quantity in 1855.[41]

Albert's role in the China tea trade was also significant. China was the main supplier of Liverpool's tea imports in the 1850s and 1860s, although the trade fell off thereafter. Some tea came from India, and some from the United States, although the latter would have originally come across the Pacific from China. Although tea packaging was notoriously lacking in standardisation, by any available measure Albert far outstripped the other docks in 1855, with 37,616 out of 40,035 'chests' (the most common unit of measurement). In 1863, Albert was still exercising a virtual monopoly, with 13,188 out of 13,192 'boxes' of China tea, 11,793 out of 11,795 'packages', and 672 of 674 'chests'.[42]

Bulky goods like cotton and wool posed more of a dilemma for the port authority's warehouse managers, however, because the attractiveness of the facility threatened to be its undoing. Even in the early stages of planning the warehouse dock, it was anticipated that some restriction might be necessary on bulk items in order to make room for even more lucrative cargoes.[43] Cotton posed a particular problem to warehouse managers because of the habit of stockpiling which marked Liverpool's cotton trade in this period. At the end of 1852, stocks warehoused in the city ran to almost 600,000 bales, equivalent to just under one-third of the year's imports.[44] If the administrative regime of the dock warehouses were not carefully worked out, cotton could swamp the facilities.

Indeed, cotton's distribution across the dock system in mid-century demonstrates the port's need to spread the commodity across ever-more docks in order to cope with increasing volumes of traffic. In the mid-1850s, there was clearly a concerted effort to focus the cotton trade on four key docks: Bramley-Moore, Albert, Waterloo and Huskisson. In total, these four handled 67% of the port's cotton imports in 1855, and the fourth dock (Huskisson) handled more than twice as much as the fifth

39   Dock revenue statements (1855, 1863, 1870).
40   Baines, *Liverpool in 1859*, p. 99.
41   BPP, Liverpool Docks (1848), evidence of Percival Austen, p. 18; BE (1855).
42   BE (1855, 1863).
43   Warehouse report (1839), p. 6.
44   B. Poole, *The commerce of Liverpool*, Liverpool, 1854, p. 3.

(Stanley). By 1870, the differences were much less pronounced. Albert was the port's largest single cotton dock, but ten docks had between 5% and 12% of the total, pointing to a much more even distribution.[45]

Despite this wider distribution, the warehouse docks remained the main focus of cotton imports: Albert and Stanley topped the list in 1870. About 40% of Albert's cotton was part of its primary trade with the Far East, but over half came from the southern United States, suggesting that the warehouses were able to attract particular commodities from regional trades that otherwise had little connection with the dock. Albert occupied an important niche in the American cotton trade, carried in smaller sailing vessels from the southern states. Increasing quantities of American cotton carried by steam used Huskisson, which was consistently Liverpool's fourth cotton dock. Trade with the southern states averaged 16% of Albert's revenue in the five years before the American Civil War began in 1861. Reduced to virtually nothing by the conflict, traffic in American cotton gradually recovered, but only really began to expand rapidly again in the early 1870s. By the end of that decade, and into the 1880s, US trade was contributing around one-quarter of Albert's total revenue, and cotton remained the key commodity.[46]

Albert continued to be an important dock throughout mid-century, therefore, but in the longer term is an excellent example of specialised infrastructure that proved too difficult to adapt to changing needs. Although the warehouses remained attractive to Far East trades in particular, those trades were increasingly carried in larger steamships after the opening of the Suez Canal. Longer, deeper steamers found Albert difficult to use, partly because of the shallowness of its entrances, but also because of the extensive manoeuvring required in negotiating the tight corners of the passages between Albert and its neighbouring docks. In addition, Albert's traditional partner docks, into which empty ships went to load their outgoing cargoes, were also small. This became an increasing problem as Manchester's textile industries began to expand their exports to the East, and the sheer quantity of cotton goods for export arriving at the docks by railway required more commodious facilities than those around Albert. Birkenhead, with its rail links to Manchester, began to make significant inroads during the 1870s. There was also a reversion to older patterns: some of the Far East traders at this time split their operations between London, where tea and spices were unloaded, and Birkenhead, where exports were collected.[47] It was, therefore, the transition from sail to steam in Albert's key trade that made the dock increasingly obsolete as the century progressed. By the mid-1880s, the Birkenhead system was handling one-third of the Mersey's traffic with the Far East, and most of the rest went through the more modern northern docks on the Liverpool side.[48]

---

45 There was no universally accepted weight for a cotton bale in this period: New Orleans bales, for example, weighed much more than Bombay bales. For the purpose of this analysis, bales were converted into lb weight using the conversion table in R. Stephens, *On the stowage of ships and their cargoes*, 5th edn, London, 1869, p. 145; BE (1855, 1870).

46 Dock revenue statements.

47 F. E. Hyde, *Far Eastern trade, 1860–1914*, London, 1973, p. 179.

48 Dock revenue statements (1885).

It should be stressed, though, that as well as earning considerable revenue from shipping, the warehouse docks were bringing in storage revenue to the Dock Board. This had been one of the original aims of the Dock Trust, which believed that warehousing was a 'tolerably profitable business' in mid-century Liverpool: while docks themselves would not make money, their attendant warehouses might.[49] Initial evidence from Albert seemed promising: at the end of its first decade of operation, Dock Committee chairman Charles Turner reported to Parliament on Liverpool's 'handsome return' on the investment in Albert, which he estimated at 7%.[50]

The evidence seems to support Turner's view. It is clear that during Albert's busiest period as a dock, in the 1850s and 1860s, the warehouses were earning more than the dock was. The figures are hard to corroborate, but between 1854 and 1870 – when comparative figures are available and use of the dock was at its height – Albert's warehouses contributed an average of £26,776 each year to the Board's coffers (after expenditure), while the dock dues averaged only £21,544 (before expenditure).[51] More specialised warehousing, managed for official purposes, also brought in revenue. Liverpool took in £6,484 annually from the Treasury for the tobacco warehouse in the later 1840s.[52]

The place of warehouse docks in the revenue hierarchy therefore indicates that secure storage not only generated income in its own right through warehouse rents, but also attracted shipping to docks that might otherwise have been more rapidly abandoned for more modern and convenient facilities elsewhere in the system. Although docks like Albert were costly, they gave the dock estate large, secure warehouse assets in the heart of Liverpool. That facility continued to attract valuable overseas trade through the dock beyond the point at which most docks of a similar size had switched to less lucrative coastal traffic. In the still longer term, far beyond the scope of this volume, Albert's warehouses were of such solid construction and in such a prime location that they continued to offer distinct advantages for the storage of goods, even when cargoes had to be taken to them by railway or cart rather than by ship.

It was clear, though, that the port authority could not push this model too far. The Prince's transit sheds, for example, were never converted into warehouses, despite the potential earnings. Although opened in 1821, Prince's revenue rose steadily from the mid-1850s to the early 1870s, with a number of important trades contributing to its traffic, and it earned around 7% of the total system revenue throughout the period.[53] It specialised in high-value cargoes which needed a secure handling environment, but which came from parts of the world where sailing ships could still hold their own. South America, the West Indies and the Far East were central to the work

49 BPP, Liverpool Docks (1848), evidence of John Bramley Moore, p. 13.
50 BPP, Liverpool Docks (1855), evidence of Charles Turner, p. 11.
51 Figures derived from tabulated data in MMM Archives, MDHB, annual reports of the Dock Engineer's Department (1854–70).
52 BPP, Liverpool Docks (1851), evidence of George Maxwell, p. 165.
53 Calculated from Dock revenue statements.

of Prince's, and cotton from the southern United States became an important element in the rise in the dock's revenue in the later 1860s.

It was already evident in the 1840s, however, that working practices in Prince's made it difficult for the port authority to recoup its investment in the transit sheds. Goods had to be removed from the sheds within 48 hours or pay rent, but all this did was give the trading community two days' free warehousing: had the sheds been converted into warehouses, they could have earned money.[54] The Board had to walk a fine line, though, between the provision of services that could be justified by demand, and moves which might alienate the trading community. The Prince's sheds were popular, many traders claimed to prefer such sheds to warehouses, and the Board settled for the extra shipping attracted to the dock rather than seek warehouse revenue also.

Specialisation in dock construction and use – whether in steam, timber or warehousing – therefore offered the port authority a way of raising revenue while managing change in a manner amenable to key users of the docks. It was also a risky strategy, based on the assumption that resources would be available to modernise and replace specialist facilities. Failure to sustain that element of the equation could rapidly alienate traders forced to use inadequate facilities, especially if other members of the community appeared to be receiving preferential treatment in new, purpose-built docks. In addition, the Board had to consider the relative contribution made by different trades to its revenue, which did not always correlate with the political influence of those groups: chapter nine will consider some of these issues in more detail.

INTEGRATION AND EFFICIENCY

Having to manage increasing and changing traffic in a broadly static dock estate brought questions of efficiency onto the port authority agenda with new urgency in mid-century. Management of traffic within the dock system was not easy, nor is it a straightforward matter for historians to explore. There are numerous examples of ships that were able to pass in and out of the docks in record time, and of ships that suffered seemingly endless delays. Gathering a reliable set of statistics to cast light on the 'normal' experience of a vessel using the Liverpool docks is fraught with difficulty, however. At the same time, it is clear from the Dock Board's figures that some parts of the estate brought in more revenue than others did. The reasons for this, and efforts by the port authority to make sections of the estate operate more effectively, offer another angle on the pressures facing the managers of an increasingly complex range of facilities.

First, the question of effective traffic management within the dock system. This is an issue rarely studied by historians, in large part because of a scarcity of records. While the volume of shipping using most ports can usually be calculated from a number of sources, Liverpool is unusual in having a comprehensive record of traffic

54   BPP, Liverpool Docks (1851), evidence of George Maxwell, p. 165.

movement *within* the dock system.[55] One of the central practical problems facing the port authority was that many ships arriving in Liverpool from long-distance voyages did not just require one berth, but, in a sense, three: one to unload, a second in a graving dock for routine repair and maintenance, and a third to load. Ensuring that the vessel could move from one to another without spending too much time waiting was a major logistical issue for the port authority, and a financial headache for shipowners. Overall in 1870, just under half of vessels in overseas trades stayed in the same dock from the time they arrived in Liverpool until they left for their outward voyages. A bare majority (52%) of vessels unloaded in one dock and then went to at least one other dock before leaving the system.[56] This figure means that we need to add half again to any total of arriving shipping to get a more accurate picture of the true implications for the port managers in their efforts to deal with increasing traffic.

Any movement in the system was a potential problem, especially when the port had to play host to larger vessels. Matters were improved somewhat by the advent of steam – having their own power, steamers were often more manoeuvrable than sailing ships. This was not always true, though, especially in the case of the largest and clumsiest steamers of mid-century. Even the routine business of getting from an entrance basin into one of the neighbouring docks could be a tricky process. The US Collins Line steamers of the mid-1850s usually stayed in the river, but occasionally struggled to use Huskisson:

> We go into the Sandon Basin first of all, and then into the Huskisson Dock. We go in about high water; we cannot go in much before, or after … we work the ship in by steam and ropes … sometimes we use a small steamer to pull the ship's head around, as we have to turn so many short corners.

This complex process took about forty-five minutes, and effectively blocked any other traffic movement in that part of the system.[57]

If the process was so problematic, why were docks systems set up in this manner? Looked at from other angles, moving vessels around in the dock system could help rather than hinder the overall efficiency of the estate. There are two main issues here. First, dock engineers preferred to have a minimum number of direct access points to the river, and, rather, to have passages from one dock to the next. This reduced the engineering difficulties associated with building and maintaining gates into the river. It was also better for shipping, in that going from one dock to another was almost always easier and safer than going out into the river and back into another dock. Ships had to take on ballast before risking the Mersey, which was obviously an additional cost and delay to most vessels. Over time, expansion of the dock estate led to complex systems of 'shunting' vessels from dock to dock, balancing the needs of moving traffic with those of vessels berthed at the quays. The second factor was

---

55   This material was recorded in the Liverpool Dock Registers (DR).

56   Figures in this paragraph are calculated from DR (1870).

57   BPP, Birkenhead Docks (1852), evidence of Captain Luce, p. 275.

closely tied to the specialisation strategy discussed earlier in the chapter. Docks designed to unload a particular commodity naturally had no facilities for loading the outgoing cargo, so vessels had to move elsewhere in the system.

It was possible to design a system that offered the best of both worlds. The Liverpool port authority aimed to do just that with a strategy of integrated dock use in mid-century, creating clusters of docks that were designed to strike an efficient balance between specialisation and flexibility. Each dock could perform a specialised function, but ships did not have to travel far through the system to reach the next stage in the process. The Albert complex is probably the state of the art of its time. As has been noted, Albert itself was an unloading dock only: high-value goods were taken from ships and stored in the secure warehouses. The ships then moved elsewhere to load or have maintenance work done. This system was not without its critics, who argued that such strictly regimented operations gave too much control to the port authority, and did not necessarily add to the efficiency of the port. Not only were vessels forced to move from Albert immediately after unloading – whether convenient to the operator or not – but Albert's water area was likely to be under-used. Critics used to seeing sailing ships berthed three or four deep in the Liverpool docks accused the port authority of wasting Albert's capacity: the dock could have accommodated fifty to eighty vessels, it was claimed, but often only had a dozen berthed at one time.[58]

They were missing the point, of course. The rationale behind Albert in its heyday was that throughput of vessels was more important than the number that could be accommodated in the dock at one time, and that vessels should only have to move to nearby docks to be loaded. In addition, the series of gates and bridges linking Albert to its surrounding docks allowed this traffic to move without going into the river: Albert itself had no direct river access. There is evidence from Albert's first decade of working that it and its neighbouring docks were operating with some success as an integrated system. In 1855, three in every four vessels leaving Albert for a loading berth only had to go as far as the neighbouring Salthouse Dock. Already, however, one element in the pattern was less positive for the port authority. Just over one-quarter of vessels leaving Albert in 1855 went to a graving dock for maintenance rather than going immediately to a loading berth. Unfortunately for the system planners, less than half of them went to the neighbouring Canning graving docks. The others had to go further afield, to facilities at Prince's, Clarence and Sandon. By 1870, Albert's traffic was even more likely to go to a graving dock, but in turn still less likely to be accommodated at Canning.[59]

There are two points here, one especially relevant to Albert's traffic and one more general. The graving-dock problem is another example of the need to consider the type of shipping using the port as well as the overall tonnage. As has been seen, most of the increase in Liverpool's sail traffic, and virtually all of its steam, consisted of iron ships. The increasing use of iron vessels on long-haul voyages from the Far

58 BPP, Liverpool Docks (1848), evidence of Thomas Dower, p. 33.
59 DR (Albert, 1855, 1870).

East, Africa and South America placed great strain on ships, not just because of the length of time spent at sea, but also because of the presence in tropical waters of a range of organisms harmful to ships' hulls. It was accepted practice in this period that iron ships on the Far East trades needed repainting with red lead after every voyage, a process that took five to six days in the early 1860s. Even in the relatively friendly waters of the Mediterranean, iron ships needed painting every two months, and the increasing reliance of Liverpool operators on these vessels in mid-century has already been demonstrated. In contrast, ship-repairers recommended that the copper plating on wooden ships in Eastern trades should be renewed every two or three years, so the demand for graving dock space was clearly accelerating even faster than the simple growth in shipping tonnage.[60]

Given Albert's specialisation in precisely the long-haul shipping that required regular maintenance, it is hardly surprising that the elderly graving docks at Canning could not accommodate all the traffic leaving Albert in search of maintenance facilities. More generally, though, Liverpool seems to have had a problem with graving docks – there is a good deal of evidence that graving docks were the weak link in the system by mid-century. The Board's income from graving docks was remarkably static then, at a time when most other indicators showed distinct rises. Dock rates levied by tonnage rose from £204,000 to £259,000 between 1860 and 1870, while moneys raised on cargo went from £344,000 to £456,000. Graving dock rents, however, started the period at £27,000, and had reached only £33,000 by 1870.[61] This was clearly not a priority area for the Board, despite the regular complaints from traders.

Contemporaries claimed that the Dock Board neglected the development of its graving docks because they did not earn enough, bringing in little over half of the 4.5% needed to service the loans with which they were funded.[62] Liverpool's sixteen graving docks could accommodate about fifty vessels at any given time in the 1850s, but there were generally half as many again on the books waiting for a place.[63] Matters grew worse in the following decade. By 1873, the Dock Board took some £2,000 in forfeited graving dock fees from vessels that registered for a place on arrival in the port but then could not wait for a place to become available.[64] Assuming half of this total was from sail and half from steam, this would give a rough estimate of more than 500 ships denied access to the overcrowded graving docks in that year. By the late 1860s, there is evidence that congestion in graving docks was not entirely the Board's fault, because shipowners were using the docks for major refitting rather than routine maintenance. Owners discovered that iron ships could safely be made much longer than their wooden counterparts, and some decided to adapt their existing ships as well as order new ones: 'a species of mania set in for lengthening vessels',

---

60   BPP, MDHB Bill (1864), evidence of W. H. Potter, qq. 1,076–82.
61   Mountfield, Western gateway, p. 203.
62   BPP, Unseaworthy ships (1874), evidence of Charles Grayson, qq. 15,917–18.
63   BPP, Liverpool Docks (1855), evidence of James Smith, p. 51.
64   Fees were 2 guineas for sail, 5 guineas for steam. BPP, Unseaworthy ships (1874), evidence of Charles Grayson, q. 15,897.

so much so that the Dock Board eventually banned such work from being undertaken in its graving docks.[65]

Other areas of the port's activity operated more smoothly in mid-century. Steamships tended to work directly from a single dock and rarely had to make complex journeys within the dock system: 76% of vessels unloading in Nelson in 1870 stayed there to load, and then left the port directly. In addition, steamers already had short stays in the docks in the 1850s, and while some slippage is evident, the system seems to have maintained those broad levels in the following decade. Nelson managed to reduce its average steamer stay from five days in 1855 to four in 1870, although Huskisson's had risen from five to six. Given that Huskisson absorbed the greatest proportion of the considerable increase in the volume of steam traffic using the port, however, such figures represent a real efficiency gain for the dock. The port also managed to provide major steamship firms with their own berths in this period through the appropriation system. Only rarely did a major operator have to seek berths elsewhere in the system, and they were usually able to find something close to their normal base if necessary. Cunard's steamers were probably the most widely scattered in this sector in 1870, and even they were split more or less evenly between adjacent docks, Huskisson and Canada. Most of the others managed to operate from one dock, and often from one berth.[66]

Sailing docks were also achieving efficiencies by the 1860s. The median length of time spent in Albert fell from fourteen days in 1855 to eight in 1870. Prince's, always under heavy pressure because of its popular central location, trimmed unloading times from 15 to 13 days, and was even more effective at turning round vessels that were being both unloaded and loaded in the same berth – the figures there were 39 and 28 days respectively. In addition, Prince's was sending a far higher proportion of vessels to other docks for loading by the end of the period, and was, in effect, becoming more like Albert in its operating practices.

Varying patterns of use and activity across the dock system point to another indicator of efficiency and effectiveness. Contemporaries were well aware that different sections of the system brought in different levels of revenue to the port authority – such differences were often brought into the political arena in disputes between traders and the Board. The Dock Board often used tonnage and revenue statistics in relation to the length of quay space available in each dock. While a rather crude measure, it is useful in this section because the range of different values allow a brief analysis of the characteristics of high- and low-earning docks. Table 4.1 shows the revenue and tonnage of Liverpool's docks in relation to quay length in the late 1850s and early 1870s.

Some patterns are immediately apparent. One group of docks shows low revenue but high tonnage: Collingwood, Clarence, and Trafalgar are the most obvious examples. These are a useful demonstration of the way port facilities could rapidly

65 A. Holt, 'Review of the progress of steam shipping during the last quarter of a century,' *Minutes of proceedings of the Institution of Civil Engineers*, Vol. 51, 1877–8, pp. 2–135, p. 4.

66 DR (1870).

Table 4.1 Mersey docks, revenue and tonnage by linear yard of quay

	1858/59	1858/59	1873/74	1873/74
	£/yd	ton/yd	£/yd	ton/yd
Albert	35.4	201.8	34.5	212.5
Birkenhead	0.3	6.5	3.8	38.4
Bramley-Moore	47.3	324.1	31.0	220.4
Brunswick	18.0	167.9	18.9	146.1
Canada	1.5	25.0	35.7	321.0
Canning	3.1	103.7	2.2	85.6
Clarence	7.0	352.9	7.7	409.3
Coburg	17.7	158.5	14.6	100.6
Collingwood	10.4	457.7	10.0	487.5
George's	11.0	94.1	10.6	79.2
Harrington	4.6	102.6	0.0	2.4
Huskisson	21.7	224.2	34.9	266.4
King's	17.9	153.2	16.2	121.5
Nelson	23.9	218.1	38.0	395.7
Prince's	15.2	93.6	31.7	198.8
Queen's	13.5	108.2	15.4	107.4
Salisbury	3.2	35.9	2.3	64.1
Salthouse	4.8	4.2	4.6	9.2
Sandon	4.2	48.4	20.1	141.3
Stanley	34.8	263.8	32.6	227.4
Toxteth	3.3	43.7	1.2	35.7
Trafalgar	5.2	260.5	5.6	224.5
Victoria	17.7	121.5	17.9	140.3
Wapping	8.2	50.3	16.4	106.9
Waterloo	42.3	280.8	38.1	245.0
Wellington	14.6	108.0	28.6	216.0

Source: Revenue and tonnage figures from Dock Revenue Statements, quay length from MDHB pocket yearbook, 1920, printed in A. Jarvis, *Liverpool central docks*, pp. 230–34.

appear antiquated in the face of changing technology. Clarence, it will be recalled, had initially been designed as a cutting-edge steam dock in the late 1820s. Collingwood, opened two decades later, was designed to accommodate the smaller elements in the port's overseas traffic. By the 1850s, both were capable of handling nothing larger than coasters, which did not pay duties on cargo, and paid a reduced rate on the tonnage of the vessel. Needless to say, it was in the port authority's interest to cram as much coastal traffic as possible into its oldest docks, and it seems to have succeeded rather well in this period. The Trafalgar/Clarence complex was in a valuable strategic location just to the north of the town centre, but remained unmodified for almost a century, serving niche trades that needed – and got – relatively little infrastructural investment.[67]

Docks with high tonnage and high revenue fall into two broad categories, reflecting the importance of the warehousing and steam questions discussed previously. Warehousing and storage were clearly factors in the revenue-earning capabilities of docks, even before the warehouse rent itself is included in the equation. Albert and Stanley with their warehouses, and Prince's with its transit sheds, all cluster around the £30/yd mark. Most of the other docks operating at that level, such as Huskisson and Nelson, were dominated by the steam trades. Canada, with its earnings from timber and steam, was clearly an efficient revenue raiser, as was Waterloo, initially busy with the United States sail trades and subsequently with its corn warehouses.

What of the docks at the bottom end of both tonnage and revenue scales? Most can be described as utility or service docks – they existed to make other parts of the system easier to use and any trade conducted in them was to a large extent a bonus for the port authority. Canning is a good example. Its main purpose was as a place to park ships during their navigation of the Albert complex, often while they waited for their turn in the adjacent Canning graving docks. Salisbury was similar, serving as an entrance to the group of docks famously opened on the same day in 1848. Indeed, Salisbury's revenue and tonnage is commendably high given the volume of traffic that passed through it on the way elsewhere, and the small length of quay space that was not taken up with gates or passages.

One special case among the very low-income docks needs further explanation. The Birkenhead docks remained a disappointment in revenue and tonnage terms, despite being a reasonably viable dock system – at least in construction terms – by the late 1860s. However, the port authority's efforts to concentrate some bulk-handling operations in Birkenhead were having some success by 1870. A range of commodities, formerly scattered over the docks, can be seen to converge on Birkenhead in this period. Most were commodities that did not have to be sold by numerous small traders working in traditional Liverpool selling practices, while others were environmentally unpleasant and evidently unwanted on the more populous Liverpool side.

Guano is a case in point. The great boom in guano imports in mid-century was accommodated in half a dozen docks, and 5,000 tons was initially recorded inward on the river in 1855, presumably because storage and handling facilities were overstretched. Brunswick, rapidly losing the timber trade, seemed a possible home for this traffic, but by 1870, Birkenhead was handling much more in both absolute and relative terms. The Birkenhead docks trebled the quantity of guano they handled between 1863 and 1870, and in the latter year were responsible for 92% of the Mersey's traffic in that commodity. This pattern also reflected a change in handling practices, as most guano was imported in bulk by 1870 rather than the earlier habit of using bags – Birkenhead again offered the space to handle and store large bulk cargoes.[68]

67 The broad activities and histories of individual docks in this and the following paragraphs are derived from the sources in note 2 above.

68 Calculated from BE (1855, 1863, 1870).

Other traffic was gradually identified for Birkenhead, generally having some specialised aspect that made it complementary to the interests of existing traders in Liverpool. It became a centre for exports of salt, logically enough, given its location near the major sources of the raw material. More important though was the fact that salt tended to be a commodity exported on its own: ships could be unloaded in Liverpool then sent to Birkenhead, in effect, as the first leg of an outward voyage, with no further need to maintain contact with Liverpool. This was the key to Birkenhead's development in mid-century – Liverpool traders could not integrate the place into their existing operations, but would use it as a specialised 'branch' system for handling some bulk goods.

Levels of efficiency across the Mersey dock system therefore varied considerably in mid-century, sometimes as an inevitable consequence of different working practices from trade to trade; sometimes because the port was struggling to overcome the legacy of ill-conceived ventures like Birkenhead; and sometimes – as in the case of graving docks – because the port authority's priorities were mistaken. Nonetheless, the effective working of large parts of the system, most of the time, make it clear that the Dock Board brought an advanced level of professional planning and management to bear on meeting the often contradictory demands of the system's users.

This survey of the operation of the Mersey dock system in mid-century points to some clear gains in efficiency in the 1850s and 1860s, despite the restrictions imposed on the port authority's decision-making processes. Efficiency was doubtless in large part driven by desperation. Nonetheless, the trading community and its port authority found ways to work available facilities more intensively, which was a good deal harder a task than the previous happy practice of building new docks on a more or less continuous basis. Intensification was not a process that could be managed in a vacuum, of course, no matter how ingenious the authority became in its strategies for specialisation and integration. The question of port accommodation became a major political issue both inside and outside the ranks of the trading community, and these issues will be developed further in chapter 9.

Part II

The dynamics of mercantile business

Part I considered the environment: part II explores some of the issues facing the trading community that worked in it. Although many studies exist of individual firms in nineteenth-century Liverpool, there have been few attempts to deal thematically with the interactions of companies and individuals, and their place within the broad web of information, finance and communication that characterised the port's business culture. These three chapters take complementary approaches, examining the boundaries between specialised firms, and the bridges that they built toward each other while seeking a working compromise between co-operation and competition, and between internal control and outside help.

Chapter 5

FUNCTION, SPECIALISATION
AND INTEGRATION

Specialisation is widely seen as a measure of economic advancement, and as an indicator that a society has reached a certain level of sophistication. 'The separation of different trades and employments', observed Adam Smith, '... is generally carried furthest in those countries which enjoy the highest degree of industry and improvement.'[1] Historians of mercantile business would agree, having identified increased specialisation as one of the clearest trends visible in the activities of traders in the modern world, although as with any trend, some ports, trades and occupations run ahead or fall behind as local circumstances dictate.

Specialisation has a broad range of implications for business, and for the more general economy. The most obvious, from the viewpoint of a trading community, is that high levels of specialisation imply high levels of interaction between firms – if firms are focusing very closely on a narrow aspect of mercantile activity, it follows that they will need to develop effective relationships with firms in related trades. A specialist wool broker, for example, will need to work closely with specialist wool importers, warehouse owners, wholesalers and/or manufacturers. Ports and trading communities with complex specialisation patterns will need well-developed mechanisms for ensuring that specialist firms are not left in economically useless isolation. At the other extreme, in a port with a small number of very general operators who manage a range of trading functions themselves, there is much less need for firms to interact with their neighbours. Specialisation, or a lack thereof, is therefore an important indicator of the characteristics of a local business culture.

This chapter uses the major systematic sources discussed in part one to assess the level and nature of specialisation in Liverpool trading, and also explores attitudes towards the issue as revealed in more qualitative evidence. The first section considers background patterns and some of the approaches adopted by business historians in dealing with this question. The next section surveys patterns of regional and commodity specialisation among merchants, leading into two sections on functional integration. The first of these considers the survival of classic integrated trading (that is, firms carrying their own goods in their own ships) in an era of expanding professional shipowning; the second breaks down the commodity trades using new evidence for the activities of brokers and other intermediaries. Finally, there is a brief discussion of the activities of shipping agents, who established valuable niches for

---

1   A. Smith, *The wealth of nations*, ed. Andrew Skinner, London, 1982, pp. 110–11.

themselves in between the shifting patterns of specialisation of the broader trading community.

PATTERNS AND PRECEDENTS

Up to the eighteenth century, most of those involved in trade were generalists, dealing in a broad range of goods and usually maintaining personal control over all aspects of their business. Such traders owned at least part of the ships their goods were carried in, handled the buying and selling of commodities, and often – especially if they were prosperous – managed extensive systems of credit for smaller traders in the absence of banks.[2] The rise of the specialist, whether shipowner, commodity merchant, broker or any of a number of related occupations, became a key trend in the decades after about 1750, and accelerated rapidly in the nineteenth century.

The increasing specialisation of shipowning is often seen as the driving force in this process. There is general agreement that shipowning itself was rarely a profitable activity prior to the later eighteenth century, and that specialised shipowning was not thought of as a separate occupation.[3] The word 'shipowner' itself was hardly ever used as an occupational label: a man called John Sadler was the sole 'shipowner' to leave a will in Liverpool during the century after 1660.[4] From around 1750, however, some traders began to see greater potential in money to be earned from the vessels themselves, and started to sell their transport services to those with insufficient capital to acquire ships of their own. A number of changes in the trading and economic environment have been suggested as having driven this trend, including an increasing demand for chartered shipping by government in time of war and imperial expansion.[5] In some ports, specialised shipping developed from whaling and fishery, where operators were always geared to working ships rather than handling cargoes.[6]

As shipping became more of a service industry in its own right, other functional specialisms developed to interact with it. Freed from the capital demands of owning ships, commodity traders could plough more of their resources into buying and selling goods. New merchants could start in business with less up-front investment – there was, in the jargon, a general lowering of entry thresholds. Others recognised the growing divide between those selling cargo space and those wanting to fill it, and set themselves up as brokers, making their living by connecting the two. As time went on, the process of specialisation became more minute until different traders

---

2   For a remarkable analysis of eighteenth-century Atlantic merchants, see D. Hancock, *Citizens of the world: London merchants and the integration of the British Atlantic community, 1735–1785*, Cambridge, 1995.

3   R. Davis, *The rise of the English shipping industry in the seventeenth and eighteenth centuries*, London, 1962, p. 81.

4   Thanks to Di Ascott for this reference.

5   S. Ville, 'The growth of specialisation in English shipowning, 1750–1850', *Economic History Review*, Vol. 46, 1993, pp. 702–22; pp. 711–16.

6   G. Jackson, *Hull in the eighteenth century*, London, 1972, pp. 170–72.

performed sharply-defined functions even within the same commodity trade, formalising their own associations, with traditions, conventions and rules. By the mid-nineteenth century, for example, Liverpool's cotton brokers and cotton importers performed completely separate functions – the former under pain of expulsion from the Cotton Brokers Association.[7]

Why is such a pattern of increased specialisation considered a good thing? Primarily, it is seen as a means of achieving economies of scale and focus. In other words, targeting resources at a narrow range of activity allows traders to become very knowledgeable about their business, streamlining procedures and establishing working methods that can be applied across the whole firm. Regular transactions with a small number of suppliers and customers were liable to be faster, more reliable and more profitable than one-off deals where each party had to learn the conventions of a different trading activity every time.[8]

So far so good. But what did this new breed of specialised trader do if his chosen commodity became unfashionable, or suffered crop failures, or some other disaster? Even in normal times, short- and medium-term trade cycles might make a particular activity less lucrative for years on end. In a complicated market, not all activities are likely to make money at the same time, and different groups do better or worse in relation to others at different times. Put crudely, shipowners and merchants often have competing interests, and when one is making money, the other may well be losing, or making less. Obviously therefore, there is an argument for being both, and taking advantage of the 'complementarities' available over a range of activities.[9] At its most extreme, this strategy meant that large firms could trade for years with part of their operation badly in the red, while making money in other activities. Some sectors might generate extreme, but very rare, profits, and other trades conducted in the meantime kept the firm in business – John Swire and Sons' China tea trade is a good example, with sufficient profit in 1879 to wipe out a decade's worth of losses prior to that. Few commodity traders could absorb losses over that length of time, however, without having steady gains from commissions, financial services or shipping to maintain the business in lean years.[10] Firms therefore had to strike fine balances. General trading spread risk but raised costs; specialisation reduced costs but also reduced flexibility.

This is a problem that mercantile and business historians need to address in more detail. In particular, attention must be given to the different measures of specialisation. The most obvious is that traders might be functional specialists, acting only as shipowners, say, or brokers or commission agents. But it was also possible to perform more than one of these *functions*, while still specialising by *commodity*, or by *region*.

7   S. Smith, *My life-work*, London, 1902, p. 17.

8   A. D. Chandler, *The visible hand: The managerial revolution in American business*, Cambridge, MA, 1977, p. 38.

9   J. Killick, 'Risk, specialisation and profit in the mercantile sector of the nineteenth century cotton trade: Alexander Brown and Sons, 1820–80', *Business History*, Vol. 16, 1974, pp. 1–16; p. 7.

10 J. Wang, 'The profitability of Anglo-Chinese trade, 1861–1913', *Business History*, Vol. 35, no. 3, 1993, pp. 39–65; p. 59.

In short, we have a broad spectrum of specialisation, from classic general merchants still working more or less in the medieval stereotype, to ultra-specialists who only handled a small link in the trading chain of a single commodity from a single region of the world.

Business historians have seen specialisation, and especially functional specialisation, as part of broader debates about vertical integration.[11] This phenomenon is often considered a crucial characteristic of modern, large-scale business. In theory, vertical integration offers firms more effective control over their affairs: a shipbuilder, for example, who makes his own blocks, tackle and rope will have closer command of his business than one who has to buy those essential components from other people. That example, though, helps to underline an important problem with the theory – it is much more obviously applicable to manufacturing firms than to mercantile firms. Long-distance trading firms bringing commodities from the other side of the world could not internalise their operations as easily as a manufacturer who chose to take over the component-making workshop round the corner.

This is not to say that it could not be done: some Liverpool firms established branches in distant ports, bought and sold goods at either end and carried them in between on their own ships. Balfour, Williamson & Co.'s operation in Liverpool and Valparaiso is a case in point. Such firms were driven by a belief that business could only be safely conducted through close personal ties, especially in overseas trading, and that failure to have distant operatives tied directly to the fortunes of the home firm left that firm vulnerable to changing market conditions, misunderstandings, negligence and fraud. Even then, there were usually commonly-accepted limits: European firms working in Central America, for example, would establish wholesaling operations in sea ports but leave retailing and inland distribution activities to the locals.[12]

The theory of firms increasingly bringing more of their activities into the control of their own partners and staff, and seeking to control as many links as possible in the chain from raw material to final sale, owes much to Alfred Chandler, whose pioneering studies of large US companies in the later nineteenth and twentieth centuries remain profoundly influential. Historians have, however, begun to question Chandler's work, or at least the interpretations placed upon it. The two main objections raised against Chandler are first, that he drew his evidence from very large industrial companies, which for all their crucial role in the modern western economy rarely reflected the experience or priorities of the great majority of people involved in business; and secondly, that his work was geographically limited to the United States, and tended to see the overall success of the US economy in the twentieth century as a vindication of the management strategies of American firms.[13]

---

11 S. Ville, 'The expansion and development of a private business: An application of vertical integration theory', *Business History*, Vol. 33, no. 4, 1991, pp. 19–42.

12 H. J. Heath, 'British merchant houses in Mexico, 1821–1860: Conforming business practices and ethics', *Hispanic American Historical Review*, Vol. 73, 1993, pp. 261–90; p. 269.

13 J. F. Wilson, *British business history, 1720–1994*, Manchester, 1995, pp. 5–8.

In the context of mid-nineteenth-century Liverpool, therefore, there must be serious questions about the applicability of vertical integration strategies, and some of these ideas will be explored in this chapter and indeed throughout part two. Small mercantile firms, of which there were a great number, were likely to have very different assumptions about credit, capital, turnover and growth compared with those of large industrial firms. In addition, vertical integration reflects a lack of trust in a firm's suppliers and customers or a lack of reliable information about their activities – if Liverpool's business environment was less hostile than that of US industrial towns, perhaps vertical integration was less useful.

It ought to be stressed that arguing about specialisation and integration is not just a theoretical game played by business historians – Liverpool's traders did it too. Specialisation was the subject of disagreements within firms, as some partners prioritised security in a familiar trade and others sought expansion and diversification. The Rathbones are a well-known example of a firm that squabbled over the appropriate level of specialisation in mid-century, although much of the argument was about regional and commodity trades rather than functional specialisation – family members were broadly agreed that they should be commission merchants, but differed on the range of commodities they should handle. One partner feared working in the 'terra incognita of breadstuffs etc. to the neglect of our old staple cotton'.[14] Elsewhere, Balfour, Williamson & Co.'s partners disagreed over copper – Balfour was convinced that the firm's safe future lay in its accustomed dry goods, and that the lucrative but risky trade in 'this horrid copper' should be left to others.[15]

There is also evidence of an increasing tendency for financial institutions to equate specialisation with security and respectability. Banks tended to advise on the creditworthiness of firms in terms of their accustomed business. Traders who experimented with new activities and suffered setbacks risked a lack of sympathy, whatever their previous record. Some trades were viewed more suspiciously than others, and speculating in bulk commodities was seen as especially likely to tempt established firms away from the safety of their own areas of expertise. In the aftermath of the American Civil War, cotton speculation was blamed for the demise of several firms, with the clear implication that they would have been safe had they stuck to their original business. Wakefield, Nash & Co. (corn and provisions dealers), Boult, English & Brandon (shipbrokers) and A. W. Powles (Latin America traders) all failed in the mid-1860s, having latterly engaged in cotton trading.[16] Boult, English & Brandon managed to resurrect themselves by returning to their old business of shipbroking, although free spending by partners led to another failure in 1870.[17] Bahr, Behrend & Co., one of Liverpool's longest established firms of shipbrokers, also fell into this trap, but with corn rather than cotton. The Bank of England agent noted with

14   S. Marriner, 'Rathbones' trading activities in the middle of the nineteenth century', *Transactions of the Historic Society of Lancashire & Cheshire*, Vol. 108, 1956, pp. 105–27; p. 109.

15   Balfour to Williamson, 1 Oct. 1864, Balfour Williamson papers, box 17/4, f. 101; Balfour to Williamson, 16 Feb. 1863, Balfour Williamson papers, box 17/4, f. 102.

16   Barings, 12, 17 May 1866, 9 Apr. 1867.

17   Bank, 5 Sept. 1868, 3 Dec. 1870.

disapproval that Bahr had lost money in corn, but overall gave the firm a clean bill of health – Behrend had not engaged in speculations, and Bahr, having learned his lesson, had 'since quietly followed his regular trade'.[18]

Of course, for every example of failure in new activities, there is usually one of success. Take the divide between cotton trading and cotton manufacturing. Robert Creighton, Pennsylvania cotton trader, was so concerned about the pitfalls of becoming involved in manufacturing that he included a warning against it in his will – he hoped his son would avoid involvement in the other side of the industry, noting that 'many commission merchants have become involved and finally got ruined by departing from this rule'.[19] On the other hand, Samuel Smith saw the acquisition of two spinning mills as a logical extension of his business as a Liverpool cotton broker.[20] There is a clear tension, therefore, between an increasing pressure from contemporary opinion in favour of specialisation and the determination of some individuals to diversify.

Specialisation was not just an issue at the extremes of success and failure, but had fundamental consequences for the working strategies of trading firms. The mid-nineteenth century, as an era of considerable change and diversification, has been seen as a period in which functional specialists jostled for position and influence over mercantile practices and patterns – the various elements were 'waging a battle to throw risks onto each other'.[21] The trading community operated in a fluid environment, with different specialisms always pushing against one another, seeking to make others take a greater portion of the overall risks of mercantile business, while at the same time retaining profits within their own sector. Of course, those taking the greatest risks also wanted the highest profits, so firms had to develop complex strategies of building relationships with clients, offering them inducements with one hand while negotiating concessions with the other.

Some aspects of specialisation are much easier to study than others. Commodity and regional specialisms are readily identifiable, because the import records are explicit about who traded what with where, and the next section of the chapter discusses the key patterns in that element of the specialisation issue. Unfortunately, many of the more subtle interactions and divisions between functional specialists are only visible in the business papers of individual trading firms, which means that we can only know in detail about a select few members of the community. The major systematic sources are much less helpful. While contemporaries were well aware of the different groups in the trading community, firms did not have to specify in the customs records whether they were acting on their own behalf or for someone else, let alone describe the complex permutations of their relationships

18 Bank, 9 Oct. 1855.
19 W. H. Chaloner, 'A Philadelphia textile merchant's trip to Europe on the eve of the Civil War: Robert Creighton, 1856–57', in *Trade and transport: Essays in economic history in honour of T. S. Willan*, ed. W. H. Chaloner and B. M. Ratcliffe, Manchester, 1977, pp. 157–72; p. 167.
20 Smith, *My life-work*, p. 74.
21 Marriner, 'Rathbones' trading activities', pp. 110–11.

with other businesses – historians are therefore confronted with large gaps in the evidence.

It is possible to go some way toward addressing the issue, however. Comparing the Ship Register with the Bills of Entry gives us a broad picture of the interaction of shipowning, ship agenting and importing. In addition, there is some internal evidence from the Bills of Entry which points to the level of intermediary activity in various trades: in other words, what percentages were handled by direct importers and by brokers of some kind. The remaining sections of the chapter survey some of the more significant branches of trading activity in mid-century Liverpool, assessing in turn the extent of their integration with, or separation from, other elements in the matrix.

REGIONAL AND COMMODITY SPECIALISATION

Most historians of trade have taken regional and commodity specialisation as a given factor in the analysis of any trading community, and with good reason. Even in the age of general merchants, some measure of regional focus was often assumed, in large part because the old charters and monopolies issued to traders by government tended to be defined on geographical lines. While demarcation lines were rarely upheld with total rigour, it is clear that a trading system based on organisations called the Levant Company, the East India Company and the Royal Africa Company must have regional assumptions underpinning it. That much is obvious. What is more important is the way traders themselves tended to form regional interest groups outside the remit of the old chartered companies, and pursue particular regional activities in their own individual businesses.

Previous studies of Liverpool's development in the later eighteenth century have identified the rise and fall of regional interest groups as a central pattern in the development of the port's trading community.[22] The growing influence of American (that is, United States) traders relative to that of the older West Indies firms in the era of the Napoleonic Wars has been seen not only as an important shift in the composition and focus of the community, but also as a significant element in the port's attitudes to broader issues of official regulation and protectionism.[23]

It has also been noted (in chapter four) that regional traders tended to seek mutual support when negotiating with the port authority. Sometimes this was done informally, but often there was an official trade organisation charged with representing the interests of a particular group. A brief survey of the port's trade organisations in mid-century reveals a combination of regional, commodity and functional specialisation. Liverpool's Chamber of Commerce aimed to represent the trading interest at all levels, although its committee was dominated by overseas traders, and it had representatives from the other trade associations active in the town. Most of these

22   F. E. Hyde, *Liverpool and the Mersey: An economic history of a port, 1700–1970*, Newton Abbot, 1971, chap. 3.

23   S. Checkland, 'American versus West Indian traders in Liverpool, 1793–1815', *Journal of Economic History*, Vol. 18, 1958, pp. 141–60; pp. 159–60.

associations were regional, such as those representing Africa; the East Indies and China; the West Indies; Brazil; the Mediterranean and the Levant; and the United States (which stressed its own importance by calling itself the American Chamber of Commerce). Rather fewer took a functional view, such as the General Brokers, the Shipowners and the Warehouse associations. Finally, commodity specialisation was represented in three groups, the Wine and Spirit, Cotton Brokers and Corn Exchange associations.[24] The use of functional specialisation as a defining theme in the Liverpool community received a boost in 1858 with the creation of the Steamship Owners' Association, but it is clear that contemporaries continued to identify traders by their regional or commodity focus.

Traders believed that there were high costs associated with breaking into a new trade, even when it seemed closely related to their existing activities. As was mentioned in chapter three, Balfour, Williamson & Co. extended their Latin American operation north into California in the late 1860s, but only after prolonged debate within the firm. Alexander Balfour believed that the new trade would require a 'perfectly distinct framework' from the original structure and practices of the firm, and it took Stephen Williamson almost five years to talk him round.[25] In other circumstances, the hurdles facing traders seeking new markets would have been more formidable still, and while young entrants with little to lose might take considerable risks to get themselves established, firms that already had good prospects in one trade needed a considerable incentive to take such chances.

The evidence available from the major systematic sources reinforces these patterns. Although a detailed assessment of specialisation in the trading community as a whole is extremely difficult, it is possible to identify clear trends from the list of importers in the Bills of Entry. A brief comment on the methodology is necessary before proceeding to discuss these results. Merchants who only appear very rarely in the samples have been excluded, because they would inflate the percentage of those seeming to be perfect specialists: obviously, a trader whose only appearance in the Bills is with one small consignment of cotton from Egypt would register as both a commodity and regional specialist, but he can hardly be viewed in the same light as a trader responsible for, say, several entire cargoes of Canadian timber. Given that large numbers of traders appear very rarely in the samples, their exclusion makes it much easier to focus on the specialisation patterns of active traders. In addition, given the large number of different ports from which cargoes arrived, and the broad range of individual commodities handled, it is necessary to devise a rough classification scheme which groups these variables into regions of the world, and into related classes of goods.[26]

The results of this analysis show marked patterns of commodity and regional specialisation. Table 5.1 shows the percentages of traders who dealt either with one region or with one group of commodities in mid-century, and who appeared at least

24   See list of associations and their officers in *Gore's Directory*, 1855.
25   Forres, *Balfour Williamson & Company*, London, 1929, pp. 33–37.
26   See the Notes on Sources at the end of the book.

Table 5.1 Regional and commodity specialisation:
Percentage of traders appearing as pure specialists

	1855	1863	1870
	n = 291	n = 473	n = 536
Regional	77	68	70
Commodity	67	63	58

Source: BE Samples. Traders appearing at least three times.

three times in each year sample: in other words, those who averaged one consignment in each month. Regional specialisation is a clear defining pattern in the activity of these traders, with at least seven in every ten targeting their business at a single region of the world. The focus on commodities was also marked, although not to quite the same extent. Diversification in goods within a single regional market was, as would be expected, easier than establishing the contacts necessary to move into other regions. Liverpool's Mediterranean traders often handled a number of categories of goods, for example, but rarely dealt with cargoes from any other region. Nonetheless, it is clear from both patterns that specialisation by region and commodity was a working assumption for Liverpool traders in mid-century.

A brief survey of particular examples demonstrates that these conclusions are safe across the scale of activity. If all those appearing to be specialists were working at the lower end of the scale, there would be a danger that the sample of the source is too small, and that general trading was more common than we think. However, those appearing as regional specialists in 1870 include E. Sofio & Co., with eight consignments a month from the Mediterranean; C. W. & F. Shand with five a month from the West Indies; and G. Campbell & Co. with four a month from the United States. It is reasonable to assume that if firms appearing with this frequency were also importing from other regions, evidence of that activity would emerge in the sample.

It is worth noting, however, that both sets of figures in Table 5.1 show a slightly declining trend between 1855 and 1870. The explanation for this raises important issues of functional change and specialisation, because it is tied to the rise of steam shipping in Liverpool, and the increasing activities of forwarding cargo agents, who handled the importation of goods from one part of the world and then supervised their transshipment to an outgoing steam service. Such firms usually did not market the commodities themselves, but earned their revenue from small commissions on each item of cargo. They became key elements in a rapidly growing global network of steam packet services, by which goods could be shipped from and to almost anywhere, but only by passing through an important steam hub like Liverpool. Indeed Liverpool's traffic patterns seem to have been particularly suited to this activity: by 1870, Liverpool had 96 firms calling themselves forwarding agents, compared with 61 in London.[27]

27 Anon., *The broker's guide and shipping directory*, Birmingham, 1870, pp. 75–76.

Many forwarding agents were also managing agents of steamship lines. In particular, some of the managers of Atlantic steam lines appear as consignees for miscellaneous parts of the cargoes of steamers from the continental ports – much of this cargo was clearly being transferred for outward transit to America, but not always on the firm's own ships. There are some cases of firms shipping items by third parties, which indicates that once a firm had the contacts and bureaucratic mechanisms in place to handle a packet service on its own vessels, it was possible to seek a wider share of this increasing sector.

An example of this activity offers useful insights. In 1867 Guion & Co., managing agents for the transatlantic Liverpool & Great Western steamship line, received 70 cases of 'glonoin oil' from a contact in Hamburg, with the request that they be forwarded to San Francisco. Guion did not have ships on that route, but arranged freight with the West India & Pacific Steam Ship Co., handled the relevant paperwork, and reckoned to have made a profit of about £5 on what was evidently a routine transaction. The only reason we know about this case is that the cargo, which turned out to be nitro-glycerine, exploded when the ship was in Panama, killing 50 people and causing enormous property damage.[28]

Most instances of forwarding agent activity had less tragic consequences. Indeed, the packet services offered by steamship companies and forwarding agents were beginning to have a liberating effect on the old regional demarcation lines by 1870. Such activity did not involve the great leaps of faith required by the older trading companies in establishing new regional markets from scratch, but nonetheless created a service by which smaller traders could exploit the widening reach of steamship routes. The growing importance of such patterns must be noted, but not exaggerated, because it remains clear from the figures that broad sections of the trading community retained older assumptions about regional and commodity specialisation in this period. The extent to which traditional *functional* demarcation was maintained is the subject of the next section.

SHIPPING, AGENTING AND IMPORTING: MEASURES OF CLASSIC INTEGRATION

The more complex question of functional specialisation cannot be tackled using a single source, but rather requires the linking of a number of strands of evidence. Such an approach was established a generation ago in pioneering work on Liverpool traders in the first half of the nineteenth century, which established that key primary sources studied in a complementary manner can shed light on the different functional activities of firms across the trading community.[29] This section uses similar methodology to focus on the survival of what might be called classic integrated trading.

28 *The Times*, 20 Aug. 1867, p. 9, 22 Aug. 1867, p. 11.

29 D. M. Williams, 'Liverpool merchants and the cotton trade, 1820–1850', in *Liverpool and Merseyside: Essays in the economic and social history of the port and its hinterland*, ed. J. R. Harris, Liverpool, 1969, pp. 182–211; pp. 199–200.

What proportion of Liverpool's trade in mid-century was still being conducted according to traditional patterns by traders who owned ships, took care of all the bureaucratic requirements of their vessel in port (ensuring Customs clearance, paying port fees and the like), and also had at least part of the vessel's cargo consigned to them? To ask the question another way, in terms of the available sources, what level of activity was being conducted by firms that appear in the Bills of Entry as consignees for cargo on a particular ship, *and* in the Bills of Entry as agents for the vessel, *and* in the Ship Register as owners of the ship?

The most straightforward relationship evident in the Liverpool fleet is that between inward agenting and ownership. Indeed, the integration of these functions, and the simultaneous exclusion of the merchanting function, is an established element in the existing literature on the management of shipping in the port, and in particular is seen as characteristic of the large steam companies. Hyde gave considerable weight to the emergence of a new breed of managing agents in mid-century. Various members of the MacIver, Burns and Cunard families are probably the best known example of a group of firms that served different functions within the Cunard operation. D&C MacIver always appear as agents for the North Atlantic services, while Burns & MacIver handled the Mediterranean trades.[30]

These new managing agents certainly operated on an impressive scale, but closer study of other branches of the port's trade casts doubt on whether they were such a new departure in functional terms. Many of the port's sail trades in mid-century show a similar differentiation between ownership and inward agenting on the one hand, and importing on the other. Rather than assuming major shifts in functional specialisation to accommodate steam, it is necessary to survey the range of activity performed by Liverpool's traders in different sectors, and offer an analysis from the point of view of function rather than shipping type.

Just as Liverpool's steam fleets usually had an established agent with a close relationship to the owners, so the great majority of Liverpool-registered sailing ships were handled by their owners or by closely related firms when in the port. Just over 80% of arriving Liverpool-registered sail tonnage across the period had one of the vessel's owners listed as agent.[31] In addition, at least part of the remaining tonnage was agented by closely related firms, and an exhaustive trace of all members of firms and their relations would undoubtedly reveal other connections – the trend, however, is clear enough. In functional terms, Liverpool's shipowners were familiar with the integration of inward agenting long before the major steam firms were established.

On one level, this is surprising. Inward agenting was a routine, but technically exacting, task that involved considerable time and paperwork: a prime candidate, it might seem, for contracting out to a specialist. The bureaucratic demands on ships' agents were extensive, with detailed paperwork having to be compiled for the Customs and the port authority. Indeed, the work of the ship's agent was so complicated that 'how-to' books on the subject were published in the nineteenth

---

30   Hyde, *Liverpool and the Mersey*, pp. 57–63.
31   Calculated from BE samples. The figures are 81% in 1855 and 82% in 1870.

century. These gave step-by-step accounts of the numerous procedures to be followed in handling the affairs of a vessel during its stay in port. When reporting vessels and cargo inward, or clearing outward, agents had to carry documentation from office to office in the Customs House, paying a series of separate bills and gathering a succession of certifications and signatures – in the right order, of course.

The permutations seemed endless. Crank-built vessels, which could not be totally emptied without capsizing, were allowed to load part of their outward cargo before the inward goods had been completely discharged, but only after a 'stiffening note' had been issued by the Tide Surveyor and two customs officials. Bonded commodities being exported were signed out by the Supervising Locker, who also assigned a cart follower to escort the goods.[32] Taking the wrong turn in any part of this paperwork maze could be costly, with penalties of £20 being incurred for minor breaches of the rules.[33] Even if the bureaucracy worked smoothly, the practical aspects of loading, unloading and maintaining vessels while in port generated regular accidents and mistakes which required negotiations between agents and the Dock Board. In the course of a fairly typical month's work in the early 1860s, Bahr, Behrend & Co. rejected liability for the sum of £1 18s 3d in damage caused to a block casting in Clarence graving dock, and objected to being overcharged for use of a crane in Coburg.[34]

In the face of these time-consuming and often trivial demands, some Liverpool shipowners did indeed contract out the agency function, regularly entrusting that element of their operation to others, and establishing effective business relationships with specialised agency firms. The Blaney family, for example, operated small sailing ships in the late 1860s, carrying coal to South America and returning with cotton. At least four members of the family were involved in the ownership of the vessels, but they nonetheless contracted out agenting, and consistently had their vessels handled, inward and outward, by shipbrokers W. H. Stott & Co.[35] As will be discussed in the final section of this chapter, Stott was well established in the business and had excellent Latin American contacts, making the firm's services extremely valuable to shipowners seeking access to that market.

Other individual cases offer possible explanations for the decision to employ a specialised agent. A few owners of Liverpool ships lived outside the town, and presumably preferred to have an agent who could deal more closely with vessels and other traders alike. Dennis Brundrit and Philip Whiterray, for example, owned small sailing ships in the South American trades in the 1850s, but lived in Runcorn and entrusted their vessels to a firm called Ashley Bros.[36] Other owners had more complex relationships with agency firms. James McLachrie, John Rae and Alexander Rae were co-owners of *Rosalie*, a small sailing ship working the West Indies trades:

32 Anon, *The merchant's clerk and brokers' assistant*, Liverpool, 1846, pp. 1–25.
33 See HM Customs to Daniel Williams, 17 Oct. 1862, Williams papers, no. 222.
34 MDHB, Docks & Quays Cttee., vol. 2, pp. 298, 307.
35 For example, *Marmion* (BE 10/10/1870/41, SR 1865/22, Stott charter party books 9 May 1870); Blaney Brothers (BE 24/2/1870/13, SR 1867/17, Stott charter party books 16 Nov. 1870).
36 SR 1853/214, BE 4/6/1855/25.

all three were master mariners, and they entrusted their vessel while in Liverpool to the agency firm Miners & Co.[37] Alexander Rae, however, owned another ship with John Miners, pointing to a multi-faceted connection between Rae and Miners, and a pragmatic approach to the ownership and management of different vessels depending on circumstances.[38] Although hard to quantify, such cases seem common enough and suggest that the agency function ran across a spectrum from being fully internal for some firms to being fully commercial and external for others, with a range of intermediate levels in between.

While acknowledging the complexities of some cases, it remains clear that the bulk of Liverpool's own shipowners – sail and steam – were at the internal end of the spectrum, and preferred to keep inward agency functions in-house. Part of the reason may have been cost. Employing an agent to clear up all the outstanding details that might be left over from a voyage could be expensive. Shipbrokers Boyd, Edwards & Co. submitted a detailed account for £1,091 incurred during the inward voyage of the *Baron of Bramber* in 1855, for which they had acted as ship's agent. The firm's duties had involved dealing with four other companies for various services, as well as the Dock Board. They dealt with Bushley & Co. in connection with part of the cargo that was sold *en route* in South Africa, and also the Mauritius Marine Insurance Company, presumably regarding the 120 bags lost overboard. They also paid the crew's wages.[39] Naturally, these bills would have had to be met by the owners anyway, but even at 3 to 5 percent the agent's commission on such sums was substantial.

Firms that kept agency functions in-house could hope to reduce that expense, as indeed did some visiting masters who knew the port well enough to handle their own negotiations with local firms. It is possible to contrast the handling of the *Baron of Bramber* with that of the *National Eagle*, an American sailing ship that frequented Liverpool in the late 1850s and early 1860s. While most of the *Baron's* affairs in port seem to have been handled by agents, George Matthews, master of the *National Eagle*, had a much more hands-on role, and relied on Liverpool's agenting firms for a very limited range of services. While in Liverpool between March and May 1860, Matthews spent almost £700 on services from local businesses, but kept firm control of these transactions himself. Only £149 went to Boult, English & Brandon, who acted as the ship's agent and handled outward port duties and the negotiation of a charter with Hoare, Miller & Co., Manchester. Boult, English & Brandon had a long-established relationship with Matthews, although they clearly never made much money from him – on the *National Eagle's* previous visit to Liverpool the extent of the firm's services was to advertise the vessel outward for Boston.[40]

Ownership and inward agenting were therefore closely integrated functions in Liverpool's sailing and steam fleets alike by mid-century. With few exceptions, firms

---

37 SR 1853/385, BE 3/6/1870/7.
38 *Bengairn*, SR 1861/251.
39 Stitt papers, box 3, i–xviii.
40 Matthews papers, 5 May 1860; 18 June 1858.

had found that maintaining control over the management of their vessels in port was preferable to contracting out. Shipowners, their clerks and/or their captains could, on the basis of this evidence, handle inward agency tasks more economically by internalising the function than by hiring specialists. To this extent, therefore, there is significant evidence of vertical integration in the owning and operating of Liverpool ships. The broader relationship between the management of vessels and the handling of cargo was a much more complex issue, however.

At one end of the shipping/merchanting spectrum, some of Liverpool's sail trades continued to show extensive patterns of integrated functional behaviour in mid-century, owning ships and dealing in cargoes alike. The West African, Canadian and West Indian trades were the most comprehensively integrated, although the level of integration varied even among these, especially in terms of the sub-letting of cargo space. Some examples will help establish the trends, and the Tobin family's West African operation is a useful case. Their vessels varied dramatically in age but were generally in the 400–600 ton wooden sailing ship class. *Cumberland* was 35 years old and *Margaret* only two in 1855: the Tobins clearly got the most from their capital investments, but were also conscious of the need to renew their vessels. Ownership followed a common pattern across the fleet, with Thomas and James holding 42/64ths and 22/64ths respectively in each vessel. In addition, the family firm, T. Tobin & Son, was always listed as the inward agent for these vessels.[41] Overall, ten sailing ships appear in the 1855 sample incoming from West Africa and handled by six different firms: all show this integrated pattern of ownership and importing. Similar patterns are to be found in the Canadian trade. The firm of Ritchie Bros perhaps typifies the conventional view of shipowning in the timber trade by 1870. Its ships were Canadian-built wooden sailing vessels in the 600–700 ton range, well into their teens, and used exclusively on the New Brunswick timber run. Ownership and agenting patterns were just as predictable. Vessels were either solely owned by John Ritchie or jointly owned by John and his brother David, and Ritchie Bros appear as agent for the vessels on their arrival in Liverpool.[42]

These firms also brought the consignment of cargo fully under their control. The Africa traders in particular tended to have entire cargoes, often of palm oil, consigned to themselves, rather than dealing with fellow traders for space on vessels, although steam shipping was to bring considerable changes to the management of this particular business.[43] Some timber traders worked in the same way, and were at one extreme of the integration spectrum, internalising all the key elements in their operations. While being fully integrated in functional terms, however, it should be stressed that

---

41 For example, *Cumberland*, SR 1849/084, BE 18/6/1855/8; *Princess Royal*, SR 1855/049, BE 3/10/1855/14. For the Tobins, see M. Lynn, 'Trade and politics in nineteenth century Liverpool: The Tobin and Horsfall families and Liverpool's African trade', *Transactions of the Historic Society of Lancashire & Cheshire*, Vol. 142, 1993, pp. 99–120.

42 For example, *Musgongus*, SR 1861/107, BE 30/6/1870/4; *Arbitrator*, SR 1859/186, BE 17/10/1870/24.

43 M. Lynn, 'From sail to steam: The impact of the steamship services on the British palm oil trade with West Africa, 1850–1890', *Journal of African History*, Vol. 30, 1989, pp. 227–45; pp. 237–39.

these traders remained firmly specialised regionally, emphasising the different strands to the definition of specialisation.

Closer study of integrated operations reveals some nuances and subtleties that demonstrate increasing flexibility in the accommodation of new markets and opportunities. Some timber traders, while maintaining close shipowning patterns, sought to make more efficient operational use of their vessels. Farnworth & Jardine were among the most active firms using wooden sailing ships in 1870: six of their vessels made a total of eight appearances in the three-month sample of that year's arrivals. All were large ships, from 900 to 1,400 tons. Three were owned by John Farnworth and David Jardine exclusively.[44] Of the remaining three, one had 12/64ths in the name of William Herron, master mariner; while two were split equally between Farnworth & Jardine on the one hand, and two members of the timber trading firm of James Bland & Co. on the other.[45] While they took care to limit their shipowning collaborations to other members of the timber trade, Farnworth & Jardine were nonetheless willing to deploy vessels beyond timber, thus making use of them in the winter months when Canadian ports were ice-bound. The ships were sent to the southern United States for spring cotton shipments and then to Canada for an autumn cargo of timber.[46] Success in cotton encouraged its pursuit further afield, and Farnworths also sent vessels to India.[47] Such patterns were threatened by the rising carriage of cotton by steamship, but a number of Liverpool's timber firms identified the cotton trade as one of the few complementary sources of income available to such a specialised sector.[48]

There were clear functional boundaries to Farnworth & Jardine's operation, though. They owned their ships, acted as inward agents for all their vessels, and also imported most of the timber cargoes in their own name. Cotton, however, was a different matter. Farnworth & Jardine did not extend the integration of their activities that far, and none of the cotton carried in their ships appears consigned to the firm. The firm was therefore acting as a traditional integrated trading firm in timber, but as an increasingly specialised professional shipowning operation when selling services to cotton merchants. This mixture of tradition and innovation led to more efficient operational practices and allowed firms like Farnworth & Jardine to expand operations from a solid base.

Timber traders were among the last to move in this direction. The great bulk of the port's own shipping was, by mid-century, demonstrating a marked divergence between ownership and inward agenting on the one hand, and importing on the other. In the South America trades, for example, the great majority of sail arrivals in 1855 show no apparent functional overlap between shipping and cargo. While 79% of arriving voyages show the ship's owners as inward agents, only in 19% of

---

44 *Anglo-Saxon* (SR 1856/325), *Alfred* (SR 1854/374) and *Lady Russell* (SR 1853/311).

45 *Ben Nevis* (SR 1853/294), *Her Majesty* (SR 1865/031) and *Friga* (SR 1866/286).

46 For example, *Ben Nevis* arrived in Liverpool with southern cotton in June 1870 (BE 23/06/1870/04) and with Quebec deals and staves in October (BE 19/10/1870/9).

47 *Her Majesty*, BE 18/10/1870/2.

48 BPP, Unseaworthy ships (1873), evidence of Robert Rankin, qq. 6540–45.

cases is there evidence of traders taking a step further and being involved as importers also. In Liverpool's surviving Mediterranean sailing trades, already under threat from steam in the 1850s, the pattern was even more stark – here, only 9% of arriving voyages have an overlap between ownership and importing.[49]

Many of Liverpool's sail trades had therefore already reached by mid-century the point of functional differentiation that has been seen as a defining feature of the new steamship operators. It is a measure of the evolutionary pace of such trends, however, that traditional occupational labels continued to be used throughout the period and beyond – most people working in the Liverpool markets still liked to call themselves 'merchant', and 'shipowner' was a widespread occupation long before the individuals concerned actually started using the term to describe themselves. 'Merchants' continued to dominate Liverpool wooden shipowning, a situation little different from that pertaining in the first half of the century.[50] Core owners of the new shipping technology were gradually seeing themselves in a different light by the 1860s, however. More than 20% of iron sailing tonnage was owned by people calling themselves 'shipowner' in 1870.[51] Although there is little in the way of direct evidence, 'merchant' was clearly a higher-status label than 'shipowner', and studies of other towns in this period suggest that 'merchant' was the term of choice for a broad range of those aspiring to respectability.[52] In Liverpool, a few radicals sought to highlight their new activity and run ahead of the fashion. William Inman, uniquely, went beyond even the new 'shipowner' label and referred to himself as a 'steam ship owner'. In this, as in much else, Inman was cleverly exploiting novelty and innovation.

In such an environment of professional shipowning, with little direct involvement in cargo, the difference between the function of many sail and steam operators was one of scale rather than one of kind, but this is not to belittle it – the scale was considerable. This issue can be explored by analysing the number of consignees appearing on the incoming cargo list of different kinds of vessels. In other words, how many different importing firms did the average shipowner have to deal with when filling his vessel with cargo for a voyage?

Sailing ship cargoes tended to be consigned to a small number of traders. The median figure in 1855 was two, and 80% of sailing voyages had their cargoes divided between no more than four consignees. The professional sailing ship operator of mid-century Liverpool could therefore expect to have to deal with only a handful of commodity traders when discharging his vessel. Steamship operations were much more fragmented, and owners (or their managers) had to deal with a far wider range of traders. The number of individuals appearing as consignees in the steam trades is

49 Calculated from BE samples.

50 F. Neal, 'Liverpool shipping in the early nineteenth century', in *Liverpool and Merseyside: Essays in the economic and social history of the port and its hinterland*, ed. J. R. Harris, Liverpool, 1969, pp. 147–81; pp. 161–63.

51 Calculated from SR (1870).

52 S. Nenadic, 'Businessmen, the urban middle classes and the "dominance" of manufactures in nineteenth century Britain', *Economic History Review*, Vol. 44, 1991, pp. 66–85; p. 68.

considerably higher than their equivalent in sail, and it is clear that steam services brought a new level of operation to the relationship between shipping and commodity trading. In 1855, the median number of consignees on a steam voyage was eighteen, and here, 80% of voyages had more than eight consignees.[53]

There are, as usual, considerable regional and commodity variations in the patterns underlying these broad figures, pointing to long-standing differences in the shipping/merchanting relationship between sectors of the port's trade. Some of the port's trades in mid-century dealt with luxury goods shipped on a small scale by specialist traders, and therefore had their cargoes broken down into very small consignments. This was even true in some sail trades, such as the long-standing practice of the European wine trade. The French-registered *Confiance* arrived in Liverpool from Bordeaux in October 1855 with a cargo largely consisting of wine and brandy, and consigned to no fewer than 37 firms and individuals, most of whom were only importing a few cases.[54] The wine trade was conducted by retailers, hoteliers and innkeepers, often bypassing middle-ranking wholesalers.

Such patterns, exceptional in sail, were the norm in steam. Even when bulk items were shipped by steam, as was, of course, increasingly the case in mid-century, it was common for a number of traders to import a small portion of the ship's cargo. The regular timetables and fixed routes adopted even by cargo steamers allowed traders to buy space on a number of vessels over time, to suit themselves rather than the shipping operator. Sailing ship operators might not send their ships to sea unless they were chartered for a full cargo, and they also worried about being able to secure sufficient cargo at their destination to justify a return or onward voyage. There is evidence that trading firms often had difficulty securing cargo space for their goods: 'many a charter is sent out signed by a merchant, and is returned by the captain and owner, declined'.[55] Although it has been argued previously in this book that sail was not the relaxed business that steam promoters claimed, some sail operators could nonetheless decide at a pinch that it was not worth sailing with a half cargo. Small items of cargo offered by a small merchant might not be enough to persuade a sailing ship operator to go to a particular place, but would be welcomed on a steamer that had to go there anyway as part of its published timetable.

The rise of steam therefore did lead to a shift in the functional boundary between shipping and commodity trading. It was not, however, a question of the professionalisation of shipowning. That was already an increasing element in Liverpool's sailing fleet, and especially in the new trades such as that with South America. The attitudes of many Liverpool sail and steam owners were similar in mid-century: their function was the development and management of shipping services and the sale of cargo space to commodity traders, who were an increasingly separate branch of the trading community. The key change arose in the attitude toward shipping of those handling commodities. Steam brought the assumption that smaller traders could deal

53   Calculated from BE samples.

54   BE 24/10/1855/11.

55   BPP, Merchant shipping (1860), evidence of Henry Atkinson, q. 3,537.

directly with shipping operators for the first time, and that larger traders would have more choice of shipping, and therefore more control over the process.

The profile of the Mediterranean steam trades by 1870 confirms the new ability of traders to pick and choose from the available range of competing shipping, rather than being tied to a particular service. Leading fruit, vegetable, corn and cotton traders, often with consignments arriving in Liverpool at a rate of a dozen a month, sent their goods on a broad range of vessels belonging to various operators. Ralli & Psicha, cotton importers, used seven different shipping firms, from the long-established Bibby, Moss and MacIver fleets to newer competitors such as Papayanni. Most of the top traders used three or four.[56] Similar patterns are evident in other growing steam trades, as large numbers of smaller traders recognised the opportunities presented by the lowering of entry thresholds and the increased competition between shipping providers.

The shifting relationship between shipowning and merchanting over the nineteenth century was, like most other elements in the trading matrix, a question of control and leverage. The rise of professional shipowning might have driven change, but shipping companies running to published timetables had to maintain good relationships with those dealing in cargoes. Balances of power shifted periodically, and there was to be great controversy later in the century as shipping firms formed cartels – 'conferences' – which restricted the options of merchants.[57] This further underlines the need for more detailed study of the mid-century period when the technologies and business structures of shipping were at their most fluid.

COMMODITY TRADES: IMPORTERS AND BROKERS

If the broad functional definition of those working with ships and those working with cargoes became clearer in mid-century, niches *within* any given commodity trade also developed ever-narrower boundaries. There was a profound awareness of demarcation lines between different kinds of trading functions, although many of the nuances appreciated by contemporaries are now hard to reconstruct. Evidence often survives only at the most formal level, when mutually agreed working practices in particular trades were regulated by the relevant trade association. The best-known Liverpool example is the Cotton Brokers' Association, which brought together a formal set of rules in the 1860s 'which clearly defined the functions, and plainly set forth the rights and duties, of both merchants and brokers, in their individual capacities and in their conduct towards each other': this was after a lengthy period of working to an 'unwritten code', however.[58] In most trades, relationships between different kinds of traders were dictated not by rules devised by committee, but rather by a

56   BE (1870).

57   R. Greenhill, 'Competition or co-operation in the global shipping industry: The origins and impact of the conference system for British shipowners before 1914', in *Global markets: The internationalisation of the sea transport industries since 1850*, ed. D. J. Starkey and Gelina Harlaftis, St John's, Newfoundland, 1998, pp. 53–80.

58   T. Ellison, *The cotton trade of Great Britain*, London, 1886, reprint 1968, pp. 272–74.

general concern not to offend customers or clients. In highly differentiated trades, there might be several 'layers' of functional specialisation, and traders seeking to diversify into a closely-related activity would probably find themselves competing with firms that had previously been their customers, thus upsetting established trading relationships.

Recognising the particular traditions and customs of different trades was therefore an important element in any firm's search for a viable niche. This could be an especially difficult issue for outsiders to resolve, and functional specialisation was a common cause of disagreement between firms and their overseas branches. In response to complaints that they were not pursuing lucrative opportunities, branch staff would argue that the local trading environment was such that chasing those avenues would only alienate existing contacts by encroaching on their trade.

The New York iron-trading community was evidently one such complicated forum. Liverpool's Stitt family traded with New York through an agent called Henry Mead, who imported the iron and sold it immediately to the city's major wholesalers. By the late 1850s, Stitts felt that they were losing trade because smaller New York buyers were buying less iron from these wholesalers, and were dealing directly with Staffordshire iron founders instead. Stitts believed that the wholesalers were charging too much, and suggested that Mead should approach the smaller buyers direct and offer them a better package than they were getting from the wholesalers – in short, Mead should become a wholesaler himself. While this looked attractive from Liverpool, Mead feared the plan would damage his standing in the New York market. It would antagonise the larger dealers and probably have the net effect of accelerating the loss of business rather than reversing it. In addition, it would require a quantum leap in Mead's operation – he would be obliged to keep stocks of iron, with the attendant risk of tied-up capital, and, in effect, learn a new and hitherto separate branch of the trade.[59] Similar dilemmas faced firms in many trades, working at various levels of activity. Even a major firm like Barings was aware of its niche, and determined not to risk it. Barings did not supply cereals to bakers or millers, although they believed they would make more money if they did. The problem was that sales would be slower, they would have more disputes and would incur the displeasure of their best customers, the larger cereal dealers.[60]

The point being made by these traders was that moving out of an established niche was likely to incur heavier costs than any slowdown or decline in existing business. On the basis of these examples, traders were likely to remain attached to their chosen functional specialism. On the other hand, less developed markets and trades were slower to reach this level of sophisticated specialisation, and traders developing their role could experiment with modes of operation until they found one that suited them. Balfour, Williamson & Co. initially worked as commission traders on behalf of other merchants in the South America trades, but also operated their own company accounts. By 1863, the latter aspect of their business looked to

59   Stitt papers, box 5, xv.
60   Barings, 2 Jan. 1854.

be the more appealing. Although risks were greater, there was much more independence of action, more scope for taking advantage of opportunities as they arose,
and less time and effort spent in the conduct of the business itself. Two years later,
consignment business had been reduced to only one shipment in four and the firm
was much more firmly focused on trading in its own direct interests.[61]

The problem for historians in moving beyond these few surviving examples, and
toward an assessment of the question in more general terms, has been one of lack
of evidence. It is often not explicitly clear from the official sources of trading
activity what function is being performed by which firm, and what activity is actually
being recorded. There are some clues, though. Many shipments appearing in the
Bills of Entry were simply consigned to 'order', rather than to a named importer.
Historians have bemoaned this fact for years, complaining that it leaves a significant
gap in our knowledge of the trading community by breaking the connection between
goods and importers: often, it is impossible to tell who was responsible for importing
a significant proportion of a given commodity. Looked at more positively, though,
the 'order' question casts valuable light on the functional specialisation of firms active
in different trades. Those observing particular trades at the time were well aware of
the problem, and the explanation for it. Barings, when asked by their London firm
to provide a listing of Liverpool's leading cotton traders, replied that it was impossible
to ascertain a fully accurate list, because 'so much comes to parties whose names do
not appear, for which the broker makes the customs house entry'.[62] Barings' identification of the 'order' question with the activities of brokers indicates that there is
an opportunity here to analyse the different ways in which particular commodities
were traded. The proportion of each commodity consigned to 'order' varied dramatically, suggesting significant differences in the role of brokers.

While Barings associated the 'order' question specifically with the activities of
brokers in the cotton trade, it was, in a broader sense, tied to what might be called
intermediary trading. There were various kinds of this. The increase in the use of
'order' from about the 1840s is usually ascribed to the advent of more rapid communications.[63] With fast mail ships active on the Atlantic, confirmation that a cotton ship
had left Charleston, say, could arrive in Liverpool, sometimes with samples of the
cargo, well before the slower cotton vessel itself arrived. The cargo could be traded by
brokers and a sale agreed without having the cargo to hand. As mail steamers and
telegraph networks developed rapidly after mid-century, such practices could be
extended to more trades and regions. Trade came to be a question of the 'hypothecation
of shipping documents'.[64] In other words, a ship's bill of lading – its certified list of
cargo – became a tradeable item when accompanied by bills of exchange for appropriate
sums of money, and cargoes themselves might pass 'virtually' through many hands
between their departure from New Orleans and their arrival at a Lancashire cotton
mill.

---

61 Stephen Williamson letter book, 30 June 1963, 13 Sep. 1865, Balfour Williamson papers, box 4.
62 Barings, 20 Apr. 1860.
63 Williams, 'Liverpool merchants and the cotton trade', p. 186.
64 Barings, 30 Aug. 1860.

It should not be forgotten, however, that while the use of 'order' may have become much more common with the development of faster communications, it was a long-established practice in some trades. West Indian sugar cargoes were being consigned to 'order' on the Liverpool market in the 1790s.[65] Clearly, this cannot have been associated with faster communications. What seems more likely is that those operating in major commodity trades, in which there was an established and active market, could rely on their goods being sold by an intermediary after negotiation with the ship's captain. The 'order' question is therefore not an easy issue to define or resolve, but nor is it an insurmountable obstacle to the analysis of the trading community. Indeed, by acting as an indicator (however crude) of intermediary activity and indirect trading patterns, it serves an important, and hitherto under-used, interpretative function.

How are these ideas reflected in the Liverpool evidence? There are considerable variations in the proportions of different commodities, from different regions of the world, that appear consigned to 'order'. The cotton trade is a good starting point. As Table 5.2 demonstrates, most US and Far East cotton was consigned to order in this period. These figures broadly confirm existing interpretations of the trade as one which was largely managed by intermediaries. An increasing trend of consignment of cotton to order had already been noticeable earlier in the century, and this correlated closely with contemporary opinion that brokers were becoming the key players in the cotton trade.[66]

Table 5.2 Cotton, percentage consigned to 'order'

	1855	1863	1870
US	75	31	88
Mediterranean	52	60	56
Far East	96	80	85

Source: Calculated from BE samples.

The regional and chronological variations need closer examination, however. Two issues in particular stand out: the low level of 'order' consignment in the Mediterranean trades, and the clearly anomalous figure for the US trade during the Civil War in 1863. First, the Mediterranean. Liverpool's trades with the region owed a great deal to the influence of émigré merchants who established family trading networks running from the eastern Mediterranean to northern Europe. The Chiots are the best known of these traders, having been the subject of extensive research by historians of Greek shipping and trade.[67] Such networks operated at a slight remove from other sectors of Liverpool's trade, with family members handling transactions at various

---

65   For example, as carried on the *Mary* from Barbados, *Billing's Gazette*, 28 Sep. 1795. Thanks to Sheryllynne Haggerty for this reference.

66   Williams, 'Liverpool merchants and the cotton trade', p. 186; Ellison, *Cotton trade*, pp. 176–79.

67   G. Harlaftis, *A history of Greek owned shipping: The making of an international tramp fleet*, London, 1995, pp. 39–69.

points in the chain rather than becoming integrated with local systems of intermediary trading. Direct personal control over importing, followed by transshipment of goods to other members of the family network operating in the cotton manufacturing districts, characterised much of the Mediterranean cotton trade, leading to a correspondingly lower figure for consignments to 'order'.

The maintenance of personal control over importing is also characteristic of some practitioners in the American trade, but became particularly apparent during the crisis of the Civil War. The figure for US cotton in the 1863 column of Table 5.2 includes that brought from the West Indies, because the great bulk of such cotton had been smuggled from the South. The most prominent direct importers of this cotton were Fraser, Trenholm & Co., well known for their financial support of the Confederacy. Indeed, this evidence points to the firm's ability to retain its accustomed role despite the dislocation caused by the conflict. Fraser Trenholm had also been Liverpool's leading single firm of cotton importers prior to the conflict, although of course their percentage of the total trade in the 1850s was overshadowed by the high 'order' factor and the extensive activities of brokers.

Importantly, Fraser Trenholm, along with a small number of other importers such as Leech, Harrison & Forwood, also appear prominently on the list of those responsible for entering cotton at the port's warehouses. This alternative 'register' of Liverpool's cotton traders included brokers, importers, forwarding agents and railway companies.[68] In normal years in the American trades, there is little correlation between the names on the Bills of Entry importing list and the warehousing list, because of the dominant role of brokers, who appear in the latter but not the former. During the Civil War crisis, however, the influence of the brokers was clearly greatly reduced, and firms having direct control over imports emerged as the key players.

Liverpool's cotton-broking community had therefore developed extensive and effective mechanisms for long-distance trade in the port's key commodity by mid-century, but the system remained susceptible to shocks. Broking, more or less by definition, was based on a fragile web of information and credit, which could all too easily be disrupted. In such circumstances, the capital-based buying power of some firms allowed them to take a much larger share of whatever import market was available. Brokers continued to buy and sell once the cotton had arrived in Liverpool, contributing to the speculation that worried some and enriched others, but they lacked the hard currency with which to establish alternative supply routes in times of crisis. As connections were restored after the war, so the influence of the brokers revived. The continued role of direct importers in the Mediterranean trade, however, serves as a reminder that there were always other perspectives, and that the practices of the American cotton trade are not necessarily applicable elsewhere.

If the pattern of intermediary trading in cotton saw some sudden shifts in mid-century, other key trades experienced more gradual change. Anecdotal evidence points to significant changes in the functional divisions within the timber trade during the

68   These listings are contained in the Bills of Entry, B series.

1860s. There had already been differences in the handling of Liverpool's two main regional timber trades in the 1830s, with Canadian timber handled by merchants on their own account and Baltic timber handled by intermediary commission merchants.[69] By 1870, however, Farnworth & Jardine, one of the port's leading traders, claimed that Baltic timber had for some time been handled directly by importers rather than commission merchants, and that Canadian trade was now moving in that direction.[70] A similar process, which seems to have happened between the late 1850s and the early 1870s, was reported by veteran timber trader Robert Rankin: companies that had previously bought timber through his offices had 'turned importers themselves and have dismissed us'.[71]

What supporting evidence do the systematic sources offer? Baltic timber was very heavily consigned to 'order' during the 1850s and 1860s, although there is a clear shift by 1870 toward handling of deals and similar timber by named importers: by that year, only 34% of Baltic deals were consigned to 'order'.[72] This would suggest that commission merchants specialising in timber were – like the cotton brokers – not recording their names in the Bills of Entry. The sharp drop in the proportion of 'order' consignments in certain classes of Baltic timber between 1863 and 1870 would reinforce the suggestion by Farnworth & Jardine that the Baltic trades were more likely to be handled directly by importers, although it suggests that the phenomenon was more recent than they claimed.

Liverpool's Canadian trade was conducted on a much larger scale and is more complex than that with the Baltic, but there is also a drop in the proportions of certain timber consigned to 'order'. 'Order' accounted for 32% of shipments of deals in 1855 but only 20% in 1870. The top direct importers consolidated their share of the market in this period, with the top five accounting for 43% of the trade in 1855 and 60% in 1870. The drop in 'order' consignments left a significant gap for new direct importing firms to fill. Farnworth & Jardine were by some way the most successful, taking almost one-third of the Canadian deal business by 1870; others, including Bland & Co. and Ritchie Bros, expanded their share of the trade considerably during the 1860s.[73] Indeed Farnworths may have moved with the trends, concentrating more on the importing function as that became more important to the port in general. Back in the mid-1850s, when the firm rarely appears in the Bills of Entry, Farnworth was regarded in the trade more as a 'timber broker' than a merchant.[74]

What do these changing patterns in cotton and timber trading suggest in terms of broader lessons for functional specialisation and integration? Business historians sometimes see vertical integration as an indicator of rise and decline in the life-cycles of particular industries, but as shipping historians confronting business theory have pointed out, the idea of a life-cycle in trading is not very helpful – international

---

69 Williams, 'Merchanting in the first half of the nineteenth century', pp. 110–11.
70 Farnworth & Jardine circular, 28 Jan. 1870, British Library.
71 BPP, Unseaworthy ships (1873), evidence of Robert Rankin, q. 6776.
72 Calculated from BE samples.
73 Calculated from BE samples.
74 BPP, Liverpool Docks (1855), evidence of William Anthony, p. 196.

trading is an industry several millennia old and unlikely to disappear.[75] A more sophisticated model would be to identify integration and deintegration with successive phases in economic and business policy and development, rather than assuming an inevitable rise and decline: obviously, industries go through different phases over time, but judgements about success and failure may not be feasible or helpful. The Liverpool evidence points to deintegration and functional specialisation as characteristic of trading firms in a period of expansion in the port's markets – most trades show an increase rather than a decrease in the percentage of goods consigned to 'order', and therefore handled by some form of intermediary trading. Importers contracted out certain parts of their operation to brokers, and new entrants in the trade assumed that they would work in more specialised functions than was previously the norm. It is clear, though, that expanding and secure markets were neither universal nor inevitable, and that in times of crisis, wealthier traders could and did revert to direct handling of imports from alternative sources rather than rely on brokers.

BRIDGING GAPS AND OILING WHEELS: SHIPPING AGENTS

Most of this chapter has considered the ways in which Liverpool's traders defined the boundaries between them to their mutual working convenience and – hopefully – profit. Analysis of the activities of Liverpool firms in their dealings with outsiders is a much more difficult task. Once again, the problem is in the sources. It is usually easy to trace the relationships formed by a particular firm through that firm's own records, but moving beyond the standard list of well-known examples to offer a broader assessment of the trading community is severely hampered by the available material.

There are some sectors of the port's business that can be considered in more breadth, however. Liverpool's specialised shipping agents, already mentioned briefly in the context of their relatively rare collaboration with Liverpool shipowners, had the opportunity to cater for a much wider market. As was discussed in chapter two, many of Liverpool's sailing ship operators moved up-market in the 1860s, using larger wooden and iron vessels on long-distance routes. Smaller continental sailing ships continued to use Liverpool, however, and offered important opportunities for specialist agency firms that could offer local services to such vessels. The activities of these firms demonstrate patterns of regional specialisation and adaptation to changing circumstances. In particular, firms proved adept at the identification of niche sectors, and the deployment of appropriate specialised resources was a key strategy in the shipping agent's business.

Such pivotal figures have been largely neglected by historians. Most of the company histories of shipbrokers and agents start from the late nineteenth century, and have little to say about the challenges facing agents in the complicated era of the first sail/steam transitions.[76] Such work often falls down in its general lack of context: it

---

75   Ville, 'Growth of specialisation in English shipowning', p. 720.

76   For a rare scholarly study, see P. N. Davies, *Henry Tyrer: A Liverpool shipping agent and his enterprise*, London, 1979.

is hard to determine the firm's position in relation to the trading community as a whole, and harder still to decide whether the practices it adopted were typical of firms of that type. Historians have begun to take a more serious interest in agents and brokers only recently, with work on Norway's leading firm pointing to the valuable evidence available from the study of this intermediary activity. Boundaries in this sector were also complicated: although many firms called themselves either shipbrokers or shipping agents, some bought and sold ships; others brokered deals between shipping operators and merchants; others specialised in the bureaucratic demands of incoming shipping; and still others moved into passenger bookings as the period went on.[77] This section considers some broad patterns before discussing a brief case-study of the Liverpool firm of W. H. Stott & Co.

Some shipping agents specialised in providing one of the key needs of a foreign ship's captain away from his home port – reliable and honest information. This was not a trivial issue in a port with a considerable range of available trade, conducted in several languages. The names of Liverpool's leading independent agency firms are suggestive of the origins of these companies. Firms like Bahr, Behrend & Co. may have been long established in Liverpool – the firm was into its third generation in mid-century – but they still did their core business with shipping from ancestral regions of the world. Bahr Behrend's founders were Danes and Hanoverians: it is no surprise therefore to find that Denmark, Prussia and Hamburg figured prominently in the registries of the vessels handled by the company. De Gauwin & Co. specialised in Belgian and French shipping, but also handled some Baltic vessels. Belgian-registered vessels appeared 16 times in Liverpool in the 1855 sample, and De Gauwin were agents on 15 of these occasions. Most of Browne Van Santen's agented vessels were Dutch-registered.[78]

Detailed knowledge of, and contacts in, other countries were widely recognised as vital elements in the shipbroking business. The London firm of Clarkson's sent partners on European trips to learn languages and establish new business connections, and they also actively recruited continentals to work in their offices: by the 1860s the firm had a number of departments handling business with particular countries, each headed by an expatriate specialist. Such connections could be maintained even when individuals travelled back to their home countries to set up their own businesses. Thomas Fearnley of the Norwegian firm of Fearnley & Eger was a Clarkson apprentice, and his new firm co-operated with the London business for some time after 1869.[79]

Clarkson's example also demonstrates that some firms in the intermediary trades

77 L. R. Fischer and H. Nordvik, 'The growth of Norwegian shipbroking: The practices of Fearnley and Eger as a case study, 1869–1914', in *People of the northern seas*, ed. L. R. Fischer and W. Minchinton, St John's, Newfoundland, 1992, pp. 135–55; also their 'Economic theory, information and management in shipbroking: Fearnley and Eger as a case study, 1869–1972', in *Management, finance and industrial relations in maritime industries*, ed. Simon Ville and D. M. Williams, St John's, Newfoundland, 1994, pp. 1–29.

78 Derived from BE samples.

79 Anon, *The Clarkson chronicle, 1852–1952*, London, 1952, pp. 14–20.

actively sought new business and developed new areas of knowledge and expertise. The Liverpool agency sector was not a static hangover from some past age of sail. Some firms were clearly innovative. Part of Bahr Behrend's high profile can be attributed to not resting complacently on the old business of handling Baltic sailing ships, and the firm played an increasing role as agent for a new line of Spanish steamships from the later 1850s. By 1863, Bahr Behrend handled a weekly steam service, and, like the port's largest steam operators, was involved in regular correspondence with the Dock Board over berth accommodation. The firm's reserved space gradually extended over much of the south side of Coburg Dock, with every hundred feet of additional quay the subject of extended haggling with the Board. The Docks and Quays Committee took almost five months in 1858 to approve the initial allocation of the firm's berth, calling George Bahr in to testify personally to the firm's requirements in the process.[80]

Bahr Behrend's ventures in steam brought the firm into new business opportunities, but it continued to work in its old sailing-ship functions. It should be stressed that while firms like these may have established long-standing and successful links with particular nationalities of traders, this did not mean that the vessels concerned were always trading with their home countries. Increasingly, as was noted in chapter two, continental European sailing ships visiting Liverpool were operating in cross trades with third parties – Danish, Norwegian and German vessels arriving in England with cargoes from the Americas or the East.

This raises another area of intermediary activity, which overlaps to a considerable extent with handling the needs of vessels in port, but which was not always carried out by the same firms. The brokerage of outgoing cargoes – making the connection between traders who wanted cargo shipped and shipowners with space in their holds – is notoriously difficult to trace in the official sources. Unlike the ownership of vessels, for example, it was not an area that governments needed to monitor. As an essentially private matter between traders, its analysis requires the survival of the business records of individual firms. In particular, it needs the survival of charter parties – these crucial documents were the contracts containing the instructions for the carriage of the cargo, and the movements of the vessel.

Unfortunately for historians, there was no official requirement to lodge charter parties with Customs or the port authority, and these crucial documents have only survived in the archives of individual firms. Probably the best Liverpool example is W. H. Stott & Co., which appears to have been an active firm in the late 1860s, although it is hard to place their operations in context. They appear 15 times in the Bills of Entry as incoming agents in the three-month sample for 1870, placing them eighteenth in such activity and therefore well above the average. In addition, the profile of their business suggests that handling incoming vessels was not their primary focus, and that most of their efforts were as outgoing cargo brokers rather than incoming ship's agents. Stott's own records show that the firm handled 198 charter

---

80   MDHB, Docks & Quays Cttee, vol. 1, pp. 15, 90, 92.

parties in 1870 – about four each week.[81] Some of this coincided with their work as incoming ships' agents, but sometimes the functions were separated. Overall, we can conclude that Stott was a major player in Liverpool cargo brokering.

Table 5.3 Regional profile of W. H. Stott & Co.'s business, 1870

Regional origin/destination as charter party	Number of vessels	%
South America	86	43
Mediterranean	26	13
Central America/West Indies	22	11
Baltic	20	10
Britain/Ireland	16	8
United States	12	6
Other Europe	9	4
Africa	3	2
Far East	3	2
Canada	2	1
Total	**199**	**100**

Source: Stott, Charter party books.

What was the profile of Stott's operation? Table 5.3 demonstrates the distribution of traffic handled by the firm in 1870. While the geographical range is considerable, Stott's single largest interest clearly lay in South-Central America. Trade with this region has already been identified as a major area of growth in the period, and also one in which smaller sailing ships continued to play a significant role, partly because of the bulk commodities being handled, and also because the anchorages in South America were only very slowly developed to the point where they could accommodate large steamships. As such, the region offered excellent opportunities for owners of smaller vessels to secure trade from Liverpool merchants, and firms like Stott enabled owners from further afield to get a foothold in the market. Stott handled routine and unexceptional commodities, with over half of the total traffic being in exports of coal or salt. Indeed, the firm had a pre-printed charter party form specifically for coal exports.[82]

The maintenance of connections, once established, was an important aspect to the shipping agent's work. Stott was able to achieve a good deal of repeat business with traders: of 115 different merchants appearing in the firm's books in 1870, 44 appear more than once, with 11 firms appearing at least four times in the year. Given the relatively low activity of many trading firms in this period, such connections suggest tried and tested relationships. Lyon, Comber & Co. were Stott's most frequent clients in 1870, arranging seven shipments of coal to Para in Brazil. Lyon Comber were not

81 Stott, Charter party books.
82 Stott, Charter party books, 2/148.

directly interested in the cargoes, but were themselves acting as Liverpool agents for the Manchester firm of Carruthers de Souza & Co. In addition, none of these seven vessels came near Liverpool in the course of these voyages. All were elsewhere on the west coast of Britain or France when the charter party was issued, were ordered to travel to a South Wales coal port and then proceed to Brazil.[83] Lyon Comber appear to have taken over as de Souza's agent from a firm called William Killey & Co., which handled similar traffic during the early months of 1870.[84]

Firms like W. H. Stott & Co. managed complex networks of connections, specialising in one major region of the world, but also establishing links elsewhere as opportunities allowed. Such firms were crucial to Liverpool's role as a key entrepôt: having a reputation as a port in which anything could be bought and sold, and which had contacts with all regions of the world, created an environment in which increasingly diverse commodity flows were channelled through the hands of Liverpool traders. Of course, these characteristics of the long-established sailing ship agents mirror closely the activities of the new forwarding agents and steamship managing firms discussed at the beginning of this chapter, and stress the range of influences and traditions that drove the definition of specialisation in mid-century Liverpool.

Liverpool's trading community, for the most part, followed the well-known path to ever-greater specialisation in this period. In regional and commodity terms, this was already an established pattern by mid-century, but functional demarcation became more common in the 1850s and 1860s. Overall, the verdict of contemporaries appears to have been that functional specialisation gave the community as a whole sufficient expertise and flexibility to withstand difficult times. Importers could respond to a cotton crisis in different ways from brokers; the new alliance of steamship operators and smaller merchants presented an alternative relationship to the old ties between sailing operators and larger traders; and agency firms of various kinds became expert information dealers, linking buyers and sellers of goods and services alike. Taken in the round, such developments could only help Liverpool's reputation as a magnet for trade. In the background, of course, these changes needed the development and maintenance of intricate arrangements for the dissemination of information, and the financing of multi-dimensional commodity dealing, in which the efforts of several parties had to be co-ordinated to ensure the delivery of a given cargo to its final destination. These vital threads in the trading web are the subject of the rest of part II.

---

83 Stott, Charter party books, 2/186A, 2/209, 2/216, 2/217, 2/222, 2/223, 3/022A.
84 Stott, Charter party books, 2/151, 2/160.

Chapter 6

CAPITAL, CREDIT, GROWTH
AND CONTROL

The patterns of specialisation discussed in the previous chapter offer one perspective on the activities of traders. They also suggest important alternative approaches. The relative lack of vertical integration implies that Liverpool's numerous small firms had regular and successful interaction with other firms, and with the various market structures and institutions that served as the framework for Victorian trade. Moving from that assumption to an informed analysis is problematic, however, in large part because the workings of small firms remain unclear – while business historians accept that small firms are a central element in modern capitalism, relatively little has been done to study them. As was discussed in chapter one, most business history has focused on large, very active companies that became prominent in their sector of the economy. Fundamental questions about small firms, particularly in relation to how they raised funds, maximised profits, and were able to grow, have begun to be explored in recent years, but much remains to be done.

As with the complex changes in shipping and trade discussed in part one, the multi-faceted web of interconnection between trading firms is best studied through a number of different indicators. This chapter concentrates on the raising and management of finance by small firms, and particularly on the ways in which firms either expanded their activities by making existing resources work harder, or brought in additional investment from elsewhere in the community. These factors reveal a great deal about the external influences on trading firms, but they also highlight differing attitudes to control within the firm. This is particularly important because very active and prosperous firms were often structured in much the same way as lesser players: family firms and small partnerships were the norm across a broad spectrum of activity. Such patterns are evident in commodity trading and shipowning alike, with traditional forms of business organisation being flexible enough to cope with rapid and sustained expansion in some cases. On the other hand, some shipping firms in mid-century eagerly adopted new corporate structures by forming joint-stock companies, and an assessment of such strategies enables issues of finance and personal control to be considered in a broader context than has previously been the case.

The first section of this chapter briefly surveys recent research on the financial restraints that are believed to impinge on the small firm, and offers a broad profile of the capital and credit resources available to Liverpool's traders. The second section focuses on strategies for making those funds work harder in the context of new communications technology and shifting patterns in the availability of shipping. Finally, Liverpool's shipowning practices are considered as an extended case-study of the varying methods chosen by firms seeking to maintain their own control and freedom of decision-making in the face of the ever-increasing capital requirements of iron and steam shipping.

THE PRIVATE FIRM

Historians of British business often stress that the small, private firm was the nineteenth century's most typical corporate structure, to be found across a range of economic activities. Ownership and management alike were largely the functions of one person, or at most of a small group of partners. The 1720 Bubble Act is often cited as the reason – this legislation, passed in the wake of the South Sea Bubble scandal, was designed to make the formation of joint-stock companies very difficult, and thereby reduce the risk of exploitation of gullible shareholders by ruthless business speculators. In fact, the individual, hands-on approach was always fundamental to the assumptions of those starting in mercantile business in the nineteenth century, and when the legal framework was relaxed in mid-century there was no immediate rush away from these traditions.[1]

Small-firm structures had a number of advantages. They allowed the founders of the business, or their chosen successors, to stay in control and steer the direction of the company without having to take account of the views of shareholders. The ownership and management of the small business became a central theme of debates in the Victorian period about middle-class attitudes and identity, and has remained a valuable framework for historical analysis. As well as being small, Victorian firms were overwhelmingly focused on the family and were heavily reliant on family connections for finance and advice. As will be discussed in the next chapter, community assumptions were biased in favour of family connections in business, and contemporaries believed that managing finances within a small network of family and close friends was much safer than venturing out into the risky world of bank lending and company flotation.

It would not do to have too rosy a picture – the small firm was not without its problems, especially when the partners were family members. Such close business relationships had their failings, often because of negative aspects of the very factors that gave them their strength. If the fusion of business and personal ties made traders more confident that their interests would be protected by their colleagues, it could also make rough patches in relationships harder to resolve. The very sense of personal obligation that made business links so strong in good times could complicate decisions and priorities when misunderstandings and disagreements arose. When close family members disagreed over the direction of a business, they were acutely conscious of the duality of the situation, and that such an issue had to be considered 'in its two-fold aspect – as a question of business and as a question of feeling'.[2]

The key problem identified by critics of the small firm, however, was its alleged

---

1   P. L. Payne, *British entrepreneurship in the nineteenth century*, 2nd edn, Basingstoke, 1988, p. 14.
2   J. J. Stitt to Samuel Stitt, 15 Nov. 1862, Stitt papers, box 1, xix.

lack of capacity for growth, particularly in terms of being able to bring in more capital. The law of partnership – which famously made every partner in the firm personally liable 'to his last shilling and acre' for any losses incurred by the firm – was seen as a straitjacket that limited the legitimate expansion of firms into new markets, while being little deterrent to those fraudulent and reckless traders who had few assets to lose anyway. Reform of company law was considered by some contemporaries to be just as important for the nation's expansion as free trade. Large numbers of people had money to invest, it was argued, but were currently forced either to buy government securities or to hoard their funds in the manner 'practised by old ladies during times of threatened invasion'.[3]

Company law was indeed reformed, and a range of issues relating to new joint-stock ventures in steam shipping will be considered in the final section of this chapter, and in chapter seven. Much of this chapter focuses, however, on strategies adopted by firms which sought to do business within the old private partnership structures. Many of the wealthiest and most successful firms of the nineteenth century remained family-based, or at most drew in partners from a close circle of professional, ethnic or religious connections. The flexibility of the small-firm model is remarkable, encompassing trading firms at every point on the scale from occasional dabblers to major operators with a dominant market share in their chosen sector.[4]

The levels of capital available to trading firms have posed problems for historians, because few sources survive that can offer accurate figures. One obvious problem is that capital meant different things to the various functional specialists that were discussed in chapter five. Shipowners obviously had most of their capital tied up in ships; import merchants might have extensive stocks of goods; commodity and ship brokers might have virtually no capital at all but still run an effective business on the basis of credit and reputation (which is of course another kind of capital). The capitalisation of mercantile business is therefore a complex question, because firms working in different specialist niches had different requirements for, and attitudes to, the acquisition and deployment of capital.

Some innovative work has been done with the records of banks and other financial institutions to gain an alternative, and hopefully more objective, perspective from that offered by a firm's own records or the memoirs of its founder. The general conclusion has been that most commodity trading firms operated with a modest level of capital in the mid-nineteenth century, and that there was then a great increase in expected levels of capital across the second half of the century. Major firms with £100,000 in the 1840s were, if they survived, generally trading with resources in excess

3 *The Times*, 20 Feb. 1852, p. 5.

4 Useful recent contributions are S. Nenadic, 'The small family firm in Victorian Britain', *Business History*, Vol. 35, 1993, pp. 86–114; P. L. Payne, 'Family business in Britain: An historical and analytical survey', in *Family business in the era of industrial growth*, ed. A. Okochi and S. Yasaoka, Tokyo, 1984, pp. 171–206; M. B. Rose, 'Family firm, community and business culture: A comparative perspective on the British and American cotton industries', in *Business history and business culture*, ed. A. Godley and O. Westall, Manchester, 1996, pp. 162–89.

of £1m by the early 1900s, and therefore appear to have started from a relatively low base.[5]

It is clear, however, that £100,000 was an exceptional level of capital in mid-century, and that many important members of the Liverpool trading community operated on considerably less. Table 6.1 shows levels of capitalisation for trading firms as recorded by the Bank of England's local agent in three years between 1855 and 1870. The nature of the sample is obviously skewed in a number of directions. The Bank's agent was, to a large extent, only commenting on firms in response to requests for information from his superiors in London. In addition, he was much more willing to comment on the credit-worthiness of firms than on their capital, suggesting that figures for capital were harder to come by and (probably) less reliable. Nonetheless, the list does point to a considerable range of capitalisation across all sectors of the trading community, and to the ability of some traders to operate with only a fraction of the capital held by the major players.

As might be expected, firms with the strongest capital base were in Liverpool's lucrative American trades. Denniston & Co., Newall & Clayton, and Blessig, Braun & Co. were all responsible for major consignments of goods across the Atlantic: Newall & Clayton were second only to Fraser, Trenholm & Co. as direct importers of blockade-running US cotton in 1863, and their record level of capitalisation at the end of the decade reflects their staying-power in difficult times.[6] As is clear from the lower end of the table, however, it was possible for firms to work in these trades, and in many others, with a fraction of the capital of the major players. It was also possible to start small and build capital with some speed. Shipbrokers English & Brandon were a recently established firm with £2,000 when they came to the Bank's attention in 1855, but within three years, and with the addition of a third partner, the new firm of Boult, English & Brandon could claim capital resources of £15,000.[7] Balfour, Williamson & Co., who started as commission merchants but moved into direct commodity trading and shipping, started with £10,000 borrowed from friends in their native Fife in the early 1850s, and put their available capital at £250,000 after twenty years in the business.[8]

Credit-worthiness is much better recorded in bank sources than capital, but of course there are many variables at work which make establishing patterns difficult. Wine merchants seem to have worked with much lower levels of credit than cotton brokers, for example. A sample from the Bank of England papers includes five wine merchants with credit levels between £200 and £500, and eight cotton brokers with ratings from £2,000 to £8,000, with most around £5,000. Liverpool's wine merchants may well have been deeply untrustworthy compared with its cotton brokers, but the

5   S. Chapman, *Merchant enterprise in Britain: From the industrial revolution to World War I*, Cambridge, 1992, appendix.

6   BE (1863).

7   Bank, 29 Jan. 1855, 19 Mar. 1858.

8   Forres, *Balfour Williamson & Company and associated firms: Memoirs of a merchant house*, London, 1929, p. 8; Stephen Williamson letter book, 10 June 1871, Balfour Williamson papers, box 4.

Table 6.1 Capitalisation of Liverpool trading firms, 1855–70

Firm	Capital (£)	Main trade	Year
Newall & Clayton	400,000	Cotton broker	1870
Alex Denniston	300,000	US trade	1855
Blessig Braun	200,000	Commission merchants	1870
George Warren	180,000	United States	1870
Henry Morre	100,000	East and West Indies	1855
Rathbone Brs	100,000	Commission merchants	1855
H. Clason	85,000	Bombay	1870
James Phelps	75,000	Tin plates	1855
Jeffrey Morrish	70,000	Silk mercer	1855
Leech Harrison & Forwood	60,000	Cotton/shipping	1870
Fox Sawyers	50,000	West Coast South America	1863
J. B. Patterson	50,000	Smyrna	1870
J. & W. Robinson	45,000	Shipowning	1855
Leech Harrison & Forwood	45,000	Cotton/Shipping	1863
Richard Sheil	40,000	Tobacco	1863
David Cannon	35,000	Shipowning	1855
Bushby & Edwards	30,000	Shipowning	1863
H. J. Forrer	25,000	Commission merchants	1870
Mather Hodgson	22,000	General merchants	1863
James Pitcairn Campbell	20,000	Cotton	1863
Carlyle & Geddes	20,000	Shipbroking	1863
James Smith	15,000	Calcutta	1863
Richardson Spence	15,000	US trade	1870
Ceaser & Sobbe	10,000	Cotton broker	1863
Joseph Woodall	10,000	Fruit	1863
G. T. Soley	10,000	Shipbroking	1870
Bigland Athya	6,000	Commission merchants	1855
Rishton Cooper & Dunderdale	6,000	Spice, rice	1870
Roberts Williams & Lumley	6,000	Timber	1870
Wichelhouse & Busch	4,000	Cotton	1855
James Chambers	4,000	Provisions	1870
Barnes Davidson	4,000	Corn	1870
Belyea & Armstrong	4,000	Chandlers	1870
W. Griffiths	4,000	Guano	1870
Thomas Raymond	3,000	Canada	1855
George Richenberg	3,000	Cotton broker	1855
English & Brandon	2,000	Shipbroker	1855
Thomas Vafea	2,000	Smyrna	1870
Bennet Medley & Collings	1,400	Africa	1870
James Black	1,000	Canada	1863

Source: Collated from references in Bank, 1855, 1863, 1870.

greatest part of the explanation must lie in the established methods and traditions of the two trades. Further examples can be cited – timber dealers had a broadly similar credit rating of around £1,000, as did fruit traders, but port service firms like ships' store dealers and chandlers are usually found around the £500 mark.[9]

This clustering of credit ratings in particular trades reflects a normal level of operating credit for middling firms conducting routine business. Relatively high or low figures are generally associated with firms that were either at the very top of the trade, or suffering from particular difficulties described by the bank agent. To put these figures in some context, large cargo steamers cost around £35,000 in the mid-1850s.[10] New Orleans cotton cost about 7d per lb, or £13 per bale on the Liverpool market: importers often brought in 500 bales, or £6,500 worth, in a single shipment.[11] Levels of capital and credit alike in the Liverpool community were not therefore so great as to suggest that firms could be complacent in their finances. On the contrary, as will be discussed in the rest of this chapter, traders of all sorts sought ways of securing greater income, while always trying to maintain control over their businesses.

MAKING CAPITAL WORK HARDER

Commodity-trading firms had two approaches to growth. They could try to build up capital quickly through large profits and attempt to persuade the community that this entitled them to higher levels of credit, which would in turn allow them to be more active. In highly profitable markets like the cotton trade of the early 1860s, this was indeed an option. The alternative approach was to increase turnover, speed up transactions and gain a reputation for the rapid and reliable payment of debts, which would also permit an increase in activity. Sophisticated systems of mercantile credit could be exploited by traders to, in effect, gain credit on the 'virtual' security of promised income from somewhere else. Thus an incoming cargo, still at sea, could be traded against debts incurred in preparing another consignment for an outward voyage. Naturally, timing was everything, and there was little leeway for dealing with unexpected events. New communications technology, especially in the form of the telegraph, could help with the co-ordination of business on a global scale, but this brought its own costs and hazards. Firms experimenting with turnover and income-raising strategies worried other traders and financial institutions, but as always there was a broad spectrum of variation from the cleverly innovative to the blatantly fraudulent, and it is hard to decide where the community drew the line of acceptable practice.

New communications technology was welcomed in some mercantile quarters as a means of increasing turnover. As has been noted, the mid-nineteenth century was

9 Calculated from figures for credit-worthiness given by the Bank of England agent during 1855 and 1870: see Bank, 1855, 1870.

10 D. Haws, *The Burma Boats: Henderson & Bibby*, Uckfield, 1995, pp. 97–98.

11 An interesting contemporary chart of cotton prices is *Spence's diagram of the cotton trade of Great Britain*, Manchester, 1879, British Library, 74/1882.d2; consignment figures are from BE (1855).

an era of unprecedented change in communications capability across long distances, thanks to two key technologies: the steam engine and the telegraph. The crucial thing about both was that they enabled information to travel faster than goods. Steamships and railways carried mail faster than sailing ships and road transport could carry cargo, and the telegraph outpaced all of them. That much is obvious. What requires further discussion is the attitude of traders to these new opportunities for transmitting information and the real impact of such changes on mercantile communications. Faster communications changed the way traders thought about information, and its relationship to capital and commodities.

More conservative traders resisted fast communications: 'a mercantile man depends for his profits a great deal upon the fluctuations of the market; the quicker the communications the less will be the fluctuations'.[12] Others recognised the potential of an alternative view. Steamships carrying mail on the North Atlantic, and telegraph connections to the Far East, allowed information about key commodities to travel faster than the goods themselves. Liverpool merchants could sell goods as soon as they had been notified of the departure of the vessel from Charleston or Bombay. The process of buying and selling could be repeated many more times in a year, without the need to acquire significantly greater amounts of capital or security. One of Liverpool's most active cotton traders put it nicely: 'the wheel is always going round when you use the wire in place of waiting for the mail for advices'.[13] Thus the telegraph encouraged merchants and brokers to put their faith in rapid turnover and close control of commodity shipments rather than trust the fluctuations of the market over long periods to eventually deliver their profits.

Liverpool's Far East merchants were especially enthusiastic about the telegraph, because it gave them a level playing field with London firms, allowing them to communicate with India in much the same time as London could. In a period when the Mersey was keen to challenge London's dominance of Far Eastern trades, telegraphs helped cotton traders to deal direct rather than through London houses. Even when it was necessary to send mail to the East, the telegraph still helped Liverpool: reports of Friday's cotton deals in Manchester could be telegraphed to an agent in London to be added to that week's package of papers to go on the mail steamer.[14]

Nonetheless, mid-century was a period of transition, with all that implied in terms of false starts, wrong turnings, and high start-up costs. Trading firms were often unenthusiastic about the new communications technology for a number of reasons. In the case of the telegraph, only the briefest of messages could be carried, and there was a great deal of suspicion about the reliability of foreign lines and the honesty of their operators – it was 'a very short and uncertain [means of] communication'.[15] Tampering with messages undermined the confidence of merchants that they had

---

12 BPP, Steam communications (1851), evidence of Frederick Parbury, q. 856.
13 BPP, East India communications (1866), evidence of Gilbert McMicking, q. 1,070.
14 BPP, East India communications (1866), evidence of John Gladstone, q. 1,032.
15 BPP, Mail contracts (1868), evidence of Russell Sturgis, q. 1,222.

the information they needed, and made them still more likely to revert to mail.[16] Even when operators were honest, technical problems were common, especially when operating at the technological cutting-edge. The saga of the transatlantic cable is well known to historians, with its frequent early failures – the first attempt in 1858 was widely believed to be a hoax and traders were only gradually persuaded that the project would work at all.[17]

Even the greatest asset of the telegraph – speed – could not always be relied upon over long distances, as backlogs of messages piled up in the chain of telegraph offices between Britain and the East, for example. Various anecdotes were circulated about messages that reached Calcutta by steamer before a telegraph message sent on the same day. In March 1865, most telegraph messages sent from London to Bombay arrived in less than three days, but a worrying number took longer. One in ten messages reached Bombay nine or ten days after leaving London.[18] Absolute speed was not really the problem: if every message had taken three days or ten, traders would have been content, but problems arose when one firm's messages might reach their agents a week before another's did. It was precisely that sort of random factor in the trading process that new technology was supposed to be eliminating, not exacerbating.

The key problem was one familiar to any transitional phase in technology and business practice – duplication. Traders found themselves having to deal with mail and telegraph systems side by side. A trader could not miss the opportunity presented by having messages delivered rapidly to India and beyond, but at the same time could not rely entirely on the service. Some traders sent more than one copy of messages by telegraph (usually a couple of days apart), and sent a copy by mail as well.[19] Larger documents, samples and the like had to go by sea in any case. Traders therefore needed reliable mail *and* telegraph services, and, if both were available, would then have been able to select the appropriate service for the task at hand. It was doubling-up that added to costs.

Bigger, more active, firms could find solutions to the practical difficulties of the telegraph, because in relative terms, the costs were less significant to them. Ralli & Co. spent around £1,000 a year on telegraph messages to the East in the mid-1860s, but considered this a minor sum compared with the profits to be made – or losses avoided – by means of rapid communications. The firm also devised a code for use by all its branches and agencies, so that the problem of corrupted messages could be overcome.[20] Smaller traders, and those working in less profitable goods and services, could not easily justify the costs of the new technology.

In addition, some branches of the community already had effective methods of

---

16 BPP, East India communications (1866), evidence of John Gladstone, q. 1,042, evidence of John Green, qq. 1,155–65.

17 H. M. Field, *History of the Atlantic telegraph*, New York, 1866, pp. 247–66.

18 Calculated from BPP, East India communications (1866), p. 540.

19 BPP, East India communications (1866), evidence of Henry Nelson, q. 813.

20 BPP, East India communications (1866), evidence of John Green, q. 1,151.

maintaining contact, and did not immediately gain much benefit from the telegraph. Shipping agents might be thought to be likely beneficiaries of telecommunications, with the potential to redirect vessels and negotiate charters with distant clients, but the industry had long since worked out operating procedures that enabled communication with vessels at various points along their routes. Most charter parties for ships returning to the UK from abroad had a clause requiring the vessel to call at either Falmouth, Cowes or Queenstown for orders, before proceeding to a particular port.[21] Similar arrangements operated on some outward voyages. Sailing ships would be instructed to proceed to a particular port, to receive further instructions that had been dispatched by the steam mail services after the original vessel's departure. The telegraph meant that Liverpool agents could communicate faster with such way-stations than was possible by mail, but not by much. Revolutionary change in working practices became possible only when wireless technology enabled communication with ships *at sea*. While the system remained dependent on cables, shipping agents continued to follow much the same routines for keeping in touch with their owners and agents as they had always done. The Norwegian shipbroking firm of Fearnley & Eger did a good deal of business with the UK, but made relatively little use of the North Sea cable in its early decades.[22]

If traders had options in increasing turnover and making capital work harder, they could also try to minimise the amount of capital that was tied up in goods or equipment in the first place. This approach worked for a large cross-section of the commodity-broking community, who were attracted to this activity precisely because it did not require them to hold stocks of goods. Their expertise lay in making connections between sellers and buyers, juggling credit, and anticipating changes in the market, and they could run extensive businesses with very little capital.

The most dramatic benefits of more effective use of capital and a determined strategy of cost reduction were felt by shipowners, however. It is worth discussing some of these issues before considering more conventional routes to expansion in shipowning in the next section of this chapter. Shipowning is generally seen as the classic capital-intensive industry of the pre-industrial age, and capital demands increased through the nineteenth century with the development of steam and iron shipping. Nonetheless, some Liverpool owners were able to keep capital outlay to a minimum, operating large vessels and even fleets with much lower levels of capital tie-up than other firms. Fundamentally, there were two ways of achieving this – chartering ships, or buying second-hand.

Chartering vessels was not necessarily cheaper, and indeed was likely to be much more expensive than owning vessels outright, but it did have the great accounting advantage of shifting the vessels from the capital side of a firm's finances into the

---

21 For example, Stott, Charter party books, 2/159.

22 L. R. Fischer and H. Nordvik, 'Economic theory, information and management in shipbroking: Fearnley and Eger as a case study, 1869–1972', in *Management, finance and industrial relations in maritime industries*, ed. Simon Ville and D. M. Williams, St John's, Newfoundland, 1994, pp. 1–29; p. 9.

firm's operating credit system. The cost of chartering a vessel became just another element in the network of credit built up to maintain the operation, rather than requiring an initial outlay of capital. The activities of James Baines and Thomas Mackay in the Australian trades offer some insights. The scale of the Baines/Mackay fleet is unclear at any one time, because they supplemented their own shipowning with extensive chartering. Mackay himself was vague on the subject, claiming to be joint owner of between 70 and 80 ships in the early 1860s, while more than 400 ships carried emigrants under the firm's auspices at some time during the 1850s and 1860s.[23] As will be discussed more fully in chapter eight, Baines and Mackay benefited from steady contracts with the British and colonial governments for the transport of emigrants, but it is also clear that their working funds were severely stretched at times by the scale of their operations. In overcoming such problems, they pushed the flexibility and legality of their business structures as far as possible, incurring some suspicion in the process. Both Baines and Mackay maintained separate firms in Liverpool and London: as early as 1855 the Governors of the Bank of England were questioning whether it was appropriate for these firms to be drawing bills of exchange on each other. Although the Bank's manager in Liverpool supported Baines and Mackay – he thought that they actually owned enough ships to stand as ample security for any difficulties – Threadneedle Street feared that such transactions were a clever way of disguising inadequate capital and/or cash flow.[24] It was rarely clear to contemporaries, therefore, exactly how much of the huge Baines and Mackay fleet was a capital asset, and how much was an addition to the firm's liabilities. The two firms also had a habit of financing ship-purchases with bills drawn on cargo that was still afloat on another of their ships, a practice which had been criticised in the speculative environment of the early 1850s as 'making a very little capital go a long way' and a 'hazardous and unsound mode' of shipowning.[25] Baines and Mackay clearly liked the first part of that statement and hoped not to be caught out by the second.

Another obvious way for shipowners to reduce their capital requirements was to buy cheaper vessels, which was most easily done by specialising in used ships. The market in second-hand shipping is not easy to trace in the official sources, because the ship register is rather a fluid source – vessels were re-registered for various reasons, and checking that each re-registration stemmed from an actual sale would be prohibitively time-consuming. Sometimes, however, a particular set of circumstances created a brisk market for used shipping in Liverpool, and such events can offer useful case-studies of the attitudes of the trading community to the acquisition of used ships. The most striking in mid-century was that surrounding the American Civil War, during which a considerable tonnage of US shipping was sold to British subjects based in the UK and in Canada. Some US shipping would have been sold in Britain anyway, of course – the figure for the last year of peace, 1860, was just

---

23   BPP, MDHB Bill (1864), evidence of Thomas Mackay, qq. 1676–82; D. Hollett, *Fast passage to Australia*, London, 1986, appendices.

24   Bank, 26 Apr. 1855, 5 June 1855, 21 Jan. 1858.

25   *The Times*, 6 Jan. 1852, p. 3.

over 11,000 tons – but the volume of the trade expanded considerably during the war. In 1863, no less than 608 US vessels with a total tonnage of almost 329,000 were sold to British owners and re-registered.[26]

Who bought these ships? Many were acquired by firms that had acted as Liverpool agents for American owners prior to the Civil War. The agency firms, such as Tapscott's, and Guion & Co., were moving sideways in business, seeking to maintain as much of their previous activities as possible under radically different circumstances. However, the most important single buyer of US vessels in 1863 was – not surprisingly – the Baines and Mackay partnership, with 13 ships totalling just over 16,000 tons. The youngest was five years old in 1863, but most were twice that, and nearing the end of their useful lives in the difficult waters of the South Atlantic. Baines and Mackay sold them on quickly, usually within a year or two of purchase. Indeed, two were sold in Australia at the end of an emigrant voyage, and one of these was turned into a storage hulk shortly afterward.[27] Baines was a frequent buyer and seller of used ships, and the opportunity presented by the American Civil War was just a particularly focused period in a long-standing business strategy. In addition, several of the American vessels bought by Baines in 1863 were mortgaged, creating another thread in the fine web of finance and credit that underpinned the firm's operations. What little evidence there is of prices points to a figure of around £5/ton for the vessels Baines was buying, which was less than half the cost of new wooden sailing ships.[28]

Depreciation during the short period that the vessels were owned by Baines would therefore have been a relatively small percentage of the buying price. Such careful restriction of capital outlay, combined with the chartering strategy outlined above, enabled the firm to operate an extensive fleet of large ships on relatively little capital. The contrast with the major steam companies of the day, which had to build fleets of new steamships from scratch with enormous up-front capital investment, could hardly be more striking. With his approach, Baines could have bought more than 130 ships with the £800,000 that the Royal Mail Steam Packet Co. had to spend on its initial fleet of sixteen.[29]

Buying used ships was a particularly favoured option of those who, for whatever reason, wanted to retain personal control of their businesses, and not follow the option of bringing in more shareholders. Edward Bates was one such operator who preferred a more personal management, and who worked at some scale. Five of his ships appear in the 1870 Bills of Entry sample, ranging from 1,160 to 2,153 tons. Bates was sole owner of two, and had at least 52/64ths in the others.[30] In all, Bates

26 BPP, American vessels (1863), p. 33.
27 For the acquisition and deployment of Baines and Mackay vessels see BPP, American vessels (1863); D. Hollett, *Fast passage to Australia*, London, 1986, appendices.
28 BPP, American vessels (1863), p. 5.
29 E. Green, 'Very private enterprise: Ownership and finance in British shipping, 1825–1940', in *Business history of shipping: Strategy and structure*, ed. T. Yui and K. Nakagawa, Tokyo, 1985, pp. 219–48; p. 223.
30 *Sir Charles Napier* (SR 1861/272), *Bates Family* (SR 1859/177), *Sidney* (SR 1867/149), *Bertram* (SR 1864/285), *Mabel* (SR 1865/288).

owned 51 vessels in that year, having bought a total of 93 at some point during the previous twenty years.[31] A number of factors make Bates a special case. First, he had been in the business for a long time, having made solid connections in the Far East early in his career. He maintained these through the 1860s, making considerable money from shipping Indian cotton during the American Civil War.[32] In addition, Bates had windfall earnings from government contracts during the Abyssinian campaign in 1868.[33] The important point, though, was the way in which Bates ploughed these earnings back into the expansion of his shipping fleet. While new iron ships were expensive, Bates was a diligent buyer of second-hand shipping in the later 1860s, keeping his costs down and spreading risk across a large number of cheap ships instead of a small number of expensive vessels: shrewdly, he even bought older steamers, removed their obsolete engines, and fitted out their still-serviceable hulls as iron sailing ships. His government contract earnings in particular were spread thinly in a buying spree of second-hand ships: he bought 23 used vessels in 1869 and 1870.[34]

Personal factors also need to be considered in such cases. Bates is an extreme example in many ways, often appearing aloof from the trading community and determined to conduct his business on his own terms. There is broad agreement that he was not liked, to the point that rumours were sometimes deliberately spread that he was in financial difficulty in order to damage his credit-worthiness and reputation.[35] It is therefore entirely in character for him to take an individualistic approach to shipowning, restricting his reliance on others as far as possible, and making the best possible use of his own resources.

Liverpool's traders were broadly inventive in their strategies for making capital go further, although merchants and shipowners alike faced increased risks from such efforts. Control remained a central issue, with the individual and the small family firm maintaining a central role by finding ways of increasing turnover and income without necessarily bringing in considerable levels of new capital. It must be stressed, however, that while commodity traders had little choice, shipowners did have the legal option of seeking a broader shareholding public even before the company-law reforms of mid-century. The extent to which they pursued these options is the subject of the next section.

STRATEGIES FOR GROWTH AND THE ADOPTION OF NEW TECHNOLOGY IN SHIPOWNING

Shipowning was an unusual business in Victorian Britain, because it had a partial exemption from the legal straitjacket of unlimited liability. Traditional shipowning

---

31 A. H. Rowson, 'Edward Bates: Shipowner', in *Bates of Bellefield, Gyrn Castle and Manydown*, ed. P. E. Bates, n.p., 1994, p. 227.
32 *Bank*, 5 Oct. 1863.
33 See chapter eight.
34 Rowson, 'Edward Bates: Shipowner', p. 227.
35 *Bank*, 15 June 1850.

revolved around the 64ths system, in which vessels were divided into 64 equal shares. This convention allowed the recruitment of smaller investors in shipping at a time when most other industries had no mechanisms for bringing in such people. Historians have concluded, however, that small investors did not rush to become involved in shipowning, and that few vessels were owned by anything approaching the legal maximum of thirty-two owners. Only in particular cases, with evidence of a long tradition of co-operative shipowning, did large numbers of people gather to own shares in a particular vessel: London cheesemongers seem to have developed a tradition of clubbing together, sometimes more than twenty at a time, to own ships, but such cases are very unusual.[36]

The small-firm model was familiar to those in the shipowning business, although some contemporaries seem to have been overawed by the new companies of mid-century. Alfred Holt, no mean shipowner himself, recognised the fragmented, small-firm nature of the shipping industry, especially in comparison with the other great transport phenomenon of the age, the huge regional railway companies: 'the increase in steamers had', he believed, 'been mainly due to private individuals who owned one, two or three vessels; the great companies which had attracted most attention had probably not moved the greatest amount of cargo, or effected the greatest amount of change'.[37] The portrait that emerges from previous work is indeed of an industry based on small, local firms in the first half of the nineteenth century. It was 'atomistic', with most vessels being owned by individuals or by small groups of partners, and with most shipowners only being involved with one or two vessels. It was local, with most owners living in or near the port in question. Finally, it was a relatively closed world, with most of those involved having some connection with maritime business anyway, either as commodity traders or seamen, or through port industries like shipbuilding or chandlering.[38]

The new technology finally pushed shipowning in the direction that had always been legally possible, but rarely used, in wooden sailing ships – bringing in many more people to own a few 64ths. While three-quarters of Liverpool's wooden vessels in 1870 had four owners or less, we need to reach nine owners before accounting for the same percentage of iron sailing ships. Other patterns in 64th ownership indicate further divergence. Most importantly, there is clear evidence of a much less equal division of vessels in iron and steam. Wooden sailing ships were likely to be divided into roughly equal holdings, but iron sailing and steamships were much more likely to have one or two owners with 20 or 30/64ths, and a number of much lesser holders

36 S. Palmer, 'Investors in London shipping, 1820–1850', *Maritime History*, Vol. 2, 1972, pp. 46–68, p. 52; Green, 'Very private enterprise', p. 221.

37 A. Holt, 'Review of the progress of steam shipping during the last quarter of a century,' *Minutes of proceedings of the Institution of Civil Engineers*, Vol. 51, 1877–8, pp. 2–135; p. 6.

38 For studies of shipowning in various ports, see S. Jones, 'Shipowning in Boston, Lincolnshire, 1836–1848', *Mariner's Mirror*, Vol. 65, 1979, pp. 339–49; Palmer, 'Investors in London shipping;' F. Neal, 'Liverpool shipping in the early nineteenth century', in *Liverpool and Merseyside: Essays in the economic and social history of the port and its hinterland*, ed. J. R. Harris, Liverpool, 1969, pp. 147–81.

of 2, 4 or 8/64ths. Only 35% of owners in wooden sailing ships had 8/64ths or less, while the same measures for iron sailing and steamships were 65% and 74% respectively.[39] Not only did the new technology require more people to invest in ships, it was also a different kind of ownership – while wooden sailing ships tended to be owned by individuals or equal partnerships, the new technology was owned by core owners supported by a larger number of lesser investors.

The idea of iron and steam being owned by the entrepreneurial few with the support of a larger number of small owners is of course far from new, but it tends to be associated with the big joint-stock companies and their hundreds of small investors scattered around the country. The pattern evident in Liverpool's iron and steam ownership demonstrates that such thinking was also possible under the 64ths system on a rather more evolutionary scale, with the smaller owners almost always being involved elsewhere in the local trading community.

It must be stressed, though, that the evidence points to a spectrum of shipowning patterns, from small, equal partnerships to more diverse multi-owner structures, and not to a series of rigidly defined types of business. The statistics demonstrate that wooden sailing ships were much more likely to be at the small-partnership end of the range, and that iron and steam tended to be found with one key owner and supporting investors – but there were a large number of exceptions, and numerous examples of ownership strategies that seemed to straddle the different kinds of shipping: this was especially true in iron and wooden sailing ships. While the broad patterns are clear, it is evident that the shipowning culture of this transitional period was quite flexible at the margins.

Some examples will help to illustrate the trends. Liverpool's South American traders demonstrate the predicted pattern in their new iron sailing ships. Balfour, Williamson & Co.'s vessels in 1870 tended to have one of the partners as the major owner, with the other, and various family and friends, holding lesser shares. Alexander Balfour owned 24/64ths of *Santiago*, with Stephen Williamson and four others holding 4, 8 or 16/64ths. *Mendoza*, on the other hand, had 26/64ths in Williamson's name and the remainder shared between four others. However, an older wooden ship, *Cordillera*, was owned on the equal-partnership model, with Balfour and Williamson having 32/64ths each.[40]

Others had longer-standing patterns to which they clung during the period of transition. Take Edward Curling Friend. Friend's profile in the 1870 sample seems to bear out fully the overall pattern in iron sailing ships. His iron ship *Clevedon* – only two years old and employed in the expanding South American trades – had a complicated pattern of ownership involving ten individuals. Friend himself owned 16/64ths jointly with his father (also called Edward) and William Coleburn; he also owned 8/64ths jointly with Robert and John Evans. The remaining 40/64ths were split between five people.[41] However, Friend had always operated in this fashion: his complex shipowning

---

39   Calculated from SR (1870).
40   SR 1856/167; SR 1861/091; SR 1866/001.
41   *Clevedon* (SR 1868/147).

strategies long pre-dated the rise of iron shipping. Back in 1855, he had shares in much smaller wooden ships with seven or eight owners, and the practice reached its zenith in the 1860s when he divided a 436 ton ship between no fewer than seventeen owners.[42]

The broad statistics of shipowning patterns in Liverpool therefore point to considerable continuity in the way the 64ths system was implemented, with an evolutionary shift in the concentration of ownership when dealing with iron and steam. It is clear therefore that contemporaries did not make the leap straight from traditional sail ownership to large-scale corporate steam ownership, although of course by the end of the nineteenth century the latter form dominated the port's trades. An alternative pattern of managing growth is visible in Liverpool's new steam fleets in mid-century, with a more sophisticated balance of personal control and collaborative investment. As was discussed in chapter two, the North Atlantic and Mediterranean services were Liverpool's first areas of rapid expansion in ocean steam shipping, and firms working these routes therefore offer valuable evidence for the strategies adopted by shipowners in new and rapidly expanding trades. This section considers the core strategies of those who built large steam fleets around the 64ths model, focusing on William Inman's American services and on the Mediterranean enterprises of the Bibby and Moss families.

Table 6.2 Ownership of the Inman fleet, 1870

Owner	Occupation/residence	% of fleet tonnage
William Inman	Steamship owner, Liverpool	48.6
Thomas Birley	Merchant, Kirkham, Lancs	8.8
Charles Birley	Merchant, Kirkham, Lancs	8.0
David Tod	Engineer, Partick, Lanark	4.9
Thomas Awden	Gent, Tottenham, Middlesex	4.8
James Kay	Gent, Turton Tower, Lancs	3.8
Charles Inman	Merchant, Liverpool	3.6
William Langton	Merchant, Liverpool	3.6
Arthur Birley	Merchant, Kirkham, Lancs	3.6
Charles Lepper	Merchant, Belfast	3.0
John Cross Lepper	Merchant, Belfast	2.5
Thomas Inman	Physician, Liverpool	2.1
William Valentine	Banker, Belfast	1.2
William Stobart	Coal Proprietor, Sunderland	1.2
Edward Wakefield	Barrister, London	0.4

Source: Vessels appearing in BE (1870); SR.

Inman's fleet in 1870 reflected the development of his business in the previous two decades. Ten different Inman vessels appear in the 1870 ship register sample, all

42 For example, *Emperor* (SR 1849/240) and *May Queen* (SR 1854/058); *Constantia* (SR 1859/217).

screw-driven steamers, with a mean tonnage of 1,770 tons. Table 6.2 shows the ownership breakdown of that fleet. Although Inman was by far the largest single owner, he owned less than half of the total available 64ths, with seventeen other collaborators involved in at least one of his ships. Many of the vessels in the fleet were owned on a standard pattern, with Inman himself having 15–20/64ths, members of the Birley family having about the same between them, and the remaining shares distributed in twos and threes. Inman was therefore able to operate a large, modern fleet on the North Atlantic while being responsible for only half of the total investment in shipping.

The collaborative structure used by Inman to manage his fleet is also found in Liverpool's early Mediterranean steam services, although these take the point a step further and provide evidence of a more complex relationship between different firms. The Mediterranean trades have long been subject to a conventional house-history model, focusing on family firms making the transition from sail to steam.[43] Various members of the Bibby family ran sailing ships to the region in the first half of the nineteenth century, and then began to experiment with steamships on the same routes. The firm took gradual steps toward steam, using hybrid sail/steam vessels from the 1850s, and only gradually abandoning sail altogether. Evolving corporate structures also seem to fit the model, with, apparently, a gradual shift toward a larger, more formal company operation: Bibby was instrumental in establishing the Liverpool & Mediterranean Screw Steam Shipping Co. in the early 1850s, which rapidly emerged as one of the port's major steam services with southern Europe and the Levant. Similar patterns are visible in the career of the Moss family, and the two came to dominate the port's trade with the region in mid-century: by 1870, the firms headed by James Jenkinson Bibby and William Miles Moss were managing owners of no less than 49% of the steam tonnage arriving in Liverpool from the Mediterranean.[44]

Closer examination casts doubt on the real lessons to be learned here. An earlier analysis of these operations warned against the assumption that companies like the Liverpool & Mediterranean were centralised, bureaucratised firms on the vertically integrated model, and argued that Bibby is probably a classic example of a shipowner who took a gradual, long-term approach to the sail/steam transition in collaboration with other firms.[45] Further evidence of ownership patterns in the Mediterranean trades in mid-century allows us to take this argument still further, revealing a complex web of owners, holding varying levels of shares in sail and steam over time, and forming a much more fluid business environment than the linear, exclusionist models implied by the large market share of the firms involved.

Rather than a model in which Moss and Bibby ran separate firms in competition,

---

43 Nigel Watson, *The Bibby Line, 1807–1990*, London, 1990; Bibby Line, *Bibby Line, 1807–1957*, London, 1957.

44 BE (1870).

45 P. L. Cottrell, 'Liverpool shipowners, the Mediterranean and the transition from sail to steam during the mid-nineteenth century', in *From wheelhouse to counting house: Essays in maritime economic history in honour of Professor Peter Neville Davies*, ed. L. R. Fischer, St John's, Newfoundland, 1992, pp. 153–202, p. 197.

the evidence points instead to a Moss-Bibby network. This occupied a spectrum, running from near-exclusive ownership of some vessels at either end, through a complex area in the middle where the firms shared ownership with a dozen other, smaller, owners. It is clear from changes in registration patterns during the 1850s and 1860s that the network evolved through gradual rather than sudden changes. Table 6.3 shows the ownership patterns of typical ships from each of five clearly identifiable groups of vessels within the network in 1870. In the middle of the range (groups II and III) were the 1,000 to 1,500 ton workhorses of the Mediterranean fleets. Moss and Bibby themselves were the only common element in the ownership of these vessels. 'Bibby' vessels would have around 30/64ths owned jointly by Bibby and Frederick Leyland, and the rest by around eight smaller investors including Moss, with 6/64ths. 'Moss' vessels were a mirror image: Moss owned between 20 and 30/64ths, Bibby around 5/64ths, but a different set of smaller investors took up the remaining shares.

Table 6.3 Patterns of ownership in the Moss-Bibby steam network, 1870

Group	I	II	III	IV	V
Typical vessel	Lotus, 476 tons, 7 yrs	Isis, 1,400 tons, 5 yrs	Danube, 942 tons, 14 yrs	Iberian, 1866 tons, 3 yrs	Douro, 359 tons, 6 yrs
Owners	Moss, 48	Moss, 24	Bibby/Leyland, 34	Bibby/Leyland, 43	Bibby/Leyland, 46
	Harding, 4	Bibby, 5	Cross, 2	Cross, 2	Cross, 6
	Shirley, 4	Leyland, 3	Chapple, 8	Wormold, 2	Schwabe, 12
	Duckworth, 8	Lamport, 4	Moss, 7	Schwabe, 8	
		Holt, 4	Schwabe, 8	Weatley, 6	
		Harding, 4	Benecke, 3	Benecke, 3	
		Shirley, 4	Mylius, 2		
		Duckworth, 8			
		Rathbone, 8			

Source: SR.

Other categories of vessels appear elsewhere on the spectrum. Both Bibby and Moss owned several smaller, older steamers in the 400 ton range, but these had no overlap in ownership: Bibby would own them with Frederick Leyland and J. T. Cross, while Moss favoured George Harding and Nicholas Duckworth (groups I and V). In addition, by 1870, there are signs that Bibby in particular was moving toward a more exclusive pattern in shipowning. Bibby's newest, largest steamers had a distinct pattern, with a much more focused distribution of shares between Bibby and Leyland, and, most importantly, Moss had no share in these (group IV). Getting to this point, however, was a gradual process that had taken almost two decades, and co-operative investment in much of the matrix evolved alongside more individual initiatives.

The various small investors in the large shipping operations – whose names have been only briefly mentioned up to this point – need to be considered in more detail if we are to find out how these firms actually worked. Lesser shareholders in shipping are usually cast in the role of supporting the activities of the entrepreneurial major operators while having little dynamic input themselves. Some of the lesser investors appearing in the Inman and Moss-Bibby ownership structures were indeed classic small shareholders in steamships, recruited through family or business links and often having no other shipowning interests. Charles and Thomas Inman (physician and merchant respectively) are the most obvious familial shareowners. Such structures of investment and operational management enabled shipowners to spread risk while maintaining the advantages of trust and confidence in known collaborators.[46] This is not to say that such people were only there to provide capital. In some cases, they contributed contacts and connections. Gustav Christian Schwabe, part-owner of some of Bibby's vessels, introduced Bibby to the engineering work of Edward Harland, whose Belfast shipyard subsequently built or modified a large part of Bibby's fleet in the early 1860s.[47]

The Liverpool evidence also reveals other patterns, especially in its earlier phases. Some part-owners of Moss-Bibby and Inman ships in the 1850s were not anonymous silent partners, but active shipowners in their own right. A number of owners used different partnership structures for their different activities. One common practice was to hold major parts of sailing ships and minor shares in steamers operated by one of the larger operators. This served various purposes: it provided the major steam operators with the supporting investments they needed to operate large fleets, and it enabled sailing ship owners to invest elsewhere in their own industry without necessarily shifting the bulk of their operations to steam. Firms like Cotesworth & Co. initially separated sail and steam in their ownership structures, investing in steam through the Moss-Bibby network while maintaining and developing their sail business on other routes with a different set of collaborators. Four vessels owned by Cotesworth appear in the 1855 sample. All were elderly wooden sailing ships, between 15 and 18 years old, and around 200 tons. They were used in the South American trades, and also in the Baltic. In the 1870 sample, five sailing ships appear under his name on the South American routes: none was particularly new, but they were younger than the 1855 vessels, pointing to a continued investment in sailing ships. There is also, in 1870, evidence of a hesitant investment in iron sailing ships, also being used in South America. At the same time as this steady, uncontroversial development, however, Cotesworth owned part shares in some of Bibby's Mediterranean steam fleet in the 1850s and, in later years, integrated steam more closely within its own corporate hierarchy. Its mixed sail and steam fleet in 1870 had a common ownership pattern across the board, and some of the vessels previously part-owned with Bibby had been brought fully into Cotesworth's control.[48]

Inman's closest collaborators, the Birley family, also maintained separate long-term

46 G. H. Boyce, *Information, mediation and institutional development: The rise of large-scale enterprise in British shipping, 1870–1919*, Manchester, 1995, pp. 50–53.
47 M. Moss and J. R. Hume, *Shipbuilder to the world: 125 years of Harland and Wolff, Belfast, 1861–1986*, Belfast, 1986, pp. 14–20, 507.
48 For example, *Cintra* (SR 1854/696).

business arrangements. Charles, Arthur and Thomas Birley owned wooden sailing ships which were generally used in the cotton and timber trades with the southern United States in 1870. Their usual pattern of ownership was to jointly hold a proportion of each vessel, varying on this sample from 16 shares to all 64, in collaboration with up to four other owners. Again, the Birleys' co-owners were smaller operators still, but had maintained close connections with the family over time. Joseph Thompson and William Henry Haynes both owned shares in Birley ships in 1863 and 1870, and both appear as agents for those ships in the latter year.[49]

Collaborative networks based on the 64ths system were therefore capable of providing a suitable business framework for fleet building in Liverpool's new steam sector. They also squared a circle, as the desire for individual ownership on the one hand confronted the necessity of external investment on the other. Bibby, Moss and Inman were clearly in operational control of their vessels, and the smaller owners of 64ths also maintained control of their related enterprises, while having a share in the port's most prosperous fleets. This is an important point. Having smaller owners in the 64ths fleets who were active members of the trading community offered a potential for growth that would not have been possible had the lesser owners been passive investors with limited funds. Having at least the expectation that the smaller associated firms would expand along with the major fleet companies enabled ongoing growth without resort to an ever-broadening base of small investors.

It is possible to go a step further, and argue that these collaborative networks established patterns in shipowning business that moulded the structures of many Liverpool joint-stock ventures. Some Liverpool shipowners, equally determined to build steam fleets, chose to adopt new joint-stock company forms in the 1860s. Whether chartered firms in the 'national flagship' category like Cunard, or the new joint-stock firms made legal by changes in company law in mid-century, however, many Liverpool companies had characteristics in common with the traditional forms of personal and associational shipowning.

At the very top of the scale, Liverpool's flagship company was, obviously, Cunard. With its government mail contract and fleet of large, passenger-carrying steamers, Cunard was hardly a typical shipping operation. Yet in ownership terms it had more in common with its lowlier counterparts than might be thought. Only 33 men subscribed the £300,000 raised as capital in 1840–1, almost all of them Glasgow merchants recruited by Cunard's co-founders Burns and MacIver. Changes in the late-1850s and mid-1860s consolidated ownership in the Cunard, Burns and MacIver families, and even incorporation in 1878 maintained a large element of the original structure.[50] This stands in some contrast to the other great flagship firm P&O, which had a full range of small shareholders from gentlemen to bakers, some 2,000 in number.[51]

49 For example, *Roscoe* (SR 1860/203), BE 5/6/1863/5); *Belgravia* (SR 1861/066, BE 11/06/1870/21) and *Rattler* (SR 1861/310, BE 21/6/1870/07).

50 F. E. Hyde, *Cunard and the North Atlantic, 1840–1973: A history of shipping and financial management*, London, 1975, pp. 12–25.

51 Green, 'Very private enterprise', p. 225.

Who bought shares in Liverpool joint-stock shipping companies? There are two distinct types of share distribution in Liverpool firms. A small minority spread their shareownership very widely, at least in the initial period of speculation in shares. Most, however, had very limited shareownership, often focused on the promoters themselves. The National Steam Navigation Co. is an important example of the minority group.[52] It was launched by William Fernie in October 1863. The first call for shares asked for only £20 per share, and with 20,000 shares floated, there was a considerable demand: 3,060 individuals owned some shares during the first year of the company's operation, and it is clear that the majority of them were short-term investors who sold their shares rapidly. By February 1865, there were only 1,148 shareholders, with a marked concentration of shares in the hands of larger investors. A similar pattern, on a slightly smaller scale, is found in the West India & Pacific, which had 980 shareholders in its first year, falling by the end of the 1860s to just over 300, with a much higher average holding.[53]

Some firms made an effort to attract investment from the other end of their chosen trade routes. The British & Eastern Shipping Co., established in December 1863, had 25 shareholders in Bombay and one in Mauritius, who together owned just under one-third of the firm's shares.[54] Two New York merchants owned just over half of the total shares in the Liverpool & American Steam Navigation Co. in 1867, although the firm's vessels were owned and managed in Liverpool.[55] Others found such investment less necessary. The Liverpool & Great Western had long-established connections with New York through the activities of its manager, Stephen Guion, but only belatedly acquired any shareholders there, and even then on a small scale.[56]

Overall, though, Liverpool's joint-stock shipping companies were able to concentrate their management and finance in the Liverpool trading community. While this has been known to historians in broad statistical terms for some time, a closer look at individual firms shows that power was even more concentrated than finance – on those occasions when investment from further afield was sought, control of the firm's operations generally remained firmly located on the Mersey.[57] The National, for example, with its 3,060 initial shareholders, had investors from all parts of the country, with only about 40% resident in Liverpool. The concentration within the ranks of the largest shareholders was much more pronounced, however. Only seventy-six individuals owned more than fifty shares during the first year, and no fewer than fifty-two of those shareholders were from Liverpool. Five of the original seven promoters of the firm were from Liverpool, and shareholders resident in the

52 The following statistics are derived from the company's share registers and documentation: Public Record Office, Kew (PRO), BT31 838/727c.

53 PRO, BT31 849/790c.

54 PRO, BT31 867/854c.

55 PRO, BT31 1270/3127.

56 PRO, BT31 1271/3138.

57 P. L. Cottrell, 'The steamship on the Mersey, 1815–80: Investment and ownership', in *Shipping trade and commerce: Essays in memory of Ralph Davies*, ed. P. L. Cottrell and D. H. Aldcroft, Leicester, 1981, pp. 137–63; pp. 158–60.

port owned almost 70% of the total shares, well out of proportion to their actual numbers.[58]

It is clear, therefore, that although there was no such thing as a typical Liverpool joint-stock shipping company, certain characteristics appear common enough. Most joint-stock firms were derivative of earlier shipping enterprises that had grown up in other forms. They used the existing reputations of their directors to give a 'virtual' reputation to the new company. In addition, they often had very restricted share-ownership, attracting capital from the directors and their existing business connections rather than from a broader public.

What, though, of those few firms, like Fernie's National, that took enthusiastic advantage of the ability of joint-stock status to provide considerable amounts of capital? In fact, the National was not the only joint-stock venture promoted by the Fernies, and the financial activities of the family serve to further underline the unusual nature of the National. The Fernies are an extreme case, but the extent to which they mixed old and new forms of shipowning is a valuable example of the opportunities presented by changing circumstances in mid-century. As well as the National, William James Fernie managed the Merchant's Trading Company, one of the few joint-stock firms to specialise in the operation of sailing ships. Founded in 1866, the firm had, by the early 1870s, eleven wooden and seven iron sailing ships operating in the Far East and on the west coast of South America. Most of the firm's shares were held in trust for Fernie's wife and children, with others being owned by his brother-in-law; one of Fernie's most experienced captains; and a Liverpool tug-owner who did most of the firm's work in port. Fernie had no choice but to admit, when pressed on the nature of the firm's ownership, that the company was 'simply Mr Fernie and his family'.[59]

The National was, of course rather more than that in terms of its shareownership, but perhaps not much different in terms of the operational control of the company's fleet. Fernie himself saw no need to acquire more than his original one hundred shares bought as a founding subscriber, and was clearly happy to separate management from investment in such an enterprise (provided he was the management).[60] William James Fernie's operations also overlapped with those of his brother Henry, sometimes in old style collaborative shipowning on the 64ths model, sometimes in joint-stock ventures. The *Royal Albert*, built in 1863, and owned by various combinations of Fernies, was owned jointly by the Merchant's Trading Co. and Henry Fernie & Sons in the early 1870s.[61] In the same year as that ship was being built, William James, Henry and David Fernie promoted the Liverpool & New Orleans Mail Steam Navigation Co., in a rather premature expectation that the American Civil War would soon be over.[62]

---

58   Calculated from share registers in PRO, BT31 838/727c.
59   BPP, Unseaworthy ships (1873), qq. 5,808–20, 6,061–74.
60   PRO, BT31 838/727c.
61   BPP, Unseaworthy ships (1873), q. 6,261.
62   PRO, BT31 778/425c.

The enthusiasm of the Fernies for joint-stock operations extended beyond the shipping industry into creating institutions which would handle the ever-growing volume of transatlantic bills of exchange. William James was a founding director of the British & American Exchange Banking Corporation in 1863, along with a number of other traders and members of the banking community. The need for such financial services seemed clear enough, and the company's shares were hugely oversubscribed with over 64,000 applications for 10,000 shares.[63] Scandals soon surfaced, however: the firm changed its name, presumably to disassociate itself from bad publicity; there was a case in Chancery against Fernie over alleged share-rigging; and the company was wound up after only three years.[64]

These problems aside, the tangled affairs of the Fernies also demonstrate that historians may have been underestimating the common sense of the public when it came to deciding whether a joint-stock company had some prospect of success. The Liverpool & New Orleans venture mentioned above failed to raise capital and never came into operation, indicating that the investing public had little hope of an early end to the Civil War. Three months later, the Fernies tried again, but this time reverted to the old style of networked, collaborative shipowning. The British & American Southern was founded by the same seven directors as the Liverpool & New Orleans, but was not a limited-liability company – all the funding came from the directors themselves or from the banks. Until southern ports reopened, the firm would run its vessels to New York, and in fact absorbed a less formal service on that route that the Fernies had been experimenting with for a year.[65]

While it is clearly extreme to have such a mixture of shipowning strategies at work in the same family, pragmatic adoption of new corporate forms was a defining characteristic of Liverpool's approach to changing technology and business opportunities. Guion's Liverpool & Great Western was remarked upon at the time for its hybrid corporate structure. Ships like *Idaho* and *Nevada* were owned on the 64ths model, with 16/64ths owned personally by Guion, and 48/64ths by the company.[66] Just as other entrepreneurs gathered friends and family to own a number of 64ths, Guion created a joint-stock company to own the 64ths that he did not personally hold. This nicely symbolic example of the shifting business structures of the shipping industry allowed Guion to maintain control of his operations wearing all three hats: as managing agent appointed by the Liverpool & Great Western; as director of the Liverpool & Great Western; and as a traditional 64ths partner in the Liverpool & Great Western's shipping enterprise.[67]

The 64ths system therefore proved a flexible means of attracting new investment to the shipowning business in an era of considerable change and growth. In addition, it was possible for leading entrepreneurs to maintain operational control over such

---

63   Bank, 10–17 Jan. 1863.
64   PRO, BT31 728/170c; Bank, 2 Mar. 1865.
65   Bank, 11 Aug. 1863.
66   SR 1869/80; SR 1869/4.
67   PRO, BT31 1271/3138; Bank, 27 June 1870.

operations, even if they technically only owned a minority share in the vessels. The maintenance of individual control while tapping a broader investment pool was also the priority of those adopting joint-stock structures, and patterns of scale and dispersal in shareholding point to such firms inheriting many of the long-standing localist, industry-based assumptions of the shipping business.

Small-firm traditions remained at the core of the Liverpool trading community, and the evolutionary, hybrid direction taken by some joint-stock firms demonstrates that even those moving to new models of business organisation often remained within a broad consensus. This lends support to the views of historians who see continuity of control as a central theme in the business cultures of nineteenth-century Britain.[68] While higher levels of interaction with markets and with fellow traders inevitably threatened the autonomy of individual firms, it also offered the means to increase revenues and profits, requiring a delicate balance.

Strategies for growth were therefore ultimately dependent on the ability of entrepreneurs to persuade the community that they were sound investment prospects. This was true of core shipowners seeking more people to own 64ths, of joint-stock promoters recruiting shareholders, and of traders of all kinds trying to prove their credit-worthiness in the pursuit of increased turnover. Even when, in a few cases, it was possible for individual traders to ignore the opinions of the community as a whole and succeed on the basis of tight financial control and steady nerves, they still needed the confidence of at least a few customers. The great majority of traders had to rely on the favourable views of leading members of the community, and the complex information networks required to make this system work are the main concern of the next chapter.

68   Payne, 'Family business in Britain', p. 173.

Chapter 7

INSECURITY, INFORMATION
AND REPUTATION

On 25 July 1870, James Jenkinson Bibby made the short journey from his firm's offices in Water Street to the Bank of England building in Castle Street. He carried with him a list of his shareholdings in US government bonds, Mersey Docks & Harbour Board bonds, and a range of British and foreign railway companies including the great international ventures of the day such as the Moscow Jaroslav. He offered the Bank's agent a choice of anything on the list to stand as security for a loan, which was in turn to be spent on further stocks and bonds. Nothing about this was unusual except for its scale. Bibby wanted £100,000 from the Bank, and the list of securities he offered came to £772,868. The Bank's agent noted – with classic bank manager understatement – that Bibby's record gave him good claim to be 'liberally dealt with'.[1]

J. J. Bibby, as we saw in chapter six, was at the peak of his shipowning career, after a lifetime in the Mediterranean steam trades in which he had deftly co-ordinated the efforts of a network of family and friends to build a large fleet working one of the port's most lucrative routes. For other members of the community, reaching similar heights was possible, but staying there much harder. Edward Oliver seemed to be heading for shipowning greatness in the early 1850s, with a huge fleet and the confidence of important traders. The collapse of his firm in 1854, considered in more detail later in this chapter, stunned the port and threatened the prospects of several major businesses. Oliver's reputation vanished with his business, especially when it became clear that he was obstructing rather than assisting efforts to investigate his activities.[2]

Most members of the trading community followed paths between these extremes of success and failure, although in any given year they might swing closer to one than the other. Whatever the circumstances, their continued activity depended on their standing in the eyes of fellow traders. This was true in normal business, when they needed to maintain the all-important level of credit-worthiness. It was also necessary to build a more general reputation, however, as an insurance for difficult times, when unlucky traders might need help to stay afloat. This was particularly true because traders of all kinds tended to see their business as being characterised by risk and uncertainty in mid-century. Whether they were wealthy merchants in lucrative trades, or more humble sailing ship owners in the less glamorous world of bulk carrying, traders feared that they were always one shipwreck or bad debt away

---

1 Bank, 25 July 1870.
2 Bank, 6 Oct. 1854.

from the ruin of their firms. They were less likely to acknowledge – although their critics frequently made the point – that mercantile business had always been risky, and that the risks worked both ways, sometimes leading to considerable wealth.

This chapter considers attitudes to success and failure, and the various strategies adopted by traders to avoid excessive risk and persuade their colleagues and a broader public that they were responsible and reputable. The first section examines the backdrop of key issues cited by contemporaries in their complaints about the uncertainties of the traders' lot. The second section considers the complex networks of information that surrounded the credit-worthiness of firms, and the problems faced by traders in securing sufficiently accurate information on which to base decisions: it also notes, however, the apparent willingness of some firms to take considerable risks in their lending and credit practices. The strategies adopted to persuade a wider audience of the respectability of the new joint-stock firms are the subject of the final section, reflecting the pragmatic adaptation of traditional attitudes to the requirements of a high-profile element in the trading community.

VULNERABILITIES

Free trade and free shipping were the building blocks of the mid-nineteenth-century liberalisation of Britain's mercantile economy. Achieving these goals required the repeal of a series of long-standing laws, mainly in the course of a dramatic decade of reform around 1850. As in any period of rapid change, there was considerable uncertainty and unease amongst those most likely to be affected. In particular, the repeal of the Navigation Acts in 1849 was seen by many British shipowners as a devastating act of betrayal by government, which undermined their livelihoods and threatened the very survival of their industry. Repeal removed the complex system of protection and regulation that, for almost two centuries, had defined the shipown-ers' role as guardians of the nation's traded wealth. In the seventeenth and eighteenth centuries, British shipping had been subject to a range of regulations which enforced vessel registration, defined patterns of trade and restricted the nationality of crews. The same laws gave British shipowners a monopoly of imperial and coastal trade, and operated – most of the time – as a reasonable compromise between the interests of traders and of government. While earlier generations of historians sometimes accepted the propaganda of the American Revolution and saw British trade laws as repressive and parasitic, more recent studies have concluded that mercantile interests throughout Britain's Atlantic empire prospered under the umbrella of the Navigation Acts.[3]

What seemed reasonable in the Atlantic economy of the eighteenth century was much less appropriate to the ever-broadening global markets of the mid-nineteenth, however. Repeal of the Navigation Acts was welcomed by large parts of Britain's mercantile classes, including some shipowners who believed that their industry was

---

3 For a recent summary of the debates, see L. Sawers, 'The Navigation Acts revisited', *Economic History Review*, Vol. 45, 1992, pp. 262–84.

complacent and lacking in innovative drive. In individual ports, varying commodity and shipping priorities coloured attitudes toward repeal, creating unpredictable fault lines. Liverpool's commodity traders generally wanted a free choice of shipping, and to be able to choose the best suppliers of the service. Those dealing in North American produce were prominent in favouring repeal, as were the port's rising South American traders, who believed that their business would expand still further in a deregulated atmosphere.[4] These merchants wanted the opportunity to create more complex trading patterns, in which vessels visited foreign countries and British colonies at different points in a chain of voyages designed to make more efficient use of seasonal variations in commodities and sailing conditions. On the other side of the argument, opposition came from Liverpool's few remaining shipbuilders; allied interests in the timber sector who feared an overhaul of their comfortable niche in the Canadian trade; and the older West India traders, who had maintained integrated business structures using their own shipping. This grouping – particularly the timber trade – still wielded enough local influence to make Liverpool's MPs cautious in their public statements. The town elected Edward Cardwell to the Commons in 1847 after a clever campaign in which he made no concrete statements about the Navigation Acts, but rather, in classic Liverpool fashion, managed to mix 'commercial freedom and religious toleration' without defining either. Importantly, though, both Liverpool MPs went on to vote for repeal, and Cardwell later introduced further Bills to Parliament aimed at removing the few remaining elements of protection.[5]

Analysing the impact of these fundamental changes in the regulatory environment is fraught with difficulty. Pessimistic elements in the industry prophesied mass bankruptcies and the disappearance of the British merchant fleet in the wake of repeal, but in fact the early 1850s saw a coincidental boom in shipping, thanks to increasing emigration to Australia and North America, and to the demand for transport vessels during the Crimean War. These were both areas in which Liverpool shipowners did well, cushioning whatever blows might have resulted from repeal of the Navigation Acts. By the time the industry went into a slump later in the decade, the agenda had moved on, and only the most reactionary elements of the shipping interest still argued for protectionism: 'our shipowners need not, and the intelligent amongst them *do not*, fear competition with the world'.[6]

Some went further, arguing that the drive and motivation of Britain's shipowners had been raised by the challenge brought by broader competition. British vessels working in the American cotton trade, it was acknowledged, had been 'very inferior', in the first quarter of the nineteenth century, but had been improved beyond all recognition by the efforts of shipowners determined to overhaul the industry.[7] Under

---

4   BPP, Navigation Acts (Lords) (1848), evidence of Thomas Bouch, q. 2,130; BPP, Navigation Acts (Commons) (1848), evidence of Charles Brownell, q. 2,710.

5   S. Palmer, *Politics, shipping and the repeal of the Navigation Acts*, Manchester, 1990, pp. 109, 130, 156, 176–7.

6   W. S. Lindsay, *Our merchant shipping: Its present state considered*, London, 1860, p. 238.

7   BPP, Merchant shipping (1860), evidence of T. M. Mackay, q. 5,156.

free trade, 'everybody seemed put on his mettle ... previously the power of British shipowners to compete was under-rated, and the power of foreign shipowners turned out to be over-rated'.[8] Some of the wealthiest shipowners had certainly done their cause no good when arguing in favour of protection. Shipowners bemoaning their lot in front of Parliamentary Committees were often treated unsympathetically, with sarcastic questions designed to cast them as backward and greedy. In the debates over repeal of the Navigation Acts, some in the industry argued that 'British shipowners have not for the last twenty years made money.'[9] Apart from the obvious question of why they wanted to maintain the Navigation Acts if they were doing so little to help the industry, major shipowners were simply unconvincing in the role of poverty-stricken victims. Leading London shipowner Duncan Dunbar, who claimed that he and his colleagues were the 'worst paid people in the world', was already making his fortune in the Far East trades, and winning significant government troop-carrying contracts – he confessed when pressured that he expected a 40% profit on all his voyages. When he died in 1862, Dunbar left an estate worth £1.5m.[10]

Just how vulnerable were members of the trading community? There was, and is, a perception that many mercantile firms in Victorian England were short-lived, ill-founded ventures which were no more than a vehicle for their founders' gambling in the markets. Some of this thinking was based on the sector's earlier reputation: systematic evidence from the eighteenth century demonstrates that merchants were more likely to become bankrupt than any other occupational group, but that they also had a good chance of becoming wealthy.[11] Contemporaries believed that firms had a high rate of bankruptcy and failure, especially in the early years of their existence – it is, however, dangerous to make assumptions about the difficulties of short-lived firms when those firms are of course precisely those about which we know least.[12] Nonetheless, historians are beginning to prove that longevity was not a common characteristic of the mid-Victorian firm, even among honest traders. Recent studies taking a rounded look at local business communities have highlighted the short life-span of most firms, with many being wound up on the retirement or death of their founders, and many businessmen failing several times before finally achieving some medium-term stability.[13] When the impact of a series of economic shocks, like those of the mid-nineteenth century, is considered against this general background, the chances of many firms lasting very long seem slim.

---

8 BPP, Merchant shipping (1860), evidence of W. J. Lamport, q. 2,577.

9 BPP, Navigation Acts (Commons) (1848), evidence of William Imrie, q. 7,581.

10 BPP, Navigation Acts (Commons) (1848), evidence of Duncan Dunbar, qq. 4,303–6; W. D. Rubinstein, 'British millionaires, 1809–1949', *Bulletin of the Institute of Historical Research*, Vol. 47, 1974, pp. 202–23; p. 207.

11 J. Hoppit, *Risk and failure in English business, 1700–1800*, Cambridge, 1987, pp. 96–103.

12 P. L. Cottrell, *Industrial finance, 1830–1914: The finance and organisation of English manufacturing industry*, London, 1980, p. 35.

13 S. Nenadic, 'The small family firm in Victorian Britain', *Business History*, Vol. 35, 1993, pp. 86–114, p. 93; R. Church, 'Ossified or dynamic? Structure, markets and the competitive process in the British business system of the nineteenth century', *Business History*, Vol. 42, no. 1, 2000, pp. 1–20, p. 14.

On the other hand, it is clear that some problems in the trading environment in the 1850s and 1860s were caused by the lucrative image of shipping and trade as a profession – many more people than ever before were entering most sectors of business. Shipping, with its higher capital costs, suffered the most obvious problems of over-capacity. As increasing numbers of ships competed for trade, shipowners' incomes fell and costs rose: 'these dull times, they seem disposed to put a ship to all the expense possible'.[14] Liverpool's owners generally located responsibility for this situation within the industry itself, however, rather than blaming official regulation or trade policies. Established owners and operators bemoaned the presence in the market of excess shipping. Many of the vessels built during the mid-50s boom, it was claimed, were of poor quality and made little lasting contribution to the business: 'There are many ships, in consequence of those speculations, which are now sailing about and competing with us, which ought to be now growing in the woods of America.'[15] There was also concern that such vessels were owned by a new class of inexperienced owners and operators in mid-century, which took advantage of cheaper shipping and easy finance to acquire ships: 'Unhappily, there is too much of it, and it must in time produce a serious reaction.'[16]

Major commodity trades went the same way, with cotton speculators a favourite scapegoat for the financial crises of the period.[17] The fragmentation of the cotton market was such that major operators faced considerable competition from small firms. Barings reckoned that 25–30 Liverpool cotton houses sent representatives to Manchester weekly 'drumming for orders', and that competition drove down commissions to the point where some traders were willing to work on a no-profit, no-commission basis. In such an environment, it was all too easy for 'the man of straw to do as well within 1 or 1½% as the most wealthy operator'.[18] In addition, while the men of straw may have been vulnerable in times of crisis, there were clearly others to take their place, as reflected in the increased numbers of those handling some cotton in the later 1860s.

A broad measure of the fluidity of the trading community can be calculated from the Bills of Entry. At the crudest level, the figures are as follows. Of all cargoes in the 1870 Bills of Entry sample used throughout this book, 2,035 different firms or individuals appear as consignees. Of these, only 432 had appeared in the same sample in 1855. In other words, we can conclude, very roughly, that four in every five trading firms active in importing in 1870 had entered the business within the previous fifteen years. Of course, the qualifications that need to surround such figures are considerable. Merchants might well have been in business in different partnerships, or performing functions other than direct importing, at the time of the previous sample, and it should not be assumed that those four in every five were newly-established speculators.

14   George Matthews to Fisher & Co., 22 Dec. 1857, Matthews papers.
15   BPP, Merchant shipping (1860), evidence of W. J. Lamport, q. 2,765.
16   Tonge, Curry & Co., circular, quoted in *The Times*, 6 Jan. 1852, p. 3.
17   S. Smith, *My life-work*, London, 1902, p. 18.
18   Barings, 9 Mar. 1860.

Nonetheless, the evidence points to a considerable level of turnover in the ranks of the trading community in this period.

The following sections consider mechanisms by which traders sought to deal with that fluidity and uncertainty in mid-century Liverpool. It will already be apparent from the discussion in the last two chapters that traders had to achieve a fine balance between their desire for independence and their need to co-operate on various levels with other members of the mercantile community. An extensive web of contacts, obligations and assurances underpinned the position of any trading firm relative to the others. Some of the variables in this equation – trust and reputation, for example – are much less objectively measurable than others. Yet we cannot simply write off these issues as unknowable, because contemporaries were clearly able to reach sophisticated judgements about reliability, appropriate behaviour and investments, and the extent of blame when things went wrong.

INFORMATION, DEPENDENCE AND FINANCE

Although rarely explicitly stated, the common assumption of those overseeing financial matters in a port like Liverpool was that traders would operate in close collaboration with 'family' and 'friends', and that finance gathered from these sources was much more likely to generate a stable and prosperous business than anything raised in a wider market. The words are in inverted commas simply to highlight their slightly broader meanings: family often included quite distant relatives, while friends were often more senior members of the community willing to vouch for less-prominent traders, and were seen more as mentors than personal friends. Contemporary opinion-formers wrote approvingly of traders who had start-up capital from relatives; of younger members of the trading community who had been apprenticed with respectable firms, often allowed to do some business on their own account while still under the 'umbrella' of the older companies; and of firms that had the support and favour of the community as a whole, even, in some cases, if they had suffered some commercial embarrassment and were trying to work their way back into the business.

Keeping business in the family is probably the most widely used and best known antidote to the dangers of the market. The last two chapters have demonstrated the importance of family connections in shipowning especially. It must be stressed, however, that family-based business strategies were not limited to the most obvious approach whereby family members pooled their resources to operate a single business. Instead, members of extended families were often in related local businesses, establishing networks of firms as an alternative to concentrating all of the family's resources into one larger, more integrated operation. As has long been recognised by historians, such family networks could operate on an international scale. Early modern trade is a particularly rich source for this, with various members of mercantile families being identified in corners of Britain's Atlantic empire.[19] In the nineteenth century also,

19 For the most recent major study, see D. Hancock, *Citizens of the world: London merchants and the integration of the British Atlantic community, 1735–1785*, Cambridge, 1995.

there are numerous cases in the literature of trading companies where partners were sent on extensive tours of other countries, sometimes to establish branch houses run by family members, sometimes to cultivate links with firms at the other end of a potential trading chain that were as close as any kinship tie.[20]

This pattern not only applied to Liverpool firms expanding abroad, but also worked the other way. A number of groups are readily identifiable in the Liverpool trading community in mid-century. American and European firms in particular had extensive representation in Liverpool at that time. Alexander Brown, having moved from Ulster to Baltimore in 1800, founded a mercantile dynasty that involved sending his sons to form branches elsewhere. William Brown came to Liverpool in 1810, and subsequent branches were formed in Philadelphia and New York.[21] Perhaps the most prominent, because of their easily recognisable names, are the 'Greek' merchants. Although most attention has been paid to their operations in Manchester and London, various firms from the eastern Mediterranean had a presence in Liverpool.[22]

Such multinational merchant houses were at the extreme top end of the mercantile spectrum, of course, and few traders could claim to be supported by such impressive family networks. At the other extreme, merchants working on their own had problems appearing secure and stable enough to be trusted in business. While partnerships, family or otherwise, were considered a respectable form of business structure, traders operating with only their own resources were viewed with suspicion, or at least unease. Those who did work alone often added '& Co.' to their names anyway, or maintained an earlier form of their firm's name, for example, as it had been when a father or brother owned it. The implication of such behaviour is that the community saw partnerships as having more solid foundations and being less vulnerable to dangers than traders working on their own. The Bank of England agent usually mentioned in his reports when a trader had no partner, and such information was clearly meant to signal caution – for example, in reinforcing the alleged 'very modest means' and previous failure of one E. J. Hore.[23]

Traders at all levels made the most of contacts that they formed with senior members of the community, who could act as facilitators, making connections and easing negotiations. This activity is of course impossible to quantify, but such examples that exist suggest a widespread informal web of obligation and favour woven through the trading community. The relationship between Captain J. F. Wooley and Liverpool iron merchant James Stitt stands out as an example of the process.[24] Wooley was, apparently, in the fairly common position of a master mariner trading on his own account and working toward a career in shipowning or merchant trading. How he first established a connection with Stitt is unclear, but in

---

20 For example, S. Chapman, *Merchant enterprise in Britain: From the industrial revolution to World War I*, Cambridge, 1992, chap. 4.

21 J. Killick, 'Risk, specialisation and profit in the mercantile sector of the nineteenth century cotton trade: Alexander Brown and Sons, 1820–80', *Business History*, Vol. 16, 1974, pp. 1–16; p. 1.

22 Chapman, *Merchant enterprise*, pp. 153–66.

23 Bank, 19 July 1855.

24 The evidence relating to this case comes from Stitt papers, box 3, unless otherwise cited.

1855 Wooley was referring to Stitt as a 'friend and patron', and Stitt had held a power of attorney over Wooley's affairs (while the latter was at sea), since 1852. Wooley had clearly accumulated some debts in recent voyages, and had the sort of financial difficulty endemic in Victorian business: he had a broadly reliable operation which promised reasonable returns, but short-term problems with cash-flow tended to arise frequently.

Late in 1855, Wooley appealed to Stitt for help after a voyage from Mauritius. Wooley expressed regret at having to involve Stitt, which sounds like formulaic grovelling but may well be genuine – Wooley's *Baron of Bramber* arrived in Albert Dock on 6 October, and was in Salthouse awaiting an outward cargo by the 17th, but it was not until late November that Wooley contacted Stitt, having clearly done a good deal of work in securing his situation in the meantime.[25]

Like any other visiting ship's master, Wooley needed the services of a range of 'official' intermediaries like shipping agents, but he also needed a less formal guarantor and facilitator to vouch for his trustworthiness. By the time he approached Stitt, Wooley had already negotiated an outward charter for the vessel and a delay in paying the ship's agents for the incoming expenses, but he hoped that the proceeds of these arrangements would go further if Stitt could channel the money through his banker at lower rates than were available to lesser members of the community. Wooley would then, in effect, be able to repay more debt with the same income.

Stitt's motives in getting Wooley and the *Baron* back to sea are not evident in the surviving material. He went to some lengths, paying bills of more than £1,200 to various agents and writing to other contacts who either owed Wooley money or held some kind of security from him. On the other hand, Stitt did not drop his usual business caution, and did not make long-term or open-ended commitments. When paying bills he was always careful to stress that his involvement did not imply any liability for future losses incurred by Wooley.

However much traders may have liked the ideal of being able to operate from within the resources of family, friends or partners, many firms at some point had to move out into the broader community in pursuit of finance or services, and all of course had to seek customers and clients in the wider world. Perhaps the key area in which traders were most reliant on each other was in defining credit-worthiness. Given the nature of mercantile funding in this period, this was inevitable, but remains strangely invisible in much historical writing. Again, this is probably a symptom of our tendency to study the largest firms and neglect the smaller companies.

The central assumption of mercantile finance in this period was that business transactions would involve credit arrangements between firms, rather than between traders and banks. This was a natural evolution from a previous era in which there were no banks – medieval and early-modern merchants had to develop systems of credit and finance amongst themselves, and bills of exchange drawn by merchants on each other continued to be the backbone of commercial finance long after banks became common in the nineteenth century. Indeed, when an increasing number of

25   BE, 6 Oct., 6 Dec. 1855; DR, Albert, 6 Oct. 1855.

private, local banks did try to establish themselves in mid-century, they often took risks with their lending that reflected badly on the sector as a whole. The apparent willingness of some banks to finance the purchase of shipping in particular created fragile networks of finance, mortgage and insurance in a volatile market prone to a range of natural and man-made disasters. Loans to overextended shipping firms like Wilson & Chambers were responsible for the suspension of the Royal Bank in Liverpool in 1867.[26] Banks began to develop their deposit and overdraft business significantly only in the last quarter of the century, and the rise in trade and mercantile activity in mid-century was managed through rapid expansion of the old bill-of-exchange system. The volume of bills of exchange in circulation may have as much as quadrupled in the fifteen years after 1844.[27] Banks played a crucial role in this growth, but their key service was as information brokers rather than lenders: banks became custodians of information about traders, and the extent to which they could be trusted.

The bill-of-exchange system was, in theory, a very straightforward mechanism of assigning an agreed monetary value to goods and services without having to use cash.[28] Its implications for the conduct of trade, and for the interaction of trading communities, were far-reaching, and a number of issues need to be considered. Bills of exchange by their very nature created complicated connections between traders. At their most straightforward, bills would be drawn by one firm on another, with a cash payment made to cover the bill at its due date, usually some months after issue to allow for the delivery of the goods in question. Inevitably, however, most firms did not have such one-dimensional affairs, and would be owed sums from several parties while also owing sums to several more. Bills were therefore often signed on to a third party to cover another transaction, and perhaps to several more down the chain before finally coming full circle. Often, discounters would cash bills for a commission, earning a profit while easing the cash-flow of the firm holding the bill.

Two serious consequences emerge from these patterns. First, the entire system relied on a pool of information on the reliability and financial strength of trading firms, which enabled traders to decide whether those approaching them for extended credit where to be trusted or not. Secondly, bills of exchange, when discounted and signed on frequently in times of extreme financial speculation, could be used to construct houses of cards, liable to collapse should any of a number of parties involved in complicated transactions suffer a commercial setback.

Firms relied on powerful friends for support beyond the directly financial. It was important to maintain good relations with major traders, and especially with the banking community, because of the complex circuit of information, rumour and gossip that characterised the interplay of the trading community. Various such

---

26 *The Times*, 22 Oct. 1867, p. 5; W. Oldham, *The Ismay Line*, Liverpool, 1961, p. 28.

27 B. L. Anderson and P. L. Cottrell, 'Another Victorian capital market: A study of banking and bank investors on Merseyside', *Economic History Review*, Vol. 28, 1975, pp. 598–615; pp. 602–3.

28 R. Muir, *A practical summary of the law relating to bills of exchange and promissory notes*, Edinburgh, 1836, pp. 1–4.

information networks existed. Larger firms with branches in a number of ports devoted a notable proportion of their correspondence to assessments of the reliability and good standing of local firms with whom business was being contemplated. Barings (Liverpool and London) and the various branches of the Brown family in the US cotton ports were prodigious gatherers of such information.[29]

One of the most powerful of these information brokers in mid-century Liverpool was the Bank of England's local agent, who sought evidence of the standing of local firms from a range of sources, reporting to other members of the financial community and, of course, to the Bank in London. The agent regularly sought information on firms from other local bankers, and reported in detail – there was clearly an established protocol by which Liverpool's banks discussed their clients with one another. Occasionally, London requested information on someone unknown to the agent or his regular sources of intelligence. This required resort to less conventional methods, as in the case where the agent was asked to offer an opinion on one John Horsfall – the agent reported shortly afterwards that Horsfall appeared respectable, living in a small house which seemed 'very neatly kept'.[30]

This image of Bank of England staff prowling the streets of Liverpool taking notes on the tidiness of traders' houses would be comical, but it reflects a culture of information without which mid-Victorian business could not have functioned. As has been clear from the evidence in the last two chapters, most commodity-trading firms operated on a small scale, with a relatively small amount of capital: had they been forced to rely on their own capital as security for every transaction, most smaller firms would have done virtually no business. Active trade in goods and services was only feasible if the competence of the firm could also be counted as security – virtual collateral, as it were – with the community's good opinion of a firm allowing the company to trade on credit.

As would be expected, however, this was a world with unwritten rules and many thin lines which were easy to cross. Particularly close financial relationships between firms could attract suspicion, because it was feared that firms drawing extensive bills on each other ('cross-drafts', in the jargon) were building on unstable foundations. The practice was common enough, though, especially between shipowners and firms in the port service industries. Ships' stores dealers Cearns & Brown, for example, drew bills on shipping operators Pilkington & Wilson for provisions supplied to the latter's ships. At the same time, though, bills were being drawn in the opposite direction to cover shares that Cearns & Brown owned in Pilkington & Wilson's ships. Such incestuous financial arrangements, not subject to the scrutiny of the port's broader financial networks, worried the banks.[31]

In addition, even when financial arrangements were more widely known, the information networks constructed by the trading community were not always reliable. Mistakes could be made in assessing the activities of firms, and because the process

---

29   Killick, 'Risk, specialisation and profit', p. 10.
30   Bank, 30 Aug. 1850.
31   Bank, 6 Feb. 1855.

was really just one of glorified rumour, there was ample scope for malicious misinformation to enter the system. The Bank of England received a threatening solicitor's letter in August 1855 alleging that the agent had spread rumours of the suspension of Syers, Walker & Co., news which would certainly have spread to India and possibly done the firm considerable damage.[32] The agent denied having done so, but other examples show that it was hard to distinguish between keeping the financial community informed and simply passing on every unconfirmed and uncorroborated story.

Indeed, reputation was such a vital element in a firm's operation that zealous efforts to quash rumours and clear names sometimes led to broader publicity than the original incident. A case in 1860 in which a German vessel was erroneously charged the wrong rate of dock fees in Liverpool reached the British and German press, not because of the minor administrative mistake, but because the parties concerned were determined that no hint of malpractice should attach to them. The agents, Heyn & Co., demanded an apology for what they saw as an implication that they had bribed port officers to give the vessel preferential treatment, while the Dock Board insisted that it be clearly stated that its employees did not take bribes – what could have been settled by a simple refund of £19 became a public battle over honour and reputation.[33]

The information machine was particularly prone to leaving the rails during times of intense speculation and uncertainty in particular markets. Even when firms did everything right, however, they had to remember that they were operating in an uncertain world. When Manchester calico printers Barratt & Wilson approached the North and South Wales Bank for information on the Liverpool shipping firm of J. P. Hall & Co., they were informed that the company was 'safe for any business engagement they were likely to undertake'. Two weeks later, with a deal done for £647 worth of goods, Hall & Co. suspended operations owing £22,000. Barrett & Wilson sued the Bank, but lost – the jury argued the bank should be completely exonerated, and could not be expected to know everything about their clients' affairs.[34]

In any case, it is clear that even experienced traders either acted against the general advice of the community or allowed themselves to be swept up in a process that outgrew their control if they thought the opportunity was lucrative enough. In addition, there was a tendency to claim – once the dust had settled – that problems had long been foreseen, but some element of hindsight must be creeping in here.

The example of Edward Oliver is instructive. Liverpool's largest owner of wooden sailing ships, Oliver had built a fleet of around one hundred ships by 1854.[35] He did this by accumulating an enormous debt from his fellow shipowners, and particularly from those involved in Liverpool's timber trade. When his business collapsed under the weight of these obligations, it emerged that he owed eighty-four individuals and

---

32   Bank, 8 Mar. 1855.
33   *The Times*, 27 Apr. 1860, p. 9; 11 Dec. 1860, p. 9.
34   *The Times*, 31 Aug. 1855, p. 8.
35   *Liverpool Chronicle*, 6 Jan. 1855, p. 2.

firms a total of just over £680,000.[36] When news broke of Oliver's initial difficulties early in October 1854, the Bank of England agent reached a quick conclusion: 'this is the beginning of the catastrophe which I predicted some time ago would befall those parties who went too rashly into shipping and raised the market fully 25%'.[37] Fair enough, but if it had all been so obvious, and particularly if Oliver really lacked 'a good character for integrity and honesty of purpose', how was he able to ensnare so many major, experienced traders in such a vulnerable enterprise?[38]

Although an extreme case, the extent of Oliver's connections with the rest of the trading community illustrates patterns that are also to be found in more normal circumstances. The network of finance that surrounded Oliver was not an ill-informed and gullible mass of small investors largely ignorant of the shipping industry – quite the contrary. Leading Liverpool traders not only supported Oliver financially, but were vocal in their public support of his activities until the very end. They even went so far as to post a notice at the Liverpool Exchange condemning reports (accurate as it turned out) that Oliver was about to fail to an unprecedented extent.[39] The creditors also, inevitably, remained tied to his affairs and to each other for some time after the collapse. When some of Oliver's vessels were sold at auction, no fewer than 15 out of 18 were sold to creditors trying to salvage something solid from the business.[40]

The list of Oliver's creditors reads like a promotional directory of Liverpool's leading traders. Some were as questionable in their trading practices as he was. James McHenry was Oliver's largest single creditor, to the tune of £66,400.[41] His own business was if anything even shakier, and he recorded liabilities late in 1854 amounting to £366,000, mostly through a complex network of his own agency houses in Philadelphia and New York.[42] Not surprisingly, McHenry's situation was not sustainable, and he negotiated a compromise with his creditors by which he paid back only 2s 6d in the pound. By 1860, however, he was back in some prosperity, although operating on the fringes of the community. Barings considered his activities 'a mystery', noting that he lacked any standing in Liverpool and asked for no credit, but nonetheless managed a large business in the export of railway iron. Financial backing, he claimed, came from a trading house in Paris and from an agency negotiated with the US government, and there was evidence that he had made considerable sums from shares in the Lake Erie railroad.[43] Indeed, McHenry became a well-known figure in American railway circles, continuing to use his Liverpool connections, not always with the full approval of his collaborators, to raise finance for ventures such as the Atlantic & Great Western Railroad.[44]

---

36   Bank, 9 Oct. 1854.
37   Bank, 3 Oct. 1854.
38   Bank, 5 Oct. 1854.
39   *The Times*, 28 Aug. 1857, p. 5.
40   *The Times*, 8 Dec. 1854, p. 6.
41   Bank, 9 Oct. 1854.
42   Barings, 9 Dec. 1854.
43   Barings, 18 Sept. 1860; Bank, 25 Sept. 1863.
44   Anderson and Cottrell, 'Another Victorian capital market', p. 613.

Fernie Brothers, owed just over £31,000 by Oliver, were also high on the list of usual suspects, and were not deflected from their activities by Oliver's demise. While operating on a large scale, they were not considered safe. Applying for a discount account with the Bank of England in 1858 – at which point they claimed to have an impressive capital of £150,000 – they clearly worried the manager. The Fernies had been closely connected with the failed Borough Bank, and the community, it seemed, had not trusted explanations put forward for their role.[45] Undaunted, the Fernies, as has been noted in previous chapters, went on to launch a number of varyingly successful shipping and financial enterprises in the 1860s.

Other firms continued to have considerable liabilities with members of the community, although rarely attracting such suspicion. Traders accepted that theirs was a risky business anyway, and did not necessarily change their practices in the aftermath of a particular crisis. Kirk & Furniss, for example, might have been more careful to spread their obligations thinly after losing £37,112 to Oliver, but in fact the firm continued to operate large accounts, and suspended trading early in 1855, having held another £15,000 on the failed firm of W. H. Hammond & Co.[46]

Finally, what of the firms that lost money to Oliver, survived, and appear to have no stain on their character? Rankin Gilmour are an obvious example. The firm was owed just under £14,000 by Oliver (although Barings put the figure at £20,000), and Robert Rankin was chosen as a member of the committee of five that attempted to salvage something from the wreckage.[47] Rankins survived and continued as major players in Liverpool's Canadian trade throughout the nineteenth century, but the Oliver affair appears to have been wiped from the corporate memory of the firm. Although generally very detailed, and containing accounts of many events of the period including a number of crises, the Rankin house history makes no mention of Oliver.[48]

The Oliver case demonstrates both the best and the worst of the Liverpool community's financial networks. Traders could raise considerable sums from other members of the community; they could rely on their creditors to support them in times of difficulty; and the community as a whole could absorb a great deal of damage in times of crisis. It was also, however, an environment open to abuse, and to the deliberate manipulation of otherwise legitimate trading practices with a view to accumulating unsustainable liabilities, which might then be avoided by absconding or otherwise evading creditors.

Deciding where to draw that line between fraud and misfortune was a difficult task in mid-century, closely tied to entrenched attitudes toward success and failure, and the way each was achieved. Mercantile fortunes attracted a range of judgemental positions. Indeed, such attitudes were written into the legal system as it dealt with

45   Bank, 27 Jan. 1858.
46   Bank, 9 Oct. 1854, 10 Feb. 1855.
47   Bank, 4 Oct. 1854.
48   J. Rankin, *A history of our firm: Some account of the firm of Pollock, Gilmour & Co., and its offshoots and connections*, Liverpool, 1908.

bankruptcy and the failure of businesses. The Bankruptcy Commissioners in the 1850s were required to classify each case according to the extent of blame they felt rested with the trader in question, and issue three classes of certificate accordingly. The whole question hinged on 'unavoidable losses and misfortunes'. Bankrupts of the first class were deemed to have failed as a result of such events. For those of the second class, failure had 'not wholly arisen' from such circumstances. The implication for those of the third class was yet more damning: their losses had not arisen from forces beyond their control.[49]

Such wording was not ideal, of course. This kind of criticism by implication did not provide the trading community with the sort of clear-cut decisions it might have wanted. Some would rather have had more explicit statements of the conduct of the trader, with more stringent classification in terms of the 'legitimate pursuit of the trade', a lack of 'proper care and discretion' and, at worst, 'misconduct'. But that might have made some of those running the system still less likely to issue third-class certificates – as it was, some Commissioners were reluctant to classify a trader in a way that seemed 'equivalent to stamping him with a brand as a felon'.[50] Such problems in application of the law were compounded by a lack of direction in legislation. Bankruptcy Acts came and went with alarming rapidity in the mid-nineteenth century, as Parliament imposed a series of contradictory and unpopular measures which cumulatively did little to encourage faith in the system.[51]

Against this background, trading communities more often than not made up their own minds about the prospects of their members. The less official process by which creditors dealt with failing firms balanced the apportioning of blame against the prospect of retrieving something from the wreckage. Traders faced with a firm in trouble had to take difficult decisions. Too much pressure on a struggling firm could easily result in total failure and the recovery of virtually none of the funds owed. When a trader was in good standing with the community, and the circumstances seemed genuinely redeemable, it was generally considered better to take a lenient position in the hope of eventually securing at least some of the outstanding money.

The case of Alexander LaFone is a useful example. Well respected in the Liverpool community, LaFone worked in partnership with his brother Samuel, who was based in Monte Video. In 1858, Alexander found himself with liabilities of £246,549 and, in effect, no assets, because all the firm's property was in South America and Samuel had been too slow in shipping goods or cash to meet the accumulating debts. A meeting of creditors heard that Alexander had repeatedly urged his brother to act, and that matters were now turning round: the creditors accepted LaFone's promise to pay all debts within eighteen months, and expressed their sympathy for his predicament.[52]

49 BPP, Bankruptcy Commission (1854), evidence of William Murray, q. 1,277.

50 BPP, Bankruptcy Commission (1854), evidence of John Howell, q. 1,428; evidence of Frederick Reed, q. 1,631.

51 V. M. Batzel, 'Parliament, businessmen and bankruptcy, 1825–1883: A study in middle class alienation', *Canadian Journal of History*, Vol. 18, 1983, pp. 171–86; pp. 174–75.

52 Bank, 30 Mar. 1858.

LaFone's fellow traders were operating on a series of unspoken assumptions about the overall prosperity of the trading community. Historians of business culture have compared this approach to a public school sports philosophy, based on the premise that the existence of stronger and weaker players and teams was a natural element in the structure of any social context.[53] Total annihilation of weaker teams was counter-productive because there would in time be no-one left to play against. In business, a similar principle was maintained, in that smaller firms served functions in the broader trading environment that helped rather than hindered the market leaders.

Not everyone agreed with this view of the trading community. Some rather more individualistic traders preferred to work outside the norms, and took a particularly hard line when confronted with firms that could not pay their debts. Such characters found themselves in the paradoxical position of being less well-regarded as successes than some of their colleagues were as failures. A good example of this is Edward Bates, who amassed a considerable business despite having broadly alienated many of his contemporaries. The Bank of England's agent noted grudgingly that Bates' shipping firm had made huge profits from carrying Far East cotton during the crisis years of the early 1860s, to the point where Bates had accumulated a personal fortune of at least £200,000 – this did not, however, persuade him to withdraw a previous judgement that Bates' operations were 'dangerous'.[54] Part of the negative impression surrounding Bates stemmed from his own attitudes to other traders who fell upon difficult times. When cotton merchants Nicol, Duckworth & Co. ran into trouble in 1870, they concluded a compromise with their major creditors at 4s in the pound. The losses to the major parties were considerable – Isaac Low was owed £32,000, and five others a total of £75,000 – but they nonetheless accepted the deal as being preferable to forcing the bankruptcy of the firm and having no return at all.[55] Bates had other ideas. His own claim on Nicol Duckworth, for the charter of a ship, was only £6,000, but he threatened to bankrupt them if he was not paid in full.[56] The point about Bates is that he could not have expected much help or sympathy from the community had he himself run into trouble. As it turned out, he did not need to ask, and retired from business to embark on a Parliamentary career from his newly acquired country seat in Hampshire.[57]

For most traders, though, playing the game was the only realistic approach. Their everyday business, heavily reliant on establishing the safety of debt and credit networks, was made much easier by the favourable opinions of information brokers in the banks and the senior levels of the trading community. In addition, devoting considerable effort to the maintenance of their reputation was a sound investment

53   M. Casson, 'Culture as an economic asset', in *Business history and business culture*, ed. A. Godley and O. Westall, Manchester, 1996, pp. 48–76, p. 66.

54   Bank, 5 Oct. 1863.

55   Bank, 18 Aug. 1870.

56   Bank, 26 Sept. 1870.

57   A. H. Rowson, 'Edward Bates: Shipowner', in *Bates of Bellefield, Gyrn Castle and Manydown*, ed. P. E. Bates, n.p., 1994, pp. 5–17; p. 16.

against the day when their own failures might, for whatever reason, be subject to the scrutiny of their fellow traders.

TACTICS OF PERSUASION

Some sectors of Liverpool's trading community had an even more acute need to establish themselves as safe and reputable, and the new joint-stock shipping companies are the most prominent example in mid-century. This was not just the case with the relatively few firms that planned to sell their shares to a much wider public: even firms that retained most of their shareholdings in a small circle had to overcome the fears of their fellow traders and customers. The structures and strategies of these firms need to be analysed against a background of considerable suspicion of the new types of company. Contemporary opponents feared the launch of ill-founded and speculative joint-stock firms 'week by week, so long as the public can be persuaded to subscribe to them'.[58] Joint-stock status was also seen in some quarters as a last resort strategy for businesses that were already in trouble. Overend, Gurney & Co. tried to convert to limited liability in July 1865, seeking to raise an impressive capital of £5m.[59] This came after years of rumours about their viability and complaints about their practices – the Bank of England's Liverpool agent believed that the firm did 'more mischief in this town than any of our most determined over-traders'.[60] Overend Gurney's collapse in 1866 did little for the reputation of corporate business promoters.

High-profile figures in the traditional shipping industry were also dismissive of the new joint-stock firms, and such concerns run deeper than the predictable complaints of established owners facing unwelcome competition. They relate to the reputation of the industry, and to the small-firm heritage of shipowning. The image of the experienced, individual shipowner maintaining a close personal control over the business was a powerful, positive symbol of the integrity and reliability of the industry, especially in contrast to the sometimes shady and semi-detached activities of those who invested in joint-stock companies. Cunard's David MacIver, when discussing the political influence of shipowners, claimed that he was the only shipowning Conservative MP, although some others were 'limited liability proprietors' – clearly, the latter were not to be taken seriously as shipowners.[61]

MacIver, as director of a heavily-subsidised government-chartered steamship line, was hardly a typical shipowner, but his views reflect a broad unease about the direction of the industry. There is evidence, though, that those keen to experiment in joint-stocks were well aware of the pitfalls, and made genuine efforts to limit their activities to realistic and reputable ventures. Historians need to be much more

58 *The Times*, 29 Apr. 1864, p. 12.

59 PRO, BT31 1128/2280c.

60 Bank, 3 Feb. 1855. See also D. Kynaston, *The City of London: Volume 1, A world of its own, 1815–1890*, London, 1995, pp. 235–43.

61 A. Holt, 'Review of the progress of steam shipping during the last quarter of a century', *Minutes of proceedings of the Institution of Civil Engineers*, Vol. 51, 1877–8, pp. 2–135; p. 33.

sensitive to the variations of form and structure hidden behind generic corporate labels, especially when we move away from the heated share-dealing of London – rates of company formation were relatively low in provincial ports like Liverpool and Hull, and the failure rate of Liverpool joint-stock shipping companies was also lower than elsewhere.[62] Liverpool joint-stock firms launched a propaganda offensive to mitigate public concern, stressing their conservative approach to new technology and their determination to be seen as safe, responsible and dependable. They did this by stressing their commitment to safety in their shipping operations, but also by highlighting the nature of their ownership patterns, with a strong emphasis on family and professional ties to counteract fears of speculative, irresponsible companies.

Thus MacIver's belief in the hands-on, experienced shipowner sets a tone for much of Liverpool's attitude to corporate ventures afloat. The elements that made joint-stock companies attractive to entrepreneurs were also precisely the factors that made them appear risky to the wider public. Joint-stocks – in the worst nightmares of traditionalists at least – allowed firms to be created out of thin air, bypassing the decades-long processes of building reputations and capital that conventional partnerships had to endure. Naturally, there was a considerable controversy about the ethical implications of such enterprises, and the joint-stock shipping company prospectuses of the early 1860s stress continuity rather than change, safe moderate profits rather than risky schemes for great wealth, and approaches based on tried and tested markets and technology.

There are two broad strands to these efforts – responsibility and reputation. Responsibility comes across most strongly in terms of technology. It was not just that steamers might be seen as dangerous, but also that they were perceived as expensive and wasteful, at least as operated by the flagship firms. It was well known at the time that the ocean paddle steamers used by Cunard and the US Collins Line on the mail run to New York were expensive to run, and that without mail subsidies they would have been uneconomic. In addition, the lack of cargo space on the average Cunard mail packet was an established problem: relatively shallow paddle steamers were ill-suited for bulk trades. Even the newer screw steamers with their deeper holds could be left with inadequate cargo space if their engines were designed for speed and power and took up a disproportionate amount of space. Liverpool joint-stock companies proposing to operate new steam services in the early 1860s therefore did not stress the speed or power of their vessels – quite the contrary. Their ships would rather be a sensible compromise, with engines large enough to drive a reliable service at speeds more than adequate for most cargo, but small and economical enough not to substantially interfere with the cargo capacity.[63]

---

62 D. J. Starkey, 'Ownership structures in the British shipping industry: The case of Hull, 1820–1916', *International Journal of Maritime History*, Vol. 8, 1996, pp. 71–95; P. L. Cottrell, 'The steamship on the Mersey, 1815–80: Investment and ownership', in *Shipping trade and commerce: Essays in memory of Ralph Davies*, ed. P. L. Cottrell and D. H. Aldcroft, Leicester, 1981, pp. 137–63; pp. 151–55.

63 See, for example, company prospectuses for the National Steam Navigation Co. and the West India & Pacific Co. in *Gore's Advertiser*, 5 Nov. 1863, p. 3; 26 Nov. 1863, p. 3.

Indeed, a number of prospectuses stressed that they would continue to use sailing ships where appropriate, and hybrid steam clippers were commonly identified as favoured vessels. The Australia & Eastern Line collapsed before it began because of a scandal in the allocation of its shares, but it actually had a plausible business proposal, which had been carefully drafted to avoid any suggestion that it was attempting anything new or reckless.[64] It was to be an amalgamation of three sailing lines, all of which had long experience of the Australian emigrant trades, and which had already been experimenting with auxiliary steam clippers. Such vessels represented technical best practice on such long-haul routes in the early 1860s, and the new company planned to invest in more of them. Importantly, the prospectus stressed that the company would not be using full steam vessels, emphasising the point that this was an evolutionary development building on the success of existing practice. Similarly, the British Shipowners Co. announced that it would concentrate on the increasingly acceptable iron sailing ships of the mid-1860s, using steam only when proven appropriate on certain routes.[65]

This cautious approach often extended to the trades in which the companies planned to operate. None claimed an intention to break into new markets, but rather would provide faster and more reliable services on existing routes where the commercial possibilities were already well established. Bulk grain from North America was a favourite target. One of Liverpool's older trades, this continued to be conducted in sailing ships in mid-century, although overheating on extended voyages damaged the cargo. The National Steam Navigation Co., operating to the United States, and two firms aiming at the Canadian trades, all stressed that the shorter journey times achieved by even moderately-powered steamers would avoid such problems.[66]

The promoters of joint-stock companies recognised that recklessness was to be avoided in all areas of their operation, and they matched their technological caution with a careful effort to overcome any impression that they lacked a sound business heritage. Reputations and experience were central to the new firms' efforts to promote themselves, and they stressed their own and that of other firms wherever possible. Name-dropping in the prospectuses was common, with firms hoping that the reputations of some of Liverpool's oldest and most successful steamship operators would rub off on them. The National Steam Navigation Co. reminded potential shareholders of the success of the Inman Line, operating on the North Atlantic without government subsidy.[67] The West India & Pacific Co. planned to work with the support and under the supervision of companies already active in Liverpool's trade with that region, but it also identified major firms working elsewhere as examples to be emulated: the company would, it claimed, have 'the advantages of direct personal supervision and economy of management which have made the Cunard and Inman steamship companies successful'.[68] This was at the least rather cheeky: neither Inman nor

---

64 Cottrell, 'The steamship on the Mersey', p. 151; Kynaston, *The City of London*, p. 224.

65 *Gore's Advertiser*, 7 Jan. 1864, p. 3; 7 Apr. 1864, p. 3.

66 *Gore's Advertiser*, 5 Nov. 1863, p. 3; 28 Apr. 1864, p. 3.

67 *Gore's Advertiser*, 5 Nov. 1863, p. 3.

68 *Gore's Advertiser*, 26 Nov. 1863, p. 3.

Cunard was involved in the venture, and their operating circumstances were very different, but the new companies sought to remind the investing community that major shipping lines could operate with the highest levels of reputation.

The new companies stressed their reputations by other means too. The image conveyed by the directors of the new companies was important. Directors were carefully chosen to give the firm an air of solidity and competence. Not only would leading shipowners be present, but usually a local banker or two, and sometimes agents with experience of operating at the other end of the proposed route. The Australian & Eastern Navigation Co. is a good example of the range of directors considered necessary.[69] Tyndal Bright, James Baines and Henry Wilson represented the three shipping companies. All had established reputations in the eastern trades and were well known to the shipping and financial communities of Liverpool and beyond. Liverpool trading firms including Huth & Co. had a seat on the Board, and Liverpool's Alliance Bank and Heywood Sons & Co. represented the banking community. Banks Bros & Henderson of Melbourne, Australia, had a representative, pointing to established connections and links at the other end of the proposed routes. Butterfield Bros of Bradford represented yet another link in the new company's network of reinforcing trading connections – many emigrants for Australia in the 1860s were recruited in the English textile regions, and Australian connections with Yorkshire and Lancashire were strong enough to inspire the establishment of relief funds in the colonies to support the 'Spartan fortitude' of mill-workers facing destitution because of the American Civil War.[70] The Australian & Eastern's board thus had representatives of each link in a lengthy chain, stressing that the enterprise, while it might be new, had long-established and solid foundations.

The choice of directors therefore performed two functions. First, from the internal corporate viewpoint, it ensured that all the elements in the proposed trading network – often already operating informally – were tied into the business structure from the outset. Secondly, when it came to selling shares to the public, the existing reputations of these individuals were important. This was especially true given the conservative nature of many proposals that stressed continuity rather than change. Such patterns, it is worth noting, were adopted throughout Liverpool's mercantile community, although the shipping firms had the highest public profile. Port service industries also pursued a gradualist strategy of joint-stock formation. The Liverpool Ship-Bread & Biscuit Co. was launched in 1865 with a ships' store dealer, ale merchant, biscuit manufacturer and shipping agent on its board. The Liverpool General Warehousing Co. was founded by wool and cotton brokers.[71] These firms, and many like them, were formed by existing businesses making pragmatic use of new financial possibilities, rather than by carpetbaggers and speculators seeking gullible investors.

There is one final element of continuity that ties up the various loose ends of

69 *Gore's Advertiser*, 7 Jan. 1864, p. 3.

70 K. Penny, 'Australian relief for the Lancashire victims of the cotton famine, 1862–1863', *Transactions of the Historic Society of Lancashire and Cheshire*, Vol. 108, 1956, pp. 129–39.

71 PRO, BT31 895/991c; BT31 1053/1844c.

reputation, personal ownership and company structure. Joint-stock shipping companies were not the first elements in the Liverpool trading community to have to persuade the public of their stability and probity. In fact, the use of a less formal kind of corporate identity was already well established in Liverpool shipping before the rise of steam. Its purpose was to disguise fluid business structures which might have appeared dangerously unstable to mercantile customers, and particularly to passengers and emigrants on the American and Australian routes. As has been noted, Liverpool shipping operators were in an unusual situation in their major trade during the second quarter of the nineteenth century: most traffic between the port and the United States was in US-registered vessels which relied on Liverpool agents for cargo and passenger handling. In a variation on the theme, Liverpool's Australian emigrant services, like those of James Baines, often used vessels chartered from owners with no profile or reputation in the port. The use of a corporate identity – the 'Black Star Line', for example – enabled the agency firms to build their reputations around a successful marque, regardless of who in the end owned the particular ship being used for that week's sailing. This identity gave an air of solidity and reliability to what were often *ad hoc* arrangements.

Passengers apparently needed more persuasion on this point than merchants shipping cargoes. While the Liverpool commercial press of the 1850s is full of advertisements for shipping services to all parts of the world, the use of 'Line' names is limited almost entirely to the Australian and North American routes where emigrants and – increasingly in the latter case – the more lucrative business travellers were carried. Most were named after the easily recognisable symbols on their flags, as in Blue Ball, White Star, Black Diamond and the like.[72] While the sophistication of shipping company advertising and marketing increased rapidly after mid-century, therefore, as passenger travel and the new tourist sector emerged as central income courses for the large steam fleets, it is worth stressing that some of the basic principles had already been well established by Liverpool traders in mid-century.

Some corporate identities carried such weight and reputation that they rapidly became marketable commodities. The changing structure and status of the White Star Line demonstrates the importance of such marques. The Line was originally a sailing operation carrying emigrants to Australia. When its managing agents Wilson & Chambers folded in 1867, the name of the Line was bought by Thomas Ismay, who re-launched White Star as a joint-stock, steamship service on the North Atlantic. Although far from its original context, the marque clearly served Ismay well, and demonstrates that the system was flexible enough to handle rapid growth and change while maintaining a public face that stressed continuity and reputation.[73]

Ideas of corporate image and reputation created for the new joint-stock companies in mid-century reflect a process of evolution rather than revolution in Liverpool's business culture. In particular, the absence of any stress on novelty is striking – the

---

72   *Gore's Advertiser*, the most prominent of the port's commercial newspapers in this period, always carried several columns of detailed passage advertisements.

73   Oldham, *The Ismay Line*, pp. 28–37.

new firms worked hard to appear as rooted in the established mechanisms of their trades as any small partnership would have been. Their appeal to local identity was also well-calculated, with the Liverpool pedigree of the directors and their managing agents demonstrating as emphatically as possible that these new ventures were not the playthings of faceless money-men in London.

Information, reputation, co-operation and careful image-making were all central to the business practices of Liverpool traders. In large part, this was because traders recognised, and to some extent feared, the insecurity of their profession, especially in an era of great upheavals in world markets and of far-reaching shifts in government attitudes to regulation and protection. Much of that insecurity, however, came from within the business culture itself. The systems of debt and credit that made trade possible in this period were only as robust as the weakest links in the chain. The reputations that were vital to underwriting these chains were themselves liable to manipulation, by fraudulent, or even just over-enthusiastic, traders. Finally, the delicate web of information that linked these elements was all too fallible.

All that said, however, the various approaches developed in this and the previous two chapters point to a trading community that was capable of expansion, flexibility and the rapid exploitation of new opportunities. Such collective progress undoubtedly owed a great deal to the accumulated risks and vulnerabilities experienced by the trading firms themselves, and suggests that in an era of change and growth the pragmatic approach of Liverpool's trading community was a net asset, even if it could easily be a recipe for individual failure. The cumulative effect of Liverpool's business and financial networks was to make a considerable volume of information available to the trading classes, which, for all its uncertainties, may have produced a safer environment than later, more restricted channels of information and finance between individual firms and their bankers.[74]

---

74 For alternative models of small-firm finance over a longer period, see A. Godley and D. M. Ross, 'Introduction: Banks, networks and small firm finance', *Business History*, Vol. 38, 1996, pp. 1–10.

Part III

Institutions and influence

Liverpool rose rapidly in the eighteenth and nineteenth centuries, overtaking other provincial ports and seeking to rival London itself. Part of that process was political: Liverpool expected a voice in national debates over the development of trade and shipping, and a share in lucrative government contracts. At a local level too, the era of municipal reform and a series of disputes between Liverpool and Birkenhead gave Liverpool traders greater power, while adding burdens of responsibility. These two chapters examine Liverpool traders at work on a broader political stage, seeking contracts for mail services, troop-carrying and emigration, and struggling to manage the conflicting pressures on their own Dock Board.

Chapter 8

CONSTRAINT AND OPPORTUNITY: GOVERNMENT CONTRACTING

The relationship between the trading community and the British government was one of considerable ambivalence in the middle of the nineteenth century. Government was involved in regulating trading activity on a number of levels, from the 'macro-regulation' of international trade law down to the 'micro-regulation' of safety rules applied to individual ships. Mid-century was a period of change across the board, but not always, apparently, in the same direction. Historians have noted that while official attitudes shifted from protectionism to free trade at the macro level, various branches of government began to take a much more active interest in the micro, operational side of shipping and trade. If the repeal of the Navigation Acts removed some constraints, a range of other legislation was adopted, to the point where shipping became recognised as one of the most heavily regulated of industries – 'no other group of nineteenth-century capitalists was so confined within a legal framework'.[1] The shipping interest claimed to have the worst of both worlds, being denied the protection of government on the large scale, while being increasingly constrained by safety and other operational regulations.

At the same time, however, it was becoming clear to traders, and to shipowners especially, that if government was sometimes an interfering regulator, it could also be a generous paymaster. In an age of expanding trade and empire, governments needed reliable communication services, and increasingly entered into contracts with private shipping firms rather than using the Navy. Mail services grew rapidly, as did the need to move troops and military materiel at intercontinental distances. Finally, dramatic expansion in emigration to Australia and New Zealand in mid-century was supported in part by governments at both ends of the migration chain, and the subsidies available helped shipowners establish large-scale operations. Some shipping entrepreneurs, like William Mackinnon, seem to have based their careers on the acquisition and maintenance of government subsidy, becoming increasingly divorced from the realities of commercial operation, but managing considerable success for as long as the climate of subsidy lasted.[2]

This chapter therefore focuses on the three major issues – wartime requisitions, passenger trades, and mail – that tied Liverpool shipowners to government in a complex and multi-faceted relationship. In analysing these questions, historians must

---

1 S. Palmer, *Politics, shipping and the repeal of the Navigation Acts*, Manchester, 1990, p. 171.

2 J. F. Munro, 'Shipping subsidies and railway guarantees: William Mackinnon, eastern Africa and the Indian Ocean, 1860–93', *Journal of African History*, Vol. 28, 1987, pp. 209–30; p. 229.

unravel an intricate web of costs, subsidies, constraints and evasions, hindered as much as helped by the public pronouncements of the traders themselves. Naturally, traders were fond of painting a gloomy picture of the interference of government in their business decisions, and complained about being 'overwhelmed with useless annoyances' from the Board of Trade.[3] Government, in this as in many other contexts, was a convenient scapegoat for the failings of traders themselves, and the alleged slowness of the authorities to pay bills for contracted shipping was a common complaint – the infamous Edward Oliver even tried to implicate the late payment of a Crimean War charter in the collapse of his business, but was not widely believed.[4] Such problems were, however, only one side of an important bargain between government and the shipping industry in mid-century, and the considerable benefits available on the other side need to be explored also.

KEEPING THE WORLD POSTED

The history of mail carriage by sea is of a complicated and lengthy tussle between the private and public sectors. Postal services were clearly a matter of great national importance, especially for a country like Britain with far-flung imperial and commercial connections to maintain, and were traditionally entrusted to naval ships. By the nineteenth century, though, it was argued that the Navy was not always the cheapest or most reliable carrier of mail, and that mail should be carried on commercial ships working with government contracts and subsidies. Nevertheless, there remained a strong element of national and imperial interest in the matter, which has proved difficult for historians to assess alongside the more easily quantifiable financial questions.[5] Matters became more complicated when steam technology made it possible to employ steam packet ships on short sea routes in the 1820s. These vessels had a clear advantage over sailing ships in terms of the time they took to reach their destination, but their running costs were high. By the 1830s, mail services came under the scrutiny of Parliamentary Committees which were dedicated to cutting costs in government departments. The results of these enquiries set the mail-contract agenda for a generation – contracting mail services out to tender by private shipping companies would offer the Treasury better value for money than having the Post Office or the Admiralty build and operate its own vessels.[6] Whether this decision was correct or not remains a matter of some debate, but its impact was significant.

---

3 Comment by David MacIver in A. Holt, 'Review of the progress of steam shipping during the last quarter of a century', *Minutes of proceedings of the Institution of Civil Engineers*, Vol. 51, 1877–8, pp. 2–135; p. 33.

4 Bank, 3 Oct. 1854.

5 A. J. Arnold and R. G. Greenhill, 'Contractors' bounties or due consideration?: Evidence on the commercial nature of the Royal Mail Steam Packet Company's mail contracts, 1842–1905', in *Management, finance and industrial relations in maritime industries*, ed. S. Ville and D. M. Williams, St John's, Newfoundland, 1994, pp. 111–37; pp. 111–13.

6 F. Harcourt, 'British oceanic mail contracts in the age of steam, 1838–1914', *Journal of Transport History*, 3rd series, Vol. 9, 1988, pp. 1–18; pp. 1–2.

Shipowners recognised the opportunity to establish new services with government subsidies, or – better still – to secure considerable new income for their existing services.

The relationship between government and shipowners in connection with the mail question was rarely a simple matter of paying a particular operator to carry a certain number of mail bags to a certain destination. Indeed, straightforward carriage expenses often seemed a small part of the overall equation. In most mail contracts, shipowners had to conform to a range of conditions relating to the speed of their vessels and the reliability of their service, as well as agreeing to restrictions on the extent of additional, private business their ships could undertake while carrying the mail.

Inevitably, in the early decades of the development of ocean-going steamships, these terms and conditions could be onerous: the large paddle steamers built for Cunard's North Atlantic mail service could only match the speed and reliability requirements by having large engines and a very restricted cargo capacity. Subsidies, necessarily, were high, because the government was paying for the cutting-edge of shipbuilding. By mid-century, however, it was clear that technology and commercial initiative were rapidly overtaking the established rationale of the mail contracts. In the course of the 1860s, technological improvements gave shipowners new screw-driven steamers with better all-round performance, carrying cargo and passengers as well as offering fast transit times for the mail. As was demonstrated in chapter two, the subsidised flagship companies were no longer the only firms running large steamers on long-distance routes. Independent competitors were running shipping lines without government subsidy, often operating with similar vessels and from the same ports as the contract companies. These competitors, such as Liverpool's William Inman, argued that flagship firms like Cunard were given a subsidy for services which would in fact have paid their way by trading revenue alone. Naturally, this made it very difficult for new firms to break into the business, or stay in it for long. Government and the shipowners became tangled in an ever-more-complicated web of subsidy and contract conditions, with increasing calls for the whole edifice to be swept away and replaced with a simple freight payment.

Matters became more complex still in mid-century as imperial expansion created even more mail routes to be maintained. The British government faced rapid expansion in the Australian colonies, more direct control over India (in the aftermath of the uprising of 1857), and a series of minor but ominous disputes in China. All these forced a process of reassessment in the 1860s, with a number of enquiries into telegraphic and maritime communications with the Far East, as serious consideration had to be given to the maintenance of official communications networks on a global scale. Meanwhile, costs spiralled. By the late 1860s P&O, with its network of routes via the Mediterranean to the East, was taking an unprecedented £450,000 in annual subsidies.[7]

Liverpool's role in longer-distance mail contracts was of course strongest on the

7   D. R. Headrick, *The tentacles of progress: Technology transfer in the age of imperialism, 1850–1940*, Oxford, 1988, pp. 39–40.

North Atlantic services to the United States and Canada. Samuel Cunard established his company (officially the British & North American Royal Mail Steam Packet Co.) specifically to run the contract mail service from Liverpool to Boston and New York, and took great advantage of both the subsidy and the prestige attached to running the official mails. While Cunard's activities are relatively well known to historians, it is worth considering briefly some of the key issues raised by the prolonged debate over competition and subsidy among Liverpool's Atlantic steamship operators during the 1860s. The port's experience in this context allows a number of points to be addressed about the relative merits of competition and subsidy in a rapidly expanding and technologically advanced sector of Britain's mercantile trade. The second part of this section considers efforts to establish mail services on other routes. Most contracts for services to places other than North America were tendered to run from London, but some Liverpool owners made persistent attempts to persuade the government of the benefits of operating routes from the Mersey.

Competition for the mail business on the North Atlantic in the middle years of the century falls broadly into two parts, as far as Liverpool was concerned. The first series of events, in the 1850s, saw Cunard apparently struggling with the American Collins Line, although historians have established that the companies actually operated a secret agreement.[8] While important in terms of national prestige and the evolution of official attitudes toward regulation and subsidy, the Collins/Cunard saga was of little consequence to the activities of most Liverpool shipowners.

Real competition emerged during the 1860s, when Liverpool steam operators began to run unsubsidised services on the North Atlantic on a considerable scale. The highest profile of all the competitors belonged to William Inman. The dispute between Inman and Cunard in the mid-1860s is worthy of some discussion, because it was seen at the time as symbolic of different approaches and philosophies of business and government. It was also in a sense a test case, because the new joint-stock shipping companies which launched North American services from Liverpool in the course of the decade formed a vocal lobby on the mail-contracts issue. The National Steam Navigation Co. and Guion's Liverpool & Great Western Co. in particular competed with Cunard and Inman on the New York run, and it was becoming increasingly hard by the end of the 1860s for Cunard to argue that carrying mail by steamer on that route was impossible without a subsidy.

The battle for mail services on the North Atlantic became a clash of shipowning cultures, and of different perspectives of the national importance of such activities. Cunard had powerful friends in the Admiralty, connections that ensured the maintenance of an annual subsidy of £188,040 throughout the 1850s.[9] The Admiralty's view had little to do with the efficiency of the mail, but showed rather a desire to prove the superiority of British steamship operations, especially in relation to competitors

---

8   F. E. Hyde, *Cunard and the North Atlantic, 1840–1973: A history of shipping and financial management*, London, 1975, pp. 39–45; E. W. Sloan, 'Collins versus Cunard: The realities of a North Atlantic steamship rivalry, 1850–1858', *International Journal of Maritime History*, Vol. 4, 1992, pp. 83–100.

9   Hyde, *Cunard*, p. 35.

from the United States. Such attitudes also led to a conservative approach to technology, however, as during the 1850s the Admiralty's specifications for mail ships continued to insist on tried and tested wooden paddle steamers rather than the new and more efficient iron screw vessels. Cunard's subsidy had therefore to be used in part to pay the additional costs of an ageing fleet. Operators bidding for mail services elsewhere rejected the Admiralty's view of the new iron technology. When Liverpool's Charles Horsfall & Sons tendered for a West Africa contract in 1851, the firm argued that it could run a service with iron ships for £37,000 a year, but that it would need an extra £100,000 to do the same with wooden ships. While Horsfall was making an explicit 'protest against the employment of wood', the successful bid from Macgregor Laird also included a £10,000 premium if they were forced to use wooden ships.[10] Clearly, shipping operators even in the early 1850s were beginning to resist the Admiralty's technological conservatism.

By the mid-1860s, the view that technology and free enterprise were overtaking the rationale of the mail subsidy system was ever-more-common in government. The Post Office took over responsibility for mail contracts in 1860 and was advised by successive Parliamentary enquiries to reduce, if not abolish, the Atlantic mail contracts. Parliament found something of a popular hero in William Inman, who took great pride in his independence: 'I have been 19 years without a contract, and I can do it still.'[11]

Inman challenged Cunard on two fronts. First, he operated fast iron steam ships that made Cunard's fleet look backward. Customers complained that while Cunard's fastest vessels were excellent, the firm all too often used its slower ships – the so-called 'cargo boats' – and was regularly falling behind both Inman and the new German Atlantic lines.[12] Secondly, Inman sought to undermine Cunard's connections with government in the late 1860s, first bidding for a mail service that was complementary to Cunard's, and then outbidding Cunard for the full service. Cunard's directors did not give up easily, of course, having spent their working lives in the official contracts business, and being adept at taking advantage of government weakness and uncertainty. Much to Inman's disgust, Cunard negotiated a separate contract with a panicky Post Office during the Abyssinian War.[13] Once international affairs had settled again, Inman successfully tendered for a subsidy in 1868 to run one of three weekly mail voyages to the United States. Inman's subsidy was only £35,000 a year, and this helped to set a 'going rate' for Atlantic mail that was far lower than Cunard had been used to. Cunard, running two voyages a week, was given £70,000, which was almost £120,000 a year *less* than its subsidy back in the 1850s, when it faced much less competition.

10 BPP, West Africa mails (1852), p. 28.
11 BPP, Mail contracts (1868), evidence of William Inman, q. 1,613.
12 BPP, Mail contracts (1868), evidence of Herbert Taylor, qq. 10, 23.
13 An account of this incident, concluding that the maintenance of the existing arrangements served the public good, is in Hyde, *Cunard*, pp. 49–53. The Parliamentary Committee took a less positive view: see BPP, Mail contracts (1868), report.

John Burns, negotiating for Cunard, admitted later that he would have asked for more.[14] He could not, however, because by the late 1860s Inman and other Liverpool operators had demonstrated that unsubsidised Atlantic services were not only feasible, but in some ways superior to the conservative practices of the subsidised firm. Inman's co-operation with Cunard in 1868 was a subtle manoeuvre, gaining a new source of revenue for his own operation while greatly reducing the subsidy available to his key competitor. Cunard in turn had to co-operate because the alternative might be worse: with official thinking turning in the direction of reduced subsidies, Cunard had to appear reasonable.

Apart from the money, having a mail contract gave Inman further advantages relative to Cunard. Mail steamers on the transatlantic routes were exempt from the Passenger Acts that were designed to enforce safety standards on the industry. Inman complained in 1860 that one of his vessels lost £400 in cargo business on each voyage through what he considered arbitrary and artificial rules restricting the cargo capacity of vessels that also carried emigrants.[15] The mail contract levelled the playing field with Cunard, and was therefore, in relative terms, a considerable boost to Inman. There was also the question of prestige and public image, with mail ships being generally assumed to be faster, safer and more reliable than other vessels: 'the American public ask no questions when they know that it is a mail steamer'.[16]

Inman's complaints about safety regulations should not be taken to imply a reckless attitude to his business. In fact, reputation was one of the key issues in the maintenance of any business in such a competitive environment. Cunard was particularly obsessive about it, and while Inman was willing to take rather more chances in pursuit of profits, he could not afford to be associated with activities that would damage the name of his firm and its operations. Inman had broken with his original partners, the Quaker Richardson Brothers, when they objected to the use of the firm's vessels for military purposes during the Crimean War, but similar issues of ethics and reputation came back to haunt Inman subsequently.[17] Early in the American Civil War, for example, the trade in weapons to the United States offered traders lucrative opportunities. In 1862, Liverpool sent almost 200,000 firearms and nearly 12 million percussion caps to New York, worth more than £500,000.[18] Even in the face of such potential, Cunard refused to carry arms to New York, but Inman was willing to carry the cargo, provided it appeared in the manifests as 'hardware'. When news circulated that the Confederate navy was raiding shipping, Inman decided that even this was drawing unwelcome attention to his business, and that the munitions trade was too risky.[19]

The fact that these firms were already paying so much attention to reputation and prestige in their Atlantic services raises another important point about the nature of

14 BPP, Mail contracts (1868), evidence of John Burns, q. 1,368.
15 BPP, Packet and telegraph services (1860), evidence of William Inman, q. 2,654.
16 BPP, Mail contracts (1868), evidence of Andrew Duncan, q. 357.
17 N. R. P. Bonsor, *North Atlantic seaway*, 5 vols, Jersey, 1975–80, vol. 1, p. 220.
18 BPP, Arms shipments (1864).
19 Barings, 30 Mar. 1863.

competition on the key routes to the United States. Parliamentary Committees at the time wondered whether the subsidised firms would actually have done anything different without the government funding. Both Cunard and Inman claimed that they would run slower services to save on the considerable running costs of the fastest ships. At the same time, though, they had to admit that their speed was currently allowing them to charge higher freight rates for private cargo than their competitors on the Atlantic routes. Inman was bringing in £1 per cargo ton more than the National Co. in the late 1860s, by virtue of being able to offer shorter delivery times.[20] By the 1860s the expectation in the trading community was for large, fast, steam liners, and the leading firms were not credible when they threatened to revert to the voyage times of previous decades. Inman and Cunard, as well as the lesser firms competing on the Atlantic, recognised that their reputations depended on a combination of speed, reliability and safety, and that those reputations, in an era of diminishing subsidy, were rapidly becoming more valuable than the mail contracts.

The maturing commercial environment of the North Atlantic steam routes therefore reveals issues in the relationship between government and the shipping industry that move beyond the early assumptions about the need to subsidise cutting-edge services. Other, much less developed, routes also have useful lessons for the attitudes of the Liverpool trading community to the opportunities and constraints offered by government. If Cunard and Inman argued with government over the level of subsidy and the conditions of service, other firms had to make a more fundamental case for the existence of a mail service at all. Many trade routes seemed much less vital to British governments than the busy North Atlantic. Even if the case was accepted, Liverpool's traders had a still harder task persuading government that mail services should use their own port as a terminus. Issuing contracts to companies based in the south of England was a long-established habit of the British government, and had made much sense in the eighteenth century when empire and commerce still very much focused on London, Bristol and the manufacturing midlands. Even in the nineteenth century, imperial considerations continued to favour London and Southampton, but commercial change began to shift focus northward. The diversification of Liverpool's shipping activity into other regions of the world encouraged companies to pursue new contracts which would rival southern lines.

Liverpool firms tendered for a number of mail contracts in mid-century, in various parts of the world. They either sought to establish new mail routes in areas where they were developing commercial contacts, or hoped opportunistically to pick up some mail business on the fringes of more established operations. Important opportunities were offered by government in the early 1850s, with a Parliamentary review of Far Eastern communications. Existing services were haphazard, shared between P&O and the East India Company's own fleet, with confusing schedules and rules about what could be carried. Traders argued for a new service, and Liverpool lobbied to be the terminus. As much as 38% of the nation's trade with the East came through

20   BPP, Mail contracts (1868), evidence of William Inman, q. 1,665.

Liverpool, claimed the Liverpool East Indies & China Association, and the port was therefore an obvious hub for the communications that went with the commerce.[21] A head-on challenge to P&O's entrenched position was beyond even the most bullish Liverpool operators, though, and an entry into eastern services was sought in two ways. First, Liverpool's Mediterranean traders sought to co-operate with P&O on that part of the service, and secondly, other operators made opportunistic attacks on the Australia route, to which P&O was barely committed in any case.

As has been discussed, Liverpool's Mediterranean steamship firms had large fleets by mid-century, and extensive experience in the region. Unlike the situation on the Atlantic, where new firms directly confronted the established contract companies, firms such as Bibby & Co. did not attempt to use their resources to challenge P&O. Rather, they aimed at providing a cargo service to complement the mail and passenger services of the contract company, and gradually moved toward a more formal co-operative agreement. Bibby became P&O's Liverpool agent 'for overland cargo to India', operating what was in effect a feeder service to Egypt for goods that would be taken eastward from there by P&O ships.[22] Making money around the edges of P&O's empire was a useful element in Bibby's shipping portfolio, just as it was for the British India Steam Navigation Company in the Indian Ocean, although of course the latter had extensive mail contracts of its own for coastal services east of Suez.[23]

The slow growth of the Australian colonies in the nineteenth century generated a lengthy debate over the provision of mail services. Even with dramatically rising emigration in the 1850s, Australia remained a sparsely populated colony, and opinions varied as to whether sufficient volume of mail existed to justify contracting a serious shipping line operating on regular schedules. The Australia mails became a complicated tussle involving the government, Parliament, the colonists, and P&O. It was appealing, from the government's viewpoint, to just add the Australia service on the end of existing steam services to India, although P&O remained unenthusiastic. In comparison with their other eastern operations, the run to Australia offered P&O little: the company complained especially about the lack of return passenger traffic.[24] On the other hand, Parliamentary Committees and the colonists themselves feared the neglect of Australia, but rarely agreed on the best solution. One Select Committee argued as early as 1851 that a direct service round the Cape of Good Hope be established.[25] The colonists themselves favoured the route across the Atlantic and Pacific via Panama.[26] Although accepting the logic of the route via India, the colonists and their supporters guessed correctly that this route was not central to the

21 BPP, Steam communications (1851), evidence of Murray Gladstone, q. 3,998.

22 Anon., *The broker's guide and shipping directory*, Birmingham, 1870, p. 59.

23 J. F. Munro, 'The "Scrubby Scotch Screw Company": British India Steam Navigation Co.'s coastal services in South Asia, 1862–70', in *From wheelhouse to counting house: Essays in maritime economic history in honour of Professor Peter Neville Davies*, ed. L. R. Fischer, St John's, Newfoundland, 1992, pp. 43–72; p. 67.

24 BPP, Packet and telegraph services (1860), evidence of Charles Howell, q. 779.

25 BPP, Steam communications (1851), 1st report, pp. xiii–xiv.

26 BPP, Packet and telegraph services (1860), evidence of W. H. Stephenson, q. 470.

strategies of P&O, and therefore vulnerable: P&O dropped the service during the Crimean War, their ships having been taken up for war service. Colonists argued that it was all too indicative of the neglect of the Australian settlements, compared with other parts of the empire which were in receipt of reliable services at high subsidies – London still, it seemed, had the outdated view that Australia was a land inhabited by only the 'occasional sheep squatter'.[27]

Liverpool shipowners identified Australia as a potential mail route in the 1840s. They saw the possibility of bypassing the confused Indian Ocean mail question by running fast clipper ships on the alternative route round the Cape. Cotesworth & Wynne offered the government a monthly mail service to Sydney as early as 1846, to run alternately with London vessels, but the offer was not taken up.[28] A decade later, P&O's decision to drop its Australia service opened an opportunity for Liverpool operators who had been working the route with emigrants. James Baines was quick to see a chance to break into P&O's monopoly, and secured a temporary contract to carry mail. The continuing weaknesses of steam on the long-distance routes helped Baines. Although it was fast becoming conventional wisdom that mail services required steam, it remained the case that Baines' fast sailing ships, taking advantages of the South Atlantic trade winds, could reach Australia within a few days of the arrival of mail carried by the chain of steamships that ran via the Mediterranean and the Indian Ocean.[29] Baines' victory was short-lived, however. After the Crimean War, the routes were re-tendered, and P&O finally established the Australia service as a branch line from Ceylon, with a subsidy more to its liking.[30]

South America was also, as has been noted, a lucrative target for Liverpool traders seeking new markets, and also offered new territory for the award of mail contracts. The South American & General Steam Navigation Co. applied for a mail contract in the spring of 1852, shortly after a (hardly coincidental) memorial had been sent to the Postmaster-General by some Liverpool merchants seeking the establishment of a bi-monthly mail service from Liverpool to South America. The South American & General established its service in 1853 with no mail contract, and ran it for almost another year before the Post Office agreed terms. In fact, the South American & General did not start its service entirely as a speculative venture: it soon emerged that the company had secured a contract from the Portuguese government to carry mails from Lisbon to Brazil.[31] A decade later, the British & South American Steam Navigation Co. was keen to convince prospective shareholders that it would be profitable without mail subsidies, but also hinted that it would pursue any chances that came up. The Chilean government, it was recalled, had offered a mail subsidy on a previous occasion, and there might be 'liberal concessions' forthcoming from

27 Letter from 'A member of the Melbourne Chamber of Commerce', *The Times*, 23 Mar. 1855, p. 5.
28 BPP, Steam communications (1851), appendix 1.
29 *The Times*, 27 Mar. 1855, p. 9.
30 F. Broeze, 'Distance tamed: Steam navigation to Australia and New Zealand from its beginnings to the outbreak of the Great War', *Journal of Transport History*, Vol. 10, 1989, pp. 1–21; pp. 5–7.
31 For listings of these services, see J. N. T. Howat, *South American packets*, York, 1984.

the governments of Peru, Argentina and Brazil.[32] South America's independent states, many with growing economies, offered an important potential source of mail contracts to Liverpool firms. The Liverpool, Brazil & River Plate company sought contracts wherever it could find them. By the late 1860s, it ran one vessel a month on a contract from the Brazilian government, another on a British mail contract, and other vessels on a commercial basis.[33]

Given the acknowledged global leadership of British owners in steam shipping, seeking contracts from countries with little shipping capability of their own offered potentially significant opportunities. Perhaps inevitably, however, such avenues were limited by nationalist concerns. Most countries preferred to run their own mail systems rather than pay the British to do it for them, even if they had to buy British-built steamships anyway. Some British colonies also felt capable by mid-century of funding mail carriage, believing that this gave them a measure of control over the service. The Canadian government, for example, spent huge sums on the Allan Line's service between Liverpool and Montreal. The Canadians were unimpressed by the failure of the British authorities to force Cunard to include a serious service to Canadian ports as part of its Atlantic operations, and sought to develop their own routes.[34] The British Treasury also managed to establish the principle that New South Wales should pay half the subsidy for the mail to Sydney, despite the fact that the colony wanted the service to run via Panama.[35] Colonial contributions to mail subsidies undoubtedly pleased the Treasury, but it is not clear whether the Admiralty approved: colonies with a financial stake might also insist on input to the management and strategic direction of the services.

The final region in which Liverpool owners sought to pioneer mail contracts was in one of the port's older trades – West Africa. As on the Atlantic routes, dynamic, almost evangelical individuals promoted the concept, and in this case there was clearly much to be gained in communications terms. It has already been noted that steam brought a revolution in the trading structures of West Africa, liberating traders from the difficult currents and winds of the African coast. Even if steamers had never been able to carry anything more than the mails, though, they would still have radically changed the trading conditions of those working with the region. A reliable method of carrying bills of lading and letters, argued steamship promoter Macgregor Laird, would in itself 'convert a most uncertain and precarious trade into a regular and steady one'.[36]

Laird was clearly convinced of that, but others focused more on the 'precarious' aspects of the African trades. The government only received four tenders for the West Africa mails in 1851. One came from the existing Royal Mail Co. working the Brazil run, proposing only a branch line, and another was from a joint-stock venture

32 Gore's Advertiser, 21 Apr. 1864, p. 3.
33 Clayton Brothers, Liverpool ABC timetables and shipping directory, Liverpool, 1868, p. 116.
34 K. S. Mackenzie, '"They lost the smell": The Canadian steam merchant marine, 1853–1903', Northern Mariner, Vol. 6, 1996, pp. 1–29, pp. 3–5.
35 BPP, Packet and telegraph services (1860), evidence of W. H. Stephenson, q. 305.
36 BPP, West Africa mails (1852), Laird to Earl Grey, 25 March 1851, p. 3.

that had failed to get itself off the ground. Importantly, though, both serious proposals came from Liverpool-based traders – Macgregor Laird and Charles Horsfall & Sons. While initially rejecting all the tenders, the government finally negotiated a lower rate with Laird.[37] Laird's service initially ran from London and Plymouth, however, and it was only in 1856, when the company was in some difficulty, that its Liverpool agents took over operations.[38]

The Africa mails question underlines the determination of Liverpool shipping firms to drive the expansion of the contract mail system and, more importantly, to ensure that Liverpool was a significant player in the business. The prestige and earnings gained from mail contracts were undoubtedly appealing to Liverpool firms, and Cunard in particular relied on its contract heavily during the 1850s. That said, mail contracts were always going to be limited to a small number of major companies working important routes. Being the first firm to be awarded a mail contract on a particular route carried a great commercial advantage, and established a relationship with which governments became reluctant to tamper. Inevitably, therefore, given the limited number of realistic mail routes in mid-century, relatively few Liverpool shipowners were able to benefit from this source of income. If mail contracts were beyond what most Liverpool owners could aspire to, though, they could make bids for government money in other ways. Rather less work has been done on these other spheres in which government and shipowners entered into financial arrangements, and it is to these issues that this chapter now turns.

WARTIME CHARTERS

The role of merchant shipping in wartime was not, of course, a new issue in the mid-nineteenth century. The line between civilian and naval shipping had been thin and ill-defined throughout the early modern period: navies hired civilian transport ships for moving soldiers and supplies, merchant ships carried guns, and many conflicts saw extensive civilian involvement in privateering and piracy. The first of these has continued to be an important issue in the relationship between government and the shipping industry. The chartering of transport vessels had, by the time of the Napoleonic Wars, become a lucrative business in its own right, valued by the major shipowners, who came to appreciate the guaranteed income and security of such contracts.[39]

Liverpool's shipowners, however, had long considered themselves discriminated against by the authorities when it came to the distribution of trooping contracts. The process of tendering was very much a London business. Advertisements were posted at Lloyds, the Jerusalem Coffee House, and the Royal Exchange: there was an assumption that agents would forward the news to the other ports, but no need was

---

37   BPP, West Africa mails (1852), p. 28.

38   P. N. Davies, *The trade makers: Elder Dempster in West Africa, 1852–1972*, London, 1973, p. 48.

39   S. Ville, *English shipowning during the industrial revolution: Michael Henley and Son, London shipowners, 1770–1830*, Manchester, 1987, pp. 124–25.

felt to do this directly.[40] Ships taken on for government service in the early 1850s were also required to be inspected on the Thames. While ensuring close control over the process by officials, this did not encourage Liverpool operators. The evidence from routine troop-carrying contracts in peacetime seems conclusive: vessels chartered for carrying garrisons to Malta, the West Indies and the Cape of Good Hope in the mid-1850s were almost exclusively London-owned, by large-scale shipowners like Duncan Dunbar and Joseph Somes.[41] Not without reason did Liverpool's James Baines refer to the transport business as 'a City annuity that had lapsed into two or three firms'.[42]

The situation changed in the mid-1850s, though, when Liverpool vessels – both sail and steam – proved themselves invaluable during the Crimean conflict. By the later 1850s, the advantages of the spacious between-deck accommodation of large Liverpool ships were well recognised: 'when we require vessels for troops', noted the Navy's Paymaster, 'we send to Liverpool'.[43] Liverpool's developing role in troop carrying was not without its critics. London firms, supported as usual by *The Times*, argued that some of the contracts awarded to Liverpool owners in the Crimea had been irregular. Liverpool owners responded that it was a question of supply and demand – if London shipping could not match technical specifications, it was inevitable that the authorities would turn to those who could. When London owners could offer vessels with two passenger decks, 200 ft long by 42 ft broad and more than 7 ft high, they could expect to win back government contracts, argued James Baines.[44]

In assessing how this shift came about, this section considers the changing environment of troop carrying in mid-century, and the increasing ability of Liverpool traders to provide the services sought by government. In particular, it focuses on two major naval/military operations from mid-century in which merchant shipping played a significant part: the Crimean War in 1854–5 and the Abyssinian expedition (in present- day Ethiopia) in 1867–8. The Crimean War is relatively well known – if only for the activities of Florence Nightingale and the ill-fated Light Brigade – but Abyssinia is a largely forgotten footnote in British imperial history.[45] Occasionally, some more serious historical effort is directed at these conflicts, and there have been particularly welcome moves in recent years to place them in their broader military and political contexts.[46]

Both conflicts posed major logistical challenges for the British. Transporting an expeditionary force of soldiers, horses and artillery was difficult in itself, and keeping

40   BPP, Transport service (1860), evidence of Charles Richards, q. 398.
41   BPP, Transport service (1860), appendix 2, pp. 257–59; Palmer, *Politics, shipping*, p. 14.
42   *The Times*, 2 Apr. 1855, p. 4.
43   BPP, Transport service (1860), evidence of Charles Richards, q. 396.
44   See letters and editorial comment in *The Times*, 2 Apr. 1855, p. 4; 5 Apr. 1855, p. 8.
45   Sometimes literally a footnote – see R. Hyam, *Britain's imperial century, 1815–1914*, 2nd edn, Basingstoke, 1993, p. 154.
46   A. Lambert, *The Crimean War: British grand strategy, 1853–56*, Manchester, 1990; F. Harcourt, 'Disraeli's imperialism, 1866–1868: A question of timing', *Historical Journal*, Vol. 23, 1980, pp. 87–109.

that force supplied with provisions, ammunition and other necessities was in some ways harder still in the course of a prolonged campaign. The Crimean War was at least fought in a part of the world with readily available supplies and a significant volume of steam shipping, but Abyssinia, prior to the opening of the Suez Canal, was much harder to reach from Britain. That campaign was designed to rescue a handful of British subjects being held captive by Emperor Theodore and thus demonstrate British capabilities in the region, and it became an example of the integrated military potential of the British Empire, with Bombay being responsible for organising shipping, co-ordinating supplies and sending troops.

It is worth taking a step back to consider the logistics of troop-carrying. In theory, there should have been a three-phase process in the delivery of trooping services by mid-century. The Navy itself owned some transport ships, but if these were insufficient, the mail companies' vessels would also be used. If the crisis was of such a scale that still more capacity was needed, then open tenders would be announced for private firms to supply additional vessels. In practice, matters were naturally more complex. First, it was clear by mid-century that even in peacetime the Navy's own transport ships needed to be supplemented by chartered merchant vessels. Civilian ships carried almost 28,000 troops in 1852–3, compared with only 16,000 carried by the Navy. In 1856–8, when troops had to be moved in considerable numbers following the Crimean War and during the uprising in India, chartered vessels carried almost four times the number of troops carried by Navy ships, and had a virtual monopoly on the transport of army horses.[47]

Contemporary thinking placed great emphasis on the role of the contract mail companies. Wartime service, it was argued, should be closely linked to mail contracts: the large, fast steamers built by the mail companies could also be used in time of war for the rapid transport of regiments abroad. There was also perhaps some confusion here, in that regulations did exist which specified that the mail ships ought to be capable of being armed. The impracticality of such provisions had led to their abandonment by 1860, according to the First Lord of the Admiralty, although the idea lingered on through periodic revivals.[48] Firms like Cunard nonetheless argued that their vessels deserved subsidies for being on call to the government in times of national emergency. As well as carrying troops during the Crimean campaign, Cunard liked to remind the government of its service in the tense winter of 1861/62, when war with the United States seemed possible. Being able to provide two large ships to carry reinforcements to Canada had been the firm's 'most critical' service to the Crown, carried out at considerable risk, given that the St Lawrence river had not previously been navigated by large steamers in winter.[49]

The most obvious problem with using mail ships for troop-carrying was that it inevitably caused disruption to the mails. Sometimes this just meant that firms had to charter other ships or use some of their slower vessels for carrying the mail –

---

47 BPP, Transport service (1860), evidence of Charles Richards, q. 256.
48 BPP, Transport service (1860), evidence of the Duke of Somerset, qq. 2,892–93.
49 BPP, Mail contracts (1868), evidence of John Burns, q. 1,383.

while an irritation to the letter-writing communities at either end, it was an acceptable short-term contingency. In other cases, though, matters could be much more serious: as has been discussed, Australia lost its mail service entirely as a result of the diversion of P&O ships to the Crimea. More important, though, was the level of demand for transports. From the Crimean War onward, it was evident that most conflicts involving British ground forces would require more transport shipping than could be supplied solely by the flagship companies. While at least thirty mail ships were contracted at some point during the Crimean War, this impressive mobilisation was less than a quarter of the total tonnage provided by commercial firms during the conflict.[50] In the rush to gather an expeditionary fleet, noted one shipbroker, 'every trade was drained, to the serious detriment, in some cases, of the postal service, to secure vessels propelled by steam'.[51]

If every ship belonging to every firm with a mail contract had been hired for the Crimea, therefore, there would still not have been enough, and the nation's overseas mails would have collapsed into the bargain. In addition, mail steamers were not necessarily suitable for all the tasks involved in such an operation. Large, fast steamships could deliver troops quickly to their destination, but lacked the carrying capacity to keep them efficiently supplied. Military logistics officers needed an appropriate mix of fast steamers, slower (but larger) steamers, and slower still (but cheap) sailing ships if they were to run an effective campaign while avoiding prohibitive costs. They also, of course, had to operate in the broader world of commercial shipping and develop a keen sense of what kind of shipping was available at a reasonable rate in the part of the globe in which the conflict was taking place. As was discussed in chapter two, there were still areas of the world late in the nineteenth century where sailing ships were much more common than steamers, and where hiring a steam fleet for a military campaign would have been a difficult business.

How, then, did these issues develop in the Crimea and Abyssinia? The Crimean War was the first campaign to make extensive use of steamships, and steam tonnage outnumbered sail in government requisitions for the operation. By the mid-1850s, steam was already well established in Britain's Mediterranean trades, and Liverpool's shipowners had been pioneers of large-scale cargo services to the region. Many of the factors that made steam attractive to Mediterranean traders also appealed to military planners. The distances were short enough to make steam economic, and steamers were much less vulnerable to the Mediterranean's notoriously unpredictable winds: there was therefore clear potential for a significant improvement in the reliability of military logistical operations, with troops and supplies being delivered to the war zone on a much more predictable timetable.[52]

Steamers offered two other key benefits. There was increasing interest in the use of condensers which could generate a supply of distilled water: this clean water supply

50   Calculated from BPP, Crimea transports (1854–5), pp. 2–19.
51   Quoted in *Economist*, 5 Jan. 1856, p. 5.
52   BPP, Transport service (1860), evidence of Charles Richards, q. 373.

helped prevent the spread of water-borne diseases, and also supplied troops with sufficient water when operating in hot climates. By the time of Abyssinia, part of the tendering process specifically called for vessels capable of producing 1,000 gallons of water per day.[53] Steamers also helped to make sailing ships more useful, by towing them. There are various examples of this in both the Crimea and Abyssinia, including an operation in 1854 which had four steamers towing eight sailing ships, ensuring the reliable arrival of a dozen ships, regardless of weather.[54] More nostalgic maritime historians might bemoan the humiliating spectacle of elegant sailing clippers being towed to war, but the owners of those ships were pragmatists who welcomed the income and the reduced wear and tear on the sails.

As would be expected, mail steamers were heavily deployed in the Crimean campaign. Five firms with mail contracts provided thirty vessels totalling just over 53,000 tons, at rates of £2 10s per ton per month. For example, the South American & General's *Imperatrix* earned just over £13,000 for a three-month contract from November 1854. That firm's three ships, plus seven of Cunard's, made up Liverpool's contribution to the mail steamer requisitions. Most of the rest came from P&O and the Royal Mail Steam Packet Co. In addition to the mail steamers, another 76,000 tons of steam shipping was hired from other firms, along with 93,000 tons of sail.[55]

Unfortunately, the evidence does not readily point to the proportion of this tonnage that came from Liverpool (it is better in the case of the Abyssinian campaign, as will be discussed shortly). Nonetheless, the port's new steam operators clearly took advantage of the opportunity. At least three Bibby steamers worked in the Crimea. In addition, the firm sold two recently built vessels to the French government for use in the conflict. Bibby's collaborators James Moss & Co. had three ships chartered by the French during the conflict.[56] William Inman was also keen to have vessels chartered, and managed to have one taken up by the British and three by the French.[57] Inman clearly saw the experience as a positive one, and offered one of the vessels again three years later for carrying reinforcements after the uprising in India. Such national service carried considerable prestige, and Inman made sure that the press was well aware of the achievements of his fleet in supplying the armed forces.[58]

Some of Liverpool's prominent sail operators also welcomed the chance to have vessels chartered for the Crimea. Edward Oliver, with a huge fleet and presumably already aware of the parlous state of his finances, sought contracts for his sailing ships on a considerable scale. At least eight of his vessels were hired, totalling just under 8,000 tons, at rates of £1 10s per ton per month. Given the average contract of four months for sailing vessels, Oliver made just under £50,000 from the Crimean

---

53 BPP, Abyssinia (1869), evidence of William Meads, q. 1,450.

54 See the account in an anonymous Crimean War diary, 7 Sept. 1854, collection no. 153, Perkins Library, Duke University.

55 BPP, Crimea transports (1854–5), pp. 18–19.

56 H. C. B. Rogers, *Troopships and their history*, London, 1963, p. 116; D. Haws, *The Burma Boats: Henderson & Bibby*, Uckfield, 1995, pp. 97–101.

57 Bonsor, *North Atlantic seaway*, vol. 1, p. 238.

58 *The Times*, 15 Dec. 1857, p. 12.

War – although, as we have seen, his liabilities were more than twelve times that when his business collapsed in 1854.[59]

Oliver's activities are a reminder that even as steam was establishing its worth in the Crimea, sail remained a necessary element in official calculations. This remained the case when planning the Abyssinian campaign in 1868. By that date – before the opening of the Suez Canal – steam was not yet the dominant form of shipping in the Indian Ocean. Some shipping was needed in Britain, to carry troops based at home and as floating hospitals, but the major part of the operation was handled from India. The authorities in each place had to operate in a very different commercial environment. In Britain, the Admiralty had no difficulty recruiting eighteen large steamships, with a total tonnage of 34,284. The ten largest and most modern steamers all commenced their voyages in Liverpool, while the remaining eight – hospital ships or mule carriers – left from the Thames. Leading Liverpool owners were well represented in the former group: two of William Inman's vessels were chartered, as were two belonging to the National Steam Navigation Co., two from T. M. Mackay & Sons, and four from the West India & Pacific Co.[60]

Most of these were chartered at a rate of around 32s per ton per month. It is indicative, though, of the different commercial environment, that the authorities in India were forced to pay much more for steamers when organising their part of the Abyssinian expedition. Steam services in the Indian Ocean remained heavily dependent on subsidies, and had, roughly, the sort of profile the Atlantic services had in the 1840s. The British India Company's vessels were chartered at rates around 50s, thanks to a clause in their mail contract – roundly criticised in the subsequent enquiry – which guaranteed them a high charter price should they be used for anything other than carrying the mails.[61] Facing shortages and high rates for steam tonnage, the Indian authorities also made full use of the large sailing ships that still carried the major proportion of the East's trade with Europe. Again, as has been noted, the operation of sailing ships in the bulk carrying trades to and from the East was a speciality of Liverpool firms in the 1860s, leaving them well placed to bid for Abyssinia contracts.

Liverpool sailing ship owners therefore moved quickly to seek employment in the Abyssinian campaign. Overall, at least thirty Liverpool firms had a total of fifty vessels accepted for service, comprising just under one-third of the sailing tonnage hired in Bombay during the crisis. Liverpool firms were supplying quality as well as quantity, as reflected in the average size of vessels chosen. The overall average tonnage of sailing ships chartered from Bombay was just over 1,000 tons, but Liverpool's contribution averaged 1,200.[62] These figures have some margin for error because the surviving evidence lists local agents rather than the owners of the vessels, and some

59 BPP, Crimea transports (1854–5), pp. 2–19.
60 BPP, Abyssinia transports (1870).
61 BPP, Abyssinia (1870), p. xxiii.
62 Data on the vessels contracted for Abyssinia are abstracted from BPP, Abyssinia transports (1870).

ships cannot be traced back through Lloyd's *Register*. Nevertheless, the scale of Liverpool involvement is clear. Several firms had more than one vessel in service, and a few were much more heavily involved, reflecting both the scale of operation of some Liverpool firms in the East and their willingness to tender for government service. Edward Bates is the most prominent example of a Liverpool sailing ship operator active in the Abyssinian campaign. Bates tendered eleven vessels to the authorities in Bombay, nine of which – with a total tonnage of 10,540 – were accepted. Another of Bates' vessels was accepted in Calcutta by the transport officer there. Most of these vessels performed unexceptional cargo duties, transporting supplies from India to the expeditionary force's supply beachhead at Annesley Bay in Abyssinia.

This apparent keenness of shipowners to become involved in government contracting rang alarm bells in Parliament, where it was suspected that too much was being paid for troop-carrying. MPs were suspicious of the costs involved and of the apparent contradiction in the attitudes of major shipowners, who complained about bureaucracy and poor remuneration, but rarely missed a chance to tender for government work. If the Admiralty was operating in a buyer's market, should it not have been able to drive the costs down? Parliament believed that the owners of the largest vessels had made 'fabulous profits' from service in the Crimea.[63] 'Excessive prices seem to have been paid,' concluded the 1870 Committee investigating Abyssinia, in large part because many vessels offering low tenders were rejected for apparently arbitrary reasons.[64] Historians have also referred to the 'rich rewards' and 'windfall earnings' of mail companies involved in supplying imperial expeditions and wars.[65]

There is no doubt that there was active competition for government contracts, which the Admiralty claimed to exploit where possible. In times of particular crisis, officials could play owners off against one another, confident that an owner would accept a reduced rate in preference to no contract at all. Although rates were high at the very beginning of the Crimean conflict, the Transport Board never lacked offers for ships and its officials later claimed that they had been able to drive down costs considerably.[66] Once it was perceived that the conflict would require considerable shipping resources over a period of months, some owners bought ships specifically to charter to the government. James Baines bought the paddle steamer *Vestal* for the purpose, despite being much more focused on large sailing ships in his normal business.[67]

This determination to secure government contracts for the Crimea had side-effects that worried some observers. Britain's consular staff in Barcelona noticed a sharp increase in the amount of British goods being landed there in foreign ships: the Scandinavians and the Prussians seemed to be taking over important elements in

---

63   BPP, Merchant shipping (1860), p. ix.
64   BPP, Abyssinia (1870), p. xxii.
65   Harcourt, 'British oceanic mail contracts', pp. 12–13.
66   BPP, Transport service (1860), evidence of Edward Giffard, qq. 530, 723–29.
67   D. Hollett, *Fast passage to Australia*, London, 1986, p. 63.

European shipping at the expense of British vessels.[68] By the end of the decade, and with considerable hindsight, owners were complaining that the opportunities of the Crimean years had made them turn their backs on routine trades, which had accordingly been lost to other fleets.[69]

Nevertheless, wartime contracts remained keenly sought by British shipowners. When choosing its eighteen steamers for Abyssinia, the Admiralty was not restricted in its choice. No fewer than 129 other steam vessels were offered by British owners in response to the initial tender. Of those, 73 were rejected as not meeting the required specifications, but the Admiralty was still able to choose from a total of 74 suitable vessels. In all, just over 200,000 tons of steam shipping was offered in Britain. Average tonnage of the accepted vessels was notably higher than that of those rejected (1,904 against 1,198), and it is clear that the Admiralty was able to operate in a buyer's market as far as quality and size were concerned.[70]

The desire of shipowners to be awarded these contracts is clear from the list of vessels rejected. It has already been noted that Liverpool's T. M. Mackay & Sons, for example, had two vessels accepted for service: the firm put forward another six, only two of which met the specifications. Some owners went to even greater lengths. The British India Steam Navigation Co. offered eight steamers in London, all of which were rejected. The reason for their rejection, however, was that they were nowhere near Britain at the time: six of them were chartered shortly afterwards by the authorities in India. Others rushed to have a share, with vessels from all over the Eastern colonies making their way to India 'on the chance of being taken up; indeed, everyone was mad about it'.[71]

Steam operators in the East were particularly keen to find an alternative income, having suffered in the later 1860s because of the slump in cotton. The British India Company welcomed its windfall earnings from the Abyssinian campaign at a time when it was suffering a drop in income from its conventional activities.[72] Witnesses called before Parliament agreed that working on war contracts meant that owners could 'employ the ships in a very profitable way both for ourselves and for the Government'.[73]

A number of possibilities can be tested. Government officials believed that shipowners did not collude to fix an artificially high rate of tender – shipping was such a fragmented industry, and tenders required with such urgency, that no organised process of price-fixing was possible.[74] Ample evidence exists to bear this out. The vessels tendered as troopships for Abyssinia were offered at rates varying from 21s to 50s, bearing out the view of one shipowner that his colleagues did not trust each

68   BPP, Commercial reports (1855), pp. 137–38.
69   BPP, Merchant shipping (1860), evidence of James Smith, q. 2,492.
70   Calculated from BPP, Abyssinia transports (1870).
71   BPP, Abyssinia (1870), evidence of Capt. William Darke, q. 2,920.
72   Munro, '"Scrubby Scotch Screw Company"', p. 65.
73   BPP, Abyssinia (1870), evidence of Capt. William Darke, q. 2,891.
74   BPP, Transport service (1860), evidence of Charles Richards, q. 439.

other sufficiently to collaborate in raising rates.[75] In addition, there was often a broad range of views among shipowners as to what was actually a fair price for a particular service. Efforts by the government to establish fair rates for particular types of work met with varied opinion from shipowners throughout this period. East India brokers and shipowners responded to a questionnaire in 1860 with a marked range of prices. Acceptable rates for carrying troops to the East varied from £15 to £45 per man, in the view of the firms concerned.[76]

Even so, there is evidence that considerable savings could have been squeezed from shipowners. The vessels accepted for Abyssinia in the UK were hired for an average of 32s per ton per month. Only nine of the 56 other vessels that met the specifications had tendered at a higher rate, and most were offered at a rate of at least 5s less. One shipowner claimed later that the Admiralty could have set the price at 20s without suffering a shortage of suitable vessels.[77] This witness may have been exaggerating: his firm, Temperleys of London, had four vessels rejected at rates nearer 25s than 20s. Even that level of saving, however, could have reduced the transport service's bill for the expedition by almost £100,000.

One aspect of the wartime chartering process that aroused particular suspicion was whether owners were offering very old vessels that were reaching the end of their working lives anyway, in the hope of making considerable sums from a ship that would probably otherwise have been sold for a much smaller figure. The hospital ships used in the campaign were a particular target for critics, having been laid up for some time in the aftermath of the collapse of the London firm of Overend Gurney. The largest of them, the *Golden Fleece*, was clearly well-named in the opinion of the 1869 Committee, which argued that the government could have bought the vessel for a fraction of the £49,824 it cost for a year's charter.[78]

Other inefficiencies were identified in the subsequent enquiries. By the time of the Abyssinian campaign, shipowners benefited from a determination on the part of the authorities to ensure effective supply lines whatever the cost. The Commissary General in Chief admitted that concerns over the failure of supply and support during the Crimean War had created a culture in later years in which the authorities were keen to err on the side of over-supply.[79] The consequence was considerable waste, little of which was a problem to the shipowners, as some of it could even be turned into additional profit. *Alsager*, belonging to Gibbs, Bright & Co., was chartered in Bombay to carry a cargo of hay to Abyssinia. Only part of the cargo was needed, and the firm was allowed to sell the remainder at a profit of £400, in addition to a charter rate over seven months that clearly met the company's approval.[80]

As well as ensuring that enough supplies were secured, the authorities took pains

---

75 From prices listed in BPP, Abyssinia transports (1870); BPP, Abyssinia (1870), evidence of Capt. William Darke, q. 2,942.
76 BPP, Transport service (1860), appendices, pp. 298–99.
77 BPP, Abyssinia (1870), evidence of Capt. William Darke, q. 2,883.
78 BPP, Abyssinia (1870), evidence of R. Adm. William R. Meads, qq. 1,831–36.
79 BPP, Abyssinia (1870), evidence of Sir William Power, q. 4,515.
80 BPP, Abyssinia (1870), evidence of Tyndall Bright, qq. 2,095–146.

to stress that they were paying for high quality as well. This applied not only to shipping but to those handling the goods themselves. Gillespie & Scott of Liverpool secured a contract for the delivery of 14,000 tons of coal during the Abyssinian campaign, having been performing similar duties for the government since the Crimean War. They were paid 19s per ton in 1867/68, at a time when, the Parliamentary committee noted, coal cost about 10s per ton. This additional cost – around £6,500 – was justified on the grounds that it secured high-quality coal and committed service from the supplier.[81]

There seemed to be no way that shipowners could lose, at least within the boundaries of the contracting system, but some witnesses at the subsequent enquiries accused the Parliamentary Committees of judgement based on hindsight. The speed with which the expeditions had to be dispatched was considerable, and the transport officials clearly took some pride from their success in mobilising a large tonnage of shipping in a short period: it was a lot easier, they suggested, for the Committees to find fault in minor details than it had been to co-ordinate a complex operation in the first place.

Clearly, there are wider issues here, which would repay more detailed study by historians. For the purposes of this analysis, it is important to stress the scale and range of Liverpool's involvement in troop contracts. The diversity of shipping used by Liverpool traders in mid-century ensured that they could take advantage of opportunities across the range of vessel types and sizes needed by government. It is also worth noting the determination of the port's sailing ship operators to have a prominent role, further underlining the flexibility and pragmatism of this allegedly declining sector of the trade. This was also a key theme in Liverpool's response to the third major area of contact with government funding, emigration.

EMIGRATION

The final area of significant interaction between shipowners and government in the mid-nineteenth century was the provision of shipping for the mass migrations of the period. Again, the role of government was two-fold, as both regulator and paymaster, but the balance was rather different in this case. The regulatory function was more systematic, with inspections of emigrant vessels and a distinctly hands-on approach by the government's emigration officers. The financial question was less clear-cut. A significant proportion of emigration to Australia was financed by government charter, but other migrants paid fares themselves or were supported by charitable organisations. Emigration to the Americas was much more likely to be self-financed, but emigration officers nonetheless had a regulatory duty under the various Passenger Acts. Being subject to government rules even when the government was not paying for the service set a rather different tone for the relationship between traders and government.

Previous historians of the emigration business have stressed the often *ad hoc*

81 BPP, Abyssinia (1869), evidence of Robert Dundas, qq. 1,395–427.

evolution of the regulatory mechanisms of the state, and the surprising lack of theoretical underpinning of passenger safety laws. The development of the office of the Emigration Commissioners was not part of a grand design based on systematic planning to alleviate the dangers of the emigrant trades, but rather a series of hurried responses to particular events and incidents.[82] Other work on the topic – focused on London in the first half of the century – suggests the need to pay more attention to the activities of the entrepreneurs themselves, who did not passively wait for government to hand out contracts, but actively drummed up business and recruited emigrants.[83]

Too aggressive a pursuit of profit in emigration could be counter-productive, however. Mid-century Liverpool traders working in the field had to overcome a legacy of business practice that was at best unsavoury and at worst dangerous and fraudulent. One historian has gone so far as to draw comparisons between the transport of emigrants in the first half of the nineteenth century and that of slaves in the eighteenth century and victims of the Holocaust in the twentieth.[84] One of the problems was a lack of accountability in the way the trade was managed. Major Liverpool shipowners could, probably truthfully, claim to know little of the arrangements for transporting emigrants in the between-decks of their ships, and many passages were made at a still further level of detachment. An emigrant might buy a ticket from an agent, who had sub-let a deck from the master of a vessel that had already been chartered for cargo. British operators tended not to give priority to the emigrant traffic, but rather sold space on ordinary cargo vessels to emigration agents, who then handled the passengers.[85]

This is not to argue that Liverpool traders involved in emigration from the 1850s were paragons who swept away the old practices in a fit of philanthropic zeal, but they were operating on a different scale, determined to take advantage of the rising market in migration, and conscious that their reputations were valuable assets. The transport of emigrants ceased to be an after-thought, a bonus profit to be gained after the main cargo had been loaded – it became a vital element in the revenue of major firms, and had to be protected as such. Liverpool's shipowners made important inroads in the two major areas of mid-century migration, North America and Australia. The former was closely tied to the use of steam on the Atlantic routes, and to competition between the various steam companies. The latter was a striking new opportunity in mid-century, as the discovery of gold promised to turn the Australian colonies into a serious market for the first time.

We should first consider the contrasting scale and nature of the two main

---

82 O. Macdonagh, 'Emigration and the state, 1833–55: An essay in administrative history', *Transactions of the Royal History Society*, 5th series, Vol. 5, 1955, pp. 133–60.

83 F. Broeze, 'Private enterprise and the peopling of Australia, 1831–50', *Economic History Review*, Vol. 35, 1982, pp. 235–53.

84 R. Scally, 'Liverpool ships and Irish emigrants in the age of sail', *Journal of Social History*, Vol. 17, 1983–4, pp. 5–30.

85 BPP, Passengers Act (1851), evidence of Robert Rankin, qq. 4,478–84; evidence of T. E. Hodder, q. 1,038.

emigration trades, and then pay more attention to the interplay between shipowners and government in relation to each. Geographically, Liverpool was, of course, well placed as a centre for Atlantic emigration, with a long record of Atlantic trade and strong connections with Ireland – the source, tragically, of much emigrant traffic from the 1840s. As was discussed in chapter two, however, Liverpool's trade with the United States was dominated by US shipping prior to the American Civil War, with the result that most emigrants crossing the Atlantic went in US vessels. Large American sailing ships were prominent in the port at the time of the Irish famine in the late 1840s, and built on their reputation during the following decade. In 1850, the Atlantic emigrant trade through Liverpool was reckoned to be worth half a million pounds in ticket sales, at least two-thirds of which went to American ships.[86]

William Inman's arrival in the market in 1850 was therefore rather daring, with the application of a new technology – the screw steamship – to the emigrant business. Inman identified a market that few others would have risked. Cunard's mail contract gave it little incentive in the 1850s to move beyond its paddle steamers on the Atlantic run, which were tried and tested for the carriage of mails and the better-off passengers, but which lacked the capacity for a large steerage class of accommodation. Equally, the American ships offered many emigrants as good a service as they needed or were able to pay for. Inman set out to demonstrate that he could provide faster, healthier, and more reliable passage for emigrants with the latest steamships, and that they would be willing to pay for the service. He succeeded. In part, he guessed correctly that the emigration movement he saw increasing in the late 1840s would continue to rise, although the scale of the increase in the mid-1850s was a welcome and probably unexpected bonus. The collapse of the American merchant marine in the early 1860s was a piece of great good fortune to Liverpool shipowners, although in the short term it also coincided with a fall in emigration traffic.

Inman's timing seems even more fortunate when the experience of his main Atlantic rival is considered. Having witnessed Inman's success in the emigrant and more general trades during the 1850s, Cunard aimed to use its prestige and reputation to attract emigrant passengers from 1860. This effort only lasted for a year before being suspended in the first months of the American Civil War. Nonetheless, it was restarted in 1863, and in the decade that followed, Cunard not only secured a share of the emigrant trade, but replaced its ageing paddle fleet with large screw steamers and stopped falling behind the innovative Inman. Liverpool's joint-stock steam companies also gained a share of the trade, and competition among the firms became pronounced. The new firms sought to market their operations as being straightforward and efficient from the emigrant's viewpoint, with a recognisably modern system of ticketing and administration. By using networks of agents in Europe and North America, and by negotiating arrangements with railway companies, firms could advertise a more or less complete package. By the 1860s, therefore, emigration on

---

86   BPP, Passengers Act (1851), evidence of T. E. Hodder, q. 1,257.

the Atlantic had been transformed from a fragmented business surrounded by much odium into a high-profile trade controlled by some of Liverpool's flagship operators.

Australian emigration was also a much more professional business in the hands of Liverpool shipping operators in mid-century. Again, this was partly due to the drive of some of the port's traders and partly due to favourable external circumstances. More official funding went into Australian emigration, and the Emigration Commissioners favoured the Mersey as an effective departure point for emigrants travelling under their auspices. Like troop-carrying, the transport of emigrants always had to be conducted as an integral part of other trading patterns, and the more reasons shipowners had to send their ships to a particular port, the easier it was for those organising emigration to secure reasonable rates of passage. The emigration station at Birkenhead was ideal: there was always plenty of shipping available on the Mersey, and outward cargo waiting to go to the colonies.[87] In addition, an increasing volume of that shipping in the 1850s and 1860s was in large wood or iron sailing ships working the Latin American or Far East trades. Liverpool's shipowners working in those trades recognised that such vessels were readily adaptable to carry emigrants to Australia and then take a return bulk cargo of cotton from India. Such favourable conditions in both the Australian and US emigrant trades gave Liverpool by far the largest single share of the business in mid-century: in the early 1850s, two in every three people emigrating from the entire United Kingdom left from the Mersey.[88]

Australian emigration entered a new phase with gold strikes in New South Wales in 1851, and rapidly became big business. The busiest year for Australian emigration, 1854, saw 127 ships carry 41,000 emigrants under the auspices of the Emigration Commissioners.[89] Traffic on that scale, all monitored by a government agency, inevitably sparked some conflict between shipowners and the local emigration officers. Some shipowners complained bitterly about petty and arbitrary rules. Liverpool's James Beazely claimed to have been driven out of the Australian trade by the new Passenger Acts, which burdened British vessels with too many ill-informed safety rules.[90] One of his London counterparts, Far East trader George Marshall, argued that the ventilation requirements imposed by the Commissioners made vessels dangerous (having too many holes in the deck), and that there was a lack of consistency between the views of officials supervising each port. Anyone reading the Commissioners' rules, he believed, would 'fancy that shipowners were either mad or something very like it, to place themselves under such obligations, but competition obliges them to do it'.[91]

The regulations were indeed comprehensive. The accommodation deck had to be at least 6 ft 4 in. in height, each adult had to have 15 square feet of space, and 20 cubic feet for luggage in the hold. There were limits to the number of emigrants to

87 BPP, Transport service (1860), evidence of Charles Alexander Wood, q. 2,184.
88 BPP, Emigration report (1854), pp. 62–63.
89 BPP, Transport service (1860), evidence of Thomas Murdoch, q. 972.
90 BPP, Merchant shipping (1860), evidence of James Beazely, q. 2,213.
91 BPP, Transport service (1860), evidence of George Marshall, qq. 2,679–81.

be carried (400 'statute adults' – children were counted as a percentage); restrictions on the cargoes that could be carried by the shipowner in the rest of the vessel; and prescribed specifications for food and medicinal supplies. A surgeon had to be carried free of charge, and he – not the ship's master – had responsibility for the emigrants. While masters might well have welcomed the reduced workload, this arrangement did reduce their traditional authority over the management of their vessels. The Secretary to the Emigration Board noted in 1860 that these conditions were more onerous than those for troop transport, and that shipowners accordingly preferred to carry troops when that work was available.[92] In addition, if the travelling conditions enforced by these regulations seem sparse, they were a considerable improvement on the common practice of the 1830s, when adults could only expect 6 square feet of space on decks with 5 ft 6 in. headroom, and baggage was stowed in the living space.[93] Such improvements clearly meant that older vessels were being regulated out of the emigration trades, and that new, larger ships had to be deployed by mid-century.

Despite all this, the major Liverpool operators reached an effective working relationship with the Commissioners in mid-century, and had come to dominate the emigration trades, making it hard for smaller firms to survive. Outclassed by the large Liverpool-based fleets, London firms were reduced to complaining about the rules and slandering the build-quality of Liverpool's emigrant clippers. The long-running dispute between Liverpool and London over Lloyds classification surfaced again in this context, with London owners alleging that many large Liverpool ships were not registered at Lloyds because they were of poor quality, rather than because their owners saw Lloyds' rules as obsolete and restrictive.[94] Some of the mud stuck, though, at least until Liverpool ships had established their capabilities in all sectors of government business. By the early 1870s, the safety records of the major Liverpool operators were regarded as better testimony to the quality of their vessels than any Lloyds classification.[95]

The Commissioners and the Liverpool operators agreed that theirs was an amicable relationship. James Baines certainly devoted considerable effort to cultivating the local officials. The emigration officer was always invited to the celebratory 'déjeuner' held on board Baines' vessels before they sailed for Australia, and Baines went so far as to name one of his ships *Schomberg* after the chief Liverpool officer. Nathaniel Hawthorne found himself quite charmed by Mrs Schomberg at the party marking the transfer of the *James Baines* from US to British registry in 1854.[96] Competitors doubtless liked to believe that this relationship was rather too cosy, but Baines' ships gave him a great advantage – his vessels were newer and larger than those of his

92   BPP, Transport service (1860), S. Walcott to Maj. Gen. Sir A. Tulloch, 27 Mar. 1860, app. 5, paper 1.
93   MacDonagh, 'Emigration and the State', p. 138.
94   BPP, Transport service (1860), evidence of George Marshall, q. 2,709.
95   BPP, Unseaworthy ships (1874), evidence of Charles Grayson, q. 15,859.
96   N. Hawthorne, *The English notebooks*, New York, 1941, p. 89.

London competitors and could be made to conform to changing regulatory standards much more easily. Trying to make smaller, older vessels fit rules that were specifically designed to improve space and ventilation was bound to be harder, and less profitable, for London owners. Putting some effort into meeting the Commissioners' specifications also gave operators like Baines support in times of trouble. When vessels were lost, shipowners could readily refute allegations of negligence by pointing to the rigid standards to which they had to adhere.[97]

If Baines recognised that a friendly relationship with the Emigration Commissioners was central to the success of his business, he was nonetheless critical of broader aspects of government contracting. Baines, like others, recognised the considerable potential for overlap between emigration work and troop-carrying, because – by and large – the same vessels were suitable for both. However, the three agencies responsible for these activities in the 1850s – the Emigration Commissioners, the Admiralty and the East India Company – operated entirely separate tendering processes, with different rules. Shipowners had to deal with technical issues in the design and operation of the ships themselves, and also with difficult business decisions as a consequence of the tendering process.

Some issues seem trivial, but caused considerable difficulties in the logistical management of fleets. As has been noted, the large iron sailing ships commonly used in trade with the west coast of South America also made very effective troop and emigrant ships. However, if a vessel had been used to carry guano, the Admiralty did not consider it acceptable for subsequent employment as a troop ship. The Emigration Commissioners took a more lenient view, approving such vessels if they had been appropriately treated to remove the fumes of the cargo. Shipowners naturally sided with the latter view – the idea that ships could not be divested of the smell of guano was an 'insult to the chemists of England'.[98] Nonetheless, for an operator like Baines, buying second-hand ships and chartering others in anticipation of a steady business in government contracting, keeping an eye on such rules and ensuring that the right vessels were available to match the particular needs of the next agency to advertise, posed an administrative problem.[99]

Some rationalisation of the tendering process was actively considered in the late 1850s, but apart from the obvious jealousies of different government departments being forced to collaborate, it was unclear to the authorities whether any real benefit would be gained. The chief Emigration Commissioner Thomas Murdoch offered an assessment of the tendering process, concluding that lower costs had been maintained for emigrant voyages than for troop-carrying during the 1850s, and suggesting that economies could be made by adopting best practice.[100] However, government agencies clearly operated in a buyer's market, with no shortage of suitable vessels being tendered every time the need for shipping was advertised: a more rigid enforcement

---

97 *The Times*, 2 Oct. 1860, p. 10.
98 BPP, Transport service (1860), evidence of James Miller Mackay, q. 2,931.
99 BPP, Transport service (1860), evidence of William Phillipps, q. 2,416.
100 BPP, Transport service (1860), appendix 5, paper 1, pp. 295–97.

of the lowest possible rates might ensure sufficient economies anyway. Nor was there any expectation that a single agency would necessarily drive down costs: shipowners complained about the duplication of effort on their part caused by having to apply to the different agencies, but of course denied that they would be able to charge lower freights if the system was streamlined.[101]

As has been noted, however, the emigration business was not just a debate between government and the shipping industry, but also required active recruitment of the emigrants themselves. This was especially true of those who were paying their own way, but even emigrants financed by the state or by charities had to be persuaded to go – in this sense it was a rather different business from carrying mail or troops. The imaginative packaging of Atlantic emigration has already been mentioned, and shipowners active in the Australian emigration trades were also keen to recruit from as many directions as possible. During the crisis in the textile industry in the early 1860s, charitable funds were established to pay for the free passage of unemployed cotton spinners to Australia in co-operation with the colonial authorities in Queensland. One such effort early in 1863 aimed to send a thousand emigrants, which would have required three large vessels – predictably, James Baines & Co., happy to have this guaranteed income, were reported to be 'doing their utmost to guide those cotton spinners wishful to obtain free passages to Queensland'.[102]

Networks of financial benefactors, shipping firms and local agents grew up in mid-century, with the aim of guiding poorer migrants through the system and making sure that they did not switch to another company's ships at the last minute: through-ticketing from obscure corners of Europe to America may have been convenient for the traveller, but it was also of vital benefit to the shipping firm. The connection between Irish emigration promoter Vere Foster and Liverpool shipping agent Henry Boyd facilitated the dispatch of refugees from the Irish famine to new lives in North America.[103] Efforts to integrate operations were also made, trying to ensure that emigrants were brought under the protection of the shipping firm as early in their journeys as possible. Barton & Brown and De Wolf & Co., both active in the Australian trades, established an Emigrants' Home in Birkenhead in 1852, managed by one of De Wolf's clerks and his wife.[104]

Emigration was therefore increasingly a business that required full-time commitment and extensive networks of connections, in some contrast to the *ad hoc* and disreputable industry of the earlier part of the century. It was also an activity that fitted remarkably well with a range of other trading functions developed in Liverpool in this period, further underlining the benefits of the spin-off effect in a port with a broad spectrum of complementary trades.

---

101 BPP, Transport service (1860), evidence of James Miller Mackay, qq. 2,911–13.

102 *Gore's Advertiser*, 22 Jan. 1863, p. 1.

103 M. A. Busteed, 'A Liverpool shipping agent and Irish emigration in the 1850s: Some newly discovered documents', *Transactions of the Historic Society of Lancashire & Cheshire*, Vol. 129, 1979, pp. 145–62.

104 Hollett, *Fast passage*, p. 13.

The relationship between Liverpool traders and the contracting authorities underlines the pragmatism of the port's approach to its mid-century expansion – the process of securing contracts was greatly helped by the broad profile of Liverpool's activities, and especially by the extensive variety of shipping available to meet almost any demand from government. Nonetheless, although government contracts might have been easy money once secured, getting them in the first place required the determination of leading shipowners to challenge entrenched interests and break into hitherto restricted sources of income and prestige. It is reasonable to measure at least part of a trading community's success in this period by its ability to impress officialdom, and the inclusion of a large tonnage of Liverpool shipping in major government ventures by the 1850s is symbolic of a significant improvement in the port's reputation.

Chapter 9

INTEREST, FACTION AND
PORT MANAGEMENT

Chapter four considered the challenges facing Liverpool's port authority in the accommodation of change and diversity, and suggested that a variety of political agendas lurked behind much contemporary debate over these issues. Those managing the port had critics and supporters alike among the town's opinion-formers, and among political figures at national level. The strategic direction of the Mersey dock estate was often as much a business for Liverpool Town Hall and the House of Commons as it was for the port authority, and the consequences for those using the port were far-reaching.

A scan of the local newspapers and other contemporary testimony points to the early years of the new Mersey Docks & Harbour Board (MDHB, founded in 1858) as a period of particular administrative controversy, which comes as no surprise given the upheavals in the broader trading environment of that period. Some sectors of the press despaired of a Board that seemed to be struggling to balance the interests of competing factions, and slipping into inertia and poor management. As early as 1863, a weary reporter was informing his readers about a Board meeting during which 'a long and exceedingly desultory discussion took place relative to providing accommodation for the steam trade, but nothing of the slightest public interest was elicited'.[1] Later commentators have been equally critical of the Board in this period. Recalling the Board's activities in his youth, William Forwood claimed that the 1870s had seen bitter disputes between different trades for representation on the Board, and widespread manipulation of the election process.[2] The Board's own historian pointed to the mid-century era as a rough patch, although he argued that it was short-lived. Mountfield believed that the Board had, by the late 1860s, already set its mind 'not on sectional interests but on the commerce and trade of the whole Port'.[3]

Of course, historians have reason to be suspicious of some of this evidence. Men like Forwood had every interest in highlighting early failures, because they themselves claimed credit for reforming the work of the Board later in the century. When Forwood wrote, early in the twentieth century, that 'there is no branch of the public service of which Liverpool people are more proud', his case was helped by the

---

1   *Gore's Advertiser*, 8 Oct. 1863, p. 6.
2   W. B. Forwood, *Recollections of a busy life, being the reminiscences of a Liverpool merchant, 1840–1910*, Liverpool, 1910, pp. 37–38.
3   S. Mountfield, *Western gateway: A history of the Mersey Docks and Harbour Board*, Liverpool, 1965, p. 26.

contrast he drew with the earlier period.[4] Equally, contemporary politics casts doubt on the positive views of James Picton, who argued in the 1870s that their 'vigour, energy and prudence' placed the Board 'in the first rank of administrators in the country'.[5] Picton was a Liberal champion of the trading community's struggle against vested interests, and would therefore be expected to take just that stance.

Nonetheless, more recent scholars have also identified divisions and factionalism as real and dangerous issues in the management of the port. Historians have favoured a framework for the development of the MDHB in the nineteenth century that has the authority bombarded by external and internal pressures. The former came from various groups united only by the belief that Liverpool was taking unfair advantage of its monopoly of trading infrastructure on the Mersey. Consequently, the port faced challenges from railway companies who either set up subsidised ports in competition or levied excessive freight charges on users of existing ones. Later, the merchants of Manchester fought a long campaign to have a Ship Canal that would give them their own docks far inland. Internal pressures came from competing sections of Liverpool's own trading community, from disputes between the town and the port, and from the advocates of the port of Birkenhead. The last major study of the port of Liverpool attempted to analyse the factional dimension of the Board's activities, but struggled to distinguish between internal divisions and external threats. Hyde devoted much discussion to internal divisions which, he conceded, could be 'harmful to the interests of Merseyside's growth as a port': on the whole, however, Hyde argued that external pressure was by far the more serious threat to the Board's work.[6]

In the context of Hyde's time-frame, and especially given the activities of the Ship Canal promoters in the later nineteenth century, this judgement makes some sense, but the internal/external dichotomy is a much less helpful framework for understanding mid-century disputes. In particular, the decision-making processes of mid-century England rarely allowed local issues to stay local. Dock building and port management regularly came under Parliamentary scrutiny, and apparently internal issues rapidly acquired wider implications. Efforts to define internal and external disputes obscure the issues rather than illuminating them.

Yet the contemporaneous shifts in trade, shipping, business practices and the management of the port offer a unique opportunity to study a crucial laboratory of change. This chapter therefore analyses port management in mid-century Liverpool, using divisions and tension in the trading community as an investigative and explanatory framework, while resisting the pitfalls of artificial definitions. The changing relationship between the port authority and factional interests over the period was driven by a range of factors. Earlier chapters of the book have highlighted the diversification of shipping and goods, and the diversification also of the trading community. Both placed increased demands on the port authority in mid-century,

4 Forwood, *Recollections of a busy life*, p. 39.

5 J. A. Picton, *Memorials of Liverpool*, 2 vols, London, 1873, vol. 1, p. 585.

6 F. E. Hyde, *Liverpool and the Mersey: An economic history of a port, 1700–1970*, Newton Abbot, 1971, chap. 7, pp. 121, 132.

whether in the practicalities of accommodating a changing traffic or in the political problems of meeting the competing demands of vocal and powerful factions.

INTERESTS AND INFLUENCE

The diversification of trade and traders would have been complex in any case, but it happened in a period when the Mersey port authority was also being significantly redefined. Exactly how members of the trading community brought influence to bear on members of the port authority remains unclear, as does the level of influence considered appropriate by contemporaries, given that a number of individuals were leading traders *and* members of the Dock Board. This section highlights some general principles and patterns.

The first point to be made concerns the role of traders in the decision-making processes of the port of Liverpool by mid-century. Looked at superficially, the changing face of the port authority is almost a Whiggish stereotype of the inexorable progress of the mercantile and commercial classes. Liverpool's pioneering efforts in dock building during the eighteenth century were driven by the port's traders, who used their influence on the Town Council.[7] Under an Act of Parliament of 1762, Liverpool's slowly developing dock estate was placed under the control of a Dock Trust, which rendered more formal the existing workings of the Liverpool Town Council, and oversaw the construction of four new docks in the later eighteenth century. By the beginning of the nineteenth century, however, trading interests doubted that the Dock Trust, as manifested in the Council Dock Committee, was fully representing their priorities. The various regional trade associations began to argue for more representation, and by 1825 were demanding that at least half the Dock Committee be elected by the port's users: Liverpool trader and MP William Huskisson brokered a compromise that gave the merchants eight members out of twenty-one.[8] The Committee as a whole was clearly committed to expansion, whatever its composition: it was this Committee, chaired by South America merchant John Bramley Moore, that drove through the dramatic period of dock planning and building in the mid-1840s.

Divisions between the elected and appointed members of the Committee emerged in the later 1840s, however, over the issue of rating the dock estate. Traders opposed the measure, but the Council came to be dominated by those in favour, and they nominated members of the Dock Committee accordingly.[9] In 1851, a Reform Bill promoted by the American Chamber of Commerce would have given the Council only a quarter of the seats on the Dock Committee – this was toned down in Parliament to create a new Committee of twenty-four members, of whom twelve

7   M. J. Power, 'Councillors and commerce in Liverpool, 1650–1750', *Urban History*, Vol. 24, 1997, pp. 301–23.

8   BPP, Birkenhead Commissioners' Docks (1844), evidence of William Potter, p. 56; Mountfield, *Western gateway*, p. 14.

9   BPP, Liverpool Docks (1851), evidence of John Bramley Moore, p. 141.

were elected by port users and twelve nominated by the Council.[10] Whatever the divisions generated by local politics, this Dock Committee was clearly dominated by mercantile interests. In 1855, for example, eighteen of the twenty-four members called themselves merchants, shipowners, agents or brokers, and two of the three 'Gentlemen' were actually merchants or shipowners. With the occupations of two members being unclear, the closest the Committee seems to have had to a non- mercantile member was Henry Steel, Manager of the United Gas Company.[11]

Finally, in 1858, the mercantile classes seemingly emerged victorious from the reorganisation of the Mersey port authority – all but four of the members of the new Mersey Docks & Harbour Board were to be elected by the users of the port. In addition, this was to be a new port authority for the Mersey as a whole, amalgamating Liverpool and Birkenhead. The MDHB would continue the trend established by the old Dock Committee of gradual separation of port finance and management from that of the town of Liverpool, and would, it was hoped, apply the skills and competence demonstrated in Liverpool over a number of decades to salvaging the less than successful docks at Birkenhead.[12]

The influence of Liverpool's traders should be seen against a broader question of the relative power of competing groups in the Victorian middle classes. The idea of a retreat of the mercantile interest in this period is a common theme in the historiography, with the image of once-dominant traders giving way to the newly ascendant manufacturing barons – 'the crucial elements in the formation of the Victorian middle class' – and facing a world in which their old securities were threatened.[13] There is, however, ample evidence that the crisis of the Victorian mercantile classes is more myth than reality.

The question of decline in the mercantile classes runs into the old problem of relative and absolute trends. Economic historians have been running round this particular maze for decades, and it is not the point of this chapter to explore the convolutions. In the case of mercantile fortunes and influence, it is important to be aware of the size of the cake as well as the proportion taken by a given group. In a growing, diversifying economy, old élites will almost inevitably have to incorporate the skills and aspirations of new elements in order to encourage further growth, but historians should not fall into the trap of all-or-nothing paradigms. Consider Glasgow, probably the best-studied of Britain's major port cities. There, an increasingly heterogeneous economic development produced competing élites which were challenging the mercantile establishment by the middle of the nineteenth century. Manufacturers were an increasingly accepted element in the ranks of local decision-makers, partly

---

10 Mountfield, *Western gateway*, p. 6; Picton, *Memorials of Liverpool*, vol. 1, p. 580. Some 1,500 people – those paying more than £10 a year in dock rates – were eligible to vote in Dock Committee elections: BPP, Liverpool Docks (1851), evidence of James Aiken, p. 192.

11 Extracted from the listing in *Gore's Directory*, 1855.

12 For an outline, see Mountfield, *Western gateway*, pp. 7–12.

13 Howe, quoted in S. Nenadic, 'Businessmen, the urban middle classes and the "dominance" of manufactures in nineteenth century Britain', *Economic History Review*, Vol. 44, 1991, pp. 66–85; p. 66.

because they brought their own 'constituency' in the form of large factory labour forces.[14] Recent studies of that town's élite in the 1840s and 1880s show a rising relative role for manufacturers, but this does not mean that there was no continuing mercantile influence – which is precisely what the city's historians have identified.[15]

In Liverpool, the influence of the mercantile classes was even less threatened. The town's relative lack of industry – indeed, an active de-industrialisation from late in the eighteenth century – left the trading élite in a secure position. They had long-standing power and influence: mercantile occupations had dominated local government in Liverpool in the late seventeenth and eighteenth centuries.[16] In addition, those industrial elements that did become prominent in the port's politics in mid-century were usually tied to some branch of mercantile activity. Shipwrights and sawmill operatives were a potent voting force in Liverpool's southern waterfront wards, but their fortunes were often more closely tied to timber traders and ship-owners than to their immediate industrial bosses.[17]

In any case, not only manufacturers had workforces to provide a dependent constituency. The Victorian clerk is a stock character in the literature, aspiring to a respectable lifestyle and establishing his own commercial connections and business while in the employment of more senior traders.[18] Liverpool merchants could mobilise their clerks as an electoral force when required: in particular, clerks could be enfranchised by their employers to vote in Dock Board elections for a mere £10, which was a very minor sum to many traders.[19]

Two brief points should be stressed regarding the general role of the trading interest. First, it is important not to establish a simplistic correlation between the role of traders and the expansion of the port – even when traders were apparently in a minority on the port authority early in the nineteenth century, Liverpool still developed its port facilities. Indeed, the distinction ought to be drawn here between strategic and operational responsibilities: traders seeking more representation on the Board were not necessarily unhappy with the overall expansion of the system, but rather with the way in which it was managed on a day-to-day basis. Traders sought to curb abuses and run the system more efficiently, and did not challenge the Liverpool Council's right as Dock Trustee to decide the direction of the port – what they sought through increased representation on the Dock Committee was to implement that direction.[20]

Second, although the gradual increase in mercantile representation at the port authority fits the nineteenth-century stereotype of progress and reform, it is worth noting the existence of a counter-current, and of divisions within the trading interest.

---

14 Nenadic, 'Businessmen', p. 80.
15 R. H. Trainor, 'The elite', in *Glasgow: Volume II, 1830–1912*, ed. W. H. Fraser and I. Maver, Manchester, 1996, pp. 227–64; p. 240.
16 Power, 'Councillors and commerce'.
17 N. Collins, *Politics and elections in nineteenth century Liverpool*, Aldershot, 1994.
18 G. Anderson, *Victorian clerks*, Manchester, 1976.
19 Forwood, *Recollections of a busy life*, p. 38.
20 BPP, Birkenhead Commissioners' Docks (1844), evidence of William Potter, p. 56–57.

Traders may have seen themselves as more forward-looking than landowners, and prosperous traders as having more strategic vision than small shopkeepers and artisans, but the pursuit of mercantile wealth did not meet with universal approval. In the particular context of managing the dock estate, there was a good case for *restricting* mercantile involvement – left unchecked, the traders might reduce dock charges, giving themselves a short-term profit at the expense of long-term investment in the port. Leading traders had to work to overcome this objection, arguing that the trading professions were far-sighted, and that they would not jeopardise the future of the system: 'townspeople and the merchants are all interested in keeping the docks in proper order'.[21] Furthermore, in a revealing admission, traders argued that they would be unlikely to be able to devise a scheme that would be of benefit to them all, and that any particular trade seeking preferential treatment would be opposed by other traders, let alone the town interests.[22] At a time when many core political issues in Liverpool had mercantile overtones – protectionism, dock rates and the decline of the shipbuilding sector, for example – divisions within the trading community were clear and often as marked as any division between trade and town.[23]

How was the changing profile of the trading community reflected in the composition of the new Dock Board, and in the decision-making processes of the authority? These are not straightforward issues. Members of the Board generally denied that they were there to represent the various interests in the port. Members did not explicitly speak for the Corn Trade Association, or the Steamship Owners' Association, or any of the other groups using the port. On the other hand, there is ample evidence that at least some of the trading interests of the port had an expectation that a certain number of members would come from their trade.

The Steamship Owners' Association offers useful evidence. Formed in 1858 – explicitly to lobby the new Dock Board – the Association was already complaining in 1862 that its representation on the Board was too small. It was to be hoped, the Association stated in its annual report, that there would shortly be restored the 'former recognised status, that four parties connected with the steam trade should have seats on the Board'.[24] The Association's concerns were caused by the retirement of William Inman in the previous year, and the failure, despite some effort, of the Association to persuade any other leading shipowner to stand for election in his place.[25]

It should not, however, be assumed that the Steamship Owners saw the remaining members of the Board as opponents of the steam trade. There was, in fact, a remarkable level of agreement across the trading community as to who should sit

21 BPP, Liverpool Docks (1851), evidence of William Brown, p. 173.
22 BPP, Liverpool Docks (1851), evidence of James Aiken, p. 191.
23 For recent revisionist assessments of Liverpool politics in the 1840s, see J. Belchem, '"The church, the throne and the people, ships, colonies and commerce": Popular Toryism in early Victorian Liverpool', *Transactions of the Historic Society of Lancashire & Cheshire*, Vol. 143, 1994, pp. 35–55.
24 Liverpool Steamship Owners' Association, Annual report, 1862, p. 7, in MMM Archives, LSSOA Papers.
25 Steamship Owners, Minutes, pp. 78–79.

on the Board. The Steamship Owners and the Chamber of Commerce both published slates of twenty-four candidates approved for election to the Board in 1858: there were only four discrepancies between the two lists, and the great majority of candidates were elected.[26] Even in 1862, when the Steamship Owners were complaining about their representation, they congratulated themselves on the fact that no fewer than 22 of the 24 men on their approved list for that year had been elected.[27]

Given that the Chamber of Commerce was a body representing the widest range of traders of every scale and specialism, and that the Steamship Owners represented a much narrower interest, there was clearly a fair consensus about the leading men of the port. Particular factions did not, it seems, object to having a wide range of interests on the Board, so long as some unwritten rules about the 'appropriate' level of representation of some trades were observed.

This is reinforced by the uncontroversial nature of elections to the Board in the early years. Members tended to be re-elected without opposition, and if factions did jostle for places, they did so at an earlier point in the electoral process which remains invisible to historians. The 1859 election, at the end of the Board's first year of operation, was by far the most widely contested, with eight candidates failing to be elected. Thereafter, however, the Board settled into a comfortable routine. During the 1860s, only three sitting members failed to be re-elected, and elections to vacant seats caused by several retirements and resignations were usually uncontested. Of the twenty-eight members in 1859, eighteen were still on the Board in 1865, and thirteen were still there in 1870 – no fewer than sixteen men sat on the Board for at least ten of its first dozen years. The 1859 cohort served a median of nine years on the Board.[28] Continuity ran the other way also – fourteen of the new Board in 1858 had been on the old Dock Committee in 1855.

It seems unlikely, therefore, that the influence of particular trades and interests on the Dock Board will be readily uncovered by a Parliamentary-style analysis of elections and candidates. Rather more promising is an analysis of some of the key issues facing the port authority in mid-century, and the extent to which particular trades wielded an influence. The role played by interests and factions outside the Board is potentially significant, because the legal framework of the MDHB held it accountable to scrutiny and gave interests every opportunity to raise objections. In addition, the activities of trading interests need to be studied in a wider context. Both competition with other ports and the involvement of central government in the planning of port infrastructure were vital issues in this period, and research that focuses narrowly on the internal workings of the Dock Board is likely to miss the point.

Within this broader framework, traders had two key tactics in bringing pressure to bear on the Board. First, they were well aware that Liverpool was not the only port in Britain. One favourite ploy was to threaten to move to another port if facilities were not provided in Liverpool. Major players used this tactic throughout the

---

26 Steamship Owners, Minutes, pp. 1–4.
27 Steamship Owners, Minutes, pp. 29–31.
28 Figures derived from membership lists in the MDHB, Minutes.

mid-century period, and opponents of the Liverpool port authorities claimed that various trades would leave the port. In the mid-1850s, Birkenhead's dock engineer James Rendell argued without much evidence that the American trades would abandon the increasingly congested Liverpool docks.[29] Rendell was scaremongering and trying to promote Birkenhead, but the tactic was taken up a decade later by leading Liverpool steamship owners. James Bibby threatened to move his operations to Southampton or London if dock accommodation in Liverpool was taken away from him.[30]

The Board did not take such threats too seriously. It judged correctly that Liverpool's hinterland was far more important to traders than any problems with dock space: however impressive the railways might be, they could hardly carry bulk staples effectively enough to make Southampton a sensible entrepôt for the north-west of England. Board members accepted that there would be competition from southern ports in the passenger trades, but were not intimidated by the cargo-handling capabilities of such places: Southampton, argued Ralph Brocklebank, was 'a tea-cup as compared to Liverpool'.[31]

The Board was a great deal less secure in dealing with the other key tactic of its opponents: opposition to Parliamentary Bills. It is important to stress that the Board was severely limited in the decisions it could take at a strategic level. In particular, it had to secure Parliamentary approval for major borrowing and expenditure. This immediately moved questions of port management onto a wider, and more complicated, stage. The process of securing a Private Act was complex enough without having to deal with opposition from within the port, and the experience of the Mersey port authorities in mid-century led prominent members of the Board in the 1860s to question the whole Private Bill process. A system more akin to that of the courts was suggested as an alternative, giving the Board a right of appeal and greater confidence in the system's ability to differentiate major strategic matters from more local operational issues.[32]

The confusion between strategic planning and day-to-day operation is at the heart of the Board's difficulties in securing Private Acts. Traders who felt disadvantaged by operational decisions recognised that the Private Bill system gave them power and influence far out of proportion to their role in the port. The nuisance value of a petition against a major dock extension scheme was such that the Board would often make concessions to those who threatened to make such objections. In addition, the frequency of new schemes in the 1850s and 1860s meant that there ·was ample opportunity to threaten a Parliamentary petition rather than negotiate with the Board through more normal channels. All manner of groups took advantage of this ploy, from individuals to major trading associations. In 1855, while facing some of the most complex Parliamentary negotiations of the period, the port authority had to

29 BPP, Liverpool Docks (1855), evidence of James Rendell, p. 213.
30 BPP, MDHB Bill (1867), evidence of James Bibby, qq. 890–92.
31 Liverpool Daily Post, 30 Oct. 1861, p. 5.
32 See J. A. Tobin's comments at the Dock Board re: the 1867 Act, MDHB Disc. 1/1, p. 7.

reach a compromise with five local men who wanted a road built more quickly.[33] In 1863, an entire Bill was withdrawn because the Steamship Owners' Association lodged an objection in Parliament.[34]

This regulatory regime placed the port authority in a peculiar triple-jeopardy. Opponents of the port authority had more than one opportunity to wield their influence: if they failed to have sufficient candidates elected to the Board to carry out their wishes, and then failed to persuade those elected of the merits of their case, they could still appeal directly to Parliament next time major expenditure had to be approved. Decision-makers despaired: 'Hence all freedom of action has been taken from the Board.'[35]

The Board argued, reasonably enough, that Parliamentary Committees were suspicious of dock schemes that attracted local opposition, especially from the very people the projects were supposed to be helping. Taking a case through Parliament was difficult anyway, but if there was a hint of division – or even worse, explicit opposition to the plans from a member of the Board itself – it was unlikely that Parliament would respond positively. The Board's Chairman in 1861 bemoaned its failure to go to Parliament with 'anything like unanimous expression of opinion'.[36]

The interaction of factional interests with the scrutiny procedures of central government is therefore at least as important to understanding change in the port of Liverpool as the composition of the Board and the behaviour of its members. Three key issues from mid-century will serve to illustrate the questions at hand. They highlight the changing nature of factional division in Liverpool and its impact on the direction of the port. The first is the debate over warehouse docks conducted in the late 1830s and early 1840s, which resulted in significant success for the then Dock Committee. This is discussed briefly here, partly because it demonstrates the relative ease with which the pre-1858 port authority was able to balance interests and pressures, but also because it raises themes which were to prove more fraught in other circumstances subsequently. The second considers the much more serious dispute over the use and development of Birkenhead in the 1850s and 1860s, an issue that dominated the period before and after the creation of the MDHB in 1858. The third considers the rise to influence of the steamship owners as a vocal and powerful faction in the 1860s, and their conflicts with more established trades for dock space.

THE PROPER ROLE OF PORT AUTHORITIES:
WAREHOUSE DOCKS

As was discussed in chapter four, warehouse docks offered the port authority an important means to improve the efficiency of the system, and to generate new income. Some of Liverpool's existing trades, already expanding in the 1830s and

---

33 Letter from Dock Solicitor's Office, re: James Jack et al., 5 June 1855, MDHB Leg. A7/11.
34 Steamship Owners, Minutes, pp. 116–17.
35 Speech of Charles Turner at the Dock Board, reported in *Liverpool Chronicle*, 3 Oct. 1863, p. 7.
36 *Liverpool Daily Post*, 30 Oct. 1861, p. 4.

early 1840s, were demanding better facilities if they were to develop further: cotton merchants often complained about their bales lying in the rain on the quaysides. The port was also keen to attract new trades, some of which required more sophisticated handling and storage than the bulk staples. The Far East trades had been a London monopoly during Liverpool's rise to prominence in the eighteenth century, but by the mid-nineteenth such lucrative traffic was open to the provincial ports if they could encourage their merchants to exploit the opportunity. Liverpool accordingly cut its dock dues to attract long-haul shipping from the Far East, and began to plan the sort of secure warehouse docks needed by high-value commodity trades.[37]

However, the idea of warehouse docks brought the port authority into immediate conflict with important elements in the trading community. Objections fell broadly into two categories. The first group of objectors were trade associations which had no need for warehouses. The Canadian traders needed flat space for timber yards, and the Shipowners' Association needed space to park their vessels and facilities to unload and load them quickly: neither body had any interest in the secure storage of luxury commodities. The second group of objectors took the form of a well-organised lobby of private warehouse-owners and road hauliers. These groups feared that the convenience and security of dock warehouses would prove attractive to traders who up to that point had been forced to incur three unwelcome costs: warehouse fees, cartage fees and extensive pilfering. Port authority warehouses might lower the first and eliminate the others, leaving the private warehouse owners unable to compete. Naturally, arguments tended not to be made in such stark terms, but were dressed up as a more serious discussion of the proper role of port authorities. Port authority funds should provide a lowest common need, it was argued, and trades with more expensive requirements should seek specialised facilities in the private sector. By the 1830s the authorities had lost patience with such arguments, believing that their opponents were motivated solely by the pursuit of private profit at the expense of the trading community as a whole. Liverpool Council Finance Committee argued that opposition from private warehouse-owners was in fact the best possible reason for Albert and similar docks to be built without delay.[38]

Despite such opposition, the Dock Committee was able to go ahead with Albert (1846) and Stanley (1848). This is all the more remarkable because such facilities were extremely expensive: the warehouses at Albert doubled the cost of building the dock.[39] The Dock Trust's success in taking warehouse docks forward stemmed from a combination of internal and external factors. It was able to enlist external support for the view that warehouses should be an integral element in the port's facilities. As far back as 1821, a Customs enquiry recommended that Liverpool build 'a contiguous chain of warehouses adjoining the docks, surrounded by walls or otherwise

37   MMM, Birkenhead Docks (1848), evidence of John Bramley Moore, p. 139.
38   Warehouse report (1839), pp. 8–15.
39   N. Ritchie-Noakes, *Liverpool's historic waterfront*, London, 1984, pp. 49–54.

insulated from places of public access'.[40] The Trust was also helped by the behaviour of some of its opponents, who managed to alienate officials charged with taking a strategic view of port facilities. The Admiralty Surveying Officer James Abernethy found himself at the centre of a typical piece of Liverpool theatre when he supervised an enquiry into plans for the 1848 Dock Bill. After announcing relatively broad terms for the proceedings, he rapidly realised his mistake and struggled to curtail the efforts of warehouse owners and Birkenhead advocates to turn the enquiry into a forum for their complaints. Abernethy's conclusions backed up the earlier decisions of the Dock Trust: warehouses should be a matter of public interest, not private profit, and were a perfectly legitimate venture for a port authority.[41]

Despite having such powerful friends, the Trust continued to be the target of powerful lobbying by its opponents. Private warehouse owners Richard Harbord and Thomas Dower claimed to reflect a 'strong anxiety at Liverpool' about the new powers inherent in allowing the Dock Committee to manage warehouses.[42] The warehouse owners could also be politically astute, and contemporaries wrote with some admiration of their Machiavellian approach to Council business. One of Liverpool's favourite political games was to find a way of linking two unrelated issues and thereby carry or defeat measures by implication rather than having to confront them directly – in this case the considerable achievement of tying warehouses and bible classes together enabled 'the election of men adverse to dock warehouses, under the pretext of zeal for reading the Bible'.[43] Eyre Evans, a leading advocate of dock warehousing, lost his seat on the Town Council as the issue polarised opinion between the Dock Committee and the rest of the Council.[44] The Committee was not averse to deception and sharp practice itself, promising during the 1840s that Albert would be a one-off, and that if objections to it were dropped there would be no further plans for dock warehouses in the port: a promise forgotten, of course, once the precedent had been established.[45] The issue coloured local politics for years. The initial decision to build dock warehouses was one of various local issues blamed for the drop in the ruling Liberal Party's share of the vote in the 1839 municipal elections.[46] Warehouse owners, claiming without much evidence to be representative of the local community, thought it 'unfair' that the Town Council should 'turn traitors and take the bread out of our mouths'.[47]

The comical extremism of warehouse owners like Thomas Dower – who once told a Parliamentary Committee that he was there to represent 'widows and orphans' – played into the hands of the port authority and the broader trading community. Local satirists had an easy target, caricaturing Dower as a reactionary with a string

40   Picton, *Memorials of Liverpool*, vol. 1, p. 568.
41   Admiralty enquiry (1848), p. 23, appendix.
42   BPP, Liverpool Docks (1848), evidence of Harbord and Dower, pp. 29–32.
43   Picton, *Memorials of Liverpool*, vol. 1, p. 570.
44   BPP, Liverpool Docks (1851), evidence of Henry Chapman, pp. 198–99.
45   BPP, Liverpool Docks (1848), evidence of Richard Harbord, p. 31.
46   Collins, *Politics and elections*, p. 35.
47   BPP, Liverpool Docks (1848), evidence of Thomas Dower, p. 33.

of vested interests, from his ongoing monologues at Town Council meetings on the warehouse question, to his refusal to ride the new-fangled omnibus.[48]

If the Trust could marginalise some of its critics, it could also reassure others. The dock building programme of the 1840s offered something for almost everyone. Traders who had no use for Albert's warehouses would have facilities in the new complex of docks to the north, due to open in 1848. In acreage terms, warehouse docks comprised less than one-third of the dock space already in the planning stages when Albert opened: traders feeling left out did not have long to wait.

The port authority of the 1840s, therefore, was working in an environment of expanding resources, with support from government officials, and opponents who hardly represented the future of the port and its trade. In such circumstances, the accommodation of diversity was not perhaps a particularly difficult achievement. Conflicts in subsequent decades were to be conducted against a very different backdrop.

THE ENEMY WITHIN AND WITHOUT: BIRKENHEAD

It has already been noted that the MDHB's early record of dock building in Liverpool was not as impressive as that of its predecessor, and that much of the Board's spending in the 1860s was directed at the Birkenhead docks. This would not have been the Board's favoured approach, given a choice, and was instead forced upon it by Birkenhead's advocates, who were able to insist on extensive remedial work for the failed Birkenhead dock system. They achieved this largely by marshalling forces in Parliament and the Board of Trade, and successfully creating a perception that Liverpool was profiteering from the nation's trade. The greed of the town should be curtailed by preventing further expansion and by encouraging a competitor port across the Mersey in Birkenhead. In 1855, the Board of Trade urged Parliament to stop Liverpool's 'improvident extension in a northerly direction', and this became, in effect, the official position until the 1870s.[49]

Contemporary Liverpool opinion was fond of casting the battle as one between progressive merchants and reactionary landholders. While the Dock Board as a whole was elected by the trading community of the Mersey, the Birkenhead lobby represented landed interests on the Cheshire bank: conflict was obvious and inevitable.[50] Birkenhead's promoters ('extensive land speculators') had secured the aid of the 'Cheshire nobility and landed gentry, probably the most aristocratic and feudal in their ideas of any in the kingdom'.[51] More than 13,000 people – including 900 'principal merchants' – signed a petition against the 1857 Bill that was to force Liverpool to

48   BPP, Liverpool Docks (1848), evidence of Thomas Dower, p. 35; H. Shimmin, *Pen and ink sketches of Liverpool Town Councillors*, Liverpool, 1866, pp. 61–63.

49   Letter from James Booth, Secretary to the Board of Trade, in BPP, *Communications from the Board of Trade to H. Labouchere, respecting the Birkenhead and Liverpool Docks Bill*, 1854–55, L (333), p. 5.

50   MDHB Disc. 1/3, 1 Aug. 1867, p. 16.

51   Picton, *Memorials of Liverpool*, vol. 1, p. 575.

take over the failed Birkenhead dock system: the House of Lords rejected their views, favouring instead the argument of various northern towns that Liverpool needed to be controlled.[52] 'Liverpool', feared Dock Committee Chairman Charles Turner, 'is in bad odour at Westminster, increases too rapidly, and requires a rival to curtail its growing importance.'[53]

The Birkenhead question had more subtle aspects, which reveal important issues in the Dock Board's ability to deal with faction and interest. One key point is the changing face of the Birkenhead question over time. During the 1840s, when Birkenhead hoped to become a serious competitor, Liverpool clearly kept one eye on the rival system. Tensions rose steadily and both sides interpreted events to suit their prejudices. For example, Liverpool's practice of cutting its dock dues to attract new trades was viewed differently in Birkenhead. The cut in 1844, claimed the Dock Committee Chairman, was designed specifically to help long-haul shipping from the Far East, but Birkenhead's advocates later observed that it was 'an odd coincidence' that Liverpool tended to cut rates shortly before new docks were due to open on the Cheshire bank.[54]

Such tensions bred a long-term resentment between the two camps, although that in itself encouraged some in Liverpool to seek a conciliatory approach. By the mid-1850s, when the companies building and running the Birkenhead docks had run out of funds and were demanding to be rescued by Liverpool, some leading Liverpool figures saw this as a lesser evil than continuing disputes in the port. Charles Turner, Chairman of the Dock Committee, argued in March 1855 for the amalgamation of the Liverpool and Birkenhead docks under a single management which would operate the facilities much more efficiently by developing specialised facilities for particular trades. Turner's thinking was driven by the 'constant squabbles ... which are very injurious to the trade of the port', and which were provoked by the Birkenhead lobby.[55]

Amalgamation, however, did not solve the problem, and the Birkenhead interest's continued agitation revived the grumbling conflict between the two sides of the Mersey. The Birkenhead interest did not only fight its battles in Parliament, nor did it rest when the failed docks were taken over. Indeed, it was the only formally recognised sectional group within the new Dock Board. Continued trouble was virtually written into the Board's constitution: four seats went to government nominees rather than being open to election by the trading community in general. The government used these nominated places to ensure that advocates of further expansion in Birkenhead had guaranteed seats on the new Board, and those nominated took their role as watchdogs seriously. During the 1850s and 1860s, the nominated

---

52   Debate in the Lords as reported in *The Times*, 21 July 1857, p. 6.
53   *Liverpool Chronicle*, 3 Oct. 1863, p. 7.
54   BPP, Birkenhead Docks (1848), evidence of John Bramley Moore, p. 139; BPP, Liverpool Docks (1855), evidence of J. M. Rendell, p. 213.
55   BPP, Liverpool Docks (1855), evidence of Charles Turner, pp. 22–29. Turner was Chairman of the Dock Committee in its later years and went on to be the first Chairman of the new Board.

members hampered the Board's strategic planning at Parliamentary level, and also obstructed its operational decision-making locally. The time and effort wasted by successive Liverpool port authorities in preparing plans for projects which were rejected by Parliament was very considerable. A series of plans between 1855 and 1858, for example, which would have involved a huge northward extension of the Liverpool system, resulted eventually in the construction of only two docks, albeit important ones (Canada and Brocklebank).[56]

Until the mid-1860s, the Birkenhead lobby's priority was to get the docks on the Cheshire bank 'finished'. Unless harassed at every opportunity, feared the Birkenhead partisans, the new Dock Board would be tempted to write off the partly-built docks, and continue developing Liverpool. This would have represented a serious defeat for key individuals, motivated partly by their own financial investments in Birkenhead, but also by a real commitment to the development of industry and trade on the Cheshire bank of the Mersey.

Harold Littledale, for example, was a tireless agitator for Birkenhead, although given to playing down his role with some inspired understatement: in 1855 he remarked to a Parliamentary Committee that the subject of dock accommodation had been 'a sort of hobby' of his.[57] Littledale sometimes went to bizarre lengths. The Dock Trust's lawyers gleefully noted that Littledale's petition against the 1855 Dock Bill had lain unsigned in the Liverpool Exchange, forcing him to carry it door-to-door round Birkenhead's tradesmen. He then attempted to pass it off as a petition from the 'Merchants, shipowners, masters of vessels and others interested in the Port of Liverpool'. Littledale was responsible for another petition at the same time, which was indeed from 'Holders of Bonds on Liverpool Docks', albeit only two of them: almost three thousand others somehow neglected to sign.[58]

Such a record on the Birkenhead question made it easy for the Board to discount Littledale's views on other issues, especially when he began raising uncomfortable truths about the work of the Engineer's Department in the later nineteenth century.[59] Other Birkenhead partisans would also have played a more positive role in the Board's proceedings if they had been less identified with that single issue. John Laird, for example, was a valued member of the Board, but even he found himself sidelined for his frequent, nit-picking efforts to bring the Birkenhead question into almost any matter under discussion. The first ever Board meeting, in 1858, was well covered in the press and supposed to be a celebration of the new era. Laird, of course, took the opportunity to disrupt proceedings by opposing the election of Charles Turner to the Chair: Turner, he claimed, had been instrumental in obstructing the progress of Birkenhead. Typically, though, Laird did not nominate an alternative candidate, and his actions only served to alienate Board members.[60] By the mid-1860s, Laird's constant

56   A. Jarvis, *The Liverpool dock engineers*, Stroud, 1996, pp. 120–22.

57   BPP, Liverpool Docks Bill (1855), evidence of Harold Littledale, p. 157.

58   The petitions and commentary are in MDHB Leg. A7/25.

59   A. Jarvis, 'Harold Littledale: The man with a mission', in *A second Merseyside maritime history*, ed. H. M. Hignett, Liverpool, 1991, pp. 6–9.

60   *The Times*, 7 Jan. 1858, p. 4.

complaints about the Birkenhead question had long since proved counter-productive, serving only to irritate his colleagues and embarrass the Board in the local press. Some of the most forceful condemnations of the Birkenhead enterprise – warmly endorsed in the editorial columns – were provoked by Laird's repetitive interventions on the issue.[61]

Laird's most important work for Birkenhead was done in Parliament, however. There was already extensive opposition to further expansion in Liverpool in the Commons during the 1850s, as manifested in the Acts forcing the take-over of the bankrupt Birkenhead docks. Nonetheless, Liverpool's MPs, including leading trader Charles Horsfall, worked hard to persuade their Westminster audience that Birkenhead was not being neglected, and that both sets of docks needed continued investment.[62] Elected MP for Birkenhead after his retirement from business in 1861, Laird was able to co-ordinate opposition to Liverpool in the Commons, as well as sitting on the Dock Board.

By the later 1860s, though, even Laird had trouble arguing that Birkenhead's development had been neglected. Almost two-thirds of the Board's works expenditure between 1858 and 1867 went to Birkenhead. Such figures were enough for the Chairman of the Board's Parliamentary Committee: 'I ask any impartial man whether we have not performed our duty by Birkenhead.'[63] At this point, the Birkenhead lobby moved the goal-posts again, and the question took on yet another angle. After the Alfred Dock entrance had been opened in 1866, the Birkenhead system had deeper access than most of the Liverpool docks, a considerable overall acreage, and even some sheds and other facilities. The Birkenhead lobby began to argue that this was now, technically, a viable port, and that the resistance of the trading community to using it was based on no more than prejudice. Furthermore, it was the Board's responsibility to force traders to use Birkenhead. Laird urged a coercive pricing policy on the Board, arguing that if Liverpool's steamship lines insisted on cramming themselves into the Canada and Huskisson docks they should have to pay dearly for their berths, encouraging them to move to lower-rated docks in Birkenhead.[64]

Laird's evangelical efforts on the part of Birkenhead had little positive effect, though. However much he argued that his family's shipbuilding yard was a demonstration of the economic success that could be achieved in the place, he could not counter the reality that this was very much the exception that proved the rule – shipbuilding and a range of other specialised activities might have been at home in Birkenhead, but mainstream trading activity was not. Indeed, once the argument shifted away from 'finishing' Birkenhead to forcing trade to use it, the issues became clearer, and the flawed underpinning of the Cheshire dock scheme even more evident.

61   See, for example, Turner's speech at the Dock Board meeting on 1 Oct. 1863, *Liverpool Chronicle*, 10 Oct. 1863, p. 7.
62   Report of proceedings in the Commons, *The Times*, 16 Feb. 1859, p. 6.
63   £1,561,485 was spent on works in Liverpool, £2,731,423 on Birkenhead: MDHB Disc. 1/1, pp. 11–12.
64   BPP, MDHB Bill (1873), evidence of John Laird, q. 2,599.

Lacking the confidence of the broader commercial and mercantile community, Birkenhead had never even been able to raise the level of funds authorised by a generous and friendly Parliament – less than £500,000 against a possible £1.4m, according to the secretary of the project's trustees.[65]

Those in the wider trading community who expressed approval in principle for Birkenhead were disinclined to lead any business migration across the Mersey, and their actions reflect a more acute business sense than their words. Traders were afraid to move their operations away from the established commercial infrastructure of Liverpool itself. Laird could not even persuade his own business partner to relocate.[66] A leading Australia merchant thought that his trade could move to Birkenhead, but when pressed bemoaned the lack of storage and handling facilities, which were just as vital to traders as the docks themselves: Birkenhead, he argued, was 'a perfect Balaclava, no sheds or anything'.[67] Two of the Mersey's largest trades – timber and cotton – were often mentioned as being ideal trades for Birkenhead, although rarely by the people who actually traded in them. Those timber or cotton merchants who did approve of Birkenhead (including Harold Littledale himself) usually argued that the whole of a given trade should move, and did not volunteer to relocate their own businesses for a trial period.[68] In such circumstances, it was easy for critics to argue that Birkenhead partisanship had more to do with inflating property prices than with serious mercantile thinking: Liverpool partisans never tired of pointing to Littledale's extensive land-holdings in Wallesey, adjacent to the Birkenhead docks.[69] In a final, fitting demonstration of the true focal point of the Mersey trading community, when the Birkenhead Dock Company held its final meeting to wind itself up in 1864, it met in the Clarendon Rooms – in Liverpool.[70]

Partly to cover its back and demonstrate that it was making an effort, the Board did indeed try various tactics of persuasion to encourage traders to move their operations from Liverpool to Birkenhead. It approached individual traders, and advertised the availability of Birkenhead berths in the local press.[71] Inevitably, such efforts did not satisfy Birkenhead's advocates and only served to sour relations between the Board and leading merchants in Liverpool, who complained that even the Board's low key measures were far too much. William Lamport claimed that 'individual members of the Board have worried me out of my life to go to Birkenhead'. Corn merchant Henry Tunnicliffe felt he had been blackmailed into taking some warehouse accommodation in Birkenhead, because only then would the Board also give him some space on the Liverpool side.[72]

65 BPP, Birkenhead Docks (1856), evidence of Edward Bramah, p. 39.
66 BPP, MDHB Bill (1873), evidence of L. H. Parr, p. 470.
67 BPP, MDHB Bill (1867), evidence of Edward Thompson, q. 1,767.
68 BPP, Liverpool Docks (1855), evidence of Harold Littledale, pp. 160–62.
69 MDHB Leg. A7/25; MDHB Disc. 1/3, 1 Aug. 1867.
70 Gore's Advertiser, 24 Nov. 1864, p. 3.
71 BPP, MDHB Bill (1873), evidence of Thomas Hornby, q. 1,716.
72 BPP, MDHB Bill (1867), evidence of W. J. Lamport, q. 1,406; evidence of Henry Tunnicliffe, q. 1,831.

Such local disputes might have rumbled on interminably were it not for increasing pressure on Liverpool's facilities in the 1860s. With no prospect of new docks in Liverpool, thanks to the success of Birkenhead's voice in Parliament, traders recognised that they were competing for shares of a finite system, rather than the expanding dock estate of the 1840s and 1850s. Inevitably, they began to fight amongst themselves. This was perhaps the most invidious effect of the Birkenhead issue: it drove divisions between groups of traders who had no particular interest in the Birkenhead docks. Shipowners and merchants desperate for dock space began to pick on particular trades and suggest that they should be moved to Birkenhead. When some merchants in the Australia trade conceded that their business could, in principle, be managed from Birkenhead, the Liverpool Shipowners' Association pounced: writing to the Dock Board, the Association urged that the trade's berths in Liverpool should immediately be taken away and reassigned 'to those who so urgently require and prefer accommodation on the Liverpool side'.[73]

While it helped create a climate in which Liverpool's traders fought amongst themselves, the Birkenhead question itself became a less fraught issue in the later 1860s, largely because the investment in the Cheshire docks could not reasonably be denied. Even the manufacturing interests of east Lancashire and Yorkshire began to support the Dock Board's plans, recognising that an efficient port of Liverpool was in their interests. The list of supporters of the Board's 1867 Parliamentary Bill included the usual list of Liverpool traders and trade associations, but also, to the surprise of the Board, the Manchester and Salford Corporations.[74] This was, of course, only a brief truce before the textile districts changed their minds and agitated for the Manchester Ship Canal, but it is clear that they no longer saw Birkenhead as such a useful stick with which to beat Liverpool. John Laird's death in 1874 was another important milestone, and while others continued to accuse the Board of neglecting the Cheshire side, no-one else could muster the same combination of local and Parliamentary influence. Despite his claims to the contrary, Laird was always recognised as the dominant force among the four nominated members of the Board.[75]

The collateral damage from the Birkenhead question, however, was felt for years.[76] By the time major dock-building in Liverpool began to be approved by Parliament again in the early 1870s, the port had to catch up with almost two decades of expanding and diversifying trade. More important for this discussion, though, is the culture of conflict that the Birkenhead issue helped to create. As will be seen, this was further exacerbated by the arrival on the scene of the new, powerful steamship lobby.

73 See Shipowners' Association to MDHB, 3 July 1867, MDHB Disc. 1/1, p.2.

74 See list of supporters of 1867 Bill, MDHB Disc. 1/1, p. 27.

75 See statements by G. H. Fletcher to the Manchester Chamber of Commerce, *Manchester Guardian*, 10 June 1871, p. 7; also Laird's obituary, *The Times*, 30 Oct. 1874, p. 3.

76 For debates over other 'artificial' ports, see G. Jackson, 'Do docks make trade? The case of the port of Great Grimsby', in *From wheelhouse to counting house: Essays in maritime economic history in honour of Professor Peter Neville Davies*, ed. L. R. Fischer, St John's, Newfoundland, 1992, pp. 17–41.

THE NEW ELITE: THE RISE OF THE STEAMSHIP OWNERS

Sharply rising steam traffic in a period of stalled dock building was inevitably going to create a vociferous new lobby within the Liverpool trading community. Steamship owners felt particularly aggrieved by the lack of new docks on the Liverpool side of the river during the 1860s, arguing that Birkenhead was even less suitable for them than for sailing trades. Critics of the steamship operators accused them of special pleading and of placing their interests before those of the port as a whole. The major steam traders would have dock accommodation 'at their back doors if they could get it', complained one Board member in 1867.[77]

As was discussed in part one, however, there is good evidence to support the steamship owners' case, both in terms of technological change and in the shifting organisation of trades. Because their fleets were growing, and each year's new ships bigger than the last, the steam operators began to assume that they would have priority when the dock system was expanded. Liners handling passengers and consignments of cargo operated in a quantifiably different mercantile framework from sailing ships carrying bulk goods. Handling a large number of small cargo consignments made steam operations more complex than sail, which handled a small number of large consignments. In 1863, the median number of merchants listed as consignees for sailing ships arriving in Liverpool was four: the figure for steamers was twenty-nine.[78] In other words, steam voyages required significantly more interaction within the trading community: steamship agents had to be at the hub of complex networks of merchants, passengers and inland transport systems. Steam operators could legitimately argue that they had to be based as close as possible to the physical focus of Liverpool's trading infrastructure and networks.

This new, more integrated operational structure made steam a belligerent interest group, increasingly likely to take a hostile attitude to other port users. Liverpool's town centre docks, like Prince's, were heavily used by sail in mid-century, as they had been since they were built. They were also, of course, ideally located at the hub of the landward infrastructure so necessary for steam operations. In addition, coastal steamers worked in competition with railways on some routes and had an equally valid, if rather different reason, to demand central dock facilities. Either way, while sail trades could and did claim greater priority over each other because of the differing values of the goods they handled, steam companies injected a new dimension, claiming that their operational requirements were inherently different and deserving of special attention. At a meeting in 1858, leading steam operators resolved to lobby the port authorities for exclusive accommodation in Liverpool's north docks, but argued that they should be no further north than the new Canada Dock. The implication was clear: sail traffic would have to be moved to the margins to make way for steam in the heart of the system.[79]

---

77 MDHB Disc. 1/1, p. 63.
78 Calculated from BE (1863).
79 See account of a meeting of the steam trade, 11 Oct. 1858, MDHB Leg. A22/22.

The rise of steam therefore brought as large a shift in the factional profile of the trading community as it did in any technological or economic sense. It created an interest based on the type of shipping used – there was no unified sail lobby to match the steam interest. In the late 1860s, the Steamship Owners' Association had a broad membership from the level of MacIver and Inman down to the agents for the Isle of Man ferry company. Three of its eight-member committee in 1868 represented coastal or short-sea firms with only a fraction of the tonnage managed by the major overseas operators sitting beside them.[80] In the longer term, of course, steam became divided into different commodity trades and between liners and tramps, but in this crucial formative period it was a powerful, united group, predisposed to disputes with older users of the port.

Like much else in an age fascinated with statistics, the disputes over steam accommodation became a battle for information. It was no secret in mid-century Liverpool that some parts of the dock estate worked more tonnage than others, and/or made appreciably more money than others. Particular trades often tried to exploit such variations for their own ends, and successive Parliamentary Committees were regaled with figures from members of the trading community who were keen to demonstrate how important their traffic was to the port. In 1855, a representative of the American Chamber of Commerce painted a glowing picture of how American traders in Waterloo (built 1834) worked three times the tonnage per acre handled in King's (built 1788) or Queen's (built 1786, extended 1816).[81]

Such figures could be concocted by any trade, given an appropriate spin and a neglect of inconvenient facts. The American trader just mentioned, for example, conveniently forgot to add that other docks handling the US trades had earnings well below those of Waterloo. Most trades had peculiarities that made comparison with others difficult. The timber trade pointed to the high density of its unloading practices: being able to unload from the front of the ship rather than over the side meant that timber achieved a uniquely high tonnage to quay-length ratio. In the autumn of 1863, with timber imports at their annual peak, it was claimed that 1,155 tons of timber were being handled every day in the Canada Dock alone. This, argued leading timber trader Hilton Halhead, would stand up very well against figures for the steam trade.[82]

The steam trade naturally disagreed, but by this point the Board had realised that it would be opening Pandora's box if it began to embark on statistical debates with particular interests in the port. The Board refused a series of requests from the Steamship Owners' Association in the early 1860s for statistics that would reveal the relative contribution of sail and steam to the revenue of the port.[83] Moving beyond the needs of propaganda and into the domain of port management, it rapidly became clear to the Board that breaking the system down into trades was a futile and self-defeating exercise.

---

80 Steamship Owners, Minutes, p. 1.
81 BPP, Liverpool Docks (1855), evidence of William Barber, 20 Apr. 1855, pp. 150–54.
82 Steamship Owners, Minutes, p. 135.
83 Steamship Owners, Minutes, p. 101.

The disparity in earnings across the dock system was indeed considerable, but this did not necessarily mean that some docks were working less efficiently than others. Some parts of the dock estate, like graving-dock entrance basins, only existed to service others, and the fact that they earned any income at all on shipping and cargo was a bonus. It was also true that the system worked as a holistic entity in some ways. Even the steam magnates accepted that they could not operate without sailing ships. Five hundred coastal colliers supplied Cunard's liners with South Wales coal every year in the mid-1850s.[84] Cunard's David MacIver cited that figure on a number of occasions to underline the scale of his firm's operations, but it stands equally well as a reminder to the Board that pitting sail against steam was unlikely to yield a coherent port-management strategy.

Such tensions inevitably blurred the line between operational and strategic issues, which, as was mentioned above, remained the most difficult question facing the management of the port. The steam trade used its weight to complain about a range of issues. Appropriated berths were the most persistent ground for complaint on the part of steamship companies. Steamships, it was argued, needed to spend as little time in port as possible, because many of them were operating on published timetables, and all had a much higher level of capital tied up in them than sailing ships. Both of these points are true, although the first may be the only relevant issue: a reputation for reliability of service in the steam trade was valuable to the port as a whole, but the Dock Board could hardly be expected to discriminate in favour of a trade on grounds of how much risk it took with its capital.

In any case, the steam trade rapidly arrived at the conclusion in the 1850s that appropriated berths were the solution to its need for a rapid turnaround. Under this system, a company had a section of a given dock appropriated for the exclusive use of its steamships. As can be imagined, few companies were ever satisfied for long with their allocation, and as trade grew in the 1860s and little new dock building took place in Liverpool, correspondence between shipowners and the Board became fraught. Matters took a turn for the worse in 1862, when the Board announced plans to charge rent for appropriated berths. On this occasion, the Steamship Owners' Association acquiesced under protest, but clearly recognised a shift in attitude that established battle lines in subsequent disputes.[85]

The other issue of central concern to the steamship trade was the means of measuring tonnage for revenue purposes. There is a significant literature on this complex issue, and this section will offer only a brief outline of the wider question. Put crudely, the net tonnage of a steamship was calculated by making an allowance for the space occupied by engines, fuel and associated elements, in an attempt to measure roughly the tonnage available for carrying cargo. It was therefore obviously in the interest of steamship owners to design ships in such a way as to make the net tonnage as low as possible in relation to the overall size of the vessel, and then ensure that ports charged rates according to that net tonnage.

84   BPP, Birkenhead Docks (1856), evidence of Charles MacIver, p. 351.
85   Steamship Owners, Minutes, pp. 92–93, 108.

A growing volume of opinion argued in the early 1860s that steam was not paying its way in the port of Liverpool. Christopher Bushell, one of the nominated members, revealed to the Dock Board some surprising figures that seemed to indicate that steam was being significantly undercharged for its use of the docks – a conclusion that was 'by no means unpalatable to the bulk of the members'.[86]

This issue caused a head-on collision between the Steamship Owners and the Dock Board in the early 1860s, and is symbolic of the contradictions inherent in the relationship between shipowners and the port authority. In 1863, the Association announced that it was 'the duty of the MDHB ... forthwith to promote a well considered scheme for further accommodation to be given to the Steam Trade at Liverpool'.[87] The Board could not have agreed more, putting yet another scheme for new dock building before Parliament early in the following year. It rapidly became clear, however, that it would not have the support of the Association after all. As well as proposing new docks, the Board decided to include in the Bill provisions for increasing the revenue to be brought in from steamships by redefining the calculations for steam tonnage. By the end of February 1864 relations had deteriorated to the point where the Association considered levying a fee from its members to meet the costs of fighting the dispute over tonnage calculation at the Board of Trade or even in the courts.[88] Looked at cynically, it appears that the Steamship Owners took the position that new docks were essential, but only if they had exclusive use of them, and if other users of the port paid for them.

Steam's attitude towards the Board remained tense, and was further complicated by the sense of collective responsibility felt by the trading community toward the Board. Individual trades felt reluctant to criticise the Board, and this encouraged their existing tendency to attack one another instead. The timber trader Hilton Halhead's criticism of Cunard's David MacIver is the clearest expression of this question in mid-century, and is worth quoting at some length because of the range of subtle points being made. According to Halhead, MacIver had complained that the Board was failing to keep up with the expansion in the steam trades, but because

it was inconvenient or impolitic to say all that he wished against the Board direct, he made the most unjustifiable attack on the timber trade by which he sought to mislead the public as to the true merits of the case, and by imputing to the Board undue partiality to the timber trade induce the conclusion that improper influences were at work, an inference unworthy of Mr MacIver and alike insulting to the Mersey Docks and Harbour Board and to the timber trade.[89]

It is clear, therefore, that the conflict between steam and the port's major sail operators had two key threads. It stemmed from the genuine differences in the

---

86 *Liverpool Chronicle*, 7 Nov. 1863, p. 7.
87 Steamship Owners, Minutes, p. 129.
88 Steamship Owners, Minutes, pp. 151–66.
89 Letter from Halhead to Steamship Owners' Assoc., 13 Nov. 1863, in Steamship Owners, Minutes, p. 134.

operational requirements of the steamship companies, but was exacerbated by the trading community's attitude to the Dock Board. Having gained ownership of the port authority through the 1858 reforms, the trading community was restrained in its direct criticisms: obviously, if MacIver was too vocal in his condemnation of the Board, he would have to explain why his Association routinely approved of the great majority of those elected. An elaborate game was therefore played, in which trades accused each other of trying to influence the Board and gain unfair advantages. Even when adopting the well-proven tactic of opposing strategic plans for dock extensions in retaliation for perceived local grievances, trades were cautious. As has been noted, the Board withdrew its 1863 Private Bill following opposition from the Steamship Owners, but the Association denied that its objection had been an attack on the Board, claiming instead that it wanted wider questions of steamship-tonnage measurement aired in Parliament.[90]

The Board, in the end, got the worst of both worlds. It had to referee public conflicts between trades which were fighting, in part, so as not to appear disloyal to the Board. At the same time, it could not rely on the steamship owners, who were rapidly becoming the best organised and most vocal lobby in the port. The expansion of steam and the rapid growth in the size of steamships guaranteed that the relationship between the steam owners and the Board would be a central element in the management of the port for the rest of the century. That relationship was defined by patterns already visible in the 1860s. In particular, the issue of the steam trade's contribution to the port's revenue became ever more fraught.[91]

The implications of the rise of steam were therefore profound for the port of Liverpool. Steam gave the port's shipowners and merchants far greater control over the traffic using their port than had been the case for half a century, but if the rise of steam helped make the port of Liverpool rich, it also threatened to make it unmanageable. The steam trade created a new kind of factional interest in the port, and one that was dependent neither on sharp practice in Town Council elections, nor on the doggedly medieval landed classes of Cheshire. In contrast to the port authority's earlier opponents, steam symbolised the future of Liverpool rather than the past, and its demands were therefore much harder to counter. The pre-1858 years were a great success for the port of Liverpool, because of its successful accommodation of diversity. It was the new Dock Board's great tragedy, however, that it was created just as the demands of diversity reached a scale that could not previously have been predicted, and with a legacy from Birkenhead that forced it to divert crucial resources from its primary mission.

90 Steamship Owners, Minutes, pp. 116–17.
91 For the situation in late-century, see A. Jarvis, 'The port of Liverpool and the shipowners in the late nineteenth century', *The Great Circle*, Vol. 16, 1994, pp. 1–22.

Chapter 10

CONCLUSION:
TRADING IN INTERESTING TIMES

We have had years of commercial disaster; we have had famines; we have had a war on the other side of the Atlantic, paralysing a very great branch of our commerce; and still our progress has been remarkable ...[1]

Mid-Victorian Liverpool was proud of its trade and commerce, and with some justification. Expansion in the middle decades of the nineteenth century, against a background of dislocation and upheaval on the international stage, was seen by contemporaries as a considerable achievement. Even if Britain was generally able, thanks to its industrial and commercial power, to take advantage of crises elsewhere rather than suffer from them, individual ports, regions and sectors of the economy could spend extended periods in the doldrums due to the interruption of their staple activities. Liverpool's ability to maintain a broad prosperity in this era, particularly in contrast to some of its manufacturing neighbours elsewhere in north-west England, stands as testimony to the efforts of its trading community.

In particular, it reflects the determination of Liverpool traders to take and maintain control of their affairs. In some areas, this represented a sharp break with earlier patterns, such as the expansion of shipowning in the port to fill the vacuum left by the Americans. In other cases, it was a more subtle process, as revealed in the concentration of joint-stock company directorships among Liverpool-based traders, or the reluctance of traders to accept the advice of the Manchester Association and invest heavily in alternative cotton sources. If Liverpool traders were in control, however, it implied that someone else was not, and mercantile growth on the Mersey led to conflict with rivals, especially in London. Liverpool relished its challenge to London's traders, especially in the high-profile activities associated with government contracting, and made considerable advances from what was more or less a standing start in the 1840s. Perhaps more significantly for the bulk of the port's traders, Liverpool's success in breaking into London's old monopoly regional trades – most notably that with the Far East – was a key element in the expansion of the Mersey's trading profile in mid-century.

Making the most of such opportunities required traders to confront an increasing range of choices in mid-century. The most obvious of these was in shipping technology, but commodity, regional and functional demarcation lines within the community also required decisions from traders as to the most appropriate deployment of their efforts

1 Comments of J. A. Tobin at the Dock Board, 25 July 1867, MDHB Disc. 1/2, p. 15.

and resources. One of the community's key strengths, however, was that such choices could be built on solid foundations. Small-firm business structures in trade and shipping were able to absorb increased activity without any fundamental overhaul in their management or capitalisation strategies. Local networks of 64th-owners could be persuaded to increase their commitments slightly, enabling the purchase of new ships. An extra clerk and a telegraph account could absorb a significant increase in commodity turnover, especially in broker-dominated markets where many transactions did not require the physical transfer of goods. Such flexibility in business structure enabled traders to concentrate on external rather than internal matters, focusing on their mercantile activities rather than being constantly preoccupied with managerial issues.

The external life of the trading firm was significant in other ways. Liverpool business relied on complex information networks brokered by important local figures. Participation in these networks enabled small firms to establish reputations and levels of credit-worthiness which, especially in the case of younger traders, allowed them to develop faster than they might have done solely on the basis of their capital. The information web also enabled the community to reach decisions about success and failure, showing a great capacity for sympathy and altruism in some cases while rushing to condemn others.

On the other hand, membership of this 'club' required the sacrifice of some measure of business autonomy. Traders who told their bankers about their low level of capitalisation, or about their difficulties in replacing a retired partner, or any of a range of commercially-sensitive measures of their activity, must have known that such information might be used against them at some point. In addition, the notorious reluctance of traders to discuss their finances in front of Parliamentary Committees – and their tendency to plead poverty if pressed – suggests that wealthy members of the community may have been even more reluctant to have such information circulated than their poorer brethren.

Clearly, personal, hands-on management and business autonomy are not incompatible with a model of closely integrated trading networks. They should, however, be remembered as potential areas of tension, and as alternative threads of investigation in any explanation of the business strategies adopted in the port. They suggest the need for attention to the subtleties of competition and collaboration, and the extent to which individual traders retained personal control over their businesses while making use of an appropriate level of support from their closest associates and from the broader trading community.

Liverpool's traders therefore found evolutionary solutions to the problems of revolutionary times, and emerged from the 1850s and 1860s with a much higher national and global profile. The scale of their mobilisation of local resources, whether in trade, shipping or in the development of the dock estate, is an impressive indicator both of the level of capital available to be tapped in the north-west, and of the cohesive, collective focus of the trading community in establishing firm foundations for subsequent expansion.

Much more remains to be done. This book has demonstrated the potential of lateral approaches to the study of the trading community, but has not moved beyond the most significant commercial and business sources. Other evidence could be used in a similar fashion to develop largely unexplored aspects. Religion, for example, was a central issue in Liverpool's politics, and also in the lives of many traders. Some wealthy traders would fret about their business activities, in the light of their sincere religious beliefs: the Balfour Williamson partners are a well-known example of traders seeking to conduct business in a manner compatible with their religious ethics. Given the range of religious groups present in mid-century Liverpool, building more systematic evidence of this factor into the overall mercantile equation might make a useful test-case for Weberian thinking on faith and capitalism. Ethnicity is a closely related question, of course, and Liverpool's multi-cultural trading environment offers valuable evidence for the role of merchant diasporas. Such communities of traders, living with the stresses of acculturation and discrimination, have been most closely studied in earlier centuries, and some nineteenth-century cases would broaden the field.

This multi-dimensional view of Liverpool in the wider world is probably the best corrective to the image of the port conveyed (usually unintentionally) by the historiographically dominant company histories of large shipping firms. The importance of Liverpool steamships in the Mediterranean trades, for example, depended as much on an émigré merchant community that had brought knowledge of the Mediterranean to Liverpool, as it did on the shipowning firms that brought Liverpool to the Mediterranean. Further exploitation of the neglected commercial sources used in this book; a concerted effort to integrate them with the wide range of local associational evidence; and an extension of the analysis of information and obligation networks to the international level should be a challenge for scholars in the future.

NOTES ON SOURCES

As was discussed in chapter one, historians studying nineteenth-century Liverpool have a wide range of original sources to deal with, but much of this material has not been systematically used in previous research. It is worth offering a brief survey of the key sources, therefore, along with an outline of their contents and the methods used in extracting information from them. Perhaps the central source for this study is the Customs Bills of Entry. The Bills, which survive from most major British ports for much of the nineteenth and early twentieth centuries, were compiled for the benefit of local trading communities. In Liverpool's case, they offer a daily printed listing of all arriving vessels, with detailed itemisation of cargoes and the names of the importing merchants and ships' agents; a listing, in much less detail, of items cleared by Customs for export, and their stated destinations; and a list of vessels loading in the port, with their planned destinations. Bills from other major ports carry similar information, although some were published less frequently. The Bills enabled merchants to monitor the trade in particular commodities, and also ascertain the availability of outward vessels.

The Liverpool Bills in this period are a considerable source, both in value and in magnitude. It was therefore necessary to select a sample that could be computerised in a reasonable time, while also providing a useful range of material. For reasons discussed in chapter one, the third quarter of the nineteenth century is the main focus of this work, so incoming data were gathered for the months of February, June and October in the years 1855, 1863 and 1870. The result was a sample of about 3,200 voyages, with a total of just over 37,000 cargo records.

This sample clearly raises questions of statistical validity. There are certainly problems in some areas: the Australian trade, for example, had only a few incoming voyages each year in this period, so the sample cannot be as valuable as that of, say, the North American trade, which regularly had a few voyages each day. In addition, while broadly seasonal trades are recognisable in this spread of months, some more focused activities will be over- or under-represented. It must be stressed, however, that the generation of statistics for Liverpool's trade was not the prime objective of this study: if it had been, there are a number of other sources from the period – Parliamentary accounts, for example – that could provide the necessary figures with much less effort than a computerised sample of the Bills. Rather, the source serves two key purposes. First, it enables individual commodity traders to be connected to specific cargo items, and therefore to particular regional and commodity trades. Secondly, the brief descriptions of the ships involved enable profiles of Liverpool's traffic to be constructed, especially when used in conjunction with the second major source – the Liverpool Register of Shipping.

Like the Bills, the Register is a voluminous and systematic record of a crucial element of the port's activity. It falls, broadly, into two parts, one being a description of the vessel and the other a listing, updated over time as necessary, of its ownership. Various sampling methods are available. A chronological sample of vessels registered in certain years is the simplest type, given that the source itself is organised chronologically by date of registration. The key problem with this approach, however, stems from the fact that the register is an account of vessels as they were *registered*, not as they were *used*. A sample of all vessels registered in a given year will be skewed in a number of ways. It will reflect the characteristics of the port's newest ships rather than the fleet as a whole. Figures from a few years on either side of a boom or slump in steamship building, or of a sudden shift in freight rates which made one kind of vessel more economic than others, are likely to show a dramatic divergence between the types of vessel appearing on the register and the majority of those actually using the port.

By linking the Register with the arriving traffic records from the Bills, however, it is possible to ensure that the shipowning patterns derived from the Register are a more accurate reflection of the port's fleet as a whole, including older but still active vessels as well as the latest ships acquired by leading steam operators. Liverpool-registered ships appearing in the Bills sample were traced in the Register (which fortunately has an alphabetical index). The resulting Register sample therefore contains construction and ownership details of vessels that we know to have been operating in Liverpool at the time of the Bills sample. These two sources taken together provide the evidence for three key functions within the Liverpool overseas trading community – agenting of incoming vessels, commodity importing and shipowning – which underpins much of the analysis of business structure and change contained in the book.

Inevitably, the wide range of commodities and ports of origin listed in the Bills of Entry had to be gathered together in a classification system for interpretation purposes. This enabled patterns of regional and commodity trading to be addressed in part one, and again in chapter five. Ports of origin were divided into 15 regions (West Africa, Mediterranean, and the like), while commodities were grouped into 30 classes, such as alcohol, artworks, chemicals and so on. This process could have been much more closely refined, but a relatively broad classification was sufficient for the purposes of this study.

Location and citation of primary sources

The most important single collection of archival material specifically relating to the port of Liverpool is that of the Maritime Archives and Library, Merseyside Maritime Museum, Albert Dock, Liverpool (cited as MMM Archives). A multi-volume guide to this collection is in progress: the first volume is *Guide to the records of Merseyside Maritime Museum*, ed. Gordon Read and Michael Stammers (St Johns, Newfoundland, 1995). Elsewhere, the British Parliamentary Papers (BPP) offer a wealth of information on a wide range of topics. These were consulted in a variety of formats, including original printed volumes, the Chadwyck-Healey microfiche collection, and the volumes of minutes of evidence relating to dock construction compiled by Thomas Webster in the mid-nineteenth century. Liverpool's newspapers consulted are in the Liverpool Record Office, William Brown St., Liverpool.

NOTES ON ABBREVIATIONS

Admiralty enquiry (1848)
Admiralty Enquiry into the Liverpool Docks Bill, 1848.
MMM Archives, MDHB/Parl.

Balfour Williamson papers
Balfour Williamson collection.
University College Library, London.

Bank
Bank of England, Liverpool branch correspondence.
Bank of England archives, London, C129, vols 11–20, 1850–70.
These volumes contain, in chronological order, the letters sent by the Bank of England agent in Liverpool to the Bank in London. They are cited here by their date.

Barings
Letters from Baring Brs, Liverpool, to Baring Brs, London.
ING Barings Holdings, London, HC 3.35, boxes 19–25, 1853–70.
These letters are archived in chronological order, and are cited here by their date.

BE
Customs Bills of Entry, Liverpool, A Series.
MMM Archives.
References to 'samples' are to the months of February, June and October taken from 1855, 1863 and 1870. Specific voyages are cited as in the following example: BE 12/6/1855/03 is the third entry in the 12 June 1855 Bill of Entry.

BE (B)
Customs Bills of Entry, Liverpool, B Series.
MMM Archives.

BPP, Abyssinia (1869)
Select Committee on the Abyssinia War.
1868–69, VI (380, 380-I).

BPP, Abyssinia (1870)
Select Committee on the excess cost of the Abyssinian expedition.
1870, V (401).

BPP, Abyssinia transports (1870)
Return of the number of transports employed in the Abyssinian expedition.
1870, XLIV (71).

BPP, American vessels (1863)
A return of the number and tonnage of American (United States) vessels sold and transferred to British subjects in 1863.
1864, LV (324).

BPP, Arms shipments (1864)
Account of guns ... shipped from the port of Liverpool to America.
1864, LVII (555).

BPP, Bankruptcy Commission (1854)
Report of HM Commissioners appointed to inquire into fees, funds and establishments of the Court of Bankruptcy.
1854, XXIII (1770).

BPP, Birkenhead Commissioners' Docks (1844)
House of Commons, Birkenhead Commissioners' Docks Bill, 1844.
In *The port and dock of Birkenhead*, ed. Thomas Webster, London, 1847.

BPP, Birkenhead Company's Docks (1845)
House of Commons, Birkenhead Company's Docks Bill, 1845.
In *The port and dock of Birkenhead*, ed. Thomas Webster, London, 1847.

BPP, Birkenhead Docks (1848)
House of Commons, Birkenhead Docks' Bill, 1848.
In *Minutes of evidence ... on the Liverpool and Birkenhead dock Bills*, ed. Thomas Webster, London, 1853.

BPP, Birkenhead Docks (1852)
House of Commons, Birkenhead Docks Bill, 1852.
In *Minutes of evidence ... on the Liverpool and Birkenhead dock Bills*, ed. Thomas Webster, London, 1853.

BPP, Birkenhead Docks (1856)
House of Commons, Select Committee on Private Bills Group M, Birkenhead Docks Bill, 1856.
MMM Archives, MDHB/Parl.

BPP, Colonial reports (1855/1863/1870)
Reports ... past and present state of Her Majesty's colonial possessions.
1857 Session 1, X [2198].
1865, XXXVII [3423, 3423-I].
1872, XLII [c523, c583, c617].

BPP, Commercial reports (1855)
Reports from Her Majesty's ministers and consuls: Trade and commerce.
1856, LVII [2131]

BPP, Crimea transports (1855)
Number of transports employed in carrying troops or munitions for war in the East, between 1 October 1853 and 1 March 1855.
1854–55, XXXIV (517).

BPP, East India communication (1862)
Select Committee on the practicality of shortening voyage to Madras.
1862, VII.

BPP, East India communications (1866)
Select Committee on practical working of present system of telegraphs ... East Indies.
1866, IX (428).

BPP, Embassy reports (1857)
Reports by Her Majesty's Secretaries of Embassy.
1857–8, LV [2444].

BPP, Emigrant ships (1854)
Select Committee on Emigrant Ships.
1854, XIII (163, 349).

BPP, Emigration report (1854)
15th General report of the Colonial Land and Emigration Commissioners.
1854–55, XVII [1953].

BPP, Liverpool Docks (1848)
House of Commons, Liverpool Docks Bill, 1848.
In *Minutes of evidence ... on the Liverpool and Birkenhead dock Bills*, ed. Thomas Webster, London, 1853.

BPP, Liverpool Docks (1851)
House of Commons, Liverpool Docks Bill, 1851.
In *Minutes of evidence ... on the Liverpool and Birkenhead dock Bills*, ed. Thomas Webster, London, 1853.

BPP, Liverpool Docks (1855)
House of Commons, Liverpool Docks Bill, 1855.
In *Minutes of evidence and proceedings on the Liverpool and Birkenhead Dock Bills*, ed. Thomas Webster, London, 1857.

BPP, Mail contracts (1868)
Select Committee to inquire into contracts ... for conveyance of mails from UK to US.
1868–9, VI (106).

BPP, MDHB Bill (1864)
House of Commons, Select Committee on Private Bills Group G.
MMM Archives, MDHB/Parl.

BPP, MDHB Bill (1867) (Commons)
House of Commons, Select Committee on Private Bills (Group E).
MMM Archives, MDHB/Parl.

BPP, MDHB Bill (1867) (Lords)
House of Lords, Select Committee on MDHB Bill.
MMM Archives, MDHB/Parl.

BPP, MDHB Bill (1873)
House of Commons, Select Committee on Private Bills (Group L), MDHB (No 1) Bill.
MMM Archives, MDHB/Parl.

BPP, Merchant shipping (1860)
Select Committee on the State of Merchant Shipping.
1860, XIII (530).

BPP, Navigation Acts (Lords) (1848)
House of Lords, Select Committee to inquire into operation and policy of Navigation Laws.
1847–8, XX (340, 431, 754).

BPP, Navigation Laws (Commons) (1848)
House of Commons, Select Committee to inquire into operation and policy of Navigation Laws.
1847–8, XX (7).

BPP, Packet and telegraph services (1860)
Select Committee to inquire into contracts by Government with steam packet companies . . . and telegraphic communications.
1860, XIV (328, 407, 431).

BPP, Passengers Act (1851)
Select Committee on the Operation of the Passengers Act.
1851, XIX (632).

BPP, Ships detained (1876)
Return of . . . ships detained for alleged unseaworthiness.
1876, LXVI (374).

BPP, Steam communications (1851)
Select Committee on steam communications with India, China, Australia and New Zealand.
1851, XXI (372, 605).

BPP, Transport service (1860)
Select Committee to inquire into . . . transporting troops, convicts, emigrants and similar services.
1860, XVIII (480).

BPP, Unseaworthy ships (1873)
Royal Commission on unseaworthy ships.
1873, XXXVI (C.853).

BPP, Unseaworthy ships (1874)
Royal Commission on unseaworthy ships.
1874, XXXIV (C.1027).

BPP, West Africa (1865)
Select Committee to consider on the state of British settlements on the western coast of Africa.
1865, V (412, 412-I).

BPP, West Africa mails (1852)
Correspondence relative to the conveyance of Her Majesty's mails to the west coast of Africa.
1852, XLIX (284).

Dock Committee, Minutes
Minute books of the Liverpool Council Dock Committee.
MMM Archives, MDHB Collection.

Dock revenue statements
MDHB, Statements of Revenue from Dues and Rates, 1844–1924.
MMM Archives, MDHB Collection.

DR
Liverpool Dock Registers.
MMM Archives.
A series of large volumes recording vessel movements within the dock system. Each dock (or group of docks) has a set of volumes, with chronological entries; individual entries are cited by dock and date. Samples were taken of the same months used in the Bills of Entry samples (see above).

Matthews papers
Papers of George Matthews, master mariner.
Perkins Library, Duke University, North Carolina.

MDHB, Disc.
Discussions at the Board.
MMM Archives, MDHB collection.
These are detailed minutes of some of the Board's discussions, offering much more material than that contained in the formal minute books (below).

MDHB, Docks & Quays Cttee
Minute books of the MDHB Docks and Quays Committee.
MMM Archives, MDHB collection.

MDHB, Leg.
Legal papers.
MMM Archives, MDHB collection.
These are papers collected by the Board's lawyers during numerous Parliamentary and legal proceedings.

MDHB, Minutes
Minute books of the Mersey Docks & Harbour Board.
MMM Archives, MDHB collection.

MDHB, WUP (Unbound)
Unbound Worked-up Papers.
MMM Archives, MDHB collection.

SR
Liverpool Statutory Register of Merchant Shipping.
MMM Archives.
The register is arranged chronologically, with numbering starting from '1' each January. Therefore, a ship cited as SR 1863/76 is no. 76 for 1863.

Steamship Owners, Minutes
Minute books of the Liverpool Steamship Owners' Association, vol. 1.
MMM Archives, D/SS.

Stitt papers
Papers relating to the Stitt family, Liverpool traders.
MMM Archives, DB115, boxes 1, 3, 5 and 7.
Individual letters are catalogued by roman numeral with each box, eg. 3(ii).

Stott, Charter party books
Shipbroking records of W. H. Stott & Co., Liverpool.
MMM Archives, STOTT, vols 2 and 3 (1869–71).
Individual charter parties are cited by volume and folio number.

Underwriters, Minutes
Minute books of the Liverpool Underwriters Association.
MMM Archives, D/LUA.

Warehouse report (1839)
Report of the Finance Committee of the Town Council ... Docks and Warehouses, 21 November 1839.
MMM Archives, MDHB/Leg/h/26.

Williams papers
Correspondence of Daniel Williams, South America merchant.
MMM Archives, DB 175.

BIBLIOGRAPHY

Anderson, B. L., 'The Lancashire bill system and its Liverpool practitioners: The case of a slave merchant', in *Trade and transport: Essays in economic history in honour of T. S. Willan*, ed. W. H. Chaloner and Barrie M. Ratcliffe, Manchester, Manchester UP, 1977, pp. 59–96.

Anderson, B. L., 'Institutional investment before the First World War: The Union Marine Insurance Company', in *Business and businessmen: Studies in business, economic and accounting history*, ed. S. Marriner, Liverpool, Liverpool UP, 1978, pp. 169–97.

Anderson, B. L., and P. L. Cottrell, 'Another Victorian capital market: A study of banking and bank investors on Merseyside', *Economic History Review*, Vol. 28, 1975, pp. 598–615.

Anderson, Gregory, *Victorian clerks*, Manchester, Manchester UP, 1976.

Anon., *The broker's guide and shipping directory*, Birmingham, 1870.

Anon., *The Clarkson chronicle, 1852–1952*, London, Harley, 1952.

Arnold, A. J., and Robert G. Greenhill, 'Contractors' bounties or due consideration?: Evidence on the commercial nature of the Royal Mail Steam Packet Company's mail contracts, 1842–1905', in *Management, finance and industrial relations in maritime industries*, ed. Simon Ville and D. M. Williams, St John's, Newfoundland, International Maritime Economic History Association (IMEHA), 1994, pp. 111–37.

Ashcroft, Neil, 'British trade with the Confederacy and the effectiveness of Union maritime strategy during the Civil War', *International Journal of Maritime History*, Vol. 10, 1998, pp. 155–76.

Bagwell, Philip, 'The Post Office steam packets, 1821–36, and the development of shipping on the Irish Sea', *Maritime History*, Vol. 1, 1971, pp. 4–28.

Baines, Thomas, *History of the commerce and town of Liverpool*, London, Longman, 1852.

Baines, Thomas, *Liverpool in 1859*, London, 1859.

Batzel, V. M., 'Parliament, businessmen and bankruptcy, 1825–1883: A study in middle class alienation', *Canadian Journal of History*, Vol. 18, 1983, pp. 171–86.

Behrend, Arthur, *Portrait of a family firm: Bahr, Behrend & Co., 1793–1945*, London, Bahr Behrend & Co., 1970.

Belchem, John, 'The peculiarities of Liverpool', in *Popular politics, riot and labour: Essays in Liverpool history, 1790–1940*, ed. John Belchem, Liverpool, Liverpool UP, 1992, pp. 1–20.

Belchem, John, '"The church, the throne and the people, ships, colonies and commerce": Popular Toryism in early Victorian Liverpool', *Transactions of the Historic Society of Lancashire & Cheshire*, Vol. 143, 1994, pp. 35–55.

Belchem, John, 'Liverpool in 1848: Image, identity and issues', *Transactions of the Historic Society of Lancashire & Cheshire*, Vol. 147, 1998, pp. 1–26.

Bibby Line, *Bibby Line, 1807–1957*, London, Bibby, [1957].

Blake, George, *Gellatley's, 1862–1962: A short history of the firm*, London, Blackie, 1962.

Bonsor, N. R. P., *North Atlantic seaway*, 5 vols, Jersey, Brookside, 1975–80.

Bonsor, N. R. P., *South Atlantic seaway*, Jersey, Brookside, 1983.

Bourne, Kenneth, *Britain and the balance of power in North America, 1815–1908*, London, Longman, 1967.

Boyce, Gordon H., *Information, mediation and institutional development: The rise of large-scale enterprise in British shipping, 1870–1919*, Manchester, Manchester UP, 1995.

Broeze, Frank, 'The cost of distance: Shipping and the early Australian economy, 1788–1850', *Economic History Review*, Vol. 28, 1975, pp. 582–97.

Broeze, Frank, 'Private enterprise and the peopling of Australia, 1831–50', *Economic History Review*, Vol. 35, 1982, pp. 235–53.

Broeze, Frank, 'Distance tamed: Steam navigation to Australia and New Zealand from its beginnings to the outbreak of the Great War', *Journal of Transport History*, Vol. 10, 1989, pp. 1–21.

Broomhall, G. J. S., and John H. Hubback, *Corn trade memories, recent and remote*, Liverpool, 1930.

Busteed, M. A., 'A Liverpool shipping agent and Irish emigration in the 1850s: Some newly discovered documents', *Transactions of the Historic Society of Lancashire & Cheshire*, Vol. 129, 1979, pp. 145–62.

Carson, Edward, 'Customs Bills of Entry', *Maritime History*, Vol. 1, 1971, pp. 176–83.

Casson, Mark, 'Culture as an economic asset', in *Business history and business culture*, ed. Andrew Godley and Oliver Westall, Manchester, Manchester UP, 1996, pp. 48–76.

Casson, Mark, 'The economics of the family firm', *Scandinavian Economic History Review*, Vol. 47, 1999, pp. 10–23.

Chaloner, W. H., 'A Philadelphia textile merchant's trip to Europe on the eve of the Civil War: Robert Creighton, 1856–57', in *Trade and transport: Essays in economic history in honour of T. S. Willan*, ed. W. H. Chaloner and Barrie M. Ratcliffe, Manchester, Manchester UP, 1977, pp. 157–72.

Chandler, Alfred D., *The visible hand: The managerial revolution in American business*, Cambridge, MA, Belknap, 1977.

Chandler, George, *Liverpool shipping: A short history*, London, Pheonix, 1960.

Chapman, Stanley, *Merchant enterprise in Britain: From the industrial revolution to World War I*, Cambridge, Cambridge UP, 1992.

Checkland, S. G., 'American versus West Indian traders in Liverpool, 1793–1815', *Journal of Economic History*, Vol. 18, 1958, pp. 141–60.

Church, R. A., *The Great Victorian Boom, 1850–1873*, London, Macmillan, 1975.

Church, Roy, 'Ossified or dynamic? Structure, markets and the competitive process in the British business system of the nineteenth century', *Business History*, Vol. 42, no. 1, 2000, pp. 1–20.

Cain, P. J., and A. G. Hopkins, *British imperialism: Innovation and expansion, 1688–1914*, London, Longman, 1993.

Clayton Brothers, *Liverpool ABC timetables and shipping directory*, Liverpool, 1868.

Coleman, D., 'The uses and abuses of business history', *Business History*, Vol. 29, 1987, pp. 141–56.

Collins, N., *Politics and elections in nineteenth century Liverpool*, Aldershot, Scholar, 1994.

Cottrell, P. L., *Industrial finance, 1830–1914: The finance and organisation of English manufacturing industry*, London, 1980.

Cottrell, P. L., 'Commercial enterprise', in *The dynamics of Victorian business: Problems and perspectives to the 1870s*, ed. R. Church, London, 1980, pp. 236–49.

Cottrell, P. L., 'The steamship on the Mersey, 1815–80: Investment and ownership', in *Shipping, trade and commerce: Essays in memory of Ralph Davies*, ed. P. L. Cottrell and D. H. Aldcroft, Leicester, Leicester UP, 1981, pp. 137–63.

Cottrell, P. L., 'Liverpool shipowners, the Mediterranean and the transition from sail to steam during the mid-nineteenth century', in *From wheelhouse to counting house: Essays in maritime economic history in honour of Professor Peter Neville Davies*, ed. L. R. Fischer, St John's, Newfoundland, IMEHA, 1992, pp. 153–202.

Curtin, Philip D., *Cross-cultural trade in world history*, Cambridge, Cambridge UP, 1984.

Daggett, Kendrick P., *Fifty years of fortitude: The maritime career of Captain Jotham Blaisdell of Kennebunk, Maine, 1810–1860*, Mystic, CT, Mystic Seaport Museum, 1988.

Davies, P. N., *The trade makers: Elder Dempster in West Africa, 1852–1972*, London, Allen & Unwin, 1973.

Davies, P. N., *Henry Tyrer: A Liverpool shipping agent and his enterprise*, London, Croom Helm, 1979.

Davies, P. N., 'British shipping and world trade: Rise and decline, 1820–1939', in *Business history of shipping: Strategy and structure*, ed. T. Yui and K. Nakagawa, Tokyo, University of Tokyo Press, 1985, pp. 39–85.

Davis, Ralph, *The rise of the English shipping industry in the seventeenth and eighteenth centuries*, London, Macmillan, 1962.

Davis, Ralph, 'Maritime history: Progress and problems', in *Business and businessmen: Studies in business economic and accounting history*, ed. S. Marriner, Liverpool, Liverpool UP, 1978, pp. 169–97.

Davis, Ralph, *The industrial revolution and British overseas trade*, Leicester, Leicester UP, 1979.

Ellison, Thomas, *The cotton trade of Great Britain*, orig. 1886, reprint, London, Frank Cass, 1968.

Fairlie, Susan, 'Shipping in the Anglo-Russian grain trade, to 1870', *Maritime History*, Vol. 1, 1971, pp. 158–75; Vol. 2, 1972, pp. 31–45.

Falkus, Malcolm, *The Blue Funnel legend: A history of the Ocean Steam Ship Company, 1865–1973*, Basingstoke, Macmillan, 1990.

Farnie, D. A., *East and west of Suez: The Suez Canal in history, 1854–1956*, Oxford, Clarendon, 1969.

Farnie, D. A., *The English cotton industry and world market, 1815–1896*, Oxford, Clarendon, 1979.

Field, Henry M., *History of the Atlantic telegraph*, New York, 1866.

Fischer, L. R., and H. Nordvik, 'The growth of Norwegian shipbroking: The practices of Fearnley and Eger as a case study, 1869–1914', in *People of the northern seas*, ed. L. R. Fischer and W. Minchinton, St John's, Newfoundland, IMEHA, 1992, pp. 135–55.

Fischer, L. R., and H. Nordvik, 'Economic theory, information and management in shipbroking: Fearnley and Eger as a case study, 1869–1972', in *Management, finance and industrial relations in maritime industries*, ed. Simon Ville and D. M. Williams, St John's, Newfoundland, IMEHA, 1994, pp. 1–29.

Fletcher, Max E., 'The Suez Canal and world shipping, 1869–1914', *Journal of Economic History*, Vol. 18, 1958, pp. 556–73.

Forres, [Lord], *Balfour Williamson & Company and associated firms: Memoirs of a merchant house*, London, privately published, 1929.

Forwood, W. B., *Recollections of a busy life, being the reminiscences of a Liverpool merchant, 1840–1910*, Liverpool, 1910.

Fritz, Martin, 'Shipping in Sweden, 1850–1913', *Scandinavian Economic History Review*, Vol. 28, 1980, pp. 147–60.

Gjølberg, Ole, 'The substitution of steam for sail in Norwegian ocean shipping, 1866–1914: A study in the economics of diffusion', *Scandinavian Economic History Review*, Vol. 28, 1980, pp. 134–46.

Godley, Andrew, and Duncan M. Ross, 'Introduction: Banks, networks and small firm finance', *Business History*, Vol. 38, no. 3, 1996, pp. 1–10.

Graham, Gerald S., 'The ascendancy of the sailing ship, 1855–1885', *Economic History Review*, Vol. 9, 1956, pp. 74–88.

Green, Edwin, 'Very private enterprise: Ownership and finance in British shipping, 1825–1940', in *Business history of shipping: Strategy and structure*, ed. T. Yui and K. Nakagawa, Tokyo, University of Tokyo Press, 1985, pp. 219–48.

Greenhill, Basil, 'Merchants and the Latin American trade: An introduction', in *Business imperialism, 1840–1930: An inquiry based on British experience in Latin America*, ed. D. C. M. Platt, Oxford, Clarendon, 1977, pp. 159–97.

Greenhill, Robert G., 'Competition or co-operation in the global shipping industry: The origins and impact of the conference system for British shipowners before 1914', in *Global markets: The internationalisation of the sea transport industries since 1850*, ed. D. J. Starkey and Gelina Harlaftis, St John's, Newfoundland, IMEHA, 1998, pp. 53–80.

Hancock, David, *Citizens of the world: London merchants and the integration of the British Atlantic community, 1735–1785*, Cambridge, Cambridge UP, 1995.

Harcourt, Freda, 'Disraeli's imperialism, 1866–1868: A question of timing', *Historical Journal*, Vol. 23, 1980, pp. 87–109.

Harcourt, Freda, 'The P&O company: Flagships of imperialism', in *Charted and uncharted waters: Proceedings of a conference on the study of British maritime history*, ed. S. Palmer and G. Williams, London, National Maritime Museum, 1981, pp. 6–28.

Harcourt, Freda, 'British oceanic mail contracts in the age of steam, 1838–1914', *Journal of Transport History*, 3rd series, Vol. 9, 1988, pp. 1–18.

Harlaftis, Gelina, *A history of Greek owned shipping: The making of an international tramp fleet*, London, Routledge, 1995.

Harley, C. K., 'The shift from sailing ships to steamships, 1850–1890: A study in technological change and its diffusion', in *Essays on a mature economy: Britain after 1840*, ed. D. N. McCloskey, Princeton, Princeton UP, 1971, pp. 215–37.

Harley, C. K., 'On the persistence of old techniques: The case of North American wooden shipbuilding', *Journal of Economic History*, Vol. 33, 1973, pp. 372–98.

Harley, C. K., 'Aspects of the economics of shipping, 1850–1913', in *Change and adaptation in the North Atlantic fleets in the 19th century*, ed. L. R. Fischer and G. Panting, St John's, Newfoundland, 1984, pp. 169–86.

Harley, C. K., 'Ocean freight rates and productivity, 1740–1913: The primacy of mechanical invention reaffirmed', *Journal of Economic History*, Vol. 48, 1988, pp. 851–76.

Harley, C. K., 'Foreign trade: Comparative advantage and performance', in *The economic history of Britain since 1700*, ed. D. N. McCloskey and R. Floud, 2nd edn, 3 vols, Cambridge, Cambridge UP, 1994, Vol. 1, pp. 300–31.

Harnetty, Peter, *Imperialism and free trade: Lancashire and India in the mid-nineteenth century*, Manchester, Manchester UP, 1972.

Havinden, M., and D. Meredith, *Colonialism and development: Britain and its tropical colonies, 1850–1960*, London, Routledge, 1993.

Haws, Duncan, *The Burma Boats: Henderson & Bibby*, Uckfield, TCL, 1995.

Hawthorne, Nathaniel, *The English notebooks*, ed. R. Stewart, New York, 1941.

Headrick, D. R., *The tentacles of progress: Technology transfer in the age of imperialism, 1850–1940*, New York, Oxford UP, 1988.

Heath, Hilaire J., 'British merchant houses in Mexico, 1821–1860: Conforming business practices and ethics', *Hispanic American Historical Review*, Vol. 73, 1993, pp. 261–90.

Hollett, D., *Fast passage to Australia*, London, Fairplay, 1986.

Holt, A., 'Review of the progress of steam shipping during the last quarter of a century', *Minutes of proceedings of the Institution of Civil Engineers*, Vol. 51, 1877–8, pp. 2–135 [paper is pp. 2–11, discussion is pp. 12–135].

Hoppit, Julian, *Risk and failure in English business, 1700–1800*, Cambridge, Cambridge UP, 1987.

Hornby, Ove, and Carl-Axel Nilsson, 'The transition from sail to steam in the Danish merchant fleet, 1865–1910', *Scandinavian Economic History Review*, Vol. 28, 1980, pp. 110–34.

Howat, J. N. T., *South American packets*, York, Postal History Society, 1984.

Hudson, Pat, *Regions and industries: A perspective on the industrial revolution in Britain*, Cambridge, Cambridge UP, 1989.

Hudson, Pat, *The industrial revolution*, London, Edward Arnold, 1992.

Hughes, J. R. T., and Stanley Reiter, 'The first 1,945 British steamships', *Journal of the American Statistical Association*, Vol. 53, 1958, pp. 360–81.

Hyam, Ronald, *Britain's imperial century, 1815–1914*, 2nd edn, Basingstoke, Macmillan, 1993.

Hyde, F. E., *Blue Funnel: A history of Alfred Holt & Co. of Liverpool, 1865–1914*, Liverpool, Liverpool UP, 1957.

Hyde, F. E., *Shipping enterprise and management, 1830–1939: Harrisons of Liverpool*, Liverpool, Liverpool UP, 1967.

Hyde, F. E., *Liverpool and the Mersey: An economic history of a port, 1700–1970*, Newton Abbot, David & Charles, 1971.

Hyde, F. E., *Far Eastern trade, 1860–1914*, London, Black, 1973.

Hyde, F. E., *Cunard and the North Atlantic, 1840–1973: A history of shipping and financial management*, London, Macmillan, 1975.

Jackson, Gordon, *Hull in the eighteenth century: A study in economic and social history*, London, Oxford UP, 1972.

Jackson, Gordon, *The history and archaeology of ports*, Tadworth, World's Work, 1983.

Jackson, Gordon, 'Do docks make trade? The case of the port of Great Grimsby', in *From wheelhouse to counting house: Essays in maritime economic history in honour of Professor Peter Neville Davies*, ed. L. R. Fischer, St John's, Newfoundland, IMEHA, 1992, pp. 17–41.

Jackson, Gordon, and Charles Munn, 'Trade, commerce and finance', in *Glasgow: Volume II, 1830–1912*, ed. W. Hamish Fraser and Irene Maver, Manchester, Manchester UP, 1996, pp. 52–95.

Jarvis, Adrian, 'Harold Littledale: The man with a mission', in *A second Merseyside maritime history*, ed. H. M. Hignett, Liverpool, 1991.

Jarvis, Adrian, *Liverpool central docks, 1799–1905*, Stroud, Sutton, 1991.

Jarvis, Adrian, 'The members of the Mersey Docks and Harbour Board and their way of doing business, 1858–1905', *International Journal of Maritime History*, Vol. 6, 1994, pp. 123–39.

Jarvis, Adrian, 'The port of Liverpool and the shipowners in the late nineteenth century', *The Great Circle*, Vol. 16, 1994, pp. 1–22.

Jarvis, Adrian, 'Managing change: The organisation of port authorities at the turn of the twentieth century', *Northern Mariner*, Vol. 6, 1996, pp. 31–42.

Jarvis, Adrian, *The Liverpool dock engineers*, Stroud, Sutton, 1996.

Jenkins, Brian, *Britain and the war for the Union*, 2 vols, Montreal, 1974.

Jones, Charles A., *International business in the nineteenth century: The rise and fall of a cosmopolitan bourgeoisie*, Brighton, Wheatsheaf, 1987.

Jones, Stephanie, 'Shipowning in Boston, Lincolnshire, 1836–1848', *Mariner's Mirror*, Vol. 65, 1979, pp. 339–49.

Kaukiainen, Yrjö, 'The transition from sail to steam in Finnish shipping, 1850–1914', *Scandinavian Economic History Review*, Vol. 28, 1980, pp. 161–84.

Kaukiainen, Yrjö, 'Coal and canvas: Aspects of the competition between steam and sail, c. 1870–1914', *International Journal of Maritime History*, Vol. 4, 1992, pp. 175–91.

Kenwood, A. G., 'Fixed capital formation on Merseyside, 1800–1913', *Economic History Review*, Vol. 31, 1978, pp. 214–37.

Killick, John, 'Bolton Ogden & Co.: A case study in Anglo-American trade, 1790–1850', *Business History Review*, Vol. 48, 1974, pp. 501–19.

Killick, John, 'Risk, specialisation and profit in the mercantile sector of the nineteenth century cotton trade: Alexander Brown and Sons, 1820–80', *Business History*, Vol. 16, 1974, pp. 1–16.

Killmarx, Robert A., *America's maritime legacy: A history of the US merchant marine and shipbuilding industry since colonial times*, Boulder, Westview, 1979.

Kirkaldy, Adam W., *British shipping: Its history, organisation and importance*, London, 1914.

Kuznets, S., 'Quantitative aspects of the economic growth of nations, X, level and structure of foreign trade: Long term trends', *Economic Development and Cultural Change*, Vol. 15, no. 2, part ii, 1967, pp. 1–140.

Kynaston, David, *The City of London: Volume 1, A world of its own, 1815–1890*, London, Pimlico, 1995.

Lambert, Andrew, *The Crimean War: British grand strategy, 1853–56*, Manchester, Manchester UP, 1990.

Lane, Tony, *Liverpool: Gateway of empire*, London, Lawrence & Wishart, 1987.

Langton, J., 'Liverpool and its hinterland in the late eighteenth century', in *Commerce, industry and transport: Studies in economic change on Merseyside*, ed. B. L. Anderson and P. J. M. Stoney, Liverpool, Liverpool UP, 1983, pp. 1–25.

Lee, Robert, 'The socio-economic and demographic characteristics of port cities: A typology for comparative analysis?', *Urban History*, Vol. 25, 1998, pp. 147–72.

Lindsay, W. S., *Our merchant shipping: Its present state considered*, London, 1860.

Lynn, Martin, 'From sail to steam: The impact of the steamship services on the British palm oil trade with West Africa, 1850–1890', *Journal of African History*, Vol. 30, 1989, pp. 227–45.

Lynn, Martin, 'Trade and politics in nineteenth century Liverpool: The Tobin and Horsfall families and Liverpool's African trade', *Transactions of the Historic Society of Lancashire & Cheshire*, Vol. 142, 1993, pp. 99–120.

Lynn, Martin, 'Liverpool and Africa in the nineteenth century: The continuing connection', *Transactions of the Historic Society of Lancashire & Cheshire*, Vol. 147, 1998, pp. 27–54.

MacDonagh, Oliver, 'Emigration and the state, 1833–55: An essay in administrative history', *Transactions of the Royal History Society*, 5th series, Vol. 5, 1955, pp. 133–60.

MacKenzie, K. S., '"They lost the smell": The Canadian steam merchant marine, 1853–1903', *Northern Mariner*, Vol. 6, 1996, pp. 1–29.

Marriner, S., 'Rathbones' trading activities in the middle of the nineteenth century', *Transactions of the Historic Society of Lancashire & Cheshire*, Vol. 108, 1956, pp. 105–27.

Marriner, S., *Rathbones of Liverpool, 1845–73*, Liverpool, Liverpool UP, 1961.

Marriner, S., and F. E. Hyde, *The Senior: John Samuel Swire, 1825–98*, Liverpool, Liverpool UP, 1967.

Matthews, Keith, and Gerald Panting, eds, *Ships and shipbuilding in the North Atlantic Region*, St John's, Newfoundland, 1978.

McCarron, K., and A. Jarvis, *Give a dock a good name?*, Birkenhead, Countrywise, 1992.

McCloskey, Donald, '1780–1860: A survey', in *The economic history of Britain since 1700*, ed. D. N. McCloskey and R. Floud, 2nd edn, 3 vols, Cambridge, Cambridge UP, 1994, vol. 1, pp. 242–70.

McDonald, J., and R. Shlomowitz, 'Mortality on immigrant voyages to Australia in the 19th century', *Explorations in Economic History*, Vol. 27, 1990, pp. 84–113.

McDonald, J., and R. Shlomowitz, 'Passenger fares on sailing vessels to Australia in the nineteenth century', *Explorations in Economic History*, Vol. 28, 1991, pp. 192–208.

Morgan, Kenneth, *Bristol and the Atlantic trade in the eighteenth century*, Cambridge, Cambridge UP, 1993.

Moss, Michael, and John R. Hume, *Shipbuilder to the world: 125 years of Harland and Wolff, Belfast, 1861–1986*, Belfast, Blackstaff, 1986.

Mountfield, Stuart, *Western gateway: A history of the Mersey Docks and Harbour Board*, Liverpool, Liverpool UP, 1965.

Muir, Robert, *A practical summary of the law relating to bills of exchange and promissory notes*, Edinburgh, 1836.

Munro, J. F., 'Shipping subsidies and railway guarantees: William Mackinnon, eastern Africa and the Indian Ocean, 1860–93', *Journal of African History*, Vol. 28, 1987, pp. 209–30.

Munro, J. F., 'The "Scrubby Scotch Screw Company": British India Steam Navigation Co.'s coastal services in South Asia, 1862–70', in *From wheelhouse to counting house: Essays in maritime economic history in honour of Professor Peter Neville Davies*, ed. L. R. Fischer, St John's, Newfoundland, IMEHA, 1992, pp. 43–72.

Neal, F., 'Liverpool shipping in the early nineteenth century', in *Liverpool and Merseyside: Essays in the economic and social history of the port and its hinterland*, ed. J. R. Harris, Liverpool, 1969, pp. 147–81.

Neal, F., *Sectarian violence: The Liverpool experience, 1819–1914, an aspect of Anglo-Irish history*, Manchester, Manchester UP, 1988.

Nenadic, Stana, 'Businessmen, the urban middle classes and the "dominance" of manufactures in nineteenth century Britain', *Economic History Review*, Vol. 44, 1991, pp. 66–85.

Nenadic, Stana, 'The small family firm in Victorian Britain', *Business History*, Vol. 35, 1993, pp. 86–114.

North, Douglass C., 'Ocean freight rates and economic development, 1750–1913', *Journal of Economic History*, Vol. 18, 1958, pp. 537–55.

Oldham, Wilton J., *The Ismay Line*, Liverpool, Journal of Commerce, 1961.

Owen, E. R. J., *Cotton and the Egyptian economy, 1820–1914: A study in trade and development*, Oxford, Clarendon, 1969.

Palmer, S., 'Investors in London shipping, 1820–1850', *Maritime History*, Vol. 2, 1972, pp. 46–68.

Palmer, S., *Politics, shipping and the repeal of the Navigation Acts*, Manchester, Manchester UP, 1990.

Payne, P. L., 'Family business in Britain: An historical and analytical survey', in *Family business in the era of industrial growth*, ed. A. Okochi and S. Yasaoka, Tokyo, University of Tokyo Press, 1984, pp. 171–206.

Payne, P. L., *British entrepreneurship in the nineteenth century*, 2nd edn, Basingstoke, Macmillan, 1988.

Pelzer, J. D., 'Liverpool and the American Civil War', *History Today*, March 1990, pp. 46–52.

Penny, K., 'Australian relief for the Lancashire victims of the cotton famine, 1862–1863', *Transactions of the Historic Society of Lancashire and Cheshire*, Vol. 108, 1956, pp. 129–39.

Phillips, G. O., 'The stirrings of the mercantile community in the British West Indies after emancipation', *Journal of Caribbean History*, Vol. 23, 1989, pp. 62–95.

Picton, J. A., *Memorials of Liverpool, historical and topographical, including a history of the dock estate*, 2 vols, London, 1873.

Platt, D. C. M., *Latin America and British trade, 1806–1914*, London, Black, 1972.

Poole, Braithwaite, *The commerce of Liverpool*, Liverpool, 1854.

Pope, David, 'Shipping and trade in the port of Liverpool, 1783–1793', unpublished PhD dissertation, University of Liverpool, 1970.

Porter, A., *Victorian shipping, business and imperial policy: Donald Currie, the Castle Line and southern Africa*, Woodbridge, Boydell, 1986.

Power, M. J., 'The growth of Liverpool', in *Popular politics, riot and labour: Essays in Liverpool history, 1790–1940*, ed. John Belchem, Liverpool, Liverpool UP, 1992, pp. 21–37.

Power, M. J., 'Councillors and commerce in Liverpool, 1650–1750', *Urban History*, Vol. 24, 1997, pp. 301–23.

Rankin, John, *A history of our firm: Some account of the firm of Pollock, Gilmour & Co., and its offshoots and connections*, Liverpool, Liverpool UP, 1908.

Redford, Arthur, *Manchester merchants and foreign trade*, 2 vols, Manchester, Manchester UP, 1934, 1956.

Rideout, Eric H., 'The development of the Liverpool warehousing system', *Transactions of the Historic Society of Lancashire & Cheshire*, Vol. 82, 1930, pp. 1–41.

Ritchie-Noakes, N., *Liverpool's historic waterfront*, London, HMSO, 1984.

Ritchie-Noakes, N., and Mike Clarke, 'The dock engineer and the development of the port of Liverpool', in *Liverpool shipping, trade and industry*, ed. Valerie Burton, Liverpool, NMGM, 1989, pp. 91–108.

Rogers, H. C. B., *Troopships and their history*, London, Seeley, 1963.

Rose, Mary B., 'Family firm, community and business culture: A comparative perspective on the British and American cotton industries', in *Business history and business culture*, ed. Andrew Godley and Oliver Westall, Manchester, Manchester UP, 1996, pp. 162–89.

Rosenberg, Nathan, 'Factors affecting the diffusion of technology', *Explorations in Economic History*, Vol. 10, 1972, pp. 3–34.

Rosenberg, Nathan, *Exploring the black box: Technology, economics and history*, Cambridge, Cambridge UP, 1994.

Rowson, A. H., 'Edward Bates: Shipowner', in *Bates of Bellefield, Gyrn Castle and Manydown*, ed. P. E. Bates, n.p., 1994, pp. 5–17.

Rubinstein, W. D., 'British millionaires, 1809–1949', *Bulletin of the Institute of Historical Research*, Vol. 47, 1974, pp. 202–23.

Rubinstein, W. D., 'The size and distribution of the English middle classes in 1860', *Historical Research*, Vol. 61, 1988, pp. 65–89.

Rubinstein, W. D., *Capitalism, culture and decline in modern Britain, 1750–1990*, London, Routledge, 1993.

Safford, J. J., 'The decline of the American merchant marine, 1850–1914: A historiographical appraisal', in *Change and adaptation in maritime history*, ed. L. R. Fischer and J. A. Tague, St John's, Newfoundland, 1983.

Safford, J. J., 'The United States merchant marine in foreign trade, 1800–1939', in *Business history of shipping: Strategy and structure*, ed. T. Yui and K. Nakagawa, Tokyo, University of Tokyo Press, 1985, pp. 91–118.

Sagar, E. W., 'Labour productivity in the shipping fleets of Halifax and Yarmouth, Nova Scotia, 1863–1900', in *Working men who got wet*, ed. R. Ommer and G. Panting, St John's, Newfoundland, 1980, pp. 157–84.

Sagar, E. W., *Seafaring labour: The merchant marine of Atlantic Canada, 1820–1914*, Kingston, McGill-Queen's UP, 1989.

Samhaber, Ernst, *Merchants make history*, London, Harrap, 1963.

Sawers, Larry, 'The Navigation Acts revisited', *Economic History Review*, Vol. 45, 1992, pp. 262–84.

Scally, Robert, 'Liverpool ships and Irish emigrants in the age of sail', *Journal of Social History*, Vol. 17, 1983–4, pp. 5–30.

Shimmin, Hugh, *Pen and ink sketches of Liverpool Town Councillors*, Liverpool, 1866.

Singleton, Colin, 'The competence, training and education of the British nineteenth-century master mariner', unpublished PhD dissertation, University of London, 1996.

Sloan, Edward W., 'Collins versus Cunard: The realities of a North Atlantic steamship rivalry, 1850–1858', *International Journal of Maritime History*, Vol. 4, 1992, pp. 83–100.

Smith, Adam, *The wealth of nations*, ed. Andrew Skinner, London, Penguin, 1982.

Smith, Samuel, *My life-work*, London, Hodder & Stoughton, 1902.

Stammers, Michael, *The passage makers*, Brighton, Teredo, 1978.

Stammers, Michael, and John Kearon, *The Jhelum: A Victorian merchant ship*, Stroud, Sutton, 1992.

Starkey, David J., 'Ownership structures in the British shipping industry: The case of Hull, 1820–1916', *International Journal of Maritime History*, Vol. 8, 1996, pp. 71–95.

Stevens, Robert, *On the stowage of ships and their cargoes*, 5th edn, London, 1869.

Stuart, Reginald C., *United States expansionism and British North America, 1775–1871*, Chapel Hill, NC, UNC Press, 1988.

Swann, D., 'The pace and progress of port investment in England, 1660–1830', *Yorkshire Bulletin of Economic and Social Research*, Vol. 12, 1960, pp. 32–44.

Tolley, B. H., 'The Liverpool campaign against the Orders in Council and the War of 1812', in *Liverpool and Merseyside: Essays in the economic and social history of the port and its hinterland*, ed. J. R. Harris, Liverpool, Liverpool UP, 1969.

Trainor, Richard H., 'The elite', in *Glasgow: Volume II, 1830–1912*, ed. W. Hamish Fraser and Irene Maver, Manchester, Manchester UP, 1996, pp. 227–64.

Tull, Malcolm, *A community enterprise: The history of the port of Fremantle, 1897 to 1997*, St John's, Newfoundland, IMEHA, 1997.

Valdaliso, Jesús M., 'Growth and modernisation of the Spanish merchant marine, 1860–1935', *International Journal of Maritime History*, Vol. 3, 1991, pp. 33–58.

Valdaliso, Jesús M., 'Spanish shipowners in the British mirror: Patterns of investment, ownership and finance in the Bilbao shipping industry, 1879–1913', *International Journal of Maritime History*, Vol. 5, 1993, pp. 1–30.

Ville, Simon P., *English shipowning during the industrial revolution: Michael Henley and Son, London shipowners, 1770–1830*, Manchester, Manchester UP, 1987.

Ville, Simon, 'The expansion and development of a private business: An application of vertical integration theory', *Business History*, Vol. 33, no. 4, 1991, pp. 19–42.

Ville, Simon, 'The growth of specialisation in English shipowning, 1750–1850', *Economic History Review*, Vol. 46, 1993, pp. 702–22.

Waller, P. J., *Democracy and sectarianism: A political and social history of Liverpool, 1868–1939*, Liverpool, Liverpool UP, 1981.

Wang, Jerry L. S., 'The profitability of Anglo-Chinese trade, 1861–1913', *Business History*, Vol. 35, no. 3, 1993, pp. 39–65.

Watkinson, Charles, 'The Liberal Party on Merseyside in the nineteenth century', unpublished PhD dissertation, University of Liverpool, 1967.

Watson, Nigel, *The Bibby Line, 1807–1990*, London, Bibby, 1990.

Williams, D. M., 'The function of the merchant in specific Liverpool import trades, 1820–50', unpub. MA dissertation, University of Liverpool, 1963.

Williams, D. M., 'Merchanting in the first half of the nineteenth century: The Liverpool timber trade', *Business History*, Vol. 8, 1966, pp. 103–21.

Williams, D. M., 'Liverpool merchants and the cotton trade, 1820–1850', in *Liverpool and Merseyside: Essays in the economic and social history of the port and its hinterland*, ed. J. R. Harris, Liverpool, Liverpool UP, 1969, pp. 182–211.

Williams, D. M., 'Crew size in trans-Atlantic trades in the mid-nineteenth century', in *Working men who got wet*, ed. R. Ommer and G. Panting, St John's, Newfoundland, 1980, pp. 107–53.

Williams, D. M., 'State regulation of merchant shipping, 1839–1914: The bulk carrying trades', in *Charted and uncharted waters: Proceedings of a conference on the study of British maritime history*, ed. S. Palmer and G. Williams, London, National Maritime Museum, 1981, pp. 55–80.

Williams, D. M., 'The rise of United States merchant shipping on the North Atlantic, 1800–1850: The British perception and response', in *Global crossroads and the American seas*, ed. Clark G. Reynolds, Missoula, Montana, Pictorial Histories Publishing, 1988, pp. 67–83.

Williams, D. M., and Jonathan M. Hutchings, 'Shipowners and iron sailing ships: The first twenty years, 1838–1857', in *Peoples of the northern seas*, ed. L. R. Fischer and W. Minchinton, St John's, Newfoundland, IMEHA, 1992, pp. 115–33.

Wilson, John F., *British business history, 1720–1994*, Manchester, Manchester UP, 1995.

INDEX